SELF-REGULATION AND AUTONOMY

Self-regulation and autonomy have emerged as key predictors of health and well-being in several areas of psychology. This timely volume brings together eminent scholars at the forefront of this research, which is taking place in disciplines including social psychology, developmental psychology, educational psychology, and developmental neuroscience. The contributors present ideas and research findings on the development of self-regulation and autonomy, including their biological bases, antecedents, and consequences. Editors Bryan W. Sokol, Frederick M. E. Grouzet, and Ulrich Müller have shaped the volume's multi-disciplinary perspective on self-regulation and autonomy to reflect the legacy of Jean Piaget, the trailblazing developmental psychologist whose work drew on a diverse body of research.

Bryan W. Sokol is an associate professor in the department of psychology and the director of the Center for Service and Community Engagement at Saint Louis University. His research interests include the development of children's social understanding and socioemotional competence, moral agency, and conceptions of selfhood.

Frederick M. E. Grouzet is an associate professor of psychology at the University of Victoria. His research interests include the development of personal goals and values through socialization and personal-growth experiences and activities, as well as the relationships between goals, mental time travel, and well-being.

Ulrich Müller is an associate professor of psychology at the University of Victoria. His research focuses on the development of self-regulation in young children and the ways in which social interaction influences the development of self-regulation. Dr. Müller has co-edited several books, including *The Cambridge Companion to Piaget* (2009).

INTERDISCIPLINARY PERSPECTIVES ON KNOWLEDGE AND DEVELOPMENT: THE JEAN PIAGET SYMPOSIUM SERIES

Series Editor

Nancy Budwig
Clark University

Current Titles: Published by Cambridge University Press

Self-Regulation and Autonomy: Social and Developmental Dimensions of Human Conduct, edited by Bryan W. Sokol, Frederick M. E. Grouzet, and Ulrich Müller, 2013.
Adolescent Vulnerabilities and Opportunities: Developmental and Constructivist Perspectives, edited by Eric Amsel and Judith Smetana, 2011.

Prior Editors: Lynn S. Liben and Ellin Kofsky Scholnick

Published by Lawrence Erlbaum Associates/Taylor and Francis/ Psychology Press

Art and Human Development, edited by Constance Milbrath and Cynthia Lightfoot, 2009.
Developmental Social Cognitive Neuroscience, edited by Philip David Zelazo, Michael Chandler, and Eveline Crone, 2009.
Social Life and Social Knowledge: Toward a Process Account of Development, edited by Ulrich Müller, Jeremy I. M. Carpendale, Nancy Budwig, and Bryan Sokol, 2008.
Social Development, Social Inequalities, and Social Justice, edited by Cecilia Wainryb, Judith G. Smetana, and Elliot Turiel, 2007.
Developmental Perspectives on Embodiment and Consciousness, edited by Willis Overton, Ulrich Müller, and Judith Newman, 2007.
Play and Development: Evolutionary, Sociocultural, and Functional Perspectives, edited by Artin Goncu and Suzanne Gaskins, 2007.
Biology and Knowledge Revisited: From Neurogenesis to Psychogenesis, edited by Sue Taylor Parker, Jonas Langer, and Constance Milbrath, 2004.
Changing Conceptions of Psychological Life, edited by Cynthia Lightfoot, Michael Chandler, and Chris Lalonde, 2004.

(*continued after the index*)

Self-Regulation and Autonomy

SOCIAL AND DEVELOPMENTAL DIMENSIONS OF HUMAN CONDUCT

Edited by

Bryan W. Sokol

Saint Louis University

Frederick M. E. Grouzet

University of Victoria

Ulrich Müller

University of Victoria

CAMBRIDGE
UNIVERSITY PRESS

32 Avenue of the Americas, New York, NY 10013–2473, USA

Cambridge University Press is part of the University of Cambridge.

It furthers the University's mission by disseminating knowledge in the pursuit of education, learning, and research at the highest international levels of excellence.

www.cambridge.org
Information on this title: www.cambridge.org/9781107023697

First published 2013

Printed in the United States of America

A catalog record for this publication is available from the British Library.

Library of Congress Cataloging in Publication data
Self-regulation and autonomy : Social and developmental dimensions of human conduct /
[edited by] Bryan W. Sokol, Saint Louis University, Frederick M. E. Grouzet,
University of Victoria, Ulrich Müller, University of Victoria.
pages cm. (Jean Piaget symposium series)
Includes index.
ISBN 978-1-107-02369-7 (hardback)
1. Autonomy (Psychology) 2. Self. 3. Executive functions (Neuropsychology)
4. Developmental psychology. 5. Social psychology. I. Sokol, Bryan W.
II. Grouzet, Frederick M. E. III. Müller, Ulrich, 1949–
BF575.A88S45 2013
155.2–dc23 2013013354

ISBN 978-1-107-02369-7 Hardback

Contents

Figures and Tables

FIGURES

TABLES

Series Editor's Preface to the Book Series

In 1970, Jean Piaget participated in a workshop that instigated vigorous discussion in higher education circles about the importance of traversing the boundaries across the disciplines. The workshop, entitled "L'interdisciplinarité – Problèmes d'enseignement et de recherche dans les universities," was held in Nice, France, in September 1970 and the proceedings were published in 1972 as a monograph entitled *Interdisciplinarity: Problems of Teaching and Research in Universities* (Paris: Organisation for Economic Cooperation and Development). This workshop and the book that resulted from it set the stage for ongoing debates about how best to view work occurring at the intersection of disciplinary boundaries. Piaget's remarks made clear that new conceptual frameworks were needed, frameworks that underscored the importance of augmenting disciplinary knowledge in order to address enduring challenges of our times. Whether to do so from multi-, trans-, or interdisciplinary bases and what precisely each of these constructs adds to disciplinary discussions has been hotly debated for the ensuing four decades. What Piaget was wrestling with in 1970 and many others have been pursuing since then are two enduring issues: the complexity of knowledge and the importance of viewing knowledge construction as a process embedded in real time. Piaget understood early what has become more obvious now, namely the importance of going beyond disciplinary limitations both theoretically and methodologically. This insight has shaped modern thinking on knowledge and development in significant ways.

Around the same time that Piaget spoke at the Organisation for Economic Cooperation and Development workshop, a new society was formed: the Jean Piaget Society. Founded in 1970, it has since provided an internationally recognized forum for inquiry and advances about significant problems in the developmental sciences. The Society has had a longstanding commitment to developmental perspectives and has been deeply concerned with theories and conceptualizations of development and the ways developmental perspectives connect to and influence research. Since renamed the Jean Piaget Society for Knowledge and Development, the Society organizes and sponsors a book series, an annual meeting for plenary addresses and scholarly presentations, a scholarly journal (*Cognitive Development*), and a website (http://www.piaget.org). Across venues, participating scholars come from a range of disciplines, including departments of psychology, anthropology, linguistics, sociology, biology, philosophy, and education.

The Society has had a long-standing dedication to the publication of a book series that addresses core problems in the developmental sciences. For more than 30 years, Lawrence Erlbaum Press (currently Psychology Press/ Taylor and Francis) published the series. Each of the volumes in the Jean Piaget Series (JPS) engages well-recognized scholars on a set of themes that bring together divergent disciplinary perspectives. The series, which has included nearly 40 published volumes, has dealt with topics such as human understanding, developmental psychopathology, concept formation, and relations between learning and development.

In a time when there is a proliferation of edited volumes, one can ask what makes this series thrive. The high regard for these volumes has been due to the careful way interdisciplinary thinking has shed light on enduring issues with which scholars interested in human development are grappling. To a large measure the rigorous system of cultivation and review plays a significant role in arriving at cutting-edge thinking that goes beyond juxtaposition of new ideas. Careful attention is given to taking a theme at the center of developmental science (e.g., epigenesis of mind; culture, thought, and development; social development and social justice; developmental social cognitive neuroscience) and weaving scholarship from neighboring disciplines into discussions in ways that hold the potential to significantly shape ongoing scientific discourse.

Each JPS volume emanates from the Society's themed annual meeting that includes plenary addresses and invited symposia, a meeting structure that itself is the outcome of a long and rigorous academic review process. Typically, several revisions are made in the proposal before it obtains approval from the full board of directors. The annual meeting organizers also serve as editors of the volume. To supplement chapters by the five or six plenary speakers, the volume editors typically invite other contributors to the volume. The editors also inform contributors about the requirements with regard to the volume's theme and scope. Finally, the editors engage in a thorough evaluation of each contribution, providing extensive feedback and soliciting revisions until they are of the required quality. This process ensures that extraordinary scholars will contribute to the volumes. In summary, we believe the book series has provided a distinctive intellectual contribution to the study of knowledge and development by focusing on developmental inquiry from an interdisciplinary perspective. Further information about the series can be found at http://www.piaget.org/Series/series.html.

This second volume in our book series *Interdisciplinary Perspectives on Knowledge and Development: The Jean Piaget Symposium Series* with Cambridge University Press exemplifies the strong interdisciplinary approach that has been central to all of our prior volumes. Edited by Bryan W. Sokol, Frederick M. E. Grouzet, and Ulrich Müller, this volume, *Self-Regulation and Autonomy: Social and Developmental Dimensions of Human Conduct*, continues the Jean Piaget Society's tradition of providing a recognized forum for advancing inquiry about both enduring and emergent problems in the developmental sciences. The linkage between self-regulation and autonomy is truly novel, and the volume provides a space to explore the interface between these two constructs from various areas of psychology. In addition to providing new conceptual frameworks that deal with the dialectic between organism and social context, the volume provides insights into usable knowledge to the extent that theory and research about self-regulation and autonomy are applied to educational settings. As such, this second volume continues to represent the goals of the series in important ways by paving the road to further interdisciplinary scholarship at the frontiers of new knowledge about human development.

Nancy Budwig
Clark University
Worcester, MA
October 2012

Preface to the Volume

The origin of this volume was a conference entitled "Self-Regulation and Autonomy: Exploring Social, Developmental and Educational Currents of Human Conduct" that we organized in 2010. The impetus for organizing a conference on self-regulation and autonomy grew from three broad considerations. The first concerned the increasing interest in these topics from researchers of diverse backgrounds. From almost any theoretical angle, self-regulation and autonomy are considered vital for adaptive psychological functioning in human beings. The second consideration followed from the important role of self-regulation in typical and atypical development, particularly in social contexts like school or family life. Successes and failures in self-regulation are reflected in children's and adults' abilities to regulate impulses, attention, and emotions, all of which have important ramifications for individual functioning and interpersonal behavior. Finally, the third consideration derived from several key conceptual questions about the notions of self-regulation and autonomy – specifically, how should the impact of social interactions on self-regulation and autonomy be conceptualized? Should self-regulation and autonomy be conceptualized as organismic or socially acquired constructs? Are they culturally universal or specific? What are their biological bases?

We submitted a meeting proposal describing these themes to the board of directors of the Jean Piaget Society. Based on their helpful feedback, we refined the proposal and sharpened its conceptual focus. Our proposal was realized at the 40th Annual Meeting of the Jean Piaget Society, which was held June 3 to 5, 2010, in St. Louis, Missouri. This volume is based on presentations from that meeting.

We would like to thank several individuals who were helpful in bringing this project to fruition. Geoffrey Saxe (past president of the Society) was very supportive of our efforts to make both the conference and this volume a success. Larry Nucci (VP Meeting Planning), Stephanie Carlson (VP Publicity and Outreach), Christopher Lalonde (VP Information Technology), Ashley Maynard (Treasurer), and Saba Ayman-Noelley (VP Communications) put in a lot of hard work in planning, organizing, and advertising the meeting. The local arrangement committee in St. Louis, headed by Bryan W. Sokol and the graduate students at Saint Louis University's Department of Psychology, made sure that the meeting itself ran smoothly. We would also like to thank Nancy Budwig for her advice and counsel in preparing this volume.

We would like to acknowledge the generous financial support we received from the Jacobs Foundation, Saint Louis University, the Center for Character and Citizenship (University of Missouri at St. Louis), the St. Louis Academy of Science, Elsevier, and Taylor and Francis.

Bryan W. Sokol (Saint Louis, MO),
Frederick M. E. Grouzet (Victoria, BC),
Ulrich Müller (Victoria, BC),
October 2012

Chapter 1

Self-Regulation and Autonomy: An Introduction

FREDERICK M. E. GROUZET
University of Victoria
BRYAN W. SOKOL
Saint Louis University
ULRICH MÜLLER
University of Victoria

The study of self-regulation and autonomy has emerged as an important topic at the intersection of several areas in psychology. Developmental psychologists (e.g., Blair & Ursach, 2011; Carlson, 2005; Posner & Rothbart, 2007; Zelazo, Carlson, & Kesek, 2008) have identified different aspects of regulatory control and how these change over time. Social psychologists (e.g., Bandura, 1997; Deci & Ryan, 2000; Ryan & Deci, 2000) have emphasized the importance of autonomy, agency, and self-determined goal setting for healthy psycho-social functioning and academic achievement. Similarly, educational psychologists (e.g., Bodrova & Leong, 2006) consider successful self-regulation to be vital for controlling impulses, attention, cognition, and emotions relevant to academic adjustment (Calkins & Howse, 2004). This interest of developmental, social, and educational psychologists has also been accompanied by a growing understanding of the neurological features of self-regulation (Heatherton & Wagner, 2011; Hrabok & Kerns, 2010), including the role that differences in the inter- and intra-hemispheric organization of the brain, as well as different neurotransmitters, play in predicting developmental and individual differences (e.g., Converse, Pathak, Steinhauser, & Homan, 2012; Luciana, Wahlstrom, Porter, & Collins, 2012).

This volume brings together distinguished scholars from a variety of disciplines, including social psychology, developmental psychology, educational psychology, and neuroscience, to explore the many ways that self-regulation and autonomy impact human life. Given the many different contributors to theory and research on these topics, it can be challenging to find a common understanding of terms and concepts. We begin, then, by trying to better contextualize the chapters in this volume and offer a review of some of the different ways that self-regulation and autonomy have been conceptualized in psychology, all with an eye toward prominent theories of human development.

SELF-REGULATION AND AUTONOMY

In psychology the concepts of self-regulation and autonomy are sometimes considered synonymous, while at other times they are quite distinct from each other. The etymology of the term autonomy, that is, auto (self) nomy (ruling), has certainly influenced the conceptualization of autonomy as equivalent to self-regulation. In such cases, the term self-regulation has typically been used to refer to a sense of self-control, or as "the self altering its own responses or inner states" (Baumeister, Schmeichel, & Vohs, 2007, p. 517). This conceptualization tends to set self-regulatory abilities in opposition to internal impulses or desires as well as to *other*-regulation (or external regulation), which tends to establish autonomy as a kind of strict independence from others' influence and control. By contrast, a more process-oriented view of self-regulation – one that perhaps relies less on notions of selfhood as independent – does not carry the same implications for autonomy. In such cases, self-regulation is understood generally as the organism's ability to regulate itself using self-corrective adjustments when circumstances demand (e.g., Carver & Scheier, 1981). This definition allows autonomous functioning to be seen as an adaptive relationship between an organism and its environment, and, as such, suggests that a detached independence from others or environmental factors is impossible.

Both of these approaches, as it happens, are also present in philosophical discourse on self-regulation and autonomy. For example, May (1994) distinguishes between autonomy as autarkeia, or self-sufficiency, and autonomy as self-rule. Autonomy as autarkeia, a view that May (1994) – probably mistakenly (see O'Neill, 2003) – attributes to Kant, implies independence from external influences. As May (1994, p. 139) observes, however, viewing autonomy as strict independence from other forces runs counter to much of human experience, and what is considered fulfilling in life, particularly in personal relationships:

> *To act in a self-sufficient manner seems a rather austere existence, lacking many of the things we think to be a part of a full, rich, and robust life. To act for such contingent, external purposes as fulfilling the wishes of a child,*

spouse, or parent because it is what the loved-one wishes would not meet the requirement of self-sufficiency, for the determination of action would then be contingent upon the content of the loved-one's wishes. Yet such actions are often what we consider the very embodiment of a rich life.

By contrast, the conceptualization of autonomy as self-rule allows external factors to influence the determination of action. Autonomy as self-rule, which May (1994) traces back to Aristotle, does not require detachment from external (including social) influences:

Rather, it requires that the agent actively assess these influences rather than simply react to them. External influences do not cause action, but rather provide information that the agent, as "helmsman," then steers according to.

Christman (2009) further specifies that the ascription of autonomy requires that competency (e.g., capacity of rational thought, self-reflection) and authenticity conditions are fulfilled. The latter conditions include the capacity to reflectively endorse and identify with one's desires and values, which Frankfurt (1971) and others (see Sokol, Müller, & Chandler, Chapter 5) have characterized as second-order identification with first-order desires and wants. This self-rule view of autonomy allows for the possibility of bringing into balance more basic, organismic drives or needs with individuals' sociocognitive functioning (for further elaboration, see Grouzet, Chapter 3).

As we describe the complexity of the relations between self-regulation and autonomy, we hope to not only identify common misunderstandings of these terms but also important advances in understanding. The chapters in this volume provide an excellent opportunity to frame these advances with varied examples from the social, developmental, educational, and neurological sciences.

Self-Regulation: From a Single-Process Perspective to a Multi-Layered Approach

The term self-regulation has different meanings. On one hand, self-regulation refers to the regulation of affect, thoughts, and actions by the organism (or the inner self) that is guided by goals and purposes. This approach is directly related to cybernetic models that have dominated the study of self-regulation in psychology (e.g., Carver & Scheier, 1981, 1990, 1998; see also Carver et al. Chapter 12) and have been linked to Piaget's biological notions of accommodation and assimilation (e.g., Boden, 1994; see Waters & Tucker,

Chapter 13). The organism possesses the ability of self-correction in order to attain a goal, using feed-forward and feed-back systems (or assimilation and accommodation). On the other hand, self-regulation may also refer to the control of the organism's response or behavior, "replacing it with a less common but more desired response" (Baumeister et al., 2007, p. 517). This latter definition provides a more narrow type of regulation, commonly referred to as self-control (Carver & Scheier, 2011; Hofmann, Schmeichel, & Baddeley, 2012). Another difference between these two definitions resides in the conceptualization of self in self-regulation. In cybernetic models, in particular, the self can refer either to the organism or to the socially constructed self. The level of analysis does not matter; the basic adaptive processes are understood in the same way. However, when self-regulation is studied more as self-control, the term self refers to the more abstract (or "thick"; see Sokol, Müller, & Chandler, Chapter 5) representation of the self (or agent), and is related to more distinct processes seen in areas of identity development or the "personal" domain (see Nucci, Chapter 8).

In both cases, however, the concept of self-regulation is presented as an important feature of executive functioning processes that develop over time and work to promote successful growth in various social contexts (e.g., school; see Duckworth & Carlson, Chapter 10). However, the nature of the self, such as the extent to which the self is connected to the inner organism versus constructed through social influences, has a significant impact on the conceptualization of self-regulation. Similarly, the development of a self as independent from the social context does not necessarily make it autonomous; rather, how the self is socially constructed may impact the nature of the self-regulation.

Accordingly, social and developmental scientists have proposed models that are responsive to the complex relationships that form between the self and the social. Self-determination theory (SDT; Deci & Ryan, Chapter 2), for instance, has proposed a conceptualization of self-regulation that distinguishes between different degrees in which social influences are integrated within the self: introjected, identified, and integrated regulation. These forms of self-regulation can be placed on a continuum that reflects different degrees of autonomy, as well as different degrees or types of internalization (see Grouzet, Chapter 3). A similar nuanced view of selfhood is also seen in the work of Moshman (2004) who has suggested that "false selves" can guide human behavior and even be used to justify immoral conduct. Finally, Marcia's (1966) seminal account of identity statuses that may be foreclosed, diffused, in moratorium, or achieved also speaks to the complicated ways that social experiences may influence the self. When regulation is external or when the self acts as a proxy for social control (what Marcia called a "foreclosed identity" or SDT has referred to as introjected regulation), then individuals do not experience a sense of autonomy. In contrast, when an "achieved" or "integrated" self is at the origin of the goal or a person's conduct, or when the self is sometimes said to listen to its organismic "inner voice" (Sheldon & Elliott, 1999; see Grouzet, Chapter 3), then a person gains a sense of autonomy.

More layered, or nuanced, conceptualizations of self-regulation, such as those suggested here, challenge various theories and assumptions in psychology. Among them is the proposition that self-regulation tends to consume psychological resources and requires for its operation energy (or willpower), which is a limited resource. Baumeister and his colleagues (Baumeister & Heatherton, 1996; Baumeister, Heatherton, & Tice, 1994; Baumeister et al., 2007), for instance, use an energy (as exhaustible resource) model of self-regulation to explain the empirical finding that individuals perform worse on measures of self-regulation as a result of prior high intensity self-regulatory engagement. However, more recent research conducted by Moller, Deci, and Ryan (2006) found that autonomous forms of self-regulation (i.e., identified and intrinsic self-regulation) are not associated with depletion of energy and might even serve as a source of psychological vitality; only more controlled, or less autonomous, forms of self-regulation (i.e., introjected regulation) were found to be depleting.

Another influential idea that has been challenged is the assumption that the biological impulses or organismic tendencies are opposed to what is societally or culturally acceptable and therefore must be reined in by self-regulatory processes. One fundamental tenet of humanistic psychology, for instance, is that organisms – particularly human beings – possess an innate sense of what is most healthy for themselves (e.g., organismic valuing process; see Grouzet, Chapter 3). Thus, it might be too simplistic to assume that biological impulses always require some form of regulation. As we are cultural animals (Baumeister, 2005), the development of self-regulation is obviously important for adaptive functioning in our society, but muting organismic tendencies may also thwart well-being and integration (see Deci & Ryan, Chapter 2).

In this volume, it will become evident that the concept of self-regulation is used in more or less layered ways, depending on particular assumptions associated with the self. For example, Sawyer's (Chapter 4) understanding of self-regulation refers to externally controlled (or introjected) aspects of the self, which explains why he proposes an opposition between self-regulation and autonomy (the latter, in an SDT perspective, refers to autonomous self-regulation). In other chapters (e.g., Duckworth & Carlson, Chapter 10), self-regulation seems to refer to more autonomous forms of regulation.

Autonomy: Toward Context-Specific Approaches

The concept of autonomy is widely used in psychology, including personality and social psychology, developmental psychology, and clinical and applied psychology, as well as in philosophy, law, and medicine. Because of its significance to human existence (Christman, 2009; Deci & Ryan, 1985; May, 1994), autonomy is a central psychological construct in several theories and models. However, due to the lack of consensus on the conceptual and operational definitions of autonomy, there is a lively debate over its developmental origin, its general importance across the life span and different cultures, and its impact on individuals' growth and day-to-day functioning. Some researchers tried to identify commonalities and differences among the different conceptualizations in the literature (e.g., Hmel & Pincus, 2002; Ryan, Deci, Grolnick, & LaGuardia, 2006). As we have illustrated so far, a common difference concerns the conceptualization of the interaction between the self and social environment. While some approaches to autonomy focus on the separation or independence of the self from others, other approaches view autonomy as resulting from a dialectical relationship between the self and the social.

A dialectical perspective considers the organism in constant interaction with the environment. Psychological approaches such as psychodynamic, humanistic, Piagetian, and Vygotskian or sociocultural traditions support this dialectical perspective. Rather than placing autonomy in opposition to communion, autonomy is opposed to passivity in governing. The self- (auto-) governing (nomy) individual is considered to be actively involved in and consciously affirming his or her decisions, whereas individuals who are externally determined in their decision making are considered to be governed (nomy) by something other or foreign (hetero). The distinction between heteronomy and autonomy is central to Piaget's theory of moral development (1932/1965), as well as to Deci and Ryan's (Chapter 2) self-determination theory (SDT).

SDT and Piagetian theory each propose that autonomy, in some form, must be present from birth, and autonomy must not (nor cannot) be inculcated into a person. For example, in his work on infancy, Piaget (1936/1963) argued that children are intrinsically motivated to exercise their sensorimotor schemes and experience functional pleasure in doing so (see also Deci & Ryan, Chapter 2). A further common feature that is shared between SDT and Piagetian theory is that living systems, particularly human beings, are viewed as functioning according to principles of self-organization and possessing a natural tendency to grow in orderly ways (i.e., growth is a natural consequence of the interactions between organism and environment; see Deci & Ryan, Chapter 2; Grouzet, Chapter 3; Sawyer, Chapter 4). Self-organization and self-regulated growth further highlight the autonomous nature of the organism.

However, in the context of moral development, some have suggested that Piaget (1932/1965) argued for two stages of moral functioning (Kohlberg, 1981) in which children move from heteronomy to autonomy. Although this interpretation has been contested (Carpendale, 2000; Sokol & Chandler, 2004; Youniss & Damon, 1992), this stage account raises questions of how it is logically possible to move from heteronomy to autonomy, and specifically, how self-rule can emerge from other-rule (Wright, 1982). This problem is recognized by SDT, which proposes that autonomy does not emerge but is present already in infancy and the move from heteronomous morality to autonomous morality (in the form of integration) is the result of the support of the psychological need for autonomy.

Therefore, the context in which autonomy is studied may help explain aspects of its conceptualization. For example, in the context of social relationships, autonomy can be considered as independence from others. In the context of competence (and daily functioning), autonomy may refer to the ability to do things without help, and to make decision and choices. In the context of organismic regulation, autonomy is a fundamental psychological need and refers to a natural self-integration and valuing processes (e.g., Deci & Ryan, Chapter 2; Grouzet, Chapter 3). In the context of morality, autonomy is related to the concept of self-regulation and is the outcome of socialization; the development of autonomy corresponds to the ability to resist many of the temptations, coming from inside or outside (e.g., see Sokol, Müller, & Chandler, Chapter 5). In the context of identity, autonomy refers to the expression of personal interests (e.g., Nucci, Chapter 8). The list of contexts could be expanded, but contextualizing the discourse on autonomy offers a good organizational framework for the various ways that autonomy is understood.

Development of the Self: Between Organismic and Cognitive Processes

The development of the self and its self-regulatory abilities is another central theme in this volume. Referring to work by Piaget, Vygotsky, and Rogers, the chapters examine different perspectives on the development of self-regulation and autonomy. On one hand, some chapters emphasize the natural tendency for self-development, referring to concepts such as an organismic integration process (Deci & Ryan, Chapter 2), organismic valuing process (Grouzet, Chapter 3), and emergence (Sawyer, Chapter 4). Autonomous self-regulation, according to these contributors, is seen to emerge naturally when the organismic needs of autonomy, competence, and relatedness are supported (Grolnick & Raftery-Helmer, Chapter 7; Ryan & Deci, Chapter 9). On the other hand, several chapters stress the importance of cognitive development for internalization and autonomous self-regulation (i.e., identified and integrated regulation) (e.g., Krettenauer, Chapter 6; Duckworth & Carlson, Chapter 10; Kinnucan & Kuebli, Chapter 11). According to these contributors, a sense of autonomy cannot emerge without the guidance of meta-cognitive abilities that enable self-authorship and ownership, a sense of (volitional and then identified) agency, and the ability to critically examine or even explain why we do what we do. What is considered by the former group as supporting an organismic need, the latter group studies as a form of sociocognitive functioning. Although these two perspectives appear to be contradictory, they might actually complement each other as Grouzet has proposed in his dual valuing process model (Chapter 3). The combination of organismic and cognitive processes can enhance our understanding of self-regulation and autonomy and their development in social and educational contexts. This combined organismic-cognitive perspective is also supported by neurological studies of self-regulation and autonomy which show that development and learning share the same neurological mechanisms (e.g., Waters & Tucker, Chapter 13). Another integration of these two perspectives can be found in Krettenauer's three-layer model of the moral self (Chapter 6) according to which early cognitive development leads to the emergence of three levels of the moral self that, in turn, impact self-regulation.

ORGANIZATION OF THE VOLUME

The objective of this volume is to provide a comprehensive and multi-perspective overview of the concepts of self-regulation and autonomy as they are studied in social, developmental, educational, and neuro psychology. The complexity of the concepts and the richness of the chapters offer various ways to organize the volume. Based on our analysis of the different meanings of self-regulation and autonomy, we chose to organize the chapters in four sections that address (1) the dialectic between the organism and the social context, (2) the social developmental perspective, (3) the role of self-regulation and autonomy in education, and (4) the neurological foundations of self-regulation and autonomy.

Dialectic Between Organismic and Social Processes

The first part of the volume includes three chapters on important theoretical conceptualizations of self-regulation and autonomy that highlight the dialectic between organismic tendencies (i.e., organismic integration process, organismic valuing process, and emergence) and social demands as being central to self-regulatory processes. First, Edward Deci and Richard Ryan present in Chapter 2 one of the most important macro-theories in psychology, namely, self-determination theory, which assigns a central role to autonomy and self-regulation. Deci and Ryan suggest that the organismic integration process is intrinsic and explains the internalization of extrinsic motivation. More specifically, they propose that the fulfillment of three fundamental psychological needs (autonomy, competence, and relatedness) can foster intrinsic motivation and integration, which is then translated into four forms of self-regulation that are characterized as introjected, identified, integrated, and intrinsic regulation. They summarize 40 years of research using self-determination theory as a theoretical framework to study human development and self-regulation. Deci and Ryan offer a framework for understanding self-regulation as described in the other chapters because they make a clear distinction between autonomous and controlled forms of self-regulation.

In Chapter 3 Frederick Grouzet revisits the valuing processes that are proposed in humanistic and social psychology to explain the development and internalization of personal goals and values. Goals and values occupy a central role in self-regulatory processes as they reflect the dynamic between the emergent self and the social context, influence corrective adjustments, and guide daily behaviors. In congruence with self-determination theory, he proposes a model that combines Rogers's organismic valuing process and the sociocognitive valuing processes that are dealt with in social and developmental psychology. In contrast to some self-regulation models that present inner impulses as something to control, the Dual Valuing Process Model proposes that the organism is capable of autoregulation, so the "inner voice" should sometimes be listened to rather than controlled. Grouzet proposes that the dynamic between the organismic and the sociocognitive valuing processes can lead to different degrees of autonomy and authenticity.

Finally, Keith Sawyer (Chapter 4) introduces the concept of emergence in an attempt to resolve the tension between autonomy and self-regulation. Emergence figures as an important concept in the accounts of human development and creativity, both of which necessarily involve (and result from) tension between the social and the individual. From this tension emerges a higher level entity that represents the mature person who balances autonomy and self-regulation. Sawyer's conceptualization of autonomy and self-regulation is different from that in other chapters. Specifically, in his chapter autonomy refers to the individual with his own desires and interests, and self-regulation refers to introjected regulation. The conflict between autonomy and self-regulation thus results from a conceptualization of autonomy and self-regulation that differs from that in other chapters of this volume.

Social Development

The second part of the volume includes four chapters that examine autonomy and self-regulation through the lens of social development. The development of self-regulation is intimately related to the development of the self, and more specifically the moral self. In Chapter 5, Bryan Sokol, Ulrich Müller, and Michael Chandler raise fundamental questions regarding the development of the moral self and agency. Building on Piaget's suggestion that agency is rooted in perspective taking, Sokol, Müller, and Chandler distinguish between a "thin" and "thick" sense of agency, corresponding to different levels of abstraction in self-regulation (see Carver & Scheier, 1998). They use this distinction to examine the process of self-appropriation by means of which individuals commit themselves to particular values and ideals. They report a study that investigates how adolescents construct their agentive abilities.

In the following chapter, Tobias Krettenauer proposes a three-layer model of the moral self, making a distinction between intentional, volitional, and identified agent. This multi-dimensional and hierarchical approach addresses Sokol et al.'s concerns (Chapter 5) and Nucci's (2004a, 2004b) criticisms regarding the reductionist approach to morality. Krettenauer identifies a sequence in the development of the moral self, which, in the order of emergence, includes the intentional self, the volitional self, and the identified self. However, in contrast with some stage models in developmental psychology, higher levels of development do not replace the previous ones. All three forms of agency co-exist. This three-layer model offers a unique perspective on self-regulation, combining developmental principles and multi-level representations of the self. In other words, more complex aspects of the self include (rather than replace) more simple components. In this respect, the structure of Krettenauer's theory of the moral self is similar to and consistent with the evolutionary-developmental framework by Waters and Tucker (Chapter 13), according to which primitive brain structures interact with more complex structures in regulating affect and actions.

The development of the moral self, like the social self and the cultural self, is subject to the desires of others (especially parents) and to socialization processes. Parents would like to see socially and culturally desirable behaviors becoming the characteristics of the child's moral self. However, research shows that by imposing the content of the moral self (i.e., values and behaviors), parents may interfere with the development of a sense of ownership that is important for an identified agent. In Chapter 7, Wendy Grolnick and Jacquelyn Raftery-Helmer directly address this "socialization paradox." Grounded in self-determination theory, they propose that supporting autonomy enables the internalization (via identification) of values and facilitates autonomous forms of self-regulation (e.g., identified regulation). After defining autonomy, Grolnick and Raftery-Helmer describe how parents can support autonomy while teaching desirable behaviors as defined by culture. Rather than using behavioral control to introduce behaviors, they propose to provide choices and rationales and to include the child in decision making. Their review of empirical evidence supports the need for a balance between autonomy support and structure in parenting style.

In contrast to previous chapters, Larry Nucci (Chapter 8) focuses on "the personal domain" – that is, children's preferences and choices in areas of life where they believe they possess the most autonomy (i.e., they serve as their own authority). The personal domain is understood as distinct from moral and social conventional domains, which stand in a different relation to cultural authority and traditions. The personal is an important component of individuals' identity and results from the "need to establish a sense of self, personal autonomy, and individuality (uniqueness)." Nucci draws on empirical studies to illustrate how the intervention of parents in personal issues could be perceived as controlling and, as a result, negatively impact well-being. He also addresses the question of the universality of the personal, showing that the personal zone of privacy and personal choice have been observed in various cultures.

Self-Regulation and Autonomy at School

The previous section considered the development of self-regulation as a character strength and the autonomous form of self-regulation as an outcome of social development and socialization. This was particularly evident in the context of education and learning. However, as Deci and Ryan (Chapter 2) show, it is crucial to distinguish between different types of self-regulation, and, more specifically, different levels of self-determination, to understand the relationship between self-regulation and academic outcomes. In Chapter 9, Richard Ryan and Edward Deci demonstrate the positive impact of autonomous forms of self-regulation, such as intrinsic motivation, identified regulation, and integrated regulation, on learning, academic achievement, and persistence. In contrast, the controlled form of self-regulation (i.e., introjected regulation) and external regulation are associated with superficial learning, anxiety, poor performance, and school dropout. Ryan and Deci review the various educational practices that can preserve intrinsic motivation and facilitate the development of identified and integrated regulation. They conclude that "classroom practices that support autonomy, competence, and relatedness are associated with both greater intrinsic motivation and autonomous forms of extrinsic motivation" (i.e., identified and integrated regulation).

Further evidence of the role of identified regulation in education is offered in Chapter 10. Based on Baumeister et al.'s perspective on self-regulation, Angela Lee Duckworth and Stephanie Carlson define self-regulation as "the *voluntary* control of attentional, emotional, and behavioral impulses in the service of *personally valued* goals and standards." This definition of self-regulation echoes Ryan and Deci's concepts of identified and integrated regulation. Based on a comprehensive review of recent research on self-regulation in an academic context, they show how self-regulation impacts both educational attainment (e.g., years of education, high school completion) and achievement (e.g., teacher-assigned course grades, standardized achievement test scores). Duckworth and Carlson also offer a brief overview of school-based interventions that can foster (autonomous) self-regulation. In particular, they emphasize the importance of teaching meta-cognitive strategies.

As described in previous chapters (e.g., Grouzet, Grolnick & Raftery-Helmer, and Ryan & Deci), the development of identified regulation or internalization of values can be facilitated by providing rationales and explanations. This strategy for supporting autonomy can also be found in Vygotsky's theory of self-regulation. Challis Kinnucan and Janet Kuebli (Chapter 11) propose that "explanation" is central to the emergence of (autonomous) self-regulation. After reviewing Vygotsky's theory of self-regulation, they discuss the role of conversation and self-talk in internalization processes and the enhancement of self-regulation. They suggest that the ability to provide self-explanations facilitates the internalization of social and cultural norms, goals, and standards, which could lead to identification. In other words, being able to make sense of social and cultural demands, transforming them into personal goals and intentions, and reformulating them using one's own language can facilitate an autonomous form of self-regulation.

Neurological Perspective on Self-Regulation and Autonomy

This volume on self-regulation and autonomy would not be complete without examining the neurological basis of these concepts. The appeal to biological substrates of self-regulation is not entirely new in psychology (Tucker & Williamson, 1984). However, in the context of a multi-dimensional perspective on self-regulation and autonomy, the last two chapters of this volume propose new insights into the connection between these psychological constructs and neurological substrates.

In Chapter 12, Charles Carver, Sheri Johnson, and Jutta Joormann examine the role of the serotonin system in self-regulation. In particular, they propose that the level of serotonic function can influence the ability to control impulsiveness toward both rewarding and aversive stimuli. Reviewing research in genetics and biopsychology, they demonstrate that lower general or situational serotonergic function increases the likelihood of observing the automatic, reflexive, and reactive mode of self-regulation, but decreases the activation of effortful, rational, and reflective mode of self-regulation. In contrast to a common perspective that considers impulses as the source of problems in self-regulation (e.g., Baumeister et al., 2007), Carver and his colleagues show that impulses are simply the expression of the personal reaction to emotional cues. For example, the effects of low serotonergic function on aggression depend on the individual's habitual tendency to be aggressive, which represents the inner self or the organism. They also show that an impulse can be associated with an approach-oriented behavior (e.g., aggression or impulsive violence) or an avoidance-oriented behavior (e.g., depression or impulsive passivity).

Finally, Allison Waters and Don Tucker (Chapter 13) use an evolutionary developmental framework to link brain structures to self-regulation and autonomy. For example, adopting a cybernetic perspective on self-regulation, they propose that the ventral cortico-limbic circuit is associated with accommodation and feedback control, while the dorsal cortico-limbic circuit supports assimilation and feed-forward functions. Similarly, they associate the ventral stream with interdependence (or attachment) and the dorsal stream with independence (or autonomy). Furthermore, they offer support for the organization/integration principles proposed by Piaget and SDT, showing that "design of neural connections is self-organizing." Finally, their model also offers a new view on the controversy about the relation between development and learning. Similar to Vygotsky (1978), they suggest that development and learning are based on the same processes, a position that is at odds with Piaget's (1970) view that development and learning are based on different processes.

CONCLUSION

We are confident that the chapters in this volume illustrate the complexity of self-regulation and autonomy. By approaching self-regulation and autonomy from multiple perspectives, the chapters explicate how each of these perspectives contributes to our understanding of these important concepts by disclosing essential aspects of each. Taken together, the chapters in this volume demonstrate that a more comprehensive understanding of self-regulation and autonomy emerges when the different disciplinary perspectives are compared, contrasted, and coordinated.

REFERENCES

Bandura, A. (1997). *Self-efficacy: The exercise of control*. New York, NY: Freeman.

Baumeister, R. F. (2005). *The cultural animal: Human nature, meaning, and social life*. New York, NY: Oxford University Press.

Baumeister, R. F., & Heatherton, T. F. (1996). Self-regulation failure: An overview. *Psychological Inquiry*, *7*, 1–15. doi:10.1207/s15327965pli0701_1

Baumeister, R. F., Heatherton, T. F., & Tice, D. M. (1994). *Losing control: How and why people fail at self-regulation*. New York, NY: Academic Press.

Baumeister, R. F., Schmeichel, B. J., & Vohs, K. D. (2007). Self-regulation and the executive function: The self as controlling agent. In A. W. Kruglanski & E. T. Higgins (Eds.), *Social psychology: Handbook of basic principles* (2nd ed., pp. 516–539). New York, NY: Guilford Press.

Blair, C., & Ursache, A. (2011). A bidirectional model of executive functions and self-regulation. In K. D. Vohs & R. F. Baumeister (Eds.), *Handbook of self-regulation: Research, theory, and applications* (2nd ed., pp. 300–320). New York, NY: Guilford Press.

Boden, M. A. (1994). *Piaget* (2nd ed.). London: Fontana Press.

Bodrova, E., & Leong, D. J. (2005). Self-regulation as a key to school readiness. In M. Zaslow (Ed.), *Critical issues in early childhood professional development* (1st ed., pp. 203–224). Baltimore, MD: Brookes.

Calkins, S. D., & Howse, R. B. (2004). Individual differences in self-regulation: Implications for childhood adjustment. In P. Philippot & R. S. Feldman (Eds.), *The regulation of emotion* (pp. 307–332). Mahwah, NJ: Lawrence Erlbaum.

Carlson, S. M. (2005). Developmentally sensitive measures of executive function in preschool children. *Developmental Neuropsychology*, *28*, 595–616. doi:10.1207/s15326942dn2802_3

Carpendale, J. M. (2000). Kohlberg and Piaget on stages and moral reasoning. *Developmental Review*, *20*, 181–205. doi:10.1006/drev.1999.0500

Carver, C. S., & Scheier, M. F. (1981). *Attention and self-regulation: A control theory approach to human behavior*. New York, NY: Springer-Verlag.

Carver, C. S., & Scheier, M. F. (1990). Origins and functions of positive and negative affect: A control-process view. *Psychological Review*, *97*, 19–35. doi:10.1037/0033-295X.97.1.19

Carver, C. S., & Scheier, M. F. (1998). *On the self-regulation of behavior*. New York, NY: Cambridge University Press.

Carver, C. S., & Scheier, M. F. (2011). Self-regulation of action and affect. In K. D. Vohs & R. F. Baumeister (Eds.), *Handbook of self-regulation: Research, theory, and applications* (2nd ed., pp. 3–21). New York, NY: Guilford Press.

Christman, J. (2009). Autonomy in moral and political philosophy. *Stanford Encyclopedia of Philosophy*. Retrieved from http://stanford.library.usyd.edu.au/entries/autonomy-moral/ (retrieved Sept. 4, 2102).

Converse, P. D., Pathak, J., Steinhauser, E., & Homan, E. W. (2012). Repeated self-regulation and asymmetric hemispheric activation. *Basic and Applied Social Psychology*, *34*, 152–167. doi:10.1080/01973533.2012.655989

Deci, E. L., & Ryan, R. M. (1985). *Intrinsic motivation and self-determination in human behavior*. New York, NY: Plenum.

Deci, E. L., & Ryan, R. M. (2000). The "what" and "why" of goal pursuits: Human needs and the self-determination of behavior. *Psychological Inquiry*, *11*, 227–268. doi:10.1207/S15327965PLI1104_01

Frankfurt, H. G. (1971). Freedom of the will and the concept of a person. *Journal of Philosophy*, *68*, 5. doi:10.2307/2024717

Heatherton, T. F., & Wagner, D. D. (2011). Cognitive neuroscience of self-regulation failure. *Trends in Cognitive Sciences*, *15*, 132–139. doi:10.1016/j.tics.2010.12.005

Hmel, B. A., & Pincus, A. L. (2002). The meaning of autonomy: On and beyond the interpersonal circumplex. *Journal of Personality*, *70*, 277–310. doi:10.1111/1467-6494.05006

Hofmann, W., Schmeichel, B. J., & Baddeley, A. D. (2012). Executive functions and self-regulation. *Trends in Cognitive Sciences*, *16*, 174–180. doi:10.1016/j.tics.2012.01.006

Hrabok, M., & Kerns, K. A. (2010). The development of self-regulation: A neuropsychological perspective. In B. W. Sokol, U. Müller, J. I. M. Carpendale, A. R. Young, & G. Iarocci (Eds.), *Self and social regulation: Social interaction and the development of social understanding and executive functions* (pp. 129–154). New York, NY: Oxford University Press.

Kohlberg, L. (1981). *The philosophy of moral development: Moral stages and the idea of justice (Essays on Moral Development)* (1st ed., Vol. 1). San Francisco: Harper & Row.

Marcia, J. E. (1966). Development and validation of ego-identity status. *Journal of Personality and Social Psychology*, *3*, 551–558. doi:10.1037/h0023281

May, T. (1994). The concept of autonomy. *American Philosophical Quarterly*, *31*, 133–144.

Moller, A. C., Deci, E. L., & Ryan, R. M. (2006). Choice and ego-depletion: The moderating role of autonomy. *Personality and Social Psychology Bulletin*, *32*, 1024–1036. doi:10.1177/0146167206288008

Moshman, D. (2004). False moral identity: Self-serving denial in the maintenance of moral self-conceptions. In D. K. Lapsley & D. Narvaez (Eds.), *Moral development, self, and identity* (pp. 83–109). Mahwah, NJ: Lawrence Erlbaum.

Nucci, L. (2004a). The promise and limitations of the moral self construct. In C. Lightfoot, C. Lalonde, & M. Chandler (Eds.), *Changing conceptions of psychological life* (pp. 49–70). Mahwah, NJ: Lawrence Erlbaum.

Nucci, L. (2004b). Reflections on the moral self construct. In D. K. Lapsley & D. Narvaez (Eds.), *Moral development, self, and identity* (pp. 111–132). Mahwah, NJ: Lawrence Erlbaum.

O'Neill, O. (2003). Autonomy: The emperor's new clothes. *Aristotelian Society Supplementary Volume, 77*, 1–21. doi:10.1111/1467-8349.00100

Piaget, J. (1932/1965). *The moral judgment of the child*. London: Free Press.

Piaget, J. (1963). *The origins of intelligence in children* (2nd ed.). New York, NY: W.W. Norton. (Original work published 1936)

Piaget, J. (1970). Piaget's theory. In P. H. Mussen (Ed.), *Carmichael's manual of child psychology* (pp. 703–732). New York, NY: Wiley.

Posner, M. I., & Rothbart, M. K. (2007). *Educating the human brain*. Washington, DC: American Psychological Association.

Ryan, R. M., & Deci, E. L. (2000). Self-determination theory and the facilitation of intrinsic motivation, social development, and well-being. *American Psychologist, 55*, 68–78. doi:10.1037/0003-066X.55.1.68

Ryan, R. M., Deci, E. L., Grolnick, W. S., & La Guardia, J. G. (2006). The significance of autonomy and autonomy support in psychological development and psychopathology. In D. Cicchetti & D. J. Cohen (Eds.), *Developmental psychopathology: Vol. 1, Theory and method* (2nd ed., pp. 795–849). Hoboken, NJ: John Wiley.

Sheldon, K. M., & Elliot, A. J. (1999). Goal striving, need satisfaction, and longitudinal well-being: The self-concordance model. *Journal of Personality and Social Psychology, 76*, 482–497. doi:10.1037/0022-3514.76.3.482

Sokol, B. W., & Chandler, M. J. (2004). A bridge too far: On the relations between moral and secular reasoning. In J. I. M. Carpendale & U. Müller (Eds.), *Social interaction and the development of knowledge* (pp. 155–174). Mahwah, NJ: Lawrence Erlbaum.

Tucker, D. M., & Williamson, P. A. (1984). Asymmetric neural control systems in human self-regulation. *Psychological Review, 91*, 185–215. doi:10.1037/0033-295X.91.2.185

Vygotsky, L. S., & Cole, M. (1978). *Mind in society: The development of higher psychological processes*. Cambridge, MA: Harvard University Press.

Wright, D. (1982). Piaget's theory of moral development. In S. Modgil & C. Modgil (Eds.), *Jean Piaget: Consensus and controversy* (pp. 207–217). London: Holt, Rinehart & Winston.

Youniss, J., & Damon, W. (1992). Social construction in Piaget's theory. In H. Beilin & P. B. Pufall (Eds.), *Piaget's theory: Prospects and possibilities* (pp. 267–286). Hillsdale, NJ: Lawrence Erlbaum.

Zelazo, P. D., Carlson, S. M., & Kesek, A. (2008). The development of executive function in childhood. In C. A. Nelson & M. Luciana (Eds.), *Handbook of developmental cognitive neuroscience* (2nd ed., pp. 553–574). Cambridge, MA: MIT Press.

PART I

DIALECTIC BETWEEN ORGANISMIC AND SOCIAL PROCESSES

Chapter 2

The Importance of Autonomy for Development and Well-Being

EDWARD L. DECI AND RICHARD M. RYAN
University of Rochester

Piaget's many contributions to developmental psychology were extraordinary, and two of these stand out to us as being particularly important. First, the overall structure of his broad and encompassing theory of cognitive development went against the grain of most developmental approaches of that era, particularly ones within the empirical academic tradition of North American psychology that focused on phenomenon-specific mini-theories. Piaget's theory, in contrast, comprised a wide variety of phenomena related to children's growth – that is, to the changes in schemata that underlie their cognitive and, to a lesser extent, affective development. Second, and even more important, the theory was based on organismic assumptions about the nature of development that followed in the important trajectory of Werner's (1948) contributions to developmental psychology. These organismic assumptions made the quality of Piaget's work quite different from most of the empirical work in developmental psychology of that era and since.

Self-determination theory (SDT), which is a theory of motivation, personality, and development, is also a macro-theory that endorses an organismic meta-theory. Similar to the *organization principle* within Piagetian thought, SDT maintains that there are integrative processes inherent in human nature that are relevant to learning, development, and coherently regulated action. SDT begins with a focus on intrinsic motivation, which represents a prototype of our spontaneous assimilative tendencies, and we review research showing that social-contextual conditions can either enhance or diminish intrinsic motivation as a function of whether they support versus thwart satisfaction of people's basic psychological needs for autonomy, competence, and relatedness. We also discuss the internalization of extrinsic motivation, through which nonintrinsically motivated behaviors can become autonomously motivated. The effectiveness of internalization is also shown to be a function of basic psychological needs supports.

Subsequently, we address differences between intrinsic and extrinsic life goals, discussing their antecedents and consequences, and then move on to discuss attachment, pointing out that substantial variability in attachment security across a person's relational partners can be explained by variability in basic psychological need satisfaction with those partners. Finally, we discuss conditional parental regard relating it to the quality of parent-child relationships.

THE ORGANIZATION PRINCIPLE

Organismic meta-theories assume that a defining characteristic of human beings – indeed, of life more generally – is *the organization principle* (Deci & Ryan, 1985; Ryan, 1993). This assumes that individuals are naturally inclined to expand or elaborate their cognitive schema and representations of themselves and their world in a systematic and organized manner. Organization results in greater integration and inner harmony, viewed not as an end-state but as an ongoing, lifelong process that is forever elaborating, refining, and transforming experiences, cognitive structures, and psychological processes. Within Piaget's theorizing the *assimilation schema* is the primary means through which the organization principle operates.

There are several noteworthy implications of this viewpoint. First, it conveys the idea that human beings are inherently active. This activity, however, is characterized neither by random movements nor movements caused by external prods and contingencies, but instead is proactive, purposive, and organized. In these actions, many of which constitute play, children are expressing or working out inner agendas, and as they do so they are learning about themselves and the world. The agendas need not involve conscious intentions to achieve outcomes other than just doing the activity, but they do lead children toward mastery or understanding of the activity itself and perhaps of affective experiences that are integral to the activity.

Also implicit in the organization principle is the assumption that development is a natural tendency of life that promotes consistency and unity. Behavioral psychologists have argued that development is a process that happens as external environments condition individuals' actions by reinforcing and strengthening specific responses or behaviors (e.g., Skinner, 1953). Thus, whatever organization or coherence is evident in the experiences and actions of individuals would be considered to result *not* from an inner tendency to integrate or assimilate experiences and learnings but rather from environments having been consistent and organized in what they conditioned and reinforced. In a similar vein, cognitive-behavioral or social-cognitive psychologists (e.g., Bandura, 1996) assume that people's behavior is regulated by a collection of cognitions about themselves that have been internalized from teachings of the social environment and from which intentions for further actions are derived. As such, the organized behaviors that people display can be understood as resulting from their being subjected to consistent and coherent teaching and socializing practices.

Piaget, however, was clear in emphasizing that people's inner organization is inherent and results from the operation of the assimilation schema (e.g., Piaget, 1952, 1971), which is made up of the interactive processes of accommodation and assimilation. People accommodate to new stimuli by adapting their existing structures to incorporate new experiences, and they assimilate these experiences within a schema and with other existing schemata. As Piaget (1952) put it, "Organization exists within each schema of assimilation.... But there is above all total organization" (p. 142). At times the organization process may involve extensive reevaluation, reorganization, and transformation of existing structures, with the result that individuals create significantly different experiences and understandings of themselves and their worlds. Regardless of how extensive the reorganization may be, however, the overall process is ongoing; through the functioning of the assimilation schema, greater total organization of structures is constantly being achieved, and this integrated whole works to coordinate its own elements into an ever-greater harmony. Because of the assimilative tendency, organisms are naturally inclined to approach optimally assimilable stimuli – that is, they are attracted to stimuli that are somewhat new relative to their existing cognitive structures but are not so discrepant that the individuals would be unable to master them.

According to Piaget, the functioning of the assimilation schema operates naturally – it is a system-inherent process. In other words, it is in people's evolved nature to assimilate and accommodate – to bring new experiences and stimuli into coherence with schemata they have already mastered – thus developing more elaborated and refined structures as they act on their environment and respond to the environment acting on them. Within Piagetian theory, this development of cognitive structures proceeds through an invariant sequence of age-related stages, and the ongoing result is adolescents having the mature cognitive processes of formal operations and thus developing more mature representations of themselves and their experiences.

Other organismic theorists have similarly assumed an inherent developmental process although they focus on other aspects of human development, such as ego development (Loevinger, 1976) or moral development (Kohlberg, 1969).

THE BASES OF SELF-DETERMINATION THEORY

Self-determination theory, like Piaget's theory, is based in organismic thinking. Its foci are on motivation, development, personality, and well-being across both the life span and the life domains (Deci & Ryan, 1985; Ryan & Deci, 2000b). It differs from Piaget's and other organismic, developmental theories, in part because it focuses primarily on the processes of activity and integration that operate throughout life, rather than their structural precipitates. That is, within SDT, the inherent activity and integrative tendency are interpreted motivationally and examined in relation to the social environment. SDT researchers both assume and observe that people are *intrinsically motivated,* as did Piaget (1952). That is, people are intrinsically motivated by interest to be active and intentional in their interactions with the environment and, through such activity, to learn and grow. From birth, individuals are actively engaged in their own mastery and growth, in ways that are developmentally appropriate, and intrinsic motivation is the energizing basis of this active engagement. An important addition to this thinking provided by SDT is its empirical focus on how social environments play a critical role in learning and development by either supporting or diminishing people's natural intrinsic motivation.

From this perspective, people are assumed to have an inherent tendency toward growth and development. That is, people by nature act in ways that promote their own development, and this development is toward coherence and unity, toward harmony and organization. Implicit in this is the strong assertion, which is contained within all organismic theories of development, that the very concept of development implies animate beings moving in the direction of integration both within themselves and in relation to others (Angyal, 1965).

SDT thus embraces the concept of organization or, as it is called within SDT, *organismic integration,* as the manifestation of the natural tendency toward organized development (Ryan, 1993). Further, and very important, the process of organismic integration underlies *human autonomy*. As explained by biologists (e.g., Mayr, 1982), the nature of life is self-organization, and self-organization is the basis for self-regulation and autonomy (Kauffman, 2000). Like Piaget (1971), SDT has endorsed this view from the start and has proposed that the self is based in organization, synthesis, and assimilation. The self thus reflects the structures and processes that relate to and result from organismic integration. Autonomy, in other words, describes the natural inclination of human beings to be regulated by the self, with the self being viewed as an integrated set of processes and structures that continue to develop over time as intrinsic motivation energizes the functioning of the organismic integration process. Through this ongoing functioning people develop a more elaborated, refined, and coherent self; they thus regulate themselves more autonomously; and they experience greater psychological well-being. As such, SDT adds to the work of prior organismic theorists in part by proposing that people are intrinsically motivated to develop, which fosters more integrated and autonomous functioning.

The Nutrients of Development

SDT further maintains that the natural developmental tendency – that is, the organismic integration process – does not entail just the unfolding of potentials at particular ages but is a more active and complex process of individuals constructing new aspects of themselves through internalization and synthetic alteration of existing processes and structures. In addition, although organismic integration is naturally energized, neither the intrinsic motivation nor the organismic integration itself will be sustained over time without adequate nutrients. Natural processes, like life itself, require nutrition for effective functioning and well-being. SDT maintains that all human beings have fundamental psychological needs for competence, autonomy, and relatedness, and satisfying these is essential for intrinsic motivation, integrity, and wellness (Deci & Ryan, 2000; Ryan, 1995). Just as human beings have universal biological necessities such as food and water that are essential for physiological health and wellness, they also have universal psychological necessities that are essential for psychological health and wellness. Specification of these three needs, it is important to note, was not through assumption, but instead resulted from the empirical process. We found these basic needs to be necessary for providing meaningful interpretations of phenomena that have emerged from our research (see Deci & Ryan, 2000).

The importance of the SDT proposition of psychological needs as universal necessities is, in part, that it provides a way to predict and interpret the effects of social environments on healthy, and not-so-healthy, human behaviors and development. Simply stated, factors in the social environment that support satisfaction of the psychological needs for competence, autonomy, and relatedness enhance intrinsic motivation, facilitate internalization and integrated development, promote autonomous self-regulation, and buttress well-being. As well, factors that thwart these basic needs undermine intrinsic motivation, impair integration, forestall autonomous self-regulation, and diminish wellness.

As should be evident from this brief introductory discussion of SDT, the theory, with its focus on autonomy across the life span, is very much a developmental theory because the inherent developmental process of organismic integration is one of its central elements. However, SDT scholars have thus far given relatively little attention to age-related changes in motivational processes. The theory does not, of course, preclude the study of age-related changes, but few scholars have yet selected that as a primary empirical agenda.

HUMAN AUTONOMY

From the SDT perspective, autonomy describes functioning that is regulated by the integrated and integrating self. This involves a view of the nascent self that has the organismic integration process at its core and is expanded and elaborated over time as that process functions. The phenomenological experience of autonomous self-regulation involves reflectively endorsing one's actions and feeling a sense of volition and choice about what one is doing. The opposite of autonomy is heteronomy or control, which means being pressured to experience or behave in particular ways.

This view of self as a regulator of autonomous action is thus dramatically different from the view of some developmental theories that consider self to be a concept or representation. From that perspective, all of one's psychic material is considered "part of" the self in an undifferentiated way, and much of the material is said to have been learned from the social environment through various types of feedback that convey to people who they are (e.g., Bandura, 1986). In this view, despite some "active organism" language, the organism appears relatively passive as the social environment "creates" the self, whereas from the organismic perspective people are proactive and integrative and their self develops as they actively engage their physical and social environments. With this latter, SDT view, the social environment impacts integrative processes through its satisfaction versus thwarting of basic psychological needs, and thus supporting or hindering both intrinsic motivation and the integrative process.

Intrinsic Motivation

Within SDT there are two classes of behaviors that are considered autonomous: those that are intrinsically motivated and those regulated by extrinsic motivations that have been fully internalized and integrated. Intrinsic motivation is inherent to the organism and manifests as individuals of any age do what interests them without the necessity of prods or contingencies. The affective side of intrinsic motivation is interest, which energizes engagement and assimilation. Intrinsically motivated activity is the prototype of autonomous or self-determined behavior, because as individuals pursue interests they feel actively volitional. People do what interests them with a full sense of volition and choice. Children's free play is a clear example of intrinsically motivated activity, and through this play children develop. For example, Elkind (1971) argued, in line with Piaget (1952), that cognitive growth cycles are intrinsically motivated. That is, children seek out interesting stimuli, which they work with repeatedly, gate out irrelevant stimuli, store relevant information from their engagement with the interesting stimuli, and as they master the activity they play with the new skills repeatedly for awhile until they are ready to move on to new stimuli. At that point they are no longer intrinsically motivated by the activity they have mastered. Instead they are ready to use it instrumentally, in some new way. In short, intrinsic motivation is crucial for the development of new skills and capacities, and need satisfaction sustains this inherent activity.

It is not only children who are intrinsically motivated; people can be intrinsically motivated for a variety of activities throughout their lives. Learning itself can remain intrinsically motivated, for example, and other activities often done during leisure time can also be intrinsically motivated. Intrinsic motivation, that is, plays an important role in growth and revitalization across the life span (Ryan & Deci, 2008).

Research on intrinsic motivation. Research has shown clear advantages of intrinsic motivation for healthy development and functioning. For example, studies have shown that when children were more intrinsically motivated to read text material they evidenced deeper understanding of the material (Grolnick & Ryan, 1987), and when late adolescents were intrinsically motivated they displayed greater perceived comprehension and text recall (Ryan, Connell, & Plant, 1990). Intrinsic motivation has also been associated with greater creativity (Amabile, 1983), more flexible problem solving (McGraw & McCullers, 1979), and improved well-being (e.g., Deci, Schwartz, Sheinman, & Ryan, 1981). In the classroom it is facilitated by teacher supports for autonomy and competence, across age groups and cultures, and it results in deeper learning and greater engaged adjustment (e.g., Jang, Reeve, Ryan, & Kim, 2009; Kage & Namiki, 1990; Tsai, Kunter, Lüdtke, Trautwein, & Ryan, 2008).

Extrinsic Motivation

Intrinsic motivation is often contrasted with extrinsic motivation, which refers to doing an activity for instrumental reasons – in order to obtain some specific separable outcome. Extrinsic motivation includes what operant theorists refer to as reinforcements (Skinner, 1953), insofar as many classic cases of extrinsic motivation entail behaving in order to get a reward or to avoid a punishment. Research has indicated that when people become motivated by the offer of a reward or the threat of a punishment while doing an intrinsically interesting activity, their intrinsic motivation is likely to be diminished (Deci, Koestner, & Ryan, 1999). A study by Lepper, Greene, and Nisbett (1973) showed this phenomenon with children as young as 3 years old, and a study by Warneken and Tomasello (2008), although it used altruistic tendencies rather than intrinsic motivation as the dependent variable, showed negative reward effects with 20-month-old children. The rewards research, which is discussed in greater detail later, would seem to imply that when people are extrinsically motivated, they are not autonomous, but this is not the full picture. As we shall see, people often have both intrinsic and extrinsic motives, and moreover, the individuals can vary in how volitional or autonomous their extrinsic motivations might be.

Internalization of Extrinsic Motivation

In addressing the question of whether extrinsically motivated activities can be autonomous, we used the concepts of internalization and integration. We reasoned that the organismic-integration process implies that children are inclined to take in aspects of the social world, especially aspects that are endorsed by significant others such as parents. Presumably, if extrinsic motivation were internalized, it could become autonomous. We argued, however, that the standard dichotomous conceptualization of internalization – namely, that something is either external to the person or has been internalized – is not sufficiently differentiated to allow a full explication of the development of extrinsic motivation. Thus, SDT suggests that extrinsic motivation can be internalized to varying degrees, and the more fully internalized it is, the more autonomous the resulting behavior will be. SDT specifies four types of extrinsic motivation.

External regulation describes the standard extrinsic motivation – it has an external perceived locus of causality (de Charms, 1968), is controlled by the external (i.e., reward or punishment) contingencies, and leads to more shallow learning than does intrinsic motivation (Benware & Deci, 1984;

Grolnick & Ryan, 1987). External regulation does not represent autonomy; indeed, as mentioned, it tends to undermine autonomy.

Introjected regulation refers to a type of regulation that occurs when a motivation has been only "partially" internalized. With introjection, people take in external contingencies without making them their own. The result is that the regulations tend to control the individuals. Ego-involvement and contingent self-esteem are instances of introjected regulation. For example, research indicates that when parents use contingent regard as a socializing strategy to prompt particular behaviors in their children, the children tend to take in the contingency and pressure themselves to do the behaviors with expectations of feeling worthy if they do the behaviors unworthy if they do not (Assor, Roth, & Deci, 2004; Roth, Assor, Niemiec, Ryan, & Deci, 2009). Introjected regulation is quite highly correlated with external regulation and, like external regulation, tends to predict negative outcomes, such as anxiety surrounding performance and unstable self-esteem, as well as decreased intrinsic motivation (e.g., Ryan, 1982). Introjection is an important concept, for it explains the relatively ubiquitous regulations that are internal to the person but are relatively controlled and tend to have negative consequences.

Identified regulation results when people have identified with the importance of an activity and thus accepted the regulation as their own. Identification represents a somewhat fuller type of internalization and has more positive correlates and consequences than does introjected regulation. For example, identified regulation for academic behaviors was positively associated with enjoyment of school and proactive coping with failures among late-elementary-aged students whereas introjected regulation for the behaviors was positively associated with anxiety and with maladaptive coping with failures (Ryan & Connell, 1989).

Integrated regulation is the most mature form of extrinsic motivation. It results from reciprocally assimilating an identification with other aspects of one's self, and thus it is the fullest form of internalization of extrinsic motivation. When people have integrated an extrinsic motivation, the motivation becomes part of who they are authentically, so that, when they enact the behavior, it will be autonomous. Integrated regulation has many of the same correlates and consequences as intrinsic motivation, although the two types of motivation are different. Integrated extrinsic motivation involves doing an activity because it has become personally important for the people themselves. For example, learning mechanical drawing may not be interesting to a person who is planning a career as an architect, but it could be personally important to him or her and could therefore become an aspect of the person's integrated or true sense of self. In contrast, intrinsic motivation involves doing an activity because the activity itself is interesting. In the case of the aspiring architect, the activity was not interesting so the motivation would not be intrinsic, although it may well have been interesting for some other architecture students. Studies have shown that although the intrinsic and well-internalized forms of motivation have many common correlates, some activities such as those that require discipline are better predicted by identified and integrated extrinsic motivation, whereas those that tend to be interesting or fun are better predicted by intrinsic motivation (e.g., Koestner & Losier, 2002).

It is important to recognize that these four types of extrinsic motivation (i.e., regulation) are not stages of development. Instead they are aligned to form a conceptual continuum reflecting more or less autonomy. The types of regulation also co-exist dynamically in relation to the social environment, as when identification is hampered by conditional regard or other "incentives" (e.g., Roth et al., 2009). Further, there is a general age effect to the continuum in the sense that we do not expect integration to emerge at least until late adolescence. The point, however, is that it is not necessary that individuals sequentially experience each type of extrinsic motivation for an activity; it is rather that individuals can begin with or evolve into varied regulations and reasons for engagement, and these regulations vary in their relative autonomy. For example, a young adult who has become relatively autonomous in general may encounter an activity for the first time and very quickly identify with its importance and thus be relatively autonomous when performing it. Further need support could facilitate integration, whereas external control could diminish it.

It is also noteworthy that people are motivated to some degree by each type of motivation, even when performing a particular activity. For example, children can be to some degree external, to some degree introjected, to some degree identified, and to some degree intrinsic for doing their schoolwork. As such, the approach to measuring motivation for an activity or domain developed by Ryan and Connell (1989) assesses each of these four types of motivation, and with adults integration is sometimes added as a fifth subscale. Research has shown consistently that these four types of motivation do fall along an autonomy continuum as indicated by a simplex pattern in which the types of motivation closest to each other along the continuum correlate more highly than those conceptually more distant. Further, the scores on these motivational subscales can be used separately in predicting outcomes such as learning or classroom adjustment, or algebraically combined to form a relative autonomy index that can also be used to predict outcomes.

A large amount of SDT research has shown that autonomous motivation, which consists of both intrinsic motivation and identified/integrated extrinsic motivation, leads to more optimal outcomes than does controlled motivation, which consists of external and introjected types of extrinsic motivation. For example, Grolnick and Ryan (1987) found that late elementary school students' autonomous motivation was associated with better conceptual learning, whereas controlled motivation was associated only with short-term rote memorization.

Autonomy and Independence

In the psychological literature, there has been considerable confusion about the meaning of autonomy. For SDT, autonomy means to be self-governing – that is, to govern through the operation of the integrated self. Experientially, to be autonomous means to act with a full sense of willingness, a sense of volition and concurrence. In contrast to autonomy is control in which either external or internal forces pressure the person to behave in particular ways. As noted, this implies that there are internal regulatory processes that do not represent autonomy. For example, ego-involvement, in which adolescents pressure themselves to act in order to prove their worth to themselves and to others represents a very low level of autonomy, for the people act with little experience of volition and choice.

An alternative definition of autonomy, one *not* employed within SDT, is that people act *independently*, without relying on others. Autonomy construed as independence (e.g., Steinberg & Silverberg, 1986) or individuation (detaching or separating from others' guidance or support; Blos, 1979) has been more prominent in developmental psychology than has autonomy construed as volition. The opposite of autonomy when defined as independence is dependence or reliance on others. When this interpretation is viewed from the SDT perspective, however, one will recognize that people can be autonomously dependent – that is, they can turn to and volitionally rely on another when they need help or have an emotional experience to share. At other times they may be volitionally independent, as when they desire to do something on their own, without guidance or help (Ryan, La Guardia, Solky-Butzel, Chirkov, & Kim, 2005; Ryan & Lynch, 1989). That is, people's dependence can be autonomous, or the people can be pressured or coerced into relying on others. Parents who need to feel important in their children's lives may pressure their children to be dependent on them (the children will be nonautonomously dependent), whereas other parents may pressure their children to be independent – that is, not to rely on them (these children will be nonautonomously independent).

Recent research by Soenens and colleagues has examined the difference between autonomy defined in these two ways – as volition and as independence – in terms of the relations of each concept to adolescent functioning. For example, Soenens et al. (2007) found that, when parental support for volition as well as parental support for independence (these being two measures of promoting different types of "autonomy") were both used to predict adolescents' well-being (e.g., high self-esteem, low depressive symptoms, and high social functioning), volition-promotion was a significant predictor of adolescents' well-being but independence-promotion was not. Further, the adolescents' level of self-determination mediated the relationship between parental support for volition and the adjustment outcomes. Similar results were found for both middle (mean age of 15) and late (mean age of 19) adolescents.

A subsequent study of emerging adults by Soenens, Vansteenkiste, and Sierens (2009) found that promotion of independence can co-occur with parental control (parents can pressure their young adults to be independent) but promotion of volition does not co-occur with parental control. Further, promotion of volition was a stronger predictor of adjustment than was promotion of independence, as was the case in the earlier study (Soenens et al., 2007). Finally, Kins, Beyers, Soenens, and Vansteenkiste (2009) found that young adults' autonomous motivation (i.e., their volition) regarding their living arrangement (viz., living with parents or living independently) predicted their well-being more strongly than the living arrangement itself.

By clarifying the difference between autonomy and independence, another related issue emerges as salient. There are some areas of life where growing children will be developmentally prone to rapidly expand autonomy – in the sense of exercising personal discretion and choice. In other spheres, children may more readily recognize and assent to parental control – in other words they may autonomously comply. In fact, work in social domain theory (e.g., Nucci, 2001) suggests that adolescents consider activities in their personal domain as not legitimately externally regulated, whereas they more willingly accept parental authority in moral and prudential domains. This differentiation suggests that support for autonomy is related to the legitimate exercise of authority rather than an absence of parental input or regulation all together.

In sum, autonomy, which comprises intrinsic motivation and well-internalized extrinsic motivation and is experienced as volition, willingness, and choice, has been found to be associated with a variety of important outcomes such as deep learning, school engagement, creativity, and well-being. Further, we highlighted the difference between autonomy when it is defined as volition and autonomy and when it is defined in terms of independence, as well as how parental interference with autonomy is more actively resisted in some domains compared to others. Research has shown that autonomy-as-volition is an important predictor of well-being whereas autonomy-as-independence contributes less to adjustment and well-being and may be a predictor of ill-being if the independence is controlled rather than autonomous.

Goals or Aspirations

The reasons for a person's actions – that is, whether the person's motivation is autonomous or controlled – is an important predictor of effective behavior and well-being. These reasons can be thought of as the "why" of people's behavior. Adolescents may, for example, do some behaviors to please their parents, or because the behaviors are interesting and enjoyable. These are different reasons or motivations that convey why they are doing the activity. In addition to studying the why of behavior, SDT also studies the "what" of behavior – that is, what it is that individuals are attempting to accomplish. For example, a child might be trying to learn the piano to please his or her mother, or an adolescent may be working in a food pantry feeding homeless people because it seems personally important and meaningful to him or her. The piano playing and feeding the homeless can be thought of as the "what" of these young people's behaviors.

Kasser and Ryan (1996) examined six types of goals or aspirations – namely, amassing wealth, becoming famous, looking attractive, building relationships, growing personally, and contributing to the community. The researchers assessed the degree to which these were important to people and found that these six goals load on two factors. The first three (wealth, fame, and image) loaded on a factor they labeled *extrinsic aspirations*, while the last three (relationships, growth, and community) loaded on a factor they labeled *intrinsic aspirations*. Research by Grouzet et al. (2005) subsequently showed that this distinction holds across 15 countries from around the world.

Results of the Kasser and Ryan research indicated that placing strong importance on the extrinsic goals was associated negatively with well-being whereas placing strong importance on intrinsic goals was associated positively with well-being. For example, in one study (Kasser & Ryan, 1993), 18-year-old adolescents completed the Aspiration Index and were clinically interviewed by a psychologist. Results indicated that those adolescents who more strongly valued wealth relative to the intrinsic aspirations were rated by a clinician as lower in global adjustment and social functioning and higher in behavioral disorders.

A study of high school students by Williams, Cox, Hedberg, and Deci (2000) examined the relations of the students' goal importance to risk behaviors, including smoking cigarettes and chewing tobacco, smoking marijuana, having sexual intercourse, and using alcohol. For the primary analyses, an index of risk behaviors was calculated and was predicted by the students' extrinsic, relative to intrinsic, aspirations after controlling for grade level, race, gender, and fathers' education. Results indicated that those students who had stronger extrinsic aspirations tended to engage in more of the risk behaviors.

Sheldon, Ryan, Deci, and Kasser (2004) examined the relations between the "what" and "why" of behaviors with particular attention being paid to whether they each accounted for independent variance in well-being outcomes. In four studies, the researchers found that the degree to which college students valued extrinsic relative to intrinsic aspirations was correlated with their controlled motivation for pursuing those aspirations. Further, however, they found that both the reasons (i.e., the why) and the aspirations (i.e., the what) were significant independent predictors of well-being outcomes. So, it appears that, when young people develop strong controlled rather than autonomous regulations and when they develop strong extrinsic rather than intrinsic aspirations, negative psychological consequences will result.

One might wonder whether the negative psychological correlates of having strong relative extrinsic aspirations might be caused by people valuing these outcomes but being unable to attain them, so they display ill-being because they were unable to attain what they wanted and might feel incompetent. A recent study by Niemiec, Ryan, and Deci (2009) examined how the attainment (or lack thereof) of valued intrinsic and extrinsic aspirations would be related to well-being and ill-being. These researchers found that when young adults experienced increases in the attainment of intrinsic aspirations over time they also evidenced increases in well-being (e.g., self-esteem and life satisfaction) and decreases in ill-being (e.g., anxiety and physical symptoms). Further, increases in the attainment of extrinsic aspirations was not associated with increased well-being, and instead predicted increases in ill-being. It is clear therefore, that the relation of pursuing extrinsic aspirations to ill-being was not a function of failing to attain the aspirations. Further, the study indicated that attaining valued goals is not necessarily good for people. Expectancy theorists (e.g., Bandura, 1996) have argued that attaining any desired goals will have a positive effect on people's well-being, but this research argues that whereas the attainment of intrinsic aspirations does have a positive effect, the attainment of extrinsic aspirations does not; in fact, it may have a negative effect on overall psychological health.

Manipulating goals. The studies just reviewed on extrinsic and intrinsic aspirations used individual differences in goal importance and goal attainment to predict well-being outcomes. Other research has framed activities in terms of their utility for attaining intrinsic versus extrinsic goals. For example, one study of tenth- and eleventh-grade high school students who were learning the physical activity of tai-boo framed the importance of the activity in terms of either maintaining one's fitness and health or maintaining one's physical attractiveness (Vansteenkiste, Simons, Lens, Sheldon, & Deci, 2004). Being physically fit had previously been found to be an intrinsic goal and attractiveness had been found be an extrinsic one (Kasser & Ryan, 1996). The Vansteenkiste et al. study found that, when the activity in physical education classes was framed in terms of the intrinsic goal, the students were more autonomously motivated for the activity, performed better at it according to expert ratings, and persisted at the activity more over time.

PROMOTING AUTONOMOUS MOTIVATION AND INTRINSIC GOALS IN CHILDREN AND ADOLESCENTS

As already mentioned, SDT proposes that all people have needs to be competent, autonomous, and related to others and that satisfaction of these needs will promote integrity, autonomous motivation, and well-being. Thus, SDT hypothesizes that social contexts that support satisfaction of the basic psychological needs will serve to maintain or enhance intrinsic motivation, promote internalization and autonomous motivation, facilitate the development of intrinsic aspirations, support high-quality relationships, and yield psychological wellness.

Many studies have tested and supported this hypothesis. Some studies have examined satisfaction of all three needs and some have examined satisfaction of only one need. In particular, many studies have examined the effects of just autonomy support or satisfaction of just the autonomy need. Autonomy is a particularly interesting case because it turns out, first, that when people support someone's autonomy they typically also support that person's relatedness and competence, for example by providing warmth and acknowledging effective performance. Second, when someone experiences satisfaction of the autonomy need, that person typically feels free to behave in ways that yield satisfaction of the competence and relatedness needs. Not surprisingly, therefore, the studies of autonomy support have shown results very similar to the studies of support for all three needs.

Tangible Rewards and Positive Feedback

The research on social environmental effects on autonomy and well-being began with experiments on reward effects on intrinsic motivation. The first studies were done with college students, but many studies were done with children, some as young as 3 years old. The first studies (Deci, 1971) showed that monetary rewards for doing puzzle problems led the rewarded participants to show significantly less subsequent intrinsic motivation than did participants who performed the same task under the same conditions except that they were not offered a reward. A study by Lepper et al. (1973) rewarded one group of nursery school children with a good-player award for making a drawing with magic markers and construction paper, while another group also did the drawings but did not receive the award. This study also led to less subsequent motivation in the rewarded participants relative to the participants who did not receive the reward.

Some investigators who studied tangible reward effects explained them using the discounting principle from attribution theory (Kelley, 1967) which suggests that when people have multiple plausible causes for doing an activity they will tend to discount internal causes (e.g., intrinsic motivation) and attribute their behavior to external causes (e.g., the reward). However, studies by Morgan (1981) showed that use of the discounting schema does not emerge until children are about 8 years old, yet the studies also showed that rewards similarly undermined intrinsic motivation for 5-year-olds, 8-year-olds, and 11-year-olds, indicating that use of the discounting schema is not necessary for the undermining effect to occur. Our interpretation of the undermining effect, in contrast, is that it results from thwarting the need for autonomy. Rewards are widely used to control children from a very early age, and the experience of being controlled is affective and does not require specific elaborated cognitive-attributional schemas, so it can operate at earlier ages.

The early research on tangible reward effects was very controversial and resulted in more than 100 published experiments. A meta-analysis (Deci et al., 1999) of these studies showed that tangible rewards do indeed undermine intrinsic motivation and that the undermining is stronger for young children than for college students or adults.

Other research examined the effects of positive feedback (sometimes called "verbal rewards") on intrinsic motivation and found that in general, positive feedback enhanced intrinsic motivation (e.g., Deci, 1971). In all, 31 studies, one-third of which were done with children, examined positive-feedback effects on intrinsic motivation, and the meta-analysis showed significant enhancement. However, when children were separated from college students, the meta-analysis showed that positive feedback enhanced intrinsic motivation for the older group but did not have a significant effect across the 11 studies with children. In sum, then, the meta-analysis showed that tangible rewards have a strong negative effect on children's intrinsic motivation but that positive feedback did not have a reliable positive effect on their intrinsic motivation. It seems that the use of tangible rewards with children has a significant risk in terms of their motivation and autonomy. Positive feedback on the other hand is relatively neutral, although if it is administered with controlling language – for example, if it is given "for doing what you should do" – it has a negative effect (Ryan, 1982). In short, relying on rewards, whether tangible or verbal, runs a serious risk of having negative motivational consequences.

As mentioned earlier, Piaget argued that children tend to approach tasks that are optimally assimilable, and in SDT we suggest that people tend to find activities (especially learning activities) intrinsically interesting when they are optimally challenging (e.g., Deci, 1975). Danner and Lonky (1981) used elementary school children's development of classification skills (viz., dichotomous sorting, class inclusion, and combinatorial reasoning) to determine whether the children's classification skills were below, at, or above a target level the investigators had selected. They then separated children into the three classification levels (below, at, or above optimal challenge) and assigned them to one of three groups: those who got tangible rewards for doing the task, those who got positive feedback, and those who got neither rewards nor feedback. The investigators examined the level of intrinsic motivation for the classification task for the three levels in the three conditions. Initially, they found that the children with the optimally challenging task were most intrinsically motivated. Then, they found that by far the largest undermining of intrinsic motivation by tangible rewards occurred for children for whom the target activity was optimally challenging, no doubt in part because those were the children who initially found the target task most interesting. Across the groups of different cognitive levels, positive feedback did not have a main effect on intrinsic motivation.

Beyond the issue of rewards, experiments have looked at the effects of other external factors on intrinsic motivation. For example, evaluations, surveillance, competition, threats of punishment, negative feedback, and deadlines have all been found to decrease intrinsic motivation; providing choice and acknowledging the participants' feelings have been found to enhance intrinsic motivation (see Ryan & Deci, 2000a for a review). Still, most of these phenomena are complex. For example, surveillance undermines intrinsic motivation mainly when it is experienced as evaluative in intent, and competition undermines intrinsic motivation primarily when the pressure to win is strong. In a parallel fashion, choice enhances intrinsic motivation and autonomy mainly when it actually allows one to pursue a valued activity and feel volition. There are types of surveillance and competition that do not control, and there are types of choice that do not feel freeing. The collective data show, in fact, that it is the autonomy-supportive versus controlling *functional significance* or need-related meaning of these events that determines their impact on intrinsic motivation (see Deci et al., 1999; Deci & Ryan, 1985; Reeve & Deci, 1996; Ryan, Mims and Koestner, 1983).

Promoting Internalization

Although most studies of internalization have been done in the field using observational or survey approaches, experimental investigations have also explored the conditions that promote internalization. For example, Deci, Eghrari, Patrick, and Leone (1994) gave college students an uninteresting task of watching a computer screen and hitting the space bar whenever they saw a dot of light appear. In motivating them to perform this uninteresting task, Deci et al. varied three factors; providing (or not) a rationale, which was that the task could help them improve concentration as a similar task does for air traffic controllers; acknowledging (or not) the participants' feelings of not finding the task interesting; and emphasizing choice versus using controlling language. Results indicated that each of these factors – rationale, acknowledgment, and minimizing control – contributed to the facilitation of internalization, behaviorally assessed. Further, some participants in each condition evidenced behavioral internalization, so the participants were separated into two groups, those who had had two or three facilitating factors (high autonomy support) and those who had had zero or one factor (low autonomy support). The behavioral measure within each group was then correlated with participants' self-reports of perceived choice, enjoyment, and utility of the task. Results indicated that those in the high-autonomy-support group showed significantly positive correlations, meaning that the more they engaged in the behavior the more they experienced choice, enjoyment, and utility of the task, which conveys a sense that the internalization was well integrated. In contrast, those in the low-autonomy-support group showed negative correlations between the behavior and self-reports meaning that the more they did the behavior the less they experienced choice, enjoyment, and utility of the task, thus suggesting that they had introjected the behavioral regulation and were doing it because they thought they should do it and not because they believed in the value of the behavior and chose to do it.

In sum, the more the social context provided autonomy support, the more participants internalized the regulation for an uninteresting task. Further, the more the internalization was integrated, the more the subsequent behavior was autonomous.

Field studies. Many questionnaire and observational studies across various life domains have examined the links of autonomy support or support of the three needs to autonomous motivation, performance, and well-being. Autonomy support is defined as one person (usually an authority such as a parent, teacher, physician, or coach) taking the internal frame of reference of the target individual (the child, student, patient, or athlete), providing choice where possible and appropriate, encouraging self-initiation, and minimizing use of controlling language. For example, Ryan and Connell (1989) found that when teachers were more autonomy supportive regarding the students' schoolwork, the students evidenced more internalization of the regulation for doing the work. Many studies discussed in the chapters by Grolnick and by Ryan and Deci within this volume show for example that when teachers and parents are more autonomy supportive, their high school student-children display greater internalization, autonomous regulation, self-actualization, life satisfaction, and self-esteem, as well as less depression (e.g., Chirkov and Ryan, 2001). Studies also have shown that autonomy support interacted positively with intrinsic goal framing to facilitate better performance and persistence (Vansteenkiste et al., 2004).

Developing Intrinsic and Extrinsic Aspirations

Theorizing about intrinsic and extrinsic aspirations as an individual difference concept has suggested that strong extrinsic aspirations develop as a function of need thwarting and represent a compensation for the feelings of anxiety and inadequacy that result from the thwarting. By amassing wealth, fame, or image, people are able to display external indicators of worth to make up for the inner feelings of worthlessness. Two studies have provided support for this proposition. In one, Kasser, Ryan, Zax, and Sameroff (1995) found that 18-year-olds who reported strong aspirations for wealth relative to the intrinsic aspirations had mothers who reported and were judged by clinicians to be less nurturant – that is, less supportive of their children's basic psychological need satisfaction. Further, these teenagers had grown up in relatively disadvantaged socioeconomic circumstances and their mothers valued having the teenagers amass wealth. Similarly, Williams et al. (2000) reported that high school students who placed strong importance on the extrinsic aspirations also rated their parents low in autonomy support.

Promoting Secure Attachments

Attachment theory (e.g., Ainsworth, Blehar, Waters, & Wall, 1978) maintains that infants develop attachments to primary caregivers that are relatively secure versus insecure as a function of the degree to which the caregivers are responsive in their interactions with the infants. These attachments are represented as working models (Bretherton, 1987) that are individual-difference or between-person constructs reflecting Bowlby's (1973) belief that early attachment patterns display continuity into adulthood. As such, individuals are expected to develop attachments with close friends and romantic partners that mirror attachment patterns they had with caregivers.

La Guardia, Ryan, Couchman, and Deci (2000) used three samples of college students to examine two issues: (1) whether the degree to which the attachments the participants developed with the attachment figures they encountered later in their lives were consistent with those they had developed with their parents, as attachment theory would predict; and (2) whether any within-person variability that exists from partner to partner would be a function of the differentials in the degree to which the target individuals got their basic psychological needs met in their relationships with the various partners. In the La Guardia et al. research participants in the three studies provided data on four to six attachment relationships in their late adolescent years, including with their mothers, fathers, best friends, and romantic partners. Results indicated that about one-third of the variance in attachment security was at the between-person level, thus indicating that there is significant consistency in attachment security across relationships and, accordingly, providing some support for the traditional attachment theory perspective. However, the preponderance of variance was still unexplained.

La Guardia et al. assessed the degree to which the participants felt satisfaction of the needs for autonomy, competence, and relatedness within each relationship and found, using multi-level modeling, that satisfaction of the basic psychological needs within relationships was a robust predictor of within-person (i.e., relationship-specific) security of attachment with the relational partners. The researchers suggested, however, that experiencing relatedness satisfaction within a relationship was undoubtedly so closely related to the idea of attachment security that this general finding was hardly remarkable. Thus, they removed relatedness satisfaction from the analyses and examined the relations of autonomy and competence satisfactions to security of attachment. Results indicated that satisfaction of the autonomy and competence needs were themselves predictive of attachment security. In particular, satisfaction of the need for autonomy within a relationship was strongly related to attachment security in that relationship, which is an important finding because some relationship theorists have argued that to have a high-quality relationship it is necessary to relinquish autonomy in service of the relationship (Jordan, 1997). The La Guardia et al. results indicate, however, that having a high quality relationship appears to be facilitated, not hindered, by the relational partners experiencing autonomy in the relationship.

More generally, it is important to underscore the strong relations of both autonomy and relational supports in fostering attachment security and overall mental health, and in buffering risk factors for mental illness and disturbed attachment patterns. Conversely, a large literature points to the formidable etiological role played by the thwarting of these need satisfactions across a range of pathologies (Ryan, Deci, Grolnick, & LaGuardia, 2006).

Parental Conditional Regard

Sears, Maccoby, and Levin (1957) reported that parents' withdrawal of love facilitated children's internalization of pro-social behavior. They suggested, however, that this technique might lead to negative affective consequences for the children, although they reported no data to address this speculation. Subsequently, Barber (1996) included withdrawal of love as one of several factors that make up what he called parents' psychological control, and he found that the global measure did predict negative developmental outcomes. However, there had been very little work examining the specific effects on children's motivation and adjustment of withdrawal of love, or of the more general concept of parental conditional regard (PCR) which is made up of withdrawal of love when the children do not behave the way the parents want and the provision of extra attention and affection when the children do behave as the parents want. Assor et al. (2004) examined the degree to which college students perceived their parents to have been conditionally regarding when they were growing up and related that to (1) the students' current enactment of the behaviors upon which the regard had been conditional, (2) various well-being outcomes, and (3) relationship quality with the parents. Self-determination theory views PCR as a form of control that is likely to promote introjection but not autonomy. The theory further predicts that there will be negative psychological consequences of PCR just as there are for other forms of control, and finally SDT suggests that PCR will strain relationships between parents and their children.

Assor et al. found that when parents displayed conditional regard in various domains – for example, regulating emotions and playing sports – their children did tend to enact the related behaviors (viz. regulating their emotions or playing sports), so the technique did work to get the behaviors. However, the research also showed that the behavioral regulation was through introjection and thus was pressured and not autonomous, and further that it was associated with less stable self-esteem, shame and guilt after failures, and short-lived satisfaction after successes. Further, students who perceived their parents as being more conditionally regarding felt more rejected by their parents and reported having more anger toward them.

A subsequent study (Roth et al., 2009) examined ninth-grade students' perceptions of their parents' conditional regard, but for this study positive PCR (giving affection for complying) was separated from negative PCR (love withdrawal) for making predictions in the domains of emotion regulation and academics. The researchers found in general that, for both parents, positive PCR led to suppression of emotions, mediated by introjection (i.e., internal compulsion), and that negative PCR led to disregulation mediated by resentment toward parents. Further, in the academic domain, positive PCR from each parent led to grade-focused engagement (a controlled strategy), mediated by introjection, and negative PCR led to lack of engagement, mediated by resentment toward parents. Clearly, the negative PCR had more negative consequences than did positive PCR, although even the use of positive PCR is far less than optimal.

In a subsequent study, Roth et al. (2009) compared positive PCR to autonomy support as approaches to socialization. They found first that, for both parents, positive PCR led to a mix of suppressive regulation and disregulation, mediated by introjection, but that autonomy support led to integrated regulation mediated by the experience of choice (i.e., autonomy). In the academic domain, positive PCR led to grade-focused engagement, mediated by introjection, whereas autonomy support led to interest-focused engagement, mediated by choice. These analyses confirm that there are negative consequences to parents' use of conditional regard, even positive conditional regard, and that autonomy support is a much more adaptive approach to parenting, as it led to greater integration and intrinsic motivation across domains.

SUMMARY AND CONCLUSIONS

Self-determination theory, like the work of Piaget, is built on an organismic meta-theory which assumes that development is a natural, active process characterized by organization or what, in SDT, is called the organismic integration process. This integrative process is the means through which people internalize and integrate extrinsic motivation; in combination with intrinsic motivation (motivation to do what one finds interesting), these two are the bases of autonomous behavior. Controlled behavior in contrast is undergirded by external contingencies and contingencies that have been introjected (i.e., partially internalized) but not accepted as one's own. Abundant research has shown that autonomous motivation is associated with more positive outcomes than controlled motivation – with greater persistence, more effective heuristic performance, more satisfying relationships, and enhanced psychological wellness.

SDT addresses not only the motivations for behaviors (the "why" of behaviors) but also the goals people pursue (the "what" of behavior). The primary goals studied by SDT researchers are extrinsic (e.g., wealth, fame, and image) and intrinsic (e.g., growth, relationships, and community), and evidence indicates that the intrinsic goals are associated with better performance and wellness and lower developmental risk than are extrinsic goals.

SDT research, from which we selected only a few of the themes closely related to developmental psychology, has supported the view that all people have fundamental psychological needs – the needs for competence, autonomy, and relatedness. It also suggests that those needs underpin developmental thriving insofar as social environments that support, rather than thwart, these basic needs also facilitate intrinsic motivation, internalization of extrinsic motivation, more intrinsic life goals, higher-quality relationships, and greater well-being. In supporting these needs, parents, teachers, and mentors of all kinds enrich the lives and skills of the developing individuals in their charge, no matter the age or stage of these individuals.

REFERENCES

Ainsworth, M. D. S., Blehar, M. C., Waters, E., & Wall, S. (1978). *Patterns of attachment*. Hillsdale, NJ: Erlbaum.

Amabile, T. M. (1983). *The social psychology of creativity.* New York, NY: Springer-Verlag. doi:10.1007/978-1-4612-5533-8
Angyal, A. (1965). *Neurosis and treatment: A holistic theory.* New York, NY: Wiley.
Assor, A., Roth, G., & Deci, E. L. (2004). The emotional costs of parents' conditional regard: A self-determination theory analysis. *Journal of Personality, 72,* 47–88. doi: 10.1111/j.0022-3506.2004.00256.x
Bandura, A. (1986). *Social foundations of thought and action: A social cognitive theory.* Englewood Cliffs, NJ: Prentice-Hall.
Bandura, A. (1996). *Self-efficacy: The exercise of control.* New York, NY: Freeman.
Barber, B. K. (1996). Parental psychological control: Revisiting a neglected construct. *Child Development, 67,* 3296–3319. doi: 10.2307/1131780
Benware, C., & Deci, E. L. (1984). Quality of learning with an active versus passive motivational set. *American Educational Research Journal, 21,* 755–765.
Blos, P. (1979). *The adolescent passage.* New York: International Universities Press.
Bowlby, J. (1973). *Attachment and loss: Vol. 2. Separation: Anxiety anger.* New York, NY: Basic Books.
Bretherton, I. (1987). New perspectives on attachment relations: Security, communication and internal working models. In J. Osofsky (Ed.), *Handbook of infant development* (pp. 1061–1100). New York, NY: Wiley.
Chirkov, V. I., & Ryan, R. M. (2001). Parent and teacher autonomy-support in Russian and U.S. adolescents: Common effects on well-being and academic motivation. *Journal of Cross Cultural Psychology, 32,* 618–635. doi: 10.1177/0022022101032005006
Danner, F. W., & Lonky, E. (1981). A cognitive-developmental approach to the effects of rewards on intrinsic motivation. *Child Development, 52,* 1043–1052. doi: 10.2307/1129110
de Charms, R. (1968). *Personal causation: The internal affective determinants of behavior.* New York, NY: Academic Press.
Deci, E. L. (1971). Effects of externally mediated rewards on intrinsic motivation. *Journal of Personality and Social Psychology, 18,* 105–115. doi: 10.1037/h0030644
Deci, E. L. (1975). *Intrinsic motivation.* New York, NY: Plenum. doi: 10.1007/978-1-4613-4446-9
Deci, E. L., Eghrari, H., Patrick, B. C., & Leone, D. R. (1994). Facilitating internalization: The self-determination theory perspective. *Journal of Personality, 62,* 119–142. doi: 10.1111/j.1467-6494.1994.tb00797.x
Deci, E. L., Koestner, R., & Ryan, R. M. (1999). A meta-analytic review of experiments examining the effects of extrinsic rewards on intrinsic motivation. *Psychological Bulletin, 125,* 627–668. doi: 10.1037/0033-2909.125.6.627
Deci, E. L., & Ryan, R. M. (1985). *Intrinsic motivation and self-determination in human behavior.* New York, NY: Plenum.
Deci, E. L., & Ryan, R. M. (2000). The "what" and "why" of goal pursuits: Human needs and the self-determination of behavior. *Psychological Inquiry, 11,* 227–268. doi: 10.1207/S15327965PLI1104_01
Deci, E. L., Schwartz, A. J., Sheinman, L., & Ryan, R. M. (1981). An instrument to assess adults' orientations toward control versus autonomy with children:

Reflections on intrinsic motivation and perceived competence. *Journal of Educational Psychology, 73*, 642–650. doi: 10.1037/0022-0663.73.5.642

Elkind, D. (1971). Cognitive growth cycles in mental development. In J. K. Cole (Ed.), *Nebraska symposium on motivation* (Vol. 19, pp. 1–31). Lincoln: University of Nebraska Press.

Grolnick, W. S., & Ryan, R. M. (1987). Autonomy in children's learning: An experimental and individual difference investigation. *Journal of Personality and Social Psychology, 52*, 890–898. doi: 10.1037/0022-3514.52.5.890

Grouzet, F. M., Kasser, T., Ahuvia, A., Dols, J. M., Kim, Y., Lau, S., Ryan, R. M., Saunders, S., Schmuck, P. & Sheldon, K. M. (2005). The structure of goals across 15 cultures. *Journal of Personality and Social Psychology, 89*, 800–816. doi: 10.1037/0022-3514.89.5.800

Jang, H., Reeve, J., Ryan, R. M., & Kim, A. (2009). Can self-determination theory explain what underlies the productive, satisfying learning experiences of collectivistically oriented Korean students? *Journal of Educational Psychology, 101*, 644–661. doi: 10.1037/a0014241

Jordan, J. V. (1997). Do you believe that the concepts of self and autonomy are useful in understanding women? In J. V. Jordan (Ed.), *Women's growth in diversity: More writings from the Stone Center* (pp. 29–32). New York, NY: Guilford.

Kage, M., & Namiki, H. (1990). The effects of evaluation structure on children's intrinsic motivation and learning. *Japanese Journal of Educational Psychology, 38*, 36–45.

Kasser, T., & Ryan, R. M. (1993). A dark side of the American dream: Correlates of financial success as a central life aspiration. *Journal of Personality and Social Psychology, 65*, 410–422. doi: 10.1037/0022-3514.65.2.410

Kasser, T., & Ryan, R. M. (1996). Further examining the American dream: Differential correlates of intrinsic and extrinsic goals. *Personality and Social Psychology Bulletin, 22*, 80–87. doi: 10.1177/0146167296223006

Kasser, T., Ryan, R. M., Zax, M., & Sameroff, A. J. (1995). The relations of maternal and social environments to late adolescents' materialistic and prosocial values. *Developmental Psychology, 31*, 907–914. doi: 10.1037/0012-1649.31.6.907

Kauffman, S. C. (2000). *Investigations*. New York, NY: Oxford University Press.

Kelley, H. H. (1967). Attribution theory in social psychology. In D. Levine (Ed.), *Nebraska symposium on motivation* (Vol. 15, pp. 192–238). Lincoln: University of Nebraska Press.

Kins, E., Beyers, W., Soenens, B., & Vansteenkiste, M. (2009). Patterns of home leaving and subjective well-being in emerging adulthood: The role of motivational processes and parental autonomy support. *Developmental Psychology, 45*, 1416–1429. doi: 10.1037/a0015580

Koestner, R., & Losier, G. F. (2002). Distinguishing three ways of being highly motivated: A closer look at introjection, identification, and intrinsic motivation. In E. L. Deci & R. M. Ryan (Eds.), *Handbook of self-determination research* (pp. 101–121). Rochester, NY: University of Rochester Press.

Kohlberg, L. (1969). Stage and sequence: The cognitive-developmental approach to socialization. In D. A. Goslin (Ed.), *Handbook of socialization theory and research* (pp. 347–480). New York, NY: Rand McNally.

La Guardia, J. G., Ryan, R. M., Couchman, C. E., & Deci, E. L. (2000). Within-person variation in security of attachment: A self-determination theory perspective on attachment, need fulfillment, and well-being. *Journal of Personality and Social Psychology*, *79*, 367–384. doi: 10.1037/0022-3514.79.3.367

Lepper, M. R., Greene, D., & Nisbett, R. E. (1973). Undermining children's intrinsic interest with extrinsic rewards: A test of the "overjustification" hypothesis. *Journal of Personality and Social Psychology*, *28*, 129–137. doi: 10.1037/h0035519

Loevinger, J. (1976). *Ego development*. San Francisco, CA: Jossey-Bass.

Mayr, E. (1982). *The growth of biological thought: Diversity, evolution, and inheritance*. Cambridge, MA: Harvard University Press.

McGraw, K. O., & McCullers, J. C. (1979). Evidence of a detrimental effect of extrinsic incentives on breaking a mental set. *Journal of Experimental Social Psychology*, *15*, 285–294. doi: 10.1016/0022-1031(79)90039-8

Morgan, M. (1981). The overjustification effect: A developmental test of self-perception interpretations. *Journal of Personality and Social Psychology*, *40*, 809–821. doi: 10.1037/0022-3514.40.5.809

Niemiec, C. P., Ryan, R. M., & Deci, E. L. (2009). The path taken: Consequences of attaining intrinsic and extrinsic aspirations in post-college life. *Journal of Research in Personality*, *43*, 291–306. doi: 10.1016/j.jrp.2008.09.001

Nucci, L. P. (2001). *Education in the moral domain*. Cambridge: Cambridge University Press. doi: 10.1017/CBO9780511605987

Piaget, J. (1952). *The origins of intelligence in children*. New York: International Universities Press. doi: 10.1037/11494-000

Piaget, J. (1971). *Biology and knowledge*. Chicago: University of Chicago Press.

Reeve, J., & Deci, E. L. (1996). Elements within the competitive situation that affect intrinsic motivation. *Personality and Social Psychology Bulletin*, *22*, 24–33. doi: 10.1177/0146167296221003

Roth, G., Assor, A, Niemiec, C. P., Ryan, R. M., & Deci, E. L. (2009). The emotional and academic consequences of parental conditional regard: Comparing conditional positive regard, conditional negative regard, and autonomy support as parenting practices. *Developmental Psychology*, *45*, 1119–1142. doi: 10.1037/a0015272

Ryan, R. M. (1982). Control and information in the intrapersonal sphere: An extension of cognitive evaluation theory. *Journal of Personality and Social Psychology*, *43*, 450–461. doi: 10.1037/0022-3514.43.3.450

Ryan, R. M. (1993). Agency and organization: Intrinsic motivation, autonomy and the self in psychological development. In J. Jacobs (Ed.), *Nebraska symposium on motivation: Developmental perspectives on motivation* (Vol. 40, pp. 1–56). Lincoln: University of Nebraska Press.

Ryan, R. M. (1995). Psychological needs and the facilitation of integrative processes. *Journal of Personality*, *63*, 397–427. doi: 10.1111/j.1467-6494.1995.tb00501.x

Ryan, R. M., & Connell, J. P. (1989). Perceived locus of causality and internalization: Examining reasons for acting in two domains. *Journal of Personality and Social Psychology*, *57*, 749–761. doi: 10.1037/0022-3514.57.5.749

Ryan, R. M., Connell, J. P., & Plant, R. W. (1990). Emotions in non-directed text learning. *Learning and Individual Differences*, *2*, 1–17. doi: 10.1016/1041-6080(90)90014-8

Ryan, R. M., & Deci, E. L. (2000a). Intrinsic and extrinsic motivations: Classic definitions and new directions. *Contemporary Educational Psychology*, *25*, 54–67. doi: 10.1006/ceps.1999.1020

Ryan, R. M., & Deci, E. L. (2000b). Self-determination theory and the facilitation of intrinsic motivation, social development, and well-being. *American Psychologist*, *55*, 68–78. doi: 10.1037/0003-066X.55.1.68

Ryan, R. M., & Deci, E. L. (2008). From ego depletion to vitality: Theory and findings concerning the facilitation of energy available to the self. *Social and Personality Psychology Compass*, *2*, 702–717. doi: 10.1111/j.1751-9004.2008.00098.x

Ryan, R. M., Deci, E. L., Grolnick, W. S., & LaGuardia, J. G. (2006) The significance of autonomy and autonomy support in psychological development and psychopathology. In D. Cicchetti & D. Cohen (Eds.), *Developmental psychopathology: Vol. 1. Theory and methods* (2nd ed., pp. 295–849). New York, NY: John Wiley.

Ryan, R. M., La Guardia, J. G., Solky-Butzel, J., Chirkov, V., & Kim, Y. (2005). On the interpersonal regulation of emotions: Emotional reliance across gender, relationships, and cultures. *Personal Relationships*, *12*, 145–163. doi: 10.1111/j.1350-4126.2005.00106.x

Ryan, R. M., & Lynch, J. (1989). Emotional autonomy versus detachment: Revisiting the vicissitudes of adolescence and young adulthood. *Child Development*, *60*, 340–356. doi: 10.2307/1130981

Ryan, R. M., Mims, V., & Koestner, R. (1983). Relation of reward contingency and interpersonal context to intrinsic motivation: A review and test using cognitive evaluation theory. *Journal of Personality and Social Psychology*, *45*, 736–750. doi: 10.1037/0022-3514.45.4.736

Sears, R. R., Maccoby, E., & Levin, H. (1957). *Patterns of child rearing*. Evanston, IL: Row, Peterson.

Sheldon, K. M., Ryan, R. M., Deci, E. L., & Kasser, T. (2004). The independent effects of goal contents and motives on well-being: It's both what you pursue and why you pursue it. *Personality and Social Psychology Bulletin*, *30*, 475–486. doi: 10.1177/0146167203261883

Skinner, B. F. (1953). *Science and human behavior*. New York, NY: Macmillan.

Soenens, B., Vansteenkiste, M., & Sierens, E. (2009). How are parental psychological control and autonomy-support related? A cluster-analytic approach. *Journal of Marriage and Family*, *71*, 187–202. doi: 10.1111/j.1741-3737.2008.00589.x

Soenens, B., Vansteenkiste, M., Lens, W., Luyckx, K., Goossens, L., Beyers, W., & Ryan, R. M. (2007). Conceptualizing parental autonomy support: Promoting independence versus promoting volitional functioning. *Developmental Psychology*, *43*, 633–646. doi: 10.1037/0012-1649.43.3.633

Steinberg, L., & Silverberg, S. (1986). The vicissitudes of autonomy in adolescence. *Child Development*, *57*, 841–851. doi: 10.2307/1130361

Tsai, Y., Kunter, M., Lüdtke, O., Trautwein, U., & Ryan, R. M. (2008). What makes lessons interesting? The role of situational and individual factors in three school subjects. *Journal of Educational Psychology*, *100*, 460–472. doi: 10.1037/0022-0663.100.2.460

Vansteenkiste, M., Simons, J., Lens, W., Sheldon, K. M., & Deci, E. L. (2004). Motivating learning, performance, and persistence: The synergistic effects of intrinsic goal contents and autonomy-supportive contexts. *Journal of Personality and Social Psychology*, *87*, 246–260. doi: 10.1037/0022-3514.87.2.246

Warneken, F., & Tomasello, M. (2008). Extrinsic rewards undermine altruistic tendencies in 20-month-olds. *Developmental Psychology*, *44*, 1785–1788. doi: 10.1037/a0013860

Werner, H. (1948). *Comparative psychology of mental development*. New York, NY: International Universities Press.

Williams, G. C., Cox, E. M., Hedberg, V., & Deci, E. L. (2000). Extrinsic life goals and health risk behaviors in adolescents. *Journal of Applied Social Psychology*, *30*, 1756–1771. doi: 10.1111/j.1559-1816.2000.tb02466.x

Chapter 3

Self-Regulation and Autonomy: The Dialectic Between Organismic and Sociocognitive Valuing Processes

FREDERICK M. E. GROUZET
University of Victoria

In psychology, theories and research are heavily influenced by assumptions about human functioning and development. These assumptions generate important debates and contribute to the development of new theories. One well-known debate concerns the origin of individual differences: innate qualities (nature) versus social context (nurture). Another related assumption is the existence of an intrinsic tendency to grow toward a complex organism. On this matter, some theories describe humans as being like a "clay," endowed with innate qualities that are shaped by the "hands" of the social context, while other theories propose that, like any other living entities (e.g., plants, animals), human beings possess a natural ability and drive to grow. Jean Piaget and Carl Rogers significantly contributed to the development of the second group of theories by emphasizing intrinsic growth processes and drawing on biological models.

On the one hand, Piaget's legacy to cognitive development psychology is indisputable (see Müller, Carpendale, & Smith, 2009), but one tends to forget that the starting point of his work was his (very) early interest in biology (see Messerly, 2009), publishing at the age of 10 years a short essay on his sighting of an albino sparrow, followed by papers on mollusks during adolescence, which led to the completion of doctoral research in zoology. The majority of his work was influenced by "the search for the mechanisms of biological adaptation" (Piaget, 1977, p. XI). He built a parallel between biological adaptation and knowledge acquisition, assigning to the individual (i.e., the child) an *active role* in the process of cognitive development. On the other hand, Carl Rogers was one of the founders of humanistic psychology proposing that human beings are naturally oriented toward growth and self-actualization. Rogers proposed that the organisms "know" what they need to grow and self-actualize, and they are *active* in meeting these needs. He called this biological tendency the *organismic valuing process.*

Self-determination theory (Deci & Ryan, 2000; Ryan & Deci, 2000), which, more recently, has emerged as a macro-theory in personality and social psychology, is built on a similar assumption regarding the natural tendency for self-organization (see Deci & Ryan, this volume).

In this chapter, I focus on the organismic valuing process as one of these intrinsic processes that support the assumption that human beings have an active and autonomous role in self-regulation and goal pursuit, as well as socialization and development. First, I present the organismic valuing process (OVP) and recent empirical support from research on the development of intrinsic and extrinsic goals. In the second section, I present a second valuing process that places the social context and cognitive processing in a central position. The sociocognitive valuing process (SVP) issues directly from the literature on social influence, persuasion, and socialization, including the concept of internalization. Finally, both OVP and SVP are integrated within the Dual Valuing Process Model that aims to explain goal prioritization and value development.

THE ORGANISMIC VALUING PROCESS

A great deal of biological research shows that living systems "know" what is good for them. Evolution has endowed them with the ability to make those sensory discriminations that allow the fulfillment of their basic needs. Animals tend to eat and drink things that are good for them, and they consume food in balanced proportions. Infants, too, want and like what they need (see, e.g., Narvaez, 2013). Carl Rogers (1951) extended what he called the organismic valuing process (OVP) to nonbiological needs, such as the needs for security, belongingness, and self-actualization. Maslow (1943) built his hierarchy of needs on this same principle. More recently, self-determination theory (SDT; Deci & Ryan, 2000; Ryan & Deci, 2000) has posited the existence of three basic psychological needs. Similar to the idea that the fulfillment of biological needs is essential to physical growth, SDT proposes that the fulfillment of needs of autonomy, competence, and relatedness is essential to psychological growth. The OVP thus explains the preference for goals and values that, when actively pursued, will ultimately facilitate the fulfillment of psychological needs. In the next section, I use the OVP to explain this general tendency to select and pursue intrinsic goals.

The Organismic Valuing Process and Intrinsic Goal Orientation

Almost all human actions are guided by goals, whether consciously or unconsciously. Starting in a simple form (i.e., action oriented and short term), goals become more complex and long term with age (i.e., life aspirations that also provide meaning to life). Regardless of the complexity of the goals, the OVP can explain the general preference for goals that fulfill organismic needs. Human beings tend to prioritize personal goals that will fulfill the basic psychological (or organismic) needs over goals that distract them from meeting these needs or thwart them. The content and nature of these personal goals may thus determine the individual's ability to meet psychological needs.

Self-determination theory (SDT; Deci & Ryan, 2000; Ryan & Deci, 2000) makes a qualitative distinction between intrinsic and extrinsic goals (see also Kasser, 2002). Intrinsic goals include, for example, the maintenance of physical health, the development of a sense of self-acceptance, the experience of nurturing and meaningful relationships, and the contribution to community wellness. In contrast, extrinsic goals could take the form of a desire for a wealthy and materialistic lifestyle, the pursuit of an appealing appearance, and the attainment of high levels of popularity or conformity to others. My colleagues and I (Grouzet et al., 2005) proposed that intrinsic and extrinsic goals are organized in a circumplex-like structure such that the intrinsic-extrinsic dimension is crossed by an orthogonal dimension that corresponds to James's conceptualization of the self, going from physical self to interpersonal self, to collective self, to spiritual self (see Figure 3.1). In this circumplex model, the intrinsic versus extrinsic nature of the goal is represented by a continuum rather than two categories, and both intrinsic and extrinsic goals can be related to the individual self or the collective, transcendent self.

Self-determination theory (SDT) posits that the active pursuit (and valuing) of intrinsic goals fosters personal well-being through the fulfillment of relatedness, autonomy, and competence needs, whereas the pursuit (and valuing) of extrinsic goals is less likely to be inherently satisfying and distracts people from intrinsic goals and the fulfillment of psychological needs. Direct evidence for the link between goals and need satisfaction is limited (see, e.g., Grouzet, 2012; Rijavec, Brdar, & Miljkovic, 2006), but indirect evidence and conceptual models exist (for an extensive review, see Vansteenkiste, Soenens, & Duriez, 2008). In addition, the positive relationship between intrinsic (vs. extrinsic) goals and well-being has received strong empirical support (e.g., Deci & Ryan, this volume; Grouzet, 2012; Kasser, 2002).

According to the OVP, individuals are naturally oriented toward the pursuit of intrinsic goals because this goal orientation facilitates the fulfillment of psychological needs and fosters personal growth, self-actualization, and psychological well-being. This hypothesis is supported by higher average

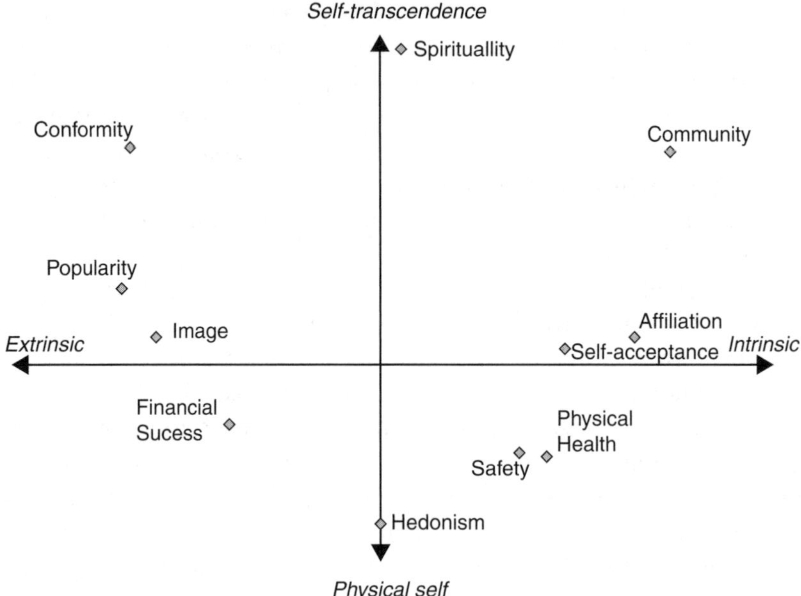

FIGURE 3.1. The Circumplex Structure of Personal Goals. Copyright © 2005 by the American Psychological Association. Reproduced with permission. The official citation that should be used in referencing this material is Grouzet, F. M. E., Kasser, T., et al. (2005). The structure of goal contents across 15 cultures. *Journal of Personality and Social Psychology, 89*, 800–816.

scores on intrinsic goals that have been found in almost all studies in which participants were asked to rate a list of intrinsic and extrinsic goals (e.g., Kasser & Ryan, 1993, 1996; Sheldon, 2005). This preference for intrinsic goals has also been observed in many different cultures (Grouzet et al., 2005; Kim, Kasser, & Lee, 2003; Ryan, Chirkov, Little, Sheldon, Timoshina, &Deci, 1999; Schmuck, Kasser, & Ryan, 2000).

The Development and Activation of the Organismic Valuing Process

Carl Rogers (1964) viewed the organismic valuing process (OVP) as an adaptive process that helps organisms to develop the ability to select the "right thing" for their own development (see also Narvaez, 2013; Narvaez & Gleason, 2012). Through trial and error, the OVP efficacy is developed and allows first infants and later adults to select actions and goals that will fulfill organismic needs. As I describe in this section, the development of the OVP can be observed in the nature of goal shift, moving toward intrinsic goals and away from extrinsic goals. However, as Rogers pointed out "a growth-promoting climate" is necessary for the activation of the OVP and the shift toward intrinsic goals. A threatening climate distracts people from the OVP, and in such climate people generally place greater emphasis on extrinsic goals (e.g., materialistic goals) rather than intrinsic goals. However, a threatening event can also be transformed into a growth experience when this event serves as a "wake-up call" and is accompanied by self-reflection. Actually, any factor that helps people to reconnect to their inner, organismic nature can activate the OVP. Among these factors, as I describe later, are cognitive (self-reflection) and experiential mechanisms.

Natural shift toward intrinsic goals. The existence of the OVP has received empirical support from the investigation of goal shifts over time. For example, Ken Sheldon (2005; Sheldon, Arndt, & Houser-Marko, 2003) showed that people tended to move toward intrinsic goals and away from extrinsic goals over periods ranging from 20 minutes to 4 years. Furthermore, this goal shift seems to operate outside of participants' awareness. For example, in one study (Sheldon et al., 2003) participants were asked to remember the importance they had placed on intrinsic and extrinsic goals 6 weeks before. The remembered importance of intrinsic goals was higher than the importance ratings 6 weeks earlier, but equal to the updated importance ratings. This memory bias also seems to be unaffected by the time between the two ratings. This move toward intrinsic goals (and away from extrinsic goals) was observed for short intervals spanning 20 minutes (Sheldon et al., 2003) as well as long intervals spanning the period from college freshman to college senior (Sheldon, 2005).

Further evidence for the OVP comes from negative correlations between chronological age and extrinsic goal importance (e.g., Kasser & Ryan, 1996; Sheldon & Kasser, 2001). In other words, older people prioritize intrinsic goals over extrinsic goals. However, it is very important to distinguish age differences from generational differences. Indeed, age differences that are observed by research using a cross-sectional design could simply be the result of a generational effect. Very recent intergenerational studies (Twenge, Campbell, & Freeman, 2012) showed that baby boomers (born between 1946 and 1961) consider extrinsic goals (financial success, image, popularity) less important and intrinsic values (self-acceptance, affiliation, community feelings) more important than generation X'ers (born between 1962 and 1981) and millennials (born after 1982). It seems that a move toward extrinsic goals (and away from intrinsic goals) occurred across most recent generations. This trend toward extrinsic goals is, however, not inconsistent with the existence of an OVP. As I discuss later in this chapter, the generational difference could be explained by the rise of materialism in Western culture (i.e., extrinsic values) (e.g., Kasser, Cohn, Kanner, & Ryan, 2007).

Supportive versus threatening social climate. Carl Rogers (1964) also specified that the OVP can be activated only in "a growth-promoting climate," which is, using SDT terms, a social climate that supports the psychological needs for autonomy, competence, and relatedness. In the context of child development, several longitudinal studies demonstrate a positive relationship between parents' support of psychological needs and children's intrinsic goal orientation (e.g., Cohen & Cohen, 1996; Kasser, Ryan, Zax, & Sameroff, 1995; Williams, Cox, Hedberg, & Deci, 2000). For example, in a 26-year longitudinal study, Kasser, Koestner, and Lekes (2002) found that 31-year-old adults were more likely to hold intrinsic goals (e.g., self-direction) when their parents reported a warm parenting style toward them while they were 5 years old. Conversely, adults were more likely to value more extrinsic goals (e.g., conformity) when their parents demonstrated a restrictive parenting style while they were children.

Conversely, a threatening climate has been shown to promote the development of materialism and extrinsic goals. Kasser and Kanner (2004) propose that materialistic pursuits may be the result of evolutionary processes that gave rise to a human tendency to seek safety through materialism when threatened. More generally, research shows that extrinsic goals and a materialistic value orientation could be a compensatory strategy to cope with various forms of insecurity, such as lower self-esteem (Chaplin & John, 2007; Kasser & Kasser, 2001), uncertainty (Chang & Arkin, 2002), existential insecurity (Arndt, Solomon, Kasser, & Sheldon, 2004; Kasser & Sheldon, 2000; Rindfleisch, Burroughs, & Wong, 2009), interpersonal threat (Kasser & Kasser, 2001; Sheldon & Kasser, 2008), and socioeconomic threat (Abramson & Inglehart, 1995; Cohen & Cohen, 1996; Sheldon & Kasser, 2008). However, it is important to note that the meaning of materialism may vary across sociocultural contexts depending on the relative sense of security or insecurity that is provided. For example, Grouzet et al. (2005) observed that although the circumplex structure of life goals is universal across cultures, financial success was slightly less extrinsic in poor countries (e.g., India, Romania) than in wealthy countries (i.e., United States, Germany).

Wake-up calls and organismic primes. The OVP is an inner mechanism that, when activated, orients human beings toward intrinsic goals. It is like an "internal voice" that can be very difficult to hear (Sheldon & Elliott, 1999). The ability to hear this internal voice (e.g., by choosing intrinsic goals) is thus directly associated with well-being. However, sometimes it may take a significant event, a "wake-up call," to direct our attention toward this inner voice. While distracted by pro-materialistic messages from the social context, a traumatic event or an important life event can serve as such a wake-up call that will activate the OVP. After a trauma, a loss, or an important life change, individuals tend to engage in meaning-making activities and re-focus on what is "really" important in life. This personal inquiry helps them to reconnect to their inner organismic needs and valuing process. In a recent conceptualization of posttraumatic growth, Joseph and Linley (2005, 2006) propose that the growth that follows a trauma arises from the OVP. There are also several lines of empirical support for the posttraumatic activation of OVP. For example, Lykins, Segerstrom, Averill, Evans, and Kemeny (2007) observed a goal shift toward intrinsic goals among survivors of the 1994 Northridge earthquake, which struck the Los Angeles area. This goal shift was particularly strong for people who had feared most for their lives during the earthquake. Similarly, Ransom, Sheldon, and Jacobsen (2008) observed a shift toward intrinsic goals from before to after a radiotherapy treatment. In this study, the actual change (i.e., difference between before and after treatment ratings), but not the perceived change (as assessed after treatment), was positively related to posttraumatic growth, which also provides support for the unconscious nature of the OVP. Other research shows that persons who had a near-death experience (i.e., an out-of-body experience, going down a tunnel, and/or meeting a deceased relative) have more intrinsic and transcendent concerns and fewer extrinsic concerns (e.g., materialism or popularity) than those who had a life-threatening experience but not a near-death experience (Groth-Marnat & Summers, 1998). It seems that the proximity to death enhances the importance of the "essential" (i.e., organismic needs).

Fortunately, a positive significant event can also be the origin of a wake-up call. For example, the birth of a first child can act like an organismic call that reminds women (but also fathers) of the importance of organismic needs. Although research on the impact of pregnancy and transition to parenthood on intrinsic goals is limited, there is some empirical evidence that shows changes in priorities after the birth of a child (e.g., Plagnol & Scott, 2011; Salmela-Aro, Nurmi, Saisto, & Halmesmäki, 2001). For example, Salmela-Aro and colleagues (2001) observed that pregnant women become less interested in achievement-related goals, especially when they are expecting their first child. Although men's personal goals also change during the transition to fatherhood, these changes are less substantial than those found among women.

Another form of "organismic call" comes from our connection to nature. Just as pregnancy can reconnect women with the OVP, immersion in nature leads individuals to endorse more intrinsic goals. For example, Weinstein, Przybylski, and Ryan (2009) immersed participants in nature by presenting slides showing natural settings versus cityscapes (Study 1–3) or by placing them in a lab room furnished with plants (Study 4). They observed that participants' immersion in nature was positively related to an increased value placed on intrinsic goals and a decreased value placed on extrinsic goals. The nature-as-an-organismic-call hypothesis takes its source in the biophilia hypothesis (Wilson, 1984, 1993; see also Kahn Jr., 1997). According to Wilson (1984), our psychological need to affiliate with other living organisms (also called biophilic instinct) influences, often unconsciously, our cognition, emotions, and behaviors.

Overall, these empirical findings suggest that any condition or environmental cue that reminds us of our organismic background (e.g., connection to other living entities) and organismic life span (from embryo to death) can activate the OVP, which is then translated into a preference for intrinsic goals over extrinsic goals. However, the association between organismic primes and intrinsic goals is also fragile. As I propose next, the inner voice that is the OVP sometimes requires self-awareness to be translated into conscious pursuits and actions. This is particularly true for conscious goal pursuit, but less true for unconscious goal pursuit.

On the importance of self-reflection and mindful awareness. Research on posttraumatic growth also illustrates that self-reflection is often necessary to make people sensitive to the internal voice. A wake-up call needs to be accompanied by profound self-reflection. For example, Lekes and colleagues (2012) recently showed that weekly reflection on intrinsic goals (vs. daily activities) was associated with an increased value placed on intrinsic goals. Cozzolino and colleagues (Cozzolino, 2006; Cozzolino, Sheldon, Schachtman, & Meyers, 2009; Cozzolino, Staples, Meyers, & Samboceti; 2004) also found that reflection on death or the end of life can attenuate materialism and foster the valuing of intrinsic goals. The opportunity to make sense of threatening events (e.g., via contemplation of death) leads people to reevaluate the situation and identify what is "really important" (i.e., organismic needs).

Similarly, mindfulness has been found to be related to OVP. For instance, Brown and Kasser (2005) found a positive correlation between mindfulness and intrinsic value orientation, but a negative relationship between mindfulness and financial desire discrepancies (the gap between current and desired states) (Brown, Kasser, Ryan, Linley, & Orzech, 2009). Pema Chödrön's (1991) conceptualization of mindfulness captures well the relationship between mindfulness and satisfaction with what we have; she wrote: "Mindfulness is loving all the details of our lives, and awareness is the natural thing that happens: life begins to open up, and you realize that you're always standing at the center of the world" (p. 28). Mindfulness also acts as a buffer against the impact of mortality salience (Niemiec, Brown, Kashdan, Cozzolino, Breen, Levesque-Bristol, & Ryan, 2010), which places people in a less defensive mental state and a more growth mind-set.

Propositions Regarding the Organismic Valuing Process

So far, I have described how the OVP, when nurtured, activated, and listened to, "pushes" people to engage in pursuits that fulfill organismic needs and contribute to flourishing and personal growth. Based on existing literature in humanistic and social psychology, I make the following propositions regarding the role of OVP in the development of intrinsic and extrinsic goals.

> *Proposition 1.1: Because human beings value what is good for the organism and its growth (organismic valuing process), they value intrinsic goals and move away from extrinsic goals.*
> *Proposition 1.2: The organismic valuing process can be activated by any environmental cue that "recalls" the organismic nature of the human being (e.g., the organismic needs, the finality of the organism, the organismic functioning, or the connections to other living organisms).*
> *Proposition 1.3: The activation of the organismic valuing process is facilitated by self-reflective activities and mindfulness.*

Limitations of the OVP. The OVP, taken by itself, has also some limitations. First, the OVP can explain and predict the development and prioritization of intrinsic over extrinsic goals. However, it does not explain the preference for the specific content of intrinsic goals (e.g., self-acceptance vs. community feelings) or different types of extrinsic goals (e.g., financial success vs. conformity). In addition, Grouzet and colleagues (2005) found that some goals are not fully intrinsic or extrinsic (e.g., spirituality and hedonism). Other factors and processes may thus explain specific goal selection.

Second, the OVP is mainly experiential and tied to phenomenological influences. As Seymour Epstein proposed in his cognitive-experiential self-theory (see, e.g., Epstein, 2003), people possess two systems: an "experiential system" and a "rational system." The rational system operates at the conscious level and may explain the role of self-reflection and mindful awareness in enhancing the OVP. Mindfulness facilitates the connection with the inner organism. However, because of this same rational system, individuals can process information from the social context, and this information can be congruent with OVP, distracting from, or in conflict with the OVP.

To get a more comprehensive picture of the valuing process, I present in the next section a second valuing process that mainly relies on the rational process and sociocognitive mechanisms.

THE SOCIOCOGNITIVE VALUING PROCESS

According to the OVP, thirsty people naturally should choose to drink water, but they often end-up drinking sweet soda or alcohol. Similarly, the OVP pushes individuals toward adopting intrinsic goals, but another process often contradicts this tendency. Humans are sociocultural creatures who have the ability to create social groups, social structures, and social norms. The importance of the social structures pushes them to engage in social regulation, social control, and socialization of the young (e.g., Boehm, 2000). Social and developmental psychologists have clearly identified the sociocultural context as a key element in human development, human functioning, and the valuing process. In social psychology, the development of values, goals, or preferences is studied through the lens of social influence, persuasion, and socialization processes.

While the OVP implies that the person "knows" what is good for the organism and pursues values and goals that can foster organismic growth, the sociocognitive valuing process (SVP) places the person in a position of informational dependence on others (Kelley & Thibaut, 1969) for evaluating what is good for him or her and/or socially appropriate However, the transmission of goals and values from social context to individuals is more than an automatic copying process. It involves a dialectical relationship between the socializee and the socializer (Kuczynski & Parkin, 2007). The nature of the relationship may also influence the form of transmission or transformation (i.e., internalization).

In this section, I present a brief overview of the literature on social influence and persuasion and the valuing process as it is studied in this literature. Then, I discuss socialization and internalization processes. Finally, I formulate propositions regarding the role of the sociocognitive valuing process in the development of intrinsic and extrinsic goals and values.

The Valuing Process in Social Psychology

Social influence and socioepistemic conflicts. Social psychology and developmental psychology propose that people's values and goals are shaped and influenced by various socialization agents and significant others. A socializer may be an authority figure, an idealized person, a sociocultural group, or a person with whom the socializee is in frequent contact (physically or symbolically). As a whole, social communities and structures, such as schools, organizations, religions, and media, can also play an important role in shaping individuals' goal prioritization. In the case of media, an individual (e.g., a pop idol) or a group (e.g., scientists) may influence people without having direct contact.

The distinction between normative and informational influence (Deutsch & Gerard, 1955) has been central to explaining the social and cognitive components of the valuing process. *Normative influence* occurs when a person or a social group that the person belongs to (e.g., students) or aspires to belong to (e.g., psychologists) conveys the socially expected values or goals, hence influencing the person's valuing process. The relationship between the source and the target is central, which results in conformity, compliance, or identification, to adopt the terminology used by Kelman (1958, 1961). *Informational influence* refers to cognitive processing of information and arguments that forms the person's knowledge and goal system. Because of the effort invested in (or depth of) processing the information, the result of the influence is accepted or internalized by the individual (cf. Kelman's concept of internalization).

Similarly, social influence literature has been marked by the distinction between majority and minority influence (Moscovici & Lage, 1976). Whereas majority influence refers to the manifest influence of a numerical majority of persons, an expert, an in-group member, or a high-status source on a target person, minority influence involves numerical or social minorities (i.e., out-group, low status, novices) that leads to latent changes and conversion. Among the various theoretical models on majority versus minority influence, Pérez and Mugny (Mugny et al., 1995; Pérez & Mugny, 1993, 1996) developed the conflict elaboration theory that is based on Moscovici's (1980, 1985) conversion theory and earlier research by Doise, Mugny, and Perret-Clermont (1975) on sociocognitive conflict. They proposed that each situation of majority and minority influence may potentially create a conflict and the nature of the conflict will determine the way influence operates and its outcomes. For example, in the presence of a consensual majority or in-group pressure, the conflict is purely social and can be resolved through compliance (or introjection, as I show later). In contrast, minority influence can generate an epistemic conflict where the established norm or knowledge is challenged by a source that cannot be ignored because of its consistency and distinctiveness. This epistemic challenge leads to divergent (vs. convergent) thinking (Nemeth, 1986), cognitive processing, and internalization (especially identification, as I show later) of the new knowledge and goals. In other words, minority influence motivates the scrutinizing of the basis of our beliefs and the reasons behind values and goals. It is worth noting that minority influence from an "authentic dissent" is more powerful than from a "devil's advocate" as evidenced in studies on jury decision making (Nemeth, Brown, & Rogers, 2001; Nemeth, Connell, Rogers, & Brown, 2001) and information-seeking situations (Schultz-Hardt, Jochims, & Frey, 2002). Because the cognitive processing may take time, its effect is considered to be latent but deeper and more stable (Mugny, 1982; Wood, Lundgren, Ouellette, Busceme, & Blackstone, 1994). For example, a child may challenge her or his parents' established goals; although the parents may not change their goals to correspond with those of their child, the fact that they engage in a discussion to explain and justify their goals may ultimately lead to some indirect and latent changes. Other theoretical models recognize the importance of internal conflicts in social influence (e.g., Erb & Bohner, 2007), but they don't necessarily emphasize the nature of the conflict. As I elaborate later, the social versus epistemic nature of the conflict is important to distinguish between different kinds of internalization (i.e., introjection vs. identification).

Persuasion and epistemic authority. In the traditional literature on persuasion the source of influence is less important than the individual's motivation and ability to cognitively process the information. In the mid-1980s two dual-process models, the Elaboration Likelihood Model (ELM; Petty & Cacioppo, 1986) and the Heuristic-Systematic Model (HSM; Chaiken, Liberman, & Eagly, 1989), proposed that an individual's motivation and cognitive capacity determine whether a peripherally based, low effort, and heuristic processing or a centrally based, high-effort, and systematic processing will dominate, with the latter leading to deeper and more stable changes. Although we might be tempted to draw a parallel between, on the one hand, normative and informational influence, and, on the other hand, heuristic versus systematic processing, Chaiken, Giner-Sorolla, and Chen (1996) suggested that an extensive processing of the argument could be motivated by desire for social approval. Therefore, the source of influence is not as important as the individual's motivational and cognitive disposition to process the information. The source of information can actually be a heuristic.

More recently, Kruglanski and his colleagues (Erb, Kruglanski, Chun, Pierro, Mannetti, & Spiegel, 2003; Kruglanski et al., 2005; Kruglanski & Thompson, 1999) proposed a more parsimonious approach to persuasion. In contrast to models and theories that make a qualitative distinction between two types of processes (i.e., ELM and HSM), they proposed a parametric unimodel (Erb et al., 2003; Kruglanski & Thompson, 1999) that views persuasion as a single process. According to this unimodel, the source of the influence (a parent, an expert, a social group, etc.) or any other heuristics are treated as information and processed like the content of the message or the arguments. Then, the "depth" (quantity) of processing will depend on (1) the subjective relevance (i.e., linkage between the evidence and the conclusion), (2) the nature of the information (i.e., easy or difficult to process; for example a peripheral cue being easier to process), (3) the willingness (i.e., epistemic motivation) and ability to process, and (4) the existence of motivational biases (e.g., processing information in a manner leading to the maintenance of the existing schema).

In addition, Kruglanski and his colleagues (2005) proposed that the concept of *epistemic authority* is central to explaining how individuals process both the information (social norms, arguments, or goals) and its source (authority, social groups, or experts). The concept of epistemic authority was first introduced in 1989 by Kruglanski. It refers to the process of relying on and accepting the source of information as valid and reliable. This source could be persons (e.g., parents, teachers, peers, etc.) or objects (e.g., media, book). In congruence with the parametric unimodel, Kruglanski and his colleagues proposed that people use both the peripheral cues (or heuristics) that are associated with social groups or experts (e.g., "if belongs to the group, then correct" or "if expert, then correct") and the arguments included in the message in order to assign an "epistemic authority" to a group, a person, or even an argument. The degree of epistemic authority that is associated with a source determines the influence that that source will have on the individual. The ascription of epistemic authority varies across the life span and life domains. Children assign epistemic authority only to the primary caregivers, and they assign it indistinguishably for all knowledge domains. However, with age individuals assign epistemic authority to different sources (e.g., peers, teachers) in different knowledge domains (including values and goals) (e.g., Leman & Duveen, 1996; Raviv, Bar-Tal, Raviv, & Houminer, 1990). Epistemic authority is so powerful that it can function as a "stopping mechanism" (Kruglanski, 1989), which means that the person will stop searching for and analyzing other arguments and accept and possibly internalize what is proposed by the epistemic authority.

Kruglanski and his colleagues (2005) also proposed that "both the self and external sources may be assigned different degrees of epistemic authority in different knowledge domains and that such assignment affects various aspects of individuals' information-processing activities, including the search for information and the readiness to base decisions on the information given" (p. 386). In the course of development, individuals may rely more on their own experience and expertise than on external sources. The degree of self-ascribed epistemic authority is particularly important for an individual to benefit from experiential learning. For example, Ellis and Kruglanski (1992) found that students with a high degree of self-ascribed epistemic authority were more ready to use their personal experience and they learned better than individuals with a low degree of self-ascribed epistemic authority. The latter learned better when principles were taught by a teacher. Self-ascription of epistemic authority allows the person to develop informational independence from others. Kruglanski et al. (2005) also noted that a child can "bestow" epistemic authority on an adult in order to seek approval in the hope that such admiration attracts the adult's attention and goodwill. This may, however, delay the development of self-ascribed epistemic authority and informational independence.

Socialization and internalization. Socialization is a broad term that encompasses several mechanisms and that has been approached from several perspectives, ranging from psychoanalysis to social anthropology (see, e.g., Bugenthal & Grusec, 2006; Macoby, 2007; Settersten Jr., 2002). With regard to valuing, several models have been developed in the domain of parental (or primary) socialization and educational/occupational (or secondary) socialization. In all these models, the central component is the continuous interaction between "elders and novices, of old hands and newcomers, as the latter with the help of the former develop the attitudes, behaviors, values, standards, and motives that enable the novices and newcomers to become part of the social community" (Grusec, 2002, p. 143). In other words, "to be socialized is to belong" (Gecas, 1981).

In the family context, Grusec (2011; Grusec & Davidov, 2010) used a domain-specific approach (Bugental, 2000) where different forms of relationships are associated with different socialization mechanisms. In short, the source (e.g., a parent) may provide the recipient (e.g., a child) with a sense of security (protective relationship) or trust (mutual reciprocity) which is translated into the recipient's (e.g., child's) compliance. The use of discipline and control (vs. warmth and supportive parenting style) can also lead to different degrees of acceptance or rejection of parents' values (this element is further developed by Grolnick & Raftery-Helmer; see 7 this volume). In addition, Grusec (2011) suggested that although the acceptance of parents' values is facilitated by a warm and supportive parenting style, it is important that parents reason in a way that is within the child's zone of proximal development (Vygotsky, 1978). Finally, in Grusec's model, adults and peers are also role models for children (e.g., Bandura, 1977), which explains how rituals and routines can foster the transmission of parents' and peers' values to children.

Models of socialization such as Grusec's domain-specific approach share a lot with social influence and persuasion theories. First, according to social influence and socialization models, the sociality of human beings leads to simple compliance and acceptance of the source's value and goals because such compliance is associated with social security and approval. However, socialization models approach social interaction from the emotional perspective rather than the perspective of a social contract. Of course, the fact that Grusec's model has been developed to explain socialization in family explains the emphasis on socioemotional processes. Nevertheless, while examining sociocognitive processes, it is important to consider the "social" as both emotional (or guilt-generator) and normative (contingency-generator). Second, both social influence and socialization models rely on the concept of internalization, which is often seen as the hallmark of successful socialization (e.g., Lepper, 1983). Internalization is thus often conceptualized as a uniform tendency to transform the external into internal. For example, Grusec and Goodnow (1994) proposed that internalization means "taking over the values and attitudes of society as one's own so that socially acceptable behavior is motivated not by anticipation of external consequences but by intrinsic or internal factors" (p. 4).

Others have proposed different kinds or degrees of internalization (for an extensive review, see Wallis & Poulton, 2001). For example, Kelman (1958, 1961) differentiated two forms of internalization. The first form of internalization is called "internalization" and occurs when "an individual accepts influence from another in order to maintain the congruence of actions and beliefs with his or her own value system" (Kelman, 2006, p. 4). The second form of internalization is called "identification" and occurs "when an individual accepts influence because he wants to establish or maintain a satisfying self-defining relationship to another person or a group" (Kelman, 1958, p. 4). Similarly, Hartmann and Loewenstein (1962) proposed two kinds of internalization: introjection and identification (see also Schafer, 1968), which have been further developed in the context of self-determination theory (SDT; Deci & Ryan, 1985; Ryan, 1995; see also Deci & Ryan, this volume). *Introjection* occurs when individuals introject the (socially contingent) desire to pursue a goal "as they should" without making it their own pursuit or understanding the rationale associated with it. Only the emotional and social contingency is internalized and translated into inner, guilt-based control and self-approval concerns. As Ryan (1995) stated, "while introjection represents a motivational impetus that is internal to the person (i.e., is intrapsychic), it nonetheless remains conflictual and external to the self" (p. 406). In contrast, *identification* occurs when the individual "fully" internalizes the goal and the associated rationale (rather than the socioemotional pressure). The individual fully endorses and is able to explain using his own words the reasons to pursue the identified goal.

One might be tempted to see similarities between Kelman's identification-internalization distinction and SDT's introjection-identification distinction, but there are important conceptual differences. Kelman's distinction between identification and internalization corresponds to the distinction between internalization of social group values and internalization of personal values. Both could be introjected or identified according to SDT's conceptualization of internalization (see Rigby et al., 1992). In addition, while Kelman describes identification and internalization as two different kinds of attitude changes, Deci and Ryan examined introjection and identification mainly in the context of behavioral regulation, placing identified and introjected regulations on a self-determination continuum ranging from extrinsic regulation to intrinsic regulation (see Deci & Ryan, this volume). According to SDT, introjection reflects partial internalization while identification involves a more complete internalization, but not as complete as integration (Deci & Ryan, 2000, 2012). It is worth noting that the self-determination continuum is not a developmental but a conceptual continuum. Therefore, internalization is not seen as a process by which individuals' external regulation becomes introjected and then identified and finally becomes integrated. An individual can demonstrate an identified form of regulation without having passed through external and introjected regulations.

The Organismic Integration Theory (OIT; a subtheory of SDT that pertains to internalization; see Deci & Ryan, 2012; Ryan & Deci, 2000) stressed the importance of psychological need support in determining the degree of internalization (from introjection to identification, to integration). First, OIT postulates that the support for competence in the behavior, the value or the goal pursuit to be internalized, and the feelings of relatedness with the socializing agents are sufficient for initiating introjection and identification. Second, Ryan and Deci (2000) proposed that further internalization and integration is possible only in the context of autonomy support: "To integrate a regulation, people must grasp its meaning and synthesize that meaning with respect to their other goals and values" (p. 74). One important element of autonomy support is informational communication, which refers to the provision of meaningful rationales so that the person understands the value associated with the behavior and ultimately internalizes it (Deci, Eghrari, Patrick, & Leone, 1994).

Finally, it is worth noting that contemporary models of socialization and internalization are bilateral and bidirectional (e.g., Kuczynski, 2003; Kuczynski & Navara, 2006; Lawrence & Valsiner, 2003) such that the socializer and the socializee influence each other and the social context changes as the result of internalization. This dialectical approach to socialization and internalization is congruent with the minority influence literature and Kruglanski's theory of external and internal epistemic authority (as discussed earlier).

Propositions Regarding the Sociocognitive Valuing Process

To summarize, the literature in social influence, persuasion, and socialization offers support for the importance of sociocognitive processes in the formation and change of knowledge, values, and personal goals. While social influence theories traditionally emphasized the source and the social situation, persuasion theories emphasized internal characteristics (motivation and cognitive capacities). However, both social and cognitive processes are important for valuing and both rely on the interaction between individuals. On one hand, Kruglanski's lay epistemic theory proposes that knowledge formation is the result of the negotiation between internal and external epistemic authorities. On the other hand, socialization models present the quality of relationships as a necessary ingredient in social influence and persuasion. It is also important to distinguish the social and cognitive aspects of the valuing process because they lead to different forms of conflict (social vs. epistemic) and different forms of internalization (introjection vs. identification).

Based on the literature on social influence, persuasion, and socialization, it is possible to state a number of proposition that account for the role of social context in the development of personal goals and values.

> *Proposition 2.1: The social context influences people's valuing of goals, regardless of the intrinsic and extrinsic nature of the goal.*

Indeed, in contrast with OVP, the sociocognitive valuing process can explain the role of social context in the development of both intrinsic and extrinsic goals. The mechanisms that are involved in the development of extrinsic goals are the same as those involved in the development of intrinsic goals. The social context can influence individuals' preferences for intrinsic or extrinsic goals. The extrinsic goals are not only viewed as distractors from OVP but also as resulting from the valuing process. It is worth noting that, as shown in the literature on minority influence, the source of influence can be perceived as illegitimate but it still forces a reevaluation of the goal system and ultimately induces goal changes. This argument is developed in another paper (Grouzet, in preparation).

Proposition 2.2: This influence can be direct or indirect (i.e., via related concepts or self-theories).

As proposed in the social influence, persuasion, and socialization literature, the sociocognitive valuing process may involve elaborative cognitive processing, especially in the case of identification (as defined by SDT; discussed later). The existence of elaborative cognitive processing means that a transformation occurs. Therefore, the social communication and transmission of values and goals cannot be reduced to a simple copying process (see, e.g., Lawrence & Valsiner, 1993).

In addition, values and goals can be developed and changed indirectly because of the development and changes of other related constructs. For example, Dweck (1999) showed that explaining success and failure by the amount of effort invested in a task may influence the development of implicit theories of intelligence, which in turn can influence the selection of mastery versus performance goals. Likewise, in a series of longitudinal and experimental studies, Grouzet and Abrami (2012) found a relationship between fixed versus malleable implicit theories of personality and intrinsic versus extrinsic goals. People who perceive personality as a malleable characteristic tended to prioritize more intrinsic than extrinsic goals. However, a situational or chronic activation of fixed theories of personality was associated with the valuing of extrinsic goals.

Similarly, the type of interpersonal relations can explain the transmission of intrinsic and extrinsic goals from one individual to another. For example, an individual who values interpersonal relationships (i.e., affiliation goal) may engage in supportive and nurturing relationships, which could be interpreted by another person as a support for the implicit theory that people are good and worth caring about. In contrast, individuals who value financial success will consider others as objects that can be used to attain a materialistic goal, which in turn will reinforce the implicit theory that materials are more important than persons (see Grouzet, 2009, 2013).

> *Proposition 2.3: The mode of influence can be verbal, symbolic, and nonverbal, via communication and modeling.*

The channels of communication that enable transmission of information from one individual (or a group of individuals) to another individual can be verbal (i.e., oral communication) but also nonverbal. For example, facial expressions can communicate approval or disapproval of the expression of goal preferences or any associated behaviors. Likewise, behaviors can indicate social approval or can provide models to imitate. Finally, any symbolic representation of goals, values, or related variables can exert a social influence on individuals' valuing process. Books, magazines, media, and art are examples of symbolic transmission of goals and values.

> *Proposition 2.4: This influence involves an inner conflict that can be either social (or socioemotional) or epistemic (or cognitive), which in turn determines the type of internalization (introjection vs. identification).*

The sociocognitive valuing process is a transformative process by which external representations (e.g., goals) become part of the "inner world." As proposed by Piaget, the starting point of any transformation is the existence of a conflict between the organism's action and cognitive schemes and the recalcitrance of the external world that resists being fitted into these schemes, issuing in a processing of accommodation. This is in line with the literature on majority and minority influence (e.g., Pérez & Mugny, 1993) that points out the importance of inner conflict in explaining manifest versus latent changes in individuals' attitudes. The distinction between social and epistemic conflict is particularly important because it determines the type of internalization that occurs. On one hand, socioemotional conflict leads to introjection. On the other hand, epistemic conflict is associated with deeper cognitive processing that is essential for identification. Although SDT/OIT approaches internalization as a continuum (from partial to full), the qualitative distinction between introjection and identification carries the conceptual advantage of being in a better position to make sense of the valuing process and associated internal conflicts. Therefore, I propose that the qualitative distinction between introjection and identification is important in studying the valuing process. What is internalized through introjection is qualitatively different from what is internalized through identification. Of course, this difference between introjections and identification can be translated into different degrees of autonomy, as proposed by SDT/OIT.

Proposition 2.5: The quality of the social context (controlling vs. nurturing) determines (1) the type of conflict (social vs. epistemic) and the type of internalization (introjection versus identification), as well as (2) the content of goals (via modeling and self-theories).

Congruent with SDT/OIT and other organismic theories (e.g., Piaget, 1971; Rogers, 1964), I propose that humans naturally internalize values and goals. However, in contrast with SDT/OIT, I propose that the fulfillment of psychological needs is not necessary for introjection because internalization is a natural process, but the support for autonomy, competence, and relatedness is important for identification. This idea finds support in the commonly observed strong positive correlation between external regulation and introjected regulation and null correlations between need support and introjection (see, e.g., Ng et al., 2012). Furthermore, recent research on parental conditional regard and internalization (e.g., Assor, Roth, Deci, 2004; Roth, 2008) confirms Rogers's (1964) hypothesis that conditional love leads to introjected values.

Consequently, any situation or relationship that stresses an individual's socioemotional dependence, a contingency, or a threat can generate a social conflict that leads to introjection; the individual internalizes only introjected values, without processing the information about the value itself except for the contingency information. In this case the transformation occurs at the emotional level. In contrast, in nurturing and supportive situations and relationships, the individual can develop a sense of security (fostered by unconditional positive regard and relatedness) and a self-ascribed epistemic authority (fostered by support of competence needs). This sense of relatedness and competence can, in turn, enable higher and autonomous cognitive reasoning (fostered by epistemic conflict or informative communication). In such situations and relationships, individuals internalize values and goals that they can identify with; the transformation occurs at the cognitive level. In other words, I propose that the support of relatedness and competence needs facilitates the effect of informative communication (part of autonomy support) and internal epistemic conflict on personal autonomy, which in turn leads to identification and profound goal system changes.

In addition, as described in Proposition 2.2, the nature of relationships can impact not only the internalization process but also the content of the goal to be internalized. Indeed, a warm and nurturing relationship can be associated with values of trust and faith in human goodness and the capacity to change and grow, which is translated into intrinsic goals (see Proposition 2.5). In contrast, a controlling environment leads individuals to the objectification of human beings and results in the belief in the impossibility of change, which is translated into extrinsic goals. This hypothesis that I proposed elsewhere (e.g., Grouzet, 2009, 2013) has recently found supports in longitudinal studies (see Grouzet, 2012).

Limitations of the SVP. The SVP operates as the result of a negotiation between internal and external realities that direct the individual to prioritize intrinsic and/or extrinsic goals. The influence of the social context on an individual's valuing activity is captured by the cognitive processing of information that results from epistemic authority and epistemic conflict. By contrast, the social climate (psychological need support vs. thwart) impacts the type of internalization because it accentuates the social rather than the epistemic nature of the conflict, making the conflict more social than epistemic. When the conflict is social, cognitive transformation of knowledge and identification are less likely to occur.

Although the individual has an active role in the valuing process, the inner reality is conceptualized as an empty space that is filled by what the social context offers; only with age does the individual become more active in the negotiation with the social context. In other words, the person tends to be conceptualized as "something of a 'handbag,' a portable repository for various identity schemas that are cued up by differing social contexts" (Ryan, 1995, p. 398). This perspective also echoes the conceptualization of autonomy as a developmental outcome such that autonomy emerges as the result of a developmental process rather than being foundational for the very process itself (see Deci & Ryan, this volume). Therefore, the SVP does not include any natural tendency toward pursuing intrinsic or extrinsic goals. However, I propose that any valuing process model should include both organismic and sociocognitive elements in order to provide adequate descriptions, explanations, and predictions of what individuals will value.

THE DUAL VALUING PROCESS MODEL: A CONCEPTUAL FRAMEWORK FOR FUTURE RESEARCH

In the earlier sections I described two valuing processes: the Organismic Valuing Process (OVP) that explains the natural tendency to value and pursue intrinsic goals, and the Sociocognitive Valuing Process (SVP) that explains the role of social context in shaping individuals' (intrinsic and extrinsic) values and goals. In the Dual Valuing Process Model these processes co-exist and interact with each other to explain the emerging preference for intrinsic or extrinsic goals. Sometimes they are congruent in pushing individuals toward intrinsic goals, and at other times they are in conflict because the SVP directs individuals toward extrinsic goals. In the following sections, I describe the dialectic between the OVP and the SVP in situations in which they are congruent and in situations in which they are in conflict. Suggestions for future research will emerge from questions that the dual valuing process model generates.

Congruence Between OVP and SVP

The OVP explains a natural move toward intrinsic goals and away from extrinsic goals. If the social context promotes intrinsic goals, congruence exists between the SVP and the OVP. Therefore, the development of intrinsic goals can be explained by both a natural, innate organismic tendency and sociocognitive processes. The role of the social context in the valuing processes is dual. First, it may, as suggested by Rogers and empirically demonstrated by Kasser and his colleagues, fulfill individuals' psychological needs, offering a nurturing climate that fosters the organismic valuing process and intrinsic goals (see Proposition 1.1). Second, the social context conveys, through social influence, persuasion, and socialization, information about intrinsic goals that can be internalized by the individual. The kind of internalization is also influenced by the quality of the social context, such that a nurturing (vs. controlling) climate is translated into identification (vs. introjection) (Proposition 2.5). In other words, a nurturing (need supportive) climate can foster both the organismic valuing process and identification. Both experiential (or organismic) and rational (or socioepistemic) processes can foster the development of intrinsic goals.

To my knowledge, no study has examined the dual valuing process in action and how a nurturing climate influences the development of intrinsic goals. Future studies are needed to distinguish the organismic and socioepistemic valuing processes that are in place in a nurturing climate. Moreover, it might be worthwhile to examine the impact of a controlling climate on promoting intrinsic goals. According to the Dual Valuing Process Model, we can expect that the individual will introject intrinsic goals. I also propose that these introjected intrinsic goals could be easily, through self-reflection, transformed into identified intrinsic goals because of the organismic nature of this type of goal.

Conflicts Between the Organismic Valuing Process and the Sociocognitive Valuing Process

While the OVP proposes that a controlling climate can distract individuals from the natural pursuit of intrinsic goals, it does not explain the actual prioritization of extrinsic goals. However, with the SVP we can explain the development of extrinsic goals. In the Dual Valuing Process Model, extrinsic goals are actually developed only through the SVP. The social context offers to individuals goals and values that are in conflict with the OVP. This conflict, which is felt but not necessarily understood by the individual, actually explains the negative relationship between extrinsic goals and well-being. Because of their dependence on social information, individuals may develop goals that will distract them from intrinsic goals and also generate unhealthy conflicts. People can also voluntarily suppress their OVP in order to meet socialization goals and cope with threats and social control.

A closer examination of the dialectic between OVP and SVP also raises some interesting questions. According to Proposition 1.1, a nurturing climate can foster OVP and intrinsic goals; according to Proposition 2.5, a nurturing climate can foster identification with any goal, including extrinsic goals. These two propositions seem to be contradictory and challenge the existence of identified extrinsic goals. Some research, however, has demonstrated the possibility of identified extrinsic goals (e.g., Sheldon, Ryan, Deci, & Kasser, 2004). Therefore, further research needs to clarify how a nurturing climate can foster identified extrinsic goals while activating the OVP and modeling relationships that are associated with intrinsic goals.

I propose that the answer to this question resides in the concept of integration that SDT proposed as a third kind of internalization. While SDT proposed that with integration, goals and values are harmoniously integrated within the self (rather than having compartmentalized identifications), I propose that integration refers to the identification of goals that are congruent with organismic needs, which are intrinsic goals. In other words, extrinsic goals can be introjected or identified, but they cannot be integrated because they are not congruent with organismic needs. Future empirical research needs to test this hypothesis.

CONCLUSION

In this chapter, I presented the Dual Valuing Process Model that integrates two valuing processes that have been suggested in different theoretical traditions. First, the Organismic Valuing Process explains the natural tendency to value intrinsic goals. Second, the Sociocognitive Valuing Process explains how people's interaction with their social context can lead them to live in congruence or in conflict with their organismic nature. The absence versus presence of conflict between what the social context offers and the organismic nature of human beings explains the impact of intrinsic versus extrinsic goals on well-being. In order to reduce this conflict, the Dual

Valuing Process Model proposes that self-reflection and mindful awareness help people to re-connect with their organismic needs and to hear their inner voice.

This model reminds us that the inclusion of the "social" in explaining human development should not let us forget the biological and organismic nature of human beings. Piaget and Rogers were aware of this and thus developed theories that borrowed important principles from biology.

ACKNOWLEDGMENT

The author gratefully acknowledges the operating grant support he has received from Social Sciences and Humanities Research Council (SSHRC).

REFERENCES

Abramson, P. R., & Inglehart, R. F. (1995). *Value change in global perspective*. Ann Arbor: University of Michigan Press.

Arndt, J., Solomon, S., Kasser, T., & Sheldon, K. M. (2004). The urge to splurge: A terror management account of materialism and consumer behavior. *Journal of Consumer Psychology*, *14*, 198–212.

Assor, A., Roth, G., & Deci, E. L. (2004). The emotional costs of parents' conditional regard: A self-determination theory analysis. *Journal of Personality*, *72*, 47–88.

Bandura, A. (1977). *Social learning theory*. Oxford, England: Prentice-Hall.

Boehm, C. (2000). Conflict and the evolution of social control. *Journal of Consciousness Studies*, *7*, 79–101.

Brown, K. W., & Kasser, T. (2005). Are psychological and ecological well-being compatible? The role of values, mindfulness, and lifestyle. *Social Indicators Research*, *74*, 349–368. doi:10.1007/s11205-004-8207-8

Brown, K. W., Kasser, T., Ryan, R. M., Alex Linley, P., & Orzech, K. (2009). When what one has is enough: Mindfulness, financial desire discrepancy, and subjective well-being. *Journal of Research in Personality*, *43*, 727–736. doi:10.1016/j.jrp.2009.07.002

Bugental, D. B. (2000). Acquisition of the algorithms of social life: A domain-based approach. *Psychological Bulletin*, *126*, 187–219. doi:10.1037/0033-2909.126.2.187

Bugental, D. B., & Grusec, J. E. (2006). Socialization processes. In N. Eisenberg, W. Damon, & R. M. Lerner (Eds.), *Handbook of child psychology: Vol. 3. Social, emotional, and personality development* (pp. 366–428). Hoboken, NJ: Wiley.

Chaiken, S., Giner-Sorolla, R., & Chen, S. (1996). Beyond accuracy: Defense and impression motives in heuristic and systematic information processing. In P. M. Gollwitzer & J. A. Bargh (Eds.), *The psychology of action: Linking cognition and motivation to behavior* (pp. 553–578). New York, NY: Guilford Press.

Chaiken, S., Liberman, A., & Eagly, A. H. (1989). Heuristic and systematic information processing within and beyond the persuasion context. In J. S. Uleman & J. A. Bargh (Eds.), *Unintended thought* (pp. 212–252). New York, NY: Guilford Press.

Chang, L., & Arkin, R. M. (2002). Materialism as an attempt to cope with uncertainty. *Psychology & Marketing, 19*, 389–406. doi:10.1002/mar.10016

Chaplin, L. N., & John, D. R. (2007). Growing up in a material world: Age differences in materialism in children and adolescents. *Journal of Consumer Research, 34*, 480–493. doi:10.1086/518546

Chödrön, P. (1991). *The wisdom of no escape: And the path of loving-kindness*. Boston, MA: Shambhala.

Cohen, P., & Cohen, J. (1996). *Life values and adolescent mental health*. Hillsdale, NJ: Erlbaum.

Cozzolino, P. J. (2006). Death contemplation, growth, and defense: Converging evidence of dual-existential systems? *Psychological Inquiry, 17*, 278–287.

Cozzolino, P. J., Sheldon, K. M., Schachtman, T. R., & Meyers, L. S. (2009). Limited time perspective, values, and greed: Imagining a limited future reduces avarice in extrinsic people. *Journal of Research in Personality, 43*, 399–408. doi:10.1016/j.jrp.2009.01.008

Cozzolino, P. J., Staples, A. D., Meyers, L. S., & Samboceti, J. (2004). Greed, death, and values: From terror management to transcendence management theory. *Personality and Social Psychology Bulletin, 30*, 278–292. doi:10.1177/0146167203260716

Deci, E. L., Eghrari, H., Patrick, B. C., & Leone, D. R. (1994). Facilitating internalization: The self-determination theory perspective. *Journal of Personality, 62*, 119–142.

Deci, E. L., & Ryan, R. M. (1985). *Intrinsic motivation and self-determination in human behavior*. New York: Plenum Press.

Deci, E. L., & Ryan, R. M. (2000). The "what" and "why" of goal pursuits: Human needs and the self-determination of behavior. *Psychological Inquiry, 11*, 227–268.

Deci, E. L., & Ryan, R. M. (2012). Self-determination theory. In P. A. M. Van Lange, A. W. Kruglanski, & E. T. Higgins (Eds.), *Handbook of theories of social psychology (Vol. 1*, pp. 416–436). Thousand Oaks, CA: Sage.

Deutsch, M., & Gerard, H. B. (1955). A study of normative and informational social influences upon individual judgment. *Journal of Abnormal and Social Psychology, 51*, 629–636. doi:10.1037/h0046408

Doise, W., Mugny, G., & Perret-Clermont, A. -N. (1975). Social interaction and the development of cognitive operations. *European Journal of Social Psychology, 5*, 367–383. doi:10.1002/ejsp.2420050309

Dweck, C. S. (1999). *Self-theories: Their role in motivation, personality, and development*. Philadelphia, PA: Psychology Press.

Ellis, S., & Kruglanski, A. W. (1992). Self as an epistemic authority: Effects on experiential and instructional learning. *Social Cognition, 10*, 357–375. doi:10.1521/soco.1992.10.4.357

Epstein, S. (2003). Cognitive-experiential self-theory of personality. In T. Millon & M. J. Lerner (Eds.), *Handbook of psychology: Vol. 5. Personality and social psychology* (pp. 159–184). Hoboken, NJ: Wiley.

Erb, H.-P., & Bohner, G. (2007). Social influence and persuasion: Recent theoretical developments and integrative attempts. In K. Fiedler (Ed.), *Social communication* (pp. 191–221). New York, NY: Psychology Press.

Erb, H.-P., Kruglanski, A., Chun, W. Y., Pierro, A., Mannetti, L., & Spiegel, S. (2003). Searching for commonalities in human judgement: The parametric unimodel and its dual mode alternatives. *European Review of Social Psychology, 14*, 1–47. doi:10.1080/10463280340000009

Gecas, V. (1981). Contexts of socialization. In M. Rosenberg & R. H. Turner (Eds.), *Social psychology: Sociological perspectives* (pp. 165–199). New York: Basic Books.

Groth-Marnat, G., & Summers, R. (1998). Altered beliefs, attitudes, and behaviors following near-death experiences. *Journal of Humanistic Psychology, 38*, 110–125. doi:10.1177/00221678980383005

Grouzet, F. M. E. (2009). Values and relationships. In H. T. Reis & S. K. Sprecher (Eds.), *Encyclopedia of human relationships* (Vol. 3, pp. 1668–1671). Thousand Oaks, CA: Sage.

Grouzet, F. M. E. (2012). *The effect of higher education on intrinsic and extrinsic goals*. Unpublished manuscript.

Grouzet, F. M. E. (2013). Future leaders' and lawyers' life values and goals: Toward a dual valuing process model. In M. Gagné (Ed.), *The Oxford handbook of work engagement, motivation, and self-determination theory*. New York: Oxford University Press.

Grouzet, F. M. E., & Abrami, J. (2012). *Personal control beliefs and personal goals*. Unpublished manuscript.

Grouzet, F. M. E., Kasser, T., Ahuvia, A., Dols, J. M. F., Kim, Y., Lau, S., Ryan, R. M., et al. (2005). The structure of goal contents across 15 cultures. *Journal of Personality and Social Psychology, 89*, 800–816. doi:10.1037/0022–3514.89.5.800

Grusec, J. E. (2002). Parental socialization and children's acquisition of values. In M. H. Bornstein (Ed.), *Handbook of parenting: Vol. 5. Practical issues in parenting* (pp. 143–167). Mahwah, NJ: Erlbaum.

Grusec, J. E. (2011). Socialization processes in the family: Social and emotional development. *Annual Review of Psychology, 62*, 243–269. doi:10.1146/annurev.psych.121208.131650

Grusec, J. E., & Davidov, M. (2010). Integrating different perspectives on socialization theory and research: A domain-specific approach. *Child Development, 81*, 687–709.

Grusec, J. E., & Goodnow, J. J. (1994). Impact of parental discipline methods on the child's internalization of values: A reconceptualization of current points of view. *Developmental Psychology, 30*, 4–19.

Hartmann, H., & Loewenstein, R. M. (1962). Notes on the superego. *Psychoanalytic Study of the Child, 17*, 42–81.

Joseph, S., & Linley, P. A. (2005). Positive adjustment to threatening events: An organismic valuing theory of growth through adversity. *Review of General Psychology, 9*, 262–280. doi:10.1037/1089-2680.9.3.262

Joseph, S., & Linley, P. A. (2006). Growth following adversity: Theoretical perspectives and implications for clinical practice. *Clinical Psychology Review, 26*, 1041–1053. doi:10.1016/j.cpr.2005.12.006

Kahn, P. H. J. (1997). Developmental psychology and the biophilia hypothesis: Children's affiliation with nature. *Developmental Review, 17*, 1–61. doi:10.1006/drev.1996.0430

Kasser, T. (2002). *The high price of materialism*. Cambridge, MA: MIT Press.

Kasser, T., Cohn, S., Kanner, A. D., & Ryan, R. M. (2007). Some costs of American corporate capitalism: A psychological exploration of value and goal conflicts. *Psychological Inquiry*, *18*, 1–22. doi:10.1080/10478400701386579

Kasser, T., & Grow Kasser, V. (2001). The dreams of people high and low in materialism. *Journal of Economic Psychology*, 22, 693–719. doi:10.1016/S0167-4870(01)00055-1

Kasser, T., & Kanner, A. D. (2004). Where is the psychology of consumer culture? In T. Kasser & A. D. Kanner (Eds.), *Psychology and consumer culture: The struggle for a good life in a materialistic world.* (pp. 3–7). Washington, DC: American Psychological Association.

Kasser, T., Koestner, R., & Lekes, N. (2002). Early family experiences and adult values: A 26-year, prospective longitudinal study. *Personality and Social Psychology Bulletin*, *28*, 826–835. doi:10.1177/0146167202289011

Kasser, T., & Ryan, R. M. (1993). A dark side of the American dream: Correlates of financial success as a central life aspiration. *Journal of Personality and Social Psychology*, *65*, 410–422. doi:10.1037/0022-3514.65.2.410

Kasser, T., & Ryan, R. M. (1996). Further examining the American dream: Differential correlates of intrinsic and extrinsic goals. *Personality and Social Psychology Bulletin*, 22, 280–287. doi:10.1177/0146167296223006

Kasser, T., Ryan, R. M., Zax, M., & Sameroff, A. J. (1995). The relations of maternal and social environments to late adolescents' materialistic and prosocial values. *Developmental Psychology*, *31*, 907–914. doi:10.1037/0012-1649.31.6.907

Kasser, T., & Sheldon, K. M. (2000). Of wealth and death: Materialism, mortality salience, and consumption behavior. *Psychological Science*, *11*, 348–351. doi:10.1111/1467-9280.00269

Kelley, H. H., & Thibaut, J. W. (1969). Group problem solving. In E. Aronson & G. Lindzey (Eds.), *Handbook of social psychology* (2nd ed., Vol. 4). Reading, MA: Addison-Wesley.

Kelman, H. C. (1958). Compliance, identification, and internalization: Three processes of attitude change. *Journal of Conflict Resolution*, *2*, 51–60.

Kelman, H. C. (1961). Processes of opinion change. *Public Opinion Quarterly*, 25, 57–78.

Kelman, H. C. (2006). Interests, relationships, identities: Three central issues for individuals and groups in negotiating their social environment. *Annual Review of Psychology*, *57*, 1–26. doi:10.1146/annurev.psych.57.102904.190156

Kruglanski, A. W. (1989). *Lay epistemics and human knowledge: Cognitive and motivational bases.* New York, NY: Plenum Press.

Kruglanski, A. W., Raviv, A., Bar-Tal, D., Raviv, A., Sharvit, K., Ellis, S., Bar, R., et al. (2005). Says who? Epistemic authority effects in social judgment. *Advances in Experimental Social Psychology*, *37*, 345–392.

Kruglanski, A. W., & Thompson, E. P. (1999). Persuasion by a single route: A view from the unimodel. *Psychological Inquiry*, *10*, 83–109. doi:10.1207/S15327965PL100201

Kuczynski, L. (2003). Beyond bidirectionality: Bilateral conceptual frameworks for understanding dynamics in parent-child relations. In L. Kuczynski (Ed.), *Handbook of dynamics in parent-child relations* (pp. 1–24). Thousand Oaks, CA: Sage.

Kuczynski, L., & Navara, G. S. (2006). Sources of innovation and change in socialization, internalization and acculturation. In M. Killen & J. G. Smetana (Eds.), *Handbook of moral development* (pp. 299–327). Mahwah, NJ: Erlbaum.

Kuczynski, L., & Parkin, C. M. (2007). Agency and bidirectionality in socialization: Interactions, transactions, and relational dialectics. In J. E. Grusec & P. D. Hastings (Eds.), *Handbook of socialization: Theory and research* (pp. 259–283). New York, NY: Guilford Press.

Lawrence, J. A., & Valsiner, J. (1993). Conceptual roots of internalization: From transmission to transformation. *Human Development, 36*, 150–167. doi:10.1159/000277333

Lawrence, J. A., & Valsiner, J. (2003). Making personal sense: An account of basic internalization and externalization processes. *Theory & Psychology, 13*, 723–752. doi:10.1177/0959354303136001

Lekes, N., Hope, N. H., Gouveia, L., Koestner, R., & Philippe, F. L. (2012). Influencing value priorities and increasing well-being: The effects of reflecting on intrinsic values. *Journal of Positive Psychology, 7*, 249–261. doi:10.1080/17439760.2012.677468

Leman, P. J., & Duveen, G. (1996). Developmental differences in children's understanding of epistemic authority. *European Journal of Social Psychology, 26*, 683–702.

Lepper, M. R. (1983). Social-control processes and the internalization of social values: An attributional perspective. In E. T. Higgins, D. N. Ruble, & W. W. Hartup (Eds.), *Social cognition and social development: A sociocultural perspective* (pp. 294–330). Cambridge, MA: Cambridge University Press.

Lykins, E. L. B., Segerstrom, S. C., Averill, A. J., Evans, D. R., & Kemeny, M. E. (2007). Goal shifts following reminders of mortality: Reconciling posttraumatic growth and terror management theory. *Personality and Social Psychology Bulletin, 33*, 1088–1099. doi:10.1177/0146167207303015

Macoby, L. (2007). Historical overview of socialization research and theory. In J. E. Grusec & P. D. Hastings (Eds.), *Handbook of socialization: Theory and research* (pp. 13–41). New York, NY: Guilford Press.

Maslow, A. H. (1943). A theory of human motivation. *Psychological Review, 50*, 370.

Messerly, J. G. (2009). Piaget's biology. In U. Müller, J. I. M. Carpendale, & L. Smith (Eds.), *The Cambridge companion to Piaget* (pp. 94–109). New York, NY: Cambridge University Press.

Moscovici, S. (1980). Toward a theory of conversion behavior. In L. Berkowitz (Ed.), *Advances in experimental social psychology* (Vol. 13, pp. 209–239). New York, NY: Academic Press.

Moscovici, S. (1985). Innovation and minority influence. In S. Moscovici, G. Mugny, & E. V. Avermaet (Eds.), *Perspectives on minority influence* (pp. 201–215). Cambridge, MA: Cambridge University Press.

Moscovici, S., & Lage, E. (1976). Studies in social influence III: Majority versus minority influence in a group. *European Journal of Social Psychology, 6*, 149–174. doi:10.1002/ejsp.2420060202

Mugny, G. (1982). *The power of minorities*. New York, NY: Academic Press.

Mugny, G., Butera, F., Sanchez-Mazas, M., & Pérez, J. A. (1995). Judgments in conflict: The conflict elaboration theory of social influence. In B. Boothe, R.

Hirsig, A. Helminger, B. Meier, & R. Volkart (Eds.), *Perception – evaluation – interpretation*. (pp. 160–168). Ashland, OH: Hogrefe & Huber.

Müller, U ., Carpendale, J. I. M., & Smith, L. (Eds.). (2009). *The Cambridge companion to Piaget*. New York, NY: Cambridge University Press.

Narvaez, D. (2013). Development and socialization within an evolutionary context: Growing up to become "A good and useful human being." In D. Fry (Ed.), *War, peace, and human nature: The convergence of evolutionary and cultural views*. New York, NY: Oxford University Press.

Narvaez, D., & Gleason, T. (2012). Developmental optimization. In D. Narvaez, J. Panksepp, A. Schore, & T. Gleason (Eds.), *Evolution, early experiences and human development: From research to practice and policy*. New York, NY: Oxford University Press.

Nemeth, C. J. (1986). Differential contributions of majority and minority influence. *Psychological Review*, *93*, 23–32. doi:10.1037/0033-295X.93.1.23

Nemeth, C. J., Brown, K., & Rogers, J. (2001). Devil's advocate versus authentic dissent: Stimulating quantity and quality. *European Journal of Social Psychology*, *31*, 707–720. doi:10.1002/ejsp.58

Nemeth, C. J., Connell, J. B., Rogers, J. D., & Brown, K. S. (2001). Improving decision making by means of dissent. *Journal of Applied Social Psychology*, *31*, 48–58. doi:10.1111/j.1559-1816.2001.tb02481.x

Ng, J. Y. Y., Ntoumanis, N., Thøgersen- Ntoumani, C., Deci, E. L., Ryan, R. M., Duda, J. L., & Williams, G. C. (2012). Self-determination theory applied to health contexts: A meta-analysis. *Perspectives on Psychological Science*, *7*, 325–340. doi:10.1177/1745691612447309

Niemiec, C. P., Brown, K. W., Kashdan, T. B., Cozzolino, P. J., Breen, W. E., Levesque-Bristol, C., & Ryan, R. M. (2010). Being present in the face of existential threat: The role of trait mindfulness in reducing defensive responses to mortality salience. *Journal of Personality and Social Psychology*, *99*, 344–365. doi:10.1037/a0019388

Pérez, J. A., & Mugny, G. (1993). *Influences sociales: la théorie de l'élaboration du conflit*. Paris: Delachaux et Niestlé.

Pérez J. A., & Mugny G. (1996). The conflict elaboration theory of social influence. In E. H. Witte, & J. H. Davies (Eds.), *Understanding group behavior: Small group processes and interpersonal relations (Vol. 2*, pp. 191–210). Mahwah, NJ: Erlbaum.

Petty, R. E., & Cacioppo, J. T. (1986). *Communication and persuasion: Central and peripheral routes to attitude change*. New York, NY: Springer-Verlag.

Piaget, J. (1971). *Biology and knowledge: An essay on the relations between organic regulations and cognitive processes*. Chicago, IL: University of Chicago Press.

Piaget, J. (1977). Foreword. In H. E. Gruber & J. Vonéche (Eds.), *The essential Piaget*. London: Routledge and Kegan Paul.

Plagnol, A. C., & Scott, J. (2011). What matters for well-being: Individual perceptions of quality of life before and after important life events. *Applied Research in Quality of Life*, *6*, 115–137. doi:10.1007/s11482-010-9119-1

Ransom, S., Sheldon, K. M., & Jacobsen, P. B. (2008). Actual change and inaccurate recall contribute to posttraumatic growth following radiotherapy. *Journal of Consulting and Clinical Psychology*, *76*, 811–819. doi:10.1037/a0013270

Raviv, A., Bar-Tal, D., Raviv, A., & Houminer, D. (1990). Development in children's perceptions of epistemic authorities. *British Journal of Developmental Psychology, 8*, 157–169. doi:10.1111/j.2044-835X.1990.tb00830.x

Rigby, C. S., Deci, E. L., Patrick, B. C., & Ryan, R. M. (1992). Beyond the intrinsic-extrinsic dichotomy: Self determination in motivation and learning. *Motivation and Emotion, 16*, 165–185.

Rijavec, M., Brdar, I., & Miljkovic, D. (2006). Extrinsic vs. intrinsic life goals, psychological needs, and well-being. In A. Delle Fave (Ed.), *Dimensions of well-being: Research and intervention* (pp. 91–103). Milano: Franco Angeli.

Rindfleisch, A., Burroughs, J. E., & Wong, N. (2009). The safety of objects: Materialism, existential insecurity, and brand connection. *Journal of Consumer Research, 36*, 1–16. doi:10.1086/595718

Rogers, C. R. (1951). *Client-centered therapy.* Oxford: Houghton Mifflin.

Rogers, C. R. (1964). Toward a modern approach to values: The valuing process in the mature person. *Journal of Abnormal and Social Psychology, 68*, 160–167. doi:10.1037/h0046419

Roth, G. (2008). Perceived parental conditional regard and autonomy support as predictors of young adults' self- versus other-oriented prosocial tendencies. *Journal of Personality, 76*, 513–534. doi:10.1111/j.1467-6494.2008.00494.x

Ryan, R. M. (1995). Psychological needs and the facilitation of integrative processes. *Journal of Personality, 63*, 397–427.

Ryan, R. M., & Deci, E. L. (2000). Self-determination theory and the facilitation of intrinsic motivation, social development, and well-being. *American Psychologist, 55*, 68–78. doi:10.1037/0003-066X.55.1.68

Salmela-Aro, K., Nurmi, J. -E., Saisto, T., & Halmesmä ki, E. (2001). Goal reconstruction and depressive symptoms during the transition to motherhood: Evidence from two cross-lagged longitudinal studies. *Journal of Personality and Social Psychology, 81*, 1144–1159. doi:10.1037//0022-3514.81.6.1144

Schafer, R. (1968). *Aspects of internalization.* Madison, CT: International Universities Press.

Schmuck, P., Kasser, T., & Ryan, R. M. (2000). Intrinsic and extrinsic goals: Their structure and relationship to well-being in German and US college students. *Social Indicators Research, 50*, 225–241. doi:10.1023/A:1007084005278

Schulz-Hardt, S., Jochims, M., & Frey, D. (2002). Productive conflict in group decision making: genuine and contrived dissent as strategies to counteract biased information seeking. *Organizational Behavior and Human Decision Processes, 88*, 563–586. doi:10.1016/S0749-5978(02)00001-8

Settersten Jr., R. A. (2002). Socialization and the life course: new frontiers in theory and research. *Advances in Life Course Research, 7*, 13–40. doi:10.1016/S1040-2608(02)80028-4

Sheldon, K. M. (2005). Positive value change during college: Normative trends and individual differences. *Journal of Research in Personality, 39*, 209–223. doi:10.1016/j.jrp.2004.02.002

Sheldon, K. M., Arndt, J., & Houser-Marko, L. (2003). In search of the organismic valuing process: The human tendency to move towards beneficial goal choices. *Journal of Personality, 71*, 835–869.

Sheldon, K. M., & Elliot, A. J. (1999). Goal striving, need satisfaction, and longitudinal well-being: The self-concordance model. *Journal of Personality and Social Psychology, 76*, 482–497. doi:10.1037/0022-3514.76.3.482

Sheldon, K. M., & Kasser, T. (2001). Getting older, getting better? Personal strivings and psychological maturity across the life span. *Developmental Psychology, 37*, 491–501. doi:10.1037//0012-1649.37.4.491

Sheldon, K. M., & Kasser, T. (2008). Psychological threat and extrinsic goal striving. *Motivation and Emotion, 32*, 37–45. doi:10.1007/s11031-008-9081-5

Sheldon, K. M., Ryan, R. M., Deci, E. L., & Kasser, T. (2004). The independent effects of goal contents and motives on well-being: It's both what you pursue and why you pursue it. *Personality and Social Psychology Bulletin, 30*, 475–486. doi:10.1177/0146167203261883

Twenge, J. M., Campbell, W. K., & Freeman, E. C. (2012). Generational differences in young adults' life goals, concern for others, and civic orientation, 1966–2009. *Journal of Personality and Social Psychology, 102*, 1045–1062. doi:10.1037/a0027408

Vansteenkiste, M., Soenens, B., & Duriez, B. (2008). Presenting a positive alternative to strivings for material success and the thin ideal: Understanding the effects of extrinsic relative to intrinsic goal pursuits. In S. J. Lopez (Ed.), *Positive psychology: Exploring the best in people: Vol. 4. Pursuing human flourishing* (pp. 57–86). Westport, CT: Praeger.

Vygotsky, L. S. (1978). *Mind in society: The development of higher psychological processes*. Cambridge, MA: Harvard University Press.

Wallis, K. C., & Poulton, J. L. (2001). *Internalization: The origins and construction of internal reality*. Buckingham, PA: Open University Press.

Weinstein, N., Przybylski, A. K., & Ryan, R. M. (2009). Can nature make us more caring? Effects of immersion in nature on intrinsic aspirations and generosity. *Personality and Social Psychology Bulletin, 35*, 1315–1329. doi:10.1177/0146167209341649

Williams, G. C., Cox, E. M., Hedberg, V. A., & Deci, E. L. (2000). Extrinsic life goals and health-risk behaviors in adolescents. *Journal of Applied Social Psychology, 30*, 1756–1771. doi:10.1111/j.1559-1816.2000.tb02466.x

Wilson, E. O. (1984). *Biophilia*. Harvard, MA: Harvard University Press.

Wilson, E. O. (1993). Biophilia and the conservation ethic. In S. R. Kellert (Ed.), *The biophilia hypothesis* (pp. 31–41). Washington, DC: Island Press.

Wood, W., Lundgren, S., Ouellette, J. A., Busceme, S., & Blackstone, T. (1994). Minority influence: A meta-analytic review of social influence processes. *Psychological Bulletin, 115*, 323–345. doi:10.1037/0033-2909.115.3.323

Chapter 4

Development as Emergence

R. KEITH SAWYER
Washington University

Perhaps the central issue facing the social sciences is the relation between the individual and the social world. How do individuals create and reproduce social order? How do social structures enable and constrain individual action? This relationship is also central in developmental psychology, and it is the central theme of this volume. As explored here, self-regulation is "children's growing competence to comply with and abide by externally imposed rules" (see Calkins & Howse, 2004; Carlson, 2005) whereas autonomy emphasizes the importance of agency and self-determined goal setting (see Grouzet, Sokol, & Müller this volume). As so defined, these concepts are in tension – with self-regulation corresponding to external constraints, and autonomy corresponding to the individual's own wishes and desires.

In this chapter, I explore the dialectic tension of self-regulation and autonomy through the theoretical lens of *emergence* (Sawyer, 2005). I argue that development is driven by a tension between self-regulation and autonomy, and that this tension can be better understood in the context of a theory of emergence, because development is at root an emergent process (Sawyer, 2003). I argue that social structures *emerge* from individuals in interaction, and that having emerged, those structures exert causal power over individuals. One mechanism through which this causal power is exerted is through socialization processes, during development, that lead to the balance of self-regulation and autonomy found in mature individuals.

An emergence theory of development argues that development is not centrally driven or programmed but instead emerges from complex interactions, both within the organism and between the organism and its environment. Further, emergence theories posit that the development of a new stage cannot be easily reduced to explanation in terms of the components of the previous stage. Theories of development that are *not* emergent include innatist or preformationist theories and social determinist theories (because they account for development by appeal to a central driving or programming force); and behaviorist theories (because they reductively explain development as a series of associations). The canonical example of an emergence theory of development is Piaget's constructivism.

I conclude by identifying five characteristics of development that are implied by the dialectic of autonomy and self-regulation that is highlighted by emergence theory: (1) the process of emergence versus the end point; (2) stage transitions and novelty; (3) domain specificity; (4) internalization of the domain; (5) emergence in social groups versus emergence in one individual's mind.

THE DIALECTIC OF AUTONOMY AND SELF-REGULATION

Deci and Ryan (this volume) draw a distinction between the autonomy that is intrinsic motivation and the autonomy that is internalized extrinsic motivation. They define autonomy as "intrinsic motivation and well-internalized extrinsic motivation." Their chapter includes an insightful account of four different degrees of internalization, which they refer to as "more or less autonomy." Deci and Ryan (this volume) say that "to be autonomous means to act with a full sense of willingness, a sense of volition and concurrence. In contrast to autonomy is control in which either external or internal forces pressure the person to behave in particular ways. As noted, this implies that there are internal regulatory processes that do not represent autonomy" (p. 29). These processes I refer to as self-regulation.

In many prominent theories of development, the dialectic between self-regulation and autonomy is what drives development. This dialectic has more than superficial parallels to Freud's classic opposition between primary process and secondary process cognition, with the superego corresponding to self-regulation, the id corresponding to autonomy (note that in Deci and Ryan's chapter, autonomy corresponds to intrinsic motivation), and the ego representing the balance of the two in the mature personality. And this dialectic is a central feature of Piaget's developmental theory (this is, of course, why this volume started as a set of papers presented at the Jean Piaget Society annual meeting). As Sokol and colleagues argue (this volume), Piaget resisted individualistic conceptions of agency and argued instead that interpersonal relationships in part constitute individual agency and autonomy. As they say, "[a]ccording to this more relational view, an individual's values, beliefs, and ideals would also be seen as originating in her or his social or communal ties" (p. 106). For Piaget, autonomy emerges in social exchanges.

The dialectic between autonomy and self-regulation also corresponds to a long-standing and classic opposition in social theory: the tension between structure and agency. In the classic formulation of Talcott Parsons, "structure" refers to the social rules, norms, entities, values, and networks of relations that exist independently of any one individual, and that perdure over generations (1937/1949, 1951). Parsons's theory came to be known as *structural-functionalism*. For structure to remain stable over long periods of time, it must *reproduce* itself, by socializing children and guiding maturing individuals into appropriate locations in the social structure (also see Corsaro, 1997). Agency (or "action" in Parsons's terminology) refers to the individual freedom to make decisions and to act within these structures; but, for the most part, structural sociologists in the Parsonsian tradition did not invest much energy in analyzing and explaining agency. Parsons himself rather uncritically adopted the Freudian model of the personality as his own theory of individual agency (e.g., Parson, 1951). Thus, in structural sociology, self-regulation is essential to explain how individuals internalize norms and values through socialization, but autonomy is undertheorized.

In the 1960s, Garfinkel's (1967) *ethnomethodology* raised a serious challenge to structural-functionalism by focusing exactly on this neglect of individual agency and autonomy. Garfinkel argued that social structures can have influence over individuals only to the extent to which the structures are perceived and interpreted by individuals. And if the causal power of social structures is always mediated by individual interpretations, then the proper study of social life should focus on individuals and their interpretations; no separate analysis of social structure is necessary, because social structure influences individual action only to the extent that it is perceived and interpreted by individuals. This general position, which I and others refer to broadly as *interpretivism* (Sawyer, 2005), became influential in social theory in the 1970s, 1980s, and 1990s, and today is often associated with the conversation analysts (e.g., Schegloff, 1968, 1986) and with Anthony Giddens's (1984) *structuration theory*.

The conversation analysts followed Garfinkel in arguing that the causal effects of macrosocial forces are not analytically distinct, but can best be understood by analyzing participants' orientations toward them as revealed in the talk itself. For example, Schegloff (1992) argued that the external context is important only to the extent that it is "demonstrably relevant to participants" (p. 215; also see Schegloff, 1991). As he put it, "if some 'external' context can be shown to be proximately (or intra-interactionally) relevant to the participants, then its external status is rendered beside the point;

and if it cannot be so shown, then its external status is rendered equivocal" (p. 197). Giddens (1984), also following in the ethnomethodology tradition, argued that the divide between structure and agency was artificial; "structure is not 'external' to individuals: as memory traces, and as instantiated in social practices, it is in a certain sense more 'internal' than exterior" (p. 25). In this modern sociological tradition, the dialectic between structure and agency is essentially that between self-regulation and autonomy, because external structural forces are considered to be necessarily mediated by the self-regulation that results from development.

Interpretivist theory has many overlaps with contemporary sociocultural theory in developmental research (Sawyer, 2002b). For example, Rogoff (1982) argued that "the child and the social world are mutually involved to an extent that precludes regarding them as independently definable" (p. 28), and that in this theoretical framework, "the boundary between individual and environment disappears" (Rogoff, 1997, p. 267). However, many sociologists have argued that interpretivist approaches undertheorize the role of social structure in social life and seem to grant individuals a greater degree of autonomy than actually exists (Archer, 1995; Sawyer, 2005). Archer (1995), for example, has called these theories "elisionist" because they "elide" the distinction between individual agency and structure.

Developmentalists have proposed various conceptions of the processes whereby external regulation becomes internalized as self-regulation, including "scaffold," "zone of proximal development," and "cultural practice." Developmentalists tend to take as a given the preexisting social relations and structures that a child encounters. Researchers who study self-regulation focus on how these external social entities are internalized, appropriated, or learned to result in increasing self-regulation (see Deci & Ryan, this volume). They generally leave it to sociologists to analyze how those structures came to be. But if the interpretivists are correct – if, as Giddens (1984) would say, structure is "more 'internal' than exterior'" (p. 25), then developmental psychologists may have a larger role to play in the analysis and explanation of social structures and forces than either sociologists or developmentalists have previously realized (also see Sawyer, 2002b). If structure is internal, then it is essentially self-regulation. And then many key sociological questions become questions for developmental psychology: How is the social order maintained and reproduced over time and across generations? (It must be through the development of self-regulation.) How do social structures constrain and enable individuals? (It must be through the tension between autonomy and self-regulation.)

THEORIES OF EMERGENCE

Emergence theory provides a helpful perspective on the dialectic between autonomy and self-regulation in development. Emergence was the focus of an influential group of British philosophers and evolutionary biologists just after World War I, a group that has been called the *British emergentists* (McLaughlin, 1992). Influential figures from this period include Broad (1925), Morgan (1923), and Whitehead (1926). Their theories shared the following properties:

- Emergence is a process that occurs through time.
- When aggregates of basic entities attain a certain level of structural complexity, properties of the aggregate emerge. New stuff does not emerge; rather, it is properties of the higher-level entities that emerge.
- What emerges are new evolutionary, historical, or developmental stages.
- What emerges is novel; it did not exist in the prior stage.
- What emerges is unpredictable and could not have been known analytically before it emerged.
- Emergent properties are irreducible to explanation in terms of the previous stage, even though they are determined by that stage.

Through the 1930s, the ideas of the British emergentists had a wide ranging impact in psychology and the social sciences and were explicitly acknowledged as influences by theorists as diverse as Wolfgang Köhler, George Herbert Mead, and Talcott Parsons. Contemporary theories of emergence largely contain these same features. In spite of their rejection of reductionism, emergentists are materialists, holding that only physical matter exists (in the 1920s, several philosophers argued for the contrasting position of *vitalism*, the belief in a nonmaterial life-giving substance). Because emergentists are materialists, they hold that emergent properties must *supervene* on microlevel properties (Sawyer, 2002a). Supervenience means that the behavior of the whole is determined by the nature and arrangement of its components. Even so, emergentists reject mechanistic theories, which held that the behavior of the whole "could, in theory at least, be *deduced* from a sufficient knowledge of how the components behave in isolation or in other wholes of a simpler kind" (Broad, 1925, p. 59).

Because the British emergentists drew on the same 19th-century influences as the founders of developmental psychology (Brent, 1978; Kitcher, 1992; Morss, 1990; Siegler, 1996), they made observations that are today usually associated with Freud's or Piaget's theoretical extensions of these same founders (e.g., Baldwin, Binet, Claparede, Darwin, Stern). For example, Morgan (1933) claimed that thought proceeds in stages that are characterized by their distinctive mental structures: "In the recurrent development of each individual mind, there is, I believe, advance through new modes of organization to further novelty in organization" (p. 79). In other words, each stage of mental development emerges from the prior stage, and this process of emergence always involves a restructuring that is novel. He referred to the study of cognitive development as both "mental evolution" and "genetic psychology" (p. 157), with "genetic" having the same emergentist connotations as Piaget's phrase "genetic epistemology"; in both cases, the term means that structures at each developmental stage emerge from interaction between the organism and its environment at the prior stage (p. 165).

A theory of development as emergent is an intermediate position between two potential alternative explanations. First, one could explain the final state of the system by arguing that it is predetermined by the initial state of the system. In evolutionary biology, this position was known as *preformationism* and this term was also frequently used in early 20th-century developmental psychology. Piaget frequently used the term in criticizing this view, which today corresponds to an overly simplistic conception of innatism as "being programmed in the genes." Preformationism needs no theory of how self-regulation and autonomy develop through internalization, because the organism is pre-programmed to develop all of its mature features, including self-regulation and autonomy.

In contrast to preformationism, in emergentism each stage emerges from activity and process at the prior stage, and thus is a result of organism-environment interaction. Without this interaction there would be no development. Emergentism rejects a preformationist position which holds that the final state of the mature organism is present in the newborn.

A second alternative to emergentism explains development by arguing that the final state of the system is determined by the environment of the organism. Such stances have been common in sociology and in the radical empiricism of behaviorist psychology. These theories are overly simplistic in their social determinism, and tend not to provide sophisticated explanations of how self-regulation develops. As already noted, structural sociology undertheorizes the autonomy and agency of the individual. The focus on the environmental determinism (as in behaviorism) allows a theorization of self-regulation, but autonomy is problematic for such theories.

In contrast, emergentism holds that an explanation of the final state of the system requires an examination of the step-by-step interaction between organism and environment, as it passes from stage to stage, because the state of the organism changes at each stage. Thus the environment is not directly imposed on or internalized by the organism; rather, development results from a constructivist process of organism-environment interaction.

The contrast with both preformationism and behaviorism reveals that the dialectic between self-regulation and autonomy is at the core of development as emergence. The term development is often contrasted with the "learning" of behaviorist theory, and the field of "cognitive development" is unified in its rejection of behaviorism. Behaviorism canonically holds that learning proceeds according to associationist mechanisms: the individual perceives two stimuli at the same time, or in succession, and after enough perceptions of the two stimuli in this relation, the mind begins to associate them. In the behaviorist framework, learning is a linear, monotonic process: skills and knowledge increase linearly with experience of the world.

Piaget's genetic psychology was opposed to behaviorist associationism (see Taylor, 1985, p. 140). The contrast with associationism is that once a child has successfully constructed a fundamental schema – such as number, equivalence, or conservation – the child's thought is fundamentally transformed; the presence of that new schema then influences the manner in which the child apprehends the world from that point forward. There are no stages nor cognitive structures in learning theories, only in developmental theories, because stages can only result from qualitative transformations in internal mental structures. This is why Piaget equated novelty with stages: "If there are novelties, then, of course, there are stages. If there are no novelties, then the concept of stages is artificial" (1971, p. 194).

Piaget's constructivism was emergentist; schemas at one stage emerge from the interaction between activity and schemas at the prior stage. His empirical research focused on the detailed incremental mechanisms of this emergence. For example, in *Play Dreams and Imitation in Childhood* (Piaget, 1945/1962), Piaget documented the microgenesis of the schema for the symbol. (In French, the book's title is *La formation du symbol chez l'enfant,* which roughly translates as "the development of the symbol in the child's mind.") By providing explanations of the emergence of mental schemas through time, Piaget rejected the claim of the Gestaltists that higher-level phenomena could be analyzed and explained without reference to their components or to the history of their emergence. And by showing how complex the processual steps were, Piaget rejected the reductionist associationism of the behaviorists.

For Piaget, the transition to the next stage always involves a moment of emergence. Piaget did not believe that these stages and their ordering was innate or preformed; although the ordering of the stages was the same in every individual, it could only be determined by documenting processes of emergence through time and it could not be found in the genetic code of the individual (Piaget, 1971a). All that must be innate is a very general ability to coordinate the actions that are needed to jump-start the whole developmental process (Piaget, 1968/1970, pp. 61–68; see Gruber & Vonèche, 1977, p. xxxv).

There has been a history of controversy about whether Piaget was an elementarist or a holist, and this relates directly to his status as an emergence theorist. Van der Veer (1996) and Kitchener (1985) both claimed that Piaget's structures were additive and thus not emergent, in contrast to gestalt structures that were nonadditive. In a sense, Piaget *was* "reductively" explaining the emergence of each stage in terms of the process whereby it emerges from the prior stage, even though this explanation did not take an associationist form. The schema is the product of past interactions, and therefore it is "a gestalt which has a history" (Piaget, 1936/1952, p. 384).

Kitchener (1985) concluded that Piaget rejected emergence because the whole is reducible to the relations between the parts, and thus the composition is reversible. However, although the 1920s emergentists were anti-reductionists, many contemporary forms of emergentism are not incompatible with reductionism, because in a sense the emergent later forms are reductively explained in terms of the dynamical relations and processes of the earlier forms (Elder-Vass, 2010; Sawyer, 2005; also see Wimsatt, 1997). Piaget referred to himself as a "relationist," and his discussion makes clear that this is a form of emergentism; Piaget is emergentist because he places his position between reductionist atomism and holism (e.g., 1967, p. 1228). Although his schemas are additive, they are always seen as evolving structures, and lower-level structures are constrained by higher-level emergent structures (see Gruber & Vonèche, 1977, p. xxxii). Piaget rejected the anti-reductionism of holists such as the Gestaltists (1968/1970, pp. 8–9) and accepted that wholes or cognitive schemas are additively composed of elements and their relations; in his view, this process is a continual dynamic and occurs through time, such that a schema cannot be reduced to its elements at a given time but must be explained in terms of its origin from elements in the past. For this reason, schemas *as wholes* are analytically prior to their elements, in that they have causal downward effects over those elements (1968/1970, p. 7).

Piaget proposed the first influential emergentist theory of development, in carving out a theoretical position in between reductionist associationism and innatist preformationism. Today, most cognitive developmentalists occupy a theoretical stance that shares more with emergentism than with either of these two alternatives, and this is the lasting legacy of Piaget.

In sum, an emergence theory of development emphasizes the core role played by the dialectic between autonomy and self-regulation. Autonomy corresponds to individual agency, and self-regulation corresponds to internalized social rules, values, and norms. For theorists who reject preformationism and behaviorism, emergence is a common thread, and it is the dialectic between autonomy and self-regulation, between agency and structure, that drives the emergence of new schemas, concepts, or stages.

FIVE CHARACTERISTICS OF EMERGENCE IN DEVELOPMENT

In the following sections, I discuss five aspects of development that are revealed by an emergence perspective and its focus on the dialectic between autonomy and self-regulation.

Process Versus Product

Emergence theories focus on process rather than on end product. A focus on process has been characteristic of many theories of development. For example, socioculturalists such as Rogoff (1990) and Cole (1996) emphasized the focus on developmental process and on microgenetic studies, in contrast to prior developmental work that focused on end points of development. And yet, this shift from endpoint to process leads to a new theoretical question: What is the relationship between developmental processes and the end points of development?

For those focused on developmental process, a promising research methodology is the *microgenetic method*, in which the child is closely observed as his or her psychological structures are changing, and frequent samples of children's mental states are obtained throughout the process (Siegler, 1996). One consistent finding of microgenetic studies of cognitive development is that children do not ordinarily substitute a more advanced for a simpler strategy (Kuhn, 1995). Older strategies continue to be used even after they are clearly seen to be less effective. A second consistent finding is that children generally think about a problem in many ways at once. This cognitive variability is most evident during a period of rapid change (Alibali & Goldin-Meadow, 1993).

This research suggests that the relation between process and end point is complex. Theories of emergence are well-suited to account for this complexity. And to a large extent, these microgenetic studies reveal the centrality of the tension between autonomy and self-regulation.

Stage Transitions and Novelty

In developmental stage theories such as Piaget's, the child is propelled to the next stage by a disturbance in the equilibrium of the prior stage. Piaget's empirical work documented the microgenesis of the emergence of the next stage from the logical necessity of the clash between the current schema and environmental interaction. Piaget also documented the process of development within a stage – which was typically a transition from a more concrete to a more abstract set of schemas (e.g., with the schema of the "symbol" in *Play, Dreams, and Imitation in Childhood*).

Late in his life, Piaget noted that we still poorly understand how stage transitions occur. He observed that the most serious unresolved problem was the issue of "novelty," how a child makes the transition to the next stage (Piaget, 1971a, p. 192). Like Piaget, many other developmentalists have argued that we have very little knowledge of what happens during stage transitions. Beginning in the 1970s and inspired by the growth of cognitive psychology, advocates of cognitive models of development claimed that they could provide new conceptual tools with which to understand the transition mechanisms of development (e.g., Case, 1985; Simon & Halford, 1995). Many of these scholars argued that Piagetian theory was largely focused on structures and thus neglected the processes of development (e.g., Case, 1985, p. 410; Klahr, 1982, p. 80), although a more recent line of Piagetian scholarship has argued that these are mischaracterizations of Piaget (Müller, Carpendale, & Smith, 2009) and that Piaget was at root a theorist of developmental process. A theory of development as emergence is consistent with this newer understanding.

Some developmentalists have proposed that there is an incubation period in between developmental stages, because it takes time for individuals "to appropriate the complex knowledge that they co-construct during social interaction" (Azmitia, 1998, p. 240). Complex ideas must "ferment" or "percolate" in our unconscious until they fully develop and begin to influence cognitive performance. These ideas are reinforced by experimental studies that have documented extended periods of stage transition during which multiple schemas and strategies are active (Siegler, 1996). In Siegler's evolutionary model, development is a process of age-related changes in the repertoire of cognitive strategies and in the preference for and ability to use different cognitive strategies. Siegler's *overlapping waves approach* proposed that the child has multiple strategies available at any one time, and that these strategies compete; over time, the more effective strategies are increasingly used (1998, p. 92). With time, the more successful strategies thrive and become more frequent, and the less successful strategies fade away. Siegler also hypothesized that children can create or discover new strategies, but he admitted that his theory is weakest in explaining the emergence of novelty (1998, p. 96).

Domain Specificity

In the 1970s, 1980s, and 1990s, developmentalists increasingly found evidence that children seemed to progress through Piagetian stages at different rates in different realms of cognitive competence (Callanan, 1999, p. 150). Piaget's theory is often thought to make the claim that stages are general properties of the child's cognition, and that when a child transitions to the next stage, the mental schemas of that stage will be manifest in all activities of the child, regardless of the topic, sensory modality, or social context. And yet, Piaget's position was much more complex and acknowledged that one child could be in different stages in different domains (Müller et al., 2009). The issue of the degree to which development is domain general or domain specific remains central in developmental psychology.

Psychologists have defined "domain" in a variety of ways:

- "a set of symbolic rules and procedures" (Csikszentmihalyi, 1996, p. 27)
- "a body of knowledge that identifies and interprets a class of phenomena assumed to share certain properties and to be of a distinct and general type" (Hirschfeld & Gelman, 1994, p. 21)
- "a given set of principles, the rules of their application, and the entities to which they apply" (Gelman & Brenneman, 1994, p. 371)
- "the set of representations sustaining a specific area of knowledge: language, number, physics, and so forth" (Karmiloff-Smith, 1992, p. 6)

At the core of all of these definitions is the idea that a domain involves an internal, symbolic language; representations; and operations on those representations. Most studies find that there are between three and seven distinct domains of human potential:

- Gardner (1983) proposed seven domains: spatial, linguistic, logical-mathematical, kinesthetic, musical, interpersonal, and intrapersonal. (Gardner 1999 added an eighth domain, naturalistic.)

- Holland (1997) proposed a model of vocational interests which contained six: realistic, investigative, artistic, social, enterprising, and conventional.
- Carson et al (2005) started with 10 domains and through a factor analysis found they grouped into three factors: expressive creativity (visual arts, writing, humor) performance creativity (dance, drama, music) and scientific creativity (invention, science, culinary) (with architecture not related to any of these three).
- Kaufman and Baer (2004) in a study of 241 college students, found that nine rated areas of creativity actually grouped into three factors: empathy/communication (interpersonal relationships, communication, solving personal problems, writing); hands-on creativity (arts, crafts, bodily/physical); and math/science creativity (math, science).

These issues continue to be actively studied in developmental psychology: What exactly are the relevant domains during cognitive development? How does development proceed differently in distinct domains? And yet, one legacy of Piaget is that similar developmental processes are thought to be responsible for development in all domains.

Internalization of the Domain

How do individuals acquire domain knowledge during development? One of the oldest and simplest theories is that the child *internalizes* domain knowledge – basically, encountering the knowledge in the external world, and then creating an iconic copy inside the mind. Internalization was a central focus of Vygotsky's developmental theory. In Vygotsky's theory, development involves a transfer of social patterns of interaction into the individual learner's mind: "an interpersonal process is transformed into an intrapersonal one" (1978, p. 57). Like Vygotsky, Lawrence and Valsiner (1993) propose a view of development as internalization: "what was originally in the interpersonal (or intermental) domain becomes intra-personal (intra-mental) in the course of development" (p. 151). As constructivists, they reject a concept of internalization as transmission ("exclusive separation"), emphasizing Vygotsky's claim that internalization involves transformation (see also Valsiner, 1989).

Piaget's theory of cognitive development presented an alternative – development results from a tension between existing schemas and external reality. From this theoretical perspective, what develops in the mind is not necessarily a direct copy of external reality. And in recent years, many

Vygotsky scholars have problematized the more simplistic accounts of internalization (cf. Lawrence & Valsiner, 1993). For example, Wertsch (1993) argues that the term "internalization" is problematic because it presupposes a "dualism between the external and the internal" (p. 168); he suggests that we can avoid this dualism using the term "mastery" (p. 169). For Wertsch, development involves "transformations in individuals' understanding (i.e., their mastery) of the meaning of cultural tools such as language" (p. 170).

For additional perspective on how domains are acquired in development, I turn to creativity research, which has addressed a similar issue (Sawyer, 2012). Creativity theorists agree that an important part of the creative process is the internalization of the language and symbols of the domain, and yet they realize this is not sufficient for creativity; it is only a prerequisite. Creativity results when the individual somehow combines these internalized elements and generates some new configuration. Thus creativity theory provides a subtly different perspective on internalization. Creativity researchers accept that much knowledge is internalized in a rather passive and direct way; the student of physics must learn Maxwell's equations and Einstein's theories as they already are, and this process does not have to be creative. Nonetheless, once the existing elements of the domain are internalized, novel combinations can be formed. Thus, creativity theory retains a conception of internalization that is compatible with creative construction and novelty.

By analogy, the child could be said to internalize many elements and components of knowledge in some domain, and this internalization could be compatible with a transformative, constructivist view of development. After internalization, the child has to go through some sort of integrative or transformative process in which those elements or components are placed into a structure or framework of knowledge.

Socioculturalists like Wertsch and Rogoff claim that there is no role for internalization in development and that constructive appropriation is always taking place. This observation can be applied to the creative process as well. Creative people rarely simply internalize; they often "transform" and "appropriate" even as they are gathering new knowledge. When an artist walks through a gallery, he views paintings very selectively, looking for ideas or inspirations that can solve creative problems that he currently is working with. This can lead the painter to see something in a painting that the creator may not have intended or been aware of. When a scientist reads a historical work by a long-dead theorist, it is a commonplace that she will read into the work whatever perspectives or issues she is currently working with. In neither case does the creative individual first simply internalize the work and then transform it; the transformation is a part of the original perception.

In sum, the common issues in creativity and development are the relations between a cognitive schema and the new knowledge that is apprehended from the world. How is the perception of the new knowledge influenced by the current schema? How can the schema be changed by the new knowledge?

The Social and the Individual

In the 1980s, developmental researchers known as socioculturalists began to examine how groups develop through time. Some ethnographers began to examine how groups create novelty by studying science lab workgroups (for example, Dunbar, 1995; Hall & Stevens, 1996; Hutchins, 1995). Rather than focusing on specific individuals in the group, they treated the group itself as an entity which develops through time, in successive stages, and as a result of interaction with its environment. More in keeping with Vygotsky than with Piaget, socioculturalists such as Rogoff proposed a social version of constructivism, arguing that knowledge is emergent from a social process (1990).

Rogoff briefly discussed adult creativity within the sociocultural framework (1990). First, the creative process "builds on the technologies already available, within existing institutions. A creative idea is in some sense a reformulation of existing ideas" (p. 198). In creativity research, a system of existing ideas is referred to as a "domain," a collection of symbols, symbol systems, and artifacts that must be internalized as the raw material of the creative process. Second, Rogoff noted that creativity always occurs within a social context, of apprentices, colleagues, coworkers, and evaluators.

In the late 1980s, in parallel with this sociocultural movement in developmental psychology, creativity researchers began to emphasize the need to move beyond a psychological study of the individual creator. Among creativity researchers, this recent development is often attributed to an article published by Mihalyi Csikszentmihalyi in 1988, in which he proposed the "systems view" of creativity. The creative system is a social system that includes three elements: the *individual*, the social institution or *field*, and the cultural symbol system or *domain* (p. 325). This tripartite model was also used by Howard Gardner in a chapter in the same 1988 volume, and he has drawn on it heavily in several books about creativity (e.g., Gardner, 1993).

There are close connections between socioculturalism and contemporary creativity theory; it is interesting that the shift from an individual to a social perspective occurred almost simultaneously in both developmental psychology and in creativity theory. At about the same time, both developmental psychology and creativity research shifted from a purely individualistic level of analysis to increasingly incorporate a social level of analysis. Many creativity researchers now focus on how individual and social factors combine during the creative process (cf. John-Steiner, 1993, p. 103; Sawyer & DeZutter, 2009). This requires the researcher to decide on an appropriate level of analysis for the phenomenon. If both individual and social levels are involved, what is the nature of the relationships and causal connections between these levels? Are there similar developmental processes at both levels of analysis?

I have already noted that these are long-standing issues in sociological theory. Particularly in the last two decades, theorists of the *micro-macro link* have attempted to reconcile the reductionism of methodological individualism, and various anti-reductionisms such as sociological realism and sociological holism (Sawyer, 2005). These issues are widely debated among socioculturalists but remain unresolved (Sawyer, 2002b).

Throughout the history of sociology, and in several influential contemporary theories, the micro-macro link has been conceived of as a relation of emergence. Social properties are thought to emerge from the collective actions and interactions of the component individuals of the system (Sawyer, 2005). In many of these theories of emergence, the social properties are thought to then take on some causal powers, such that individuals can be causally influenced by social properties, even though those social properties emerged from the actions of those same individuals (Archer, 1995, 2000; Bhaskar, 1982). Such theories can be helpful in conceiving of the dialectic between self-regulation and autonomy.

There are interesting analogies in emergence theories in development, and emergence theories in sociology. This chapter has largely focused on emergence during the development of one individual, through the dialectic of autonomy and self-regulation. But much of current theory that goes by the names of distributed cognition, or sociocultural or activity theory can be viewed as an attempt to explore the merits of applying emergentist insights to social groups. By analogy, one might speak of a dialectic tension between group autonomy and group self-regulation. In what sense might groups be said to possess agency? How do groups internalize social structures and norms during development? How does this tension drive group development and group learning?

CONCLUSION

The dialectic between self-regulation and autonomy is central to emergence theories of development. Self-regulation corresponds to an internalized social reality – the social rules and norms for behavior associated with development. Autonomy corresponds to creative, novel action on the part of the individual. Yet autonomy refers to novel action that is *appropriately* novel – that aligns with and remains within the parameters of the external social forces represented by self-regulatory processes. There is no autonomy without self-regulation, and no self-regulation without autonomy.

At the social level of analysis, the relation between individual action and social structures can be considered to be one of emergence: social properties and entities arise from individual action and interaction. At the individual level of analysis, development (of a new schema, a new concept, or whatever) can be understood as an emergence process. Constructivist and transformationist theories of development are fundamentally emergentist, in that they argue that later developmental states emerge through interactive processes at prior moments in time.

I began by summarizing several contemporary social theories that address the dialectic between structure and agency. I conclude by suggesting there is great potential in further dialogue between developmentalists and social theorists: a dialogue that centers on emergence processes, and the mechanisms whereby social phenomena result in self-regulation during development. Many social theorists argue that all social action emerges from a dialectic between structure and agency. And if so, the dialectic between self-regulation and autonomy is the central feature not only of development, but of all human social action.

REFERENCES

Alibali, M. W., & Goldin-Meadow, S. (1993). Gesture-speech mismatch and mechanisms of learning: What the hands reveal about a child's state of mind. *Cognitive Psychology, 25*, 468–523.

Archer, M. S. (1995). *Realist social theory: The morphogenetic approach*. New York, NY: Cambridge University Press.

Archer, M. S. (2000). *Being human: The problem of agency*. Cambridge, UK: Cambridge University Press.

Azmitia, M. (1998). Dissolving boundaries between collective and individual representations: A welcome contribution to developmental psychology. *Human Development, 41*, 239–244.

Bhaskar, R. (1982). Emergence, explanation, and emancipation. In P. F. Secord (Ed.), *Explaining human behavior: Consciousness, human action and social structure* (pp. 275–310). Beverly Hills, CA: Sage.

Brent, S. B. (1978). Individual specialization, collective adaptation and rate of environmental change. *Human Development, 21*, 21–33.

Broad, C. D. (1925). *The mind and its place in nature*. New York: Harcourt, Brace & Company.

Callanan, M. A. (1999). Culture, cognition, and biology: Contexts for the developing mind. *Human Development, 42*, 149–158.

Carlson, S. M. (2005). Developmentally sensitive measures of executive function in preschool children. *Developmental Neuropsychology, 28*, 595–616. doi:10.1207/s15326942dn2802_3

Carson, S. H., Peterson, J. B., & Higgins, D. M. (2005). Reliability, validity, and factor structure of the Creative Achievement Questionnaire. *Creativity Research Journal, 17*, 37–50.

Case, R. (1985). *Intellectual development: Birth to adulthood.* Orlando, FL: Academic Press.

Cole, M. (1996). *Cultural psychology: A once and future discipline*. Cambridge. MA: Harvard University Press.

Collins, A. (2006). Cognitive apprenticeship. In R. K. Sawyer (Ed.), *Cambridge handbook of the learning sciences* (pp. 47–60). New York, NY: Cambridge University Press.

Corsaro, W. A. (1997). *The sociology of childhood.* Thousand Oaks, CA: Pine Forge Press.

Csikszentmihalyi, M. (1988). Society, culture, and person: A systems view of creativity. In R. J. Sternberg (Ed.), *The nature of creativity* (pp. 325–339). New York. NY: Cambridge University Press.

Csikszentmihalyi, M. (1996). *Creativity: Flow and the psychology of discovery and invention*. New York, NY: HarperCollins.

Dunbar, K. (1995). How scientists really reason: Scientific reasoning in real-world laboratories. In R. J. Sternberg & J. E. Davidson (Eds.), *The nature of insight* (pp. 365–395). Cambridge, MA: MIT Press.

Elder-Vass, D. (2010). *The causal power of social structures: Emergence, structure and agency*. Cambridge, UK: Cambridge University Press.

Gardner, H. (1983). *Frames of mind: The theory of multiple intelligences*. New York, NY: Basic Books.

Gardner, H. (1988). Creative lives and creative works: A synthetic scientific approach. In R. J. Sternberg (Ed.), *The nature of creativity* (pp. 298–321). New York, NY: Cambridge University Press.

Gardner, H. (1993). *Creating minds*. New York, NY: Basic Books.

Gardner, H. (1999). *Intelligence reframed. Multiple intelligences for the 21st century*. New York, NY: Basic Books.

Garfinkel, H. (1967). *Studies in ethnomethodology*. Englewood Cliffs, NJ: Prentice-Hall.

Gelman, R., & Brenneman, K. (1994). First principles can support both universal and culture-specific learning about number and music. In L. A. Hirschfeld & S. A. Gelman (Eds.), *Mapping the mind: Domain specificity in cognition and culture* (pp. 369–390). New York, NY: Cambridge University Press.

Giddens, A. (1984). *The constitution of society: Outline of the theory of structuration*. Berkeley: University of California Press.

Gruber, H. E., & Vonèche, J. J. (1977). Introduction. In H. E. Gruber & J. J. Vonèche (Eds.), *The essential Piaget* (pp. xvii–xl). New York, NY: Basic Books.

Hall, R., & Stevens, R. (1996). Teaching/learning events in the workplace: A comparative analysis of their organizational and interactional structure. In G. W.

Cottrell (Ed.), *Proceedings of the Eighteenth Annual Conference of the Cognitive Science Society* (pp. 160–165). Hillsdale, NJ: Erlbaum.

Hirschfeld, L. A., & Gelman, S. A. (Eds.). (1994). *Mapping the mind: Domain specificity in cognition and culture.* New York, NY: Cambridge University Press.

Holland, J. L. (1997). *Making vocational choices: A theory of vocational personalities and work environments* (3rd ed.). Odessa, FL: Psychological Assessment Resources.

Hutchins, E. (1995). *Cognition in the wild.* Cambridge, MA: MIT Press.

John-Steiner, V. (1993). Creative lives, creative tensions. *Creativity Research Journal,* 5, 99–108.

Karmiloff-Smith, A. (1992). *Beyond modularity: A developmental perspective on cognitive science.* Cambridge, MA: MIT Press.

Kaufman, J. C., & Baer, J. (2004). Sure, I'm creative – but not in math! Self-reported creativity in diverse domains. *Empirical Studies of the Arts, 22,* 143–155.

Kitchener, R. F. (1985). Holistic structuralism, elementarism and Piaget's theory of "relationism." *Human Development, 28,* 281–294.

Kitcher, P. (1992). *Freud's dream: A complete interdisciplinary science of mind.* Cambridge, MA: MIT Press.

Klahr, D. (1982). Nonmonotone assessment of monotone development: An information processing analysis. In S. Strauss (Ed.), *U-shaped behavioral growth* (pp. 63–86). New York, NY: Academic Press.

Kuhn, D. (1995). Microgenetic study of change: What has it told us? *Psychological Science, 6,* 133–139.

Lawrence, J. A., & Valsiner, J. (1993). Conceptual roots of internalization: From transmission to transformation. *Human Development, 36,* 150–167.

McLaughlin, B. P. (1992). The rise and fall of British emergentism. In A. Beckermann, H. Flohr, & J. Kim (Eds.), *Emergence or reduction? Essays on the prospects of nonreductive physicalism* (pp. 49–93). Berlin: Walter de Gruyter.

Morgan, C. L. (1923). *Emergent evolution.* London: Williams and Norgate. (Originally presented as the 1922 Gifford lectures at the University of St. Andrews.)

Morgan, C. L. (1933). *The emergence of novelty.* London: Williams & Norgate.

Morss, J. R. (1990). *The biologising of childhood: Developmental psychology and the Darwinian myth.* Hillsdale, NJ: Erlbaum.

Müller, U., Carpendale, J. I. M., and Smith, L. (Eds.). (2009). *The Cambridge Companion to Piaget.* New York, NY: Cambridge University Press.

Parsons, T. (1937/1949). *The structure of social action.* New York, NY: Free Press.

Parsons, T. (1951). *The social system.* Glencoe, IL: Free Press.

Piaget, J. (1936/1952). *The origins of intelligence in children.* New York: International Universities Press. (Originally published as *La naissance d'intelligence chez l'enfant,* Neuchatel: Delachaux & Niestlé, 1936).

Piaget, J. (1945/1962). *Play, dreams, and imitation in childhood* (C. G. F. M. Hodgson, Trans.). New York: Norton. (Originally published as *La formation du symbole chez l'enfant: imitation, jeu et rêve, image et représentation,* Neuchâtel: Delachaux & Niestlé, 1945).

Piaget, J. (1968/1970). *Structuralism.* New York: Basic Books. (Originally published as *Le Structuralisme,* Paris: Presses Universitaires de France, 1968.)

Piaget, J. (1971). Comment on Beilin's paper. In D. R. Green, M. P. Ford, & G. B. Flamer (Eds.), *Measurement and Piaget* (pp. 192–194). New York, NY: McGraw-Hill.

Rogoff, B. (1982). Integrating context and cognitive development. In M. E. Lamb & A. L. Brown (Eds.), *Advances in developmental psychology* (Vol. 2, pp. 125–170). Hillsdale, NJ: Erlbaum.

Rogoff, B. (1990). *Apprenticeship in thinking: Cognitive development in social context.* New York, NY: Oxford University Press.

Rogoff, B. (1997). Evaluating development in the process of participation: Theory, methods, and practice building on each other. In E. Amsel & A. Renninger (Eds.), *Change and development* (pp. 265–285). Hillsdale, NJ: Erlbaum.

Sawyer, R. K. (2002a). Nonreductive individualism, Part I: Supervenience and wild disjunction. *Philosophy of the Social Sciences, 32*, 537–559.

Sawyer, R. K. (2002b). Unresolved tensions in sociocultural theory: Analogies with contemporary sociological debates. *Culture & Psychology, 8*, 283–305.

Sawyer, R. K. (2003). Emergence in creativity and development. In R. K. Sawyer, V. John-Steiner, S. Moran, R. Sternberg, D. H. Feldman, M. Csikszentmihalyi, & J. Nakamura (Eds.), *Creativity and development* (pp. 12–60). New York, NY: Oxford University Press.

Sawyer, R. K. (2005). *Social emergence: Societies as complex systems.* New York, NY: Cambridge University Press.

Sawyer, R. K. (2012). *Explaining creativity: The science of human innovation* (2nd ed.). New York, NY: Oxford University Press.

Sawyer, R. K., & DeZutter, S. (2009). Distributed creativity: How collective creations emerge from collaboration. *Psychology of Aesthetics, Creativity, and the Arts, 3*, 81–92.

Schegloff, E. A. (1968). Sequencing in conversational openings. *American Anthropologist, 70*, 1075–1095.

Schegloff, E. A. (1986). The routine as achievement. *Human Studies, 9*, 111–151.

Schegloff, E. A. (1991). Reflections on talk and social structure. In D. Boden & D. H. Zimmerman (Eds.), *Talk and social structure: Studies in ethnomethodology and conversation analysis* (pp. 44–70). Berkeley: University of California Press.

Schegloff, E. A. (1992). In another context. In A. Duranti & C. Goodwin (Eds.), *Rethinking context: Language as an interactive phenomenon* (pp. 191–227). New York, NY: Cambridge University Press.

Siegler, R. S. (1996). *Emerging minds: The process of change in children's thinking.* New York, NY: Oxford University Press.

Siegler, R. S. (1998). *Children's thinking* (3rd ed.). Upper Saddle River, NJ: Prentice-Hall.

Simon, T. J., & Halford, G. S. (Eds.). (1995). *Developing cognitive competence: New approaches to process modeling.* Hillsdale, NJ: Erlbaum.

Taylor, C. (1985). What is involved in a genetic psychology? In C. Taylor (Ed.), *Human agency and language* (pp. 139–163). New York, NY: Cambridge University Press.

van der Veer, R. (1996). Structure and development: Reflections by Vygotsky. In A. Tryphon & J. Vonèche (Eds.), *Piaget-Vygotsky: The social genesis of thought* (pp. 45–56). Hove, UK: Psychology Press.

Valsiner, J. (1989). *Human development and culture: The social nature of personality and its study*. Lexington, MA: Lexington Books.

Vygotsky, L. S. (1978). *Mind in society* (A. Kozulin, Trans.). Cambridge: Harvard University Press.

Wertsch, J. V. (1993). Commentary. *Human Development*, *36*, 168–171.

Whitehead, A. N. (1926). *Science and the modern world.* New York, NY: Macmillan.

Wimsatt, W. C. (1997). Aggregativity: Reductive heuristics for finding emergence. *Philosophy of Science, 64*, S372–S384.

PART II

SOCIAL DEVELOPMENT

Chapter 5

Constructing the Agent: Developing Conceptions of Autonomy and Selfhood

BRYAN W. SOKOL
Saint Louis University
ULRICH MÜLLER
University of Victoria
MICHAEL J. CHANDLER
University of British Columbia

Developmental scientists tend to see psychological growth as stretched out over time or spread along continua, and so, as never being quite complete. That is, very few psychological phenomena appear de novo, or like Athena, emerging from Zeus' forehead, fully formed and battle ready. Rather, psycho-social competencies of various kinds, ranging from children's self-regulation (Zelazo & Müller, 2002) to changing theories of mind (Chandler & Sokol, 1999) to conceptions of selfhood (Chandler, Lalonde, & Sokol, 2000), tend to emerge gradually, sometimes fitfully, and are consolidated, if ever, only slowly over time. In this chapter, we argue that human agency is also like that. Agency, and especially that part of human experience that eventually forms the hub of individuals' self-constituting sense of personal agency, is not some salutary, all-or-nothing, miracle that suddenly erupts fully formed. Nor, despite popular conceptions of individual "willpower" or views of "the will" as a distinct psychological faculty, is it necessarily a phenomenon that is entirely consolidated in a singular person. Instead, human agency is a distributed kind of thing, and truth be told, it is not even a *thing* at all. That is, as Frie (2008) has suggested: "agency is not a fixed entity that conforms to traditional definitions of free will. It is an active process … [which] can never be divorced from the contexts in which it exists, yet neither can it be wholly reduced to these contexts" (p. vii). As a multi-layered, psycho-social *process*, then, agency is never entirely here nor there, all because it is distributed, not only across ontogenetic time, but also across people and their relationships to each other – or what some (Mackenzie & Stoljar, 2000; Sugarman, 2008) have called "relational agency." What ultimately becomes a sense of personal agency in individuals' lives – the part of their psychological experience that gets targeted when they attempt to understand their own conduct – weaves together these various distributed strands of agentive potential from their personal, developmental histories and sociorelational contexts.

To warrant these claims about human agency, our plan for this chapter involves three steps. First, we review Piaget's (1954/1981) classical conception of the "will." Notwithstanding what now is seen as arcane terminology, Piaget describes human agency in ways that are otherwise remarkably modern. Accordingly, with the second step in this chapter, we show how Piaget's (1954/1981) account has affinities with more contemporary renderings of human agency, particularly with the process of perspective-taking (e.g., Martin, Sokol, & Elfers, 2008). Third, and finally, we argue for a view of agency that is wrapped up in individuals' identity development, or conceptions of selfhood. By elaborating on the meaning of "taking" in the perspective-taking process, we construct an account of human agency that is defined by *taking ownership* of particular perspectives that constitute one's self. We borrow from the work of Augusto Blasi (2004a), in particular, and argue that "in agency, the subjective self feels the owner" (p. 12).

MODERNIZING THE WILL

Whether human agency is a "real thing" or more a matter of "what one believes" (i.e., an ontological reality or a hypothetical construct) is perhaps not a question we can answer definitively, at least not without betraying our own ideological commitments. In our case, the title of our chapter, "Constructing the Agent," is not coincidental, and, if not otherwise evident, should reveal the constructivist underpinnings of our account. Accordingly, the first strand in our argument rehearses what Piaget (1954/1981) had to say about human agency in his writings on "the will."

Piaget makes a case for the emergence of human agency that is remarkably contemporary – a case that dispels some of the classic confusions surrounding notions about the will. One of these concerns involves whether the will is a distinct psychological faculty housed away mysteriously in our heads. Piaget rejects this view and, as a modern alternative, posits the notion that agency is a psychological process that closely resembles, and even draws on, the process of perspective-taking. Specifically, Piaget (1954/1981) maintained that the will is a shorthand term for the process of coordinating and integrating one's desires and personal values, just as perspective-taking involves coordinating and integrating multiple points of view. If there is anything mysterious or perhaps miraculous in this account, it's that the agentive potential in human actions can become the source of thoughts about an individual's own agentive abilities, and, in turn, fuel what subsequently becomes a richer sense of agency and autonomy.

Agency a la Piaget

Not surprisingly, Piaget's (1954/1981) account of agency, or "the will," has affinities with the views held by many other scholars of his own and earlier generation. William James, James Mark Baldwin, and George Herbert Mead are just some of these classic figures. A common thread that runs through these touchstone views is the role that conflict between competing desires and impulses plays in making an individual's will manifest. William James (1899/1962), for instance, characterized willful action, at least on the narrower, reflective definition that he developed, as "tak[ing] place only when there are a number of conflicting systems of ideas, and depends on having a complex field of consciousness" (pp. 85–86). In an often repeated (although fairly bloodless) example meant to illustrate such a conflict and eventual act of willful resolve, he described a university teacher preparing a lecture and combating the impulse to leave his desk to enjoy a walk outdoors (James, 1890). The "higher value" of completing his lecture wins out over the "lower impulse" to walk outside. Piaget also offers a similar description. For Piaget (1954/1981), agency or the will is structured as a "veritable logic of feelings" (p. 13) that comes to share the same "conservations and invariants" (p. 60) that arise in related areas of children's cognitive growth. That is, just as children come to appreciate the rational necessities involved in the conservation of matter, number, and volume, so too do they develop a "conservation of values" (Piaget, 1954/1981, p. 60).

The concept of value plays a central role in Piaget's theory and introduces a distinction that is frequently not appreciated in contemporary theories of self-regulation. Self-regulation, which in many respects has replaced the notion of the will in contemporary developmental theories (see Baumeister & Exline, 1999), is variously defined as "effortful control" (Blair & Ursache, 2011) or the "deliberate attempt to modulate, modify, or inhibit actions and reactions toward a more adaptive end" (McClelland, Ponitz, Messersmith,

& Tominey, 2010, p. 510). Self-regulation, for the most part, has the function of regulating the expenditure of energy. Historically speaking, this conceptualization is similar to the way that Pierre Janet (1926–1928), a contemporary of Piaget, conceived of secondary actions. For Janet, secondary actions were affective reactions that regulated primary actions. Primary actions were understood as goal-directed actions determined by cognition and characterized by successive phases such as latency, triggering, activation, and termination. Affect thus served the function to reinforce or terminate primary actions. In his critique of Janet's theory, Piaget (1954/1981) suggested that in addition to secondary actions, a second regulatory system had to be introduced: "This second system would have to do with interest and the evaluation of action" (pp. 30–31). This notion of value, Piaget argued, helped explain why persons engage in behavior that, from a mere energetics perspective, makes little sense because of the costs of depleting a person's limited energy resources. Piaget illustrated this point using the example of an infant who, after succeeding at pulling a toy through the bars of his playpen repeated the action several times until understanding how to rotate the toy to pull it through the bars. For Piaget (1954/1981), "what is important to the baby and the reason that he starts all over is that he is interested in expanding his activity and his sense of self through the conquest of the universe. This expansion involves assimilation, understanding, etc. From this point of view, value is an affective exchange with the exterior, i.e., with objects and people. It comes into play even in primary actions, and the system of values goes beyond the simply energetic regulatory system of secondary actions described by Janet" (p. 31).

Values, then, cut through the distinction between affect and cognition (Kesselring, 2010a, b, c; Turiel, 2010; Turiel & Killen, 2010; for neurophysiological evidence see Moll, de Oliveira-Souza, & Zahn, 2009). Values explain why humans engage in actions that, from an economics or energetics perspective, are too costly to be carried out (e.g., altruistic behavior; Mays, 1997). For Piaget, a human is more than a *homo economicus* – a creature that simply optimizes utilities. Values set the direction, or "finality" (Piaget, 1954/1981, p. 33) of action and are open to reflection and critical evaluation (see also Carver & Scheier, 2011).

As a developmental scientist, Piaget argued that children do not come into the world with some fully formed "scale of values" (Piaget, 1954/1981, p. 9). Rather, initially values and energetic regulations are fused, and they become differentiated over time. One indicator of the differentiation between energetic regulations and values is the emergence of a nascent hierarchy of values (Piaget, 1954/1981, p. 36) through means-ends behavior that typically enters infants' repertoire of action at the end of the first year of life. Means-ends behavior involves the coordination of two independent action schemes, with one scheme assigning an end (finality) to the action (e.g., grasping the matchbox) and the other scheme subordinated to the goal as a means (e.g., hitting the hand to lower it; see Kesselring & Müller, 2011). Means-ends behavior reflects both a cognitive and an affective decentration. It reflects *cognitive* decentration because it involves the differentiation between means and goal, and the flexible coordination of means and goal to achieve a goal determined beforehand (Piaget, 1954/1981, p. 26). It reflects *affective* decentration (i.e., the differentiation of different values and the coordination between them) because certain objects without interest in themselves take on an interest in relation to other objects that are valued: "[T]he value of the means is determined in relation to the value of a particular goal, and labile hierarchies of values arise from activity of this sort" (Piaget, 1954/1981, p. 26).

The values that infants and young children develop, however, are very fluid and often dictated by the immediate situation. Initially, then, a child's will easily wavers according to external forces, or what could be called a heteronomous configuration of the will or agency. Children's growing awareness of their own desires and preferences is, according to Piaget, what allows them to move away from this situation-bound form of agency and to conduct themselves in more autonomous ways. Like William James, Piaget (1954/1981) argued that an autonomous configuration of the will arises when "a conflict between two impulses or tendencies [is] present … [and] the impulse that is initially weaker … become[s] the stronger of the two" (p. 61). An autonomous act of agency, then, requires that an individual resist the initially dominant impulse, as Piaget (1954/1981) says, by "subordinating [it] to a permanent scale of values" (p. 65). This is where perspective-taking abilities become especially important in Piaget's (1954/1981) account. Similar to the subordination of means to ends, he explained the subordination of impulses by drawing on the notion of decentration, suggesting that autonomous agency is the intellectual equivalent to a "change of perspective" (p. 64). Similar to the perceptual manipulations occurring in Piaget's classic conservation problems, an individual masters, in the case of the will, the immediate affective configuration of a situation by "connecting it with former situations and, if need be, by anticipating future ones" (Piaget, 1954/1981, p. 63). That, according to Piaget, is how decentration within the perspective-taking process essentially operates, and, more important, how autonomous agency in the child is said to be first manifest.

Piaget does not explicitly elaborate from where the child's "permanent scale of values" might originate, although the heavy emphasis that he places on social relationships and emerging moral normativity – all in his early efforts to describe children's sociomoral growth (e.g., Piaget, 1932/1965) – provides important clues (see also Grouzet, this volume, for an extended discussion of value systems). This oft-forgotten "social Piaget" (Sokol & Hammond, 2009) offers an account that closely resembles the notions of interpersonal or relational agency represented in the work of other contemporary contributors to the agency literature (e.g., Sugarman & Sokol, 2012). Despite the cognitivist assumptions that typically attend Piagetian theory, Piaget himself would have agreed with the view, expressed by Roger Frie (2008), that "Agency is never simply the work of the intellect, nor is it strictly a solitary, private affair" (pp. 12–13). In this regard, Piaget should be seen as resisting individualistic conceptions of agency and personhood, and arguing instead for the constitutive role that interpersonal relationships play in this, just as in other, aspects of psychological growth. According to this more relational view, an individual's values, beliefs, and ideals would also be seen as originating in her or his social or communal ties. In fact, Piaget's (1932/1965) characterization of heteronomous and autonomous levels of morality is embedded in his account of the impact that different social relationships have on children's sociocognitive development. Autonomy is said by Piaget (1932/1965) to emerge in the mutual social exchanges of symmetrical peer relations; heteronomy in the unilateral social exchanges that are more typical of asymmetrical parent-child relations. While there are some problems with placing parents and peers at opposite poles of this conceptualization (for criticism, see Helwig, 2008; Wright, 1982), Piaget's insight that relationships may support or constrain autonomy is an enduring feature of his work (for further elaboration of autonomy supporting relationships, particularly between parents and children; see Grolnick & Raftery-Helmer, this volume).

AGENCY THROUGH THICK AND THIN

While Piaget uses different forms of social relationships to distinguish different levels of agency, more contemporary scholars (e.g., Jurist, 2008; Modell, 2008), using language that was popularized by Clifford Geertz (1973), have argued that agency may manifest in thick and thin ways. Specifically, a *thin* sense of agency refers here to an early patch on the developmental continuum that is preoccupied with physical, or overt, forms of goal-directed activity (i.e., those willful actions that bring about some immediate, desired effect). In contrast, a *thick* sense of agency occurs considerably further downstream, and is used here to reference other more inward, reflective actions of self-understanding and meaning-making. This thick and developmentally later-arriving variant of agency, as we mean to show in the next section of this chapter, is where perspective-taking and the processes of identity development become particularly important.

Thick and thin manifestations of agency do not necessarily preclude the social-relational concerns bound together in Piaget's (1932/1965) account, but they do seem to emphasize more person-centered, or individualistic, expressions of agency. For instance, Jurist (2008) introduces thick-and-thin terminology as a heuristic for dividing, on the one hand, minimalist conceptions of agency seen in the work of social scientists who are "inclined to think of agency in terms of the link between beliefs and action" (p. 51), from richer or more robust conceptions, on the other hand, "seeking to capture something further – like self-understanding and self-realization" (p. 51). In this scheme, a thin sense of agency offers a minimalist view of how human conduct may be guided by mental states like belief, desire, and intention – the staple, as it happens, of most theory-of-mind research concerned with young children's early understanding of others' actions (Sokol & Chandler, 2003). By contrast, a thick description of agency implies a more robust view of individuals' reflective powers, particularly as they are directed toward themselves. Martin (2008), for example, argues that such thick understandings of agency are what flourish in adolescence and emerging adulthood as a kind of "reflective, intentional agency … [that] fosters an increasingly conceptual self-understanding and … imbues life with meaning" (p. 104).

Humble Beginnings

For many developmental psychologists the puzzle is how to fit thick and thin together, or how rich and lean variants of agency might come to be situated along a common developmental continuum. One clue to this puzzle can be found again in William James' (1899/1962) remarks about the will. As he claimed: "Our acts of voluntary attention, brief and fitful as they are, are nevertheless momentous and critical, determining us, as they do, to higher or lower destinies" (p. 92). Although this may still sound too cryptic, the seemingly simple notion of being able to direct one's attention, as James suggested, has been argued by other contemporary scholars as similarly momentous in the development of human agency. More specifically, James Russell (1996) claimed that the key to human agency is the degree to which an individual can "alter at will [his or her] perceptual inputs" (1996, p. 64). While this perhaps sounds simple enough, in Russell's (1996) analysis, distinguishing between one's self and what he called the "refractoriness" of the world, allows children, in the early stages of infancy, to discover the boundaries of their agency. The way in which the world resists the child's will, or imposes constraints on his or her agency is, according to Russell (1996), what eventually drives a critical wedge between internal and external experiences of reality. What individuals *perceive as* being "inside" or "outside" of themselves is rooted in their early experience of what they can and cannot control. Coping and adjusting to the constraints and resistances encountered with the external world of other people and things are what ultimately allow for that first phenomenological experience that some actions belong to one's self, whereas others do not (see also Russell, 1999). In short, Russell offers yet another way to frame the emergence of autonomous agency, showing, just as Piaget does, how an individual's initial sense of ownership arises from very basic actions upon, and inter-actions with, the world.

OWNERSHIP AND IDENTITY

For the third, and final thread of our argument, we want to offer a friendly amendment to the more usual definitions of agency – like the one we ascribed to Piaget (1954/1981) – that rely on perspective-taking as the central psychological mechanism by which individuals are imbued with agentive possibilities. Essentially, we argue for a more robust meaning of perspective-taking, with an emphasis on "taking," and especially taking ownership of particular perspectives that define one's self. Here, we capitalize on the work of Augusto Blasi, and claim, much as Blasi (2004a) does, that "in agency, the subjective self feels the owner; the sense of mineness is its central feature" (p. 12). We illustrate some of the ramifications of a sense of ownership, or "mine-ness," for individuals' conceptions of self-unity using data from one of our own research projects (Proulx & Chandler, 2009).

"Mine-ness"

Whereas there are many developmental steps between the nascent sense of ownership that first manifests in the actions of early childhood and what later becomes the richer or thicker sense of ownership associated with closely held values and commitments in adulthood, we propose that this process primarily revolves around a person's claiming possession of his or her thoughts and deeds. Here again we are not alone. In particular, Augusto Blasi's (2004a, 2004b, 2005) work has helped fill in more pieces of our agency puzzle. He has claimed: "In willing, one appropriates certain desires ... and makes them especially one's own, investing oneself in and identifying oneself with them" (Blasi, 2004b, p. 342). Blasi proposes a protracted developmental sequence of self-appropriation (see Blasi, 2005) that begins – much as Piaget or James have suggested – with children's early experiences of desires in immediate conflict with one another, and of their being unable to successfully distance themselves from either in order to make a choice between them. In essence, Blasi has described here a situation of heteronomy, where the most urgent or salient desire stands as the child's "choice" even though none is actually made. From this heteronomous configuration of agency, Blasi (2005) goes on to argue that children accumulate experiences with, and memories of, previous desire satisfactions that gradually give rise to preferences for replicating one course of action over another. These preferences, or "second-order desires" (see also Frankfurt, 1988), are initially fragmented, but nevertheless signal a nascent form of self-appropriation – that is, of wanting some things and taking steps to acquire them, while avoiding others.

The next steps in the development of agency and self-appropriation, according to Blasi, draw heavily on advances in other areas of children's sociocognitive growth, particularly their construction of value categories that define "good" and "bad" both for themselves and others. Much like the "social Piaget" we have described, Blasi (2005) argued that such value groupings are "no doubt socially and culturally mediated," and moreover, form "the foundation for the understanding of objective values and their normativity: there are objects that one desires and wants, but there are also objects that are desirable and valuable, and should be desired and wanted also by other people" (p. 81). Normative values, however, are not all-of-one piece, nor, for that matter, are individuals' self-concepts. Accordingly, Blasi (2005) has qualified the end point of agentive development by suggesting there are many different values from which "people can choose to structure their will and center their sense of self" (p. 81). Although some of these values will become stable enough to regulate broad areas of individuals' lives, "wholehearted commitment" (Blasi, 2005, p. 82) or unwavering reference to any unified set of values or core principles continues to be rare. As a result, most people will attain self-concepts that are "defined by a variety of desires and values," devoid of wholeheartedness. Although the typical adolescent or young adult will still work to actively avoid "rejected desires" (Blasi, 2005, p. 82), when pressed about their self-concept we find, more often than not, that it is riddled with inconsistency. To illustrate how these processes of identity development might look in the lives of adolescents, consider a recent study by Proulx and Chandler (2009) that describes some of these inconsistencies.

Doing It "My Way"

Earlier we alluded to a distinction that characterized agency, on the one hand, as a real, active force in individuals' lives, and, on the other, as individuals' perceptions or beliefs *about* their agency. The study by Proulx and Chandler (2009) is distinctly about the latter, or people's beliefs about agency, and particularly how these beliefs bear on their own moral conduct.

The study (Proulx & Chandler, 2009) involved interviewing forty-five 13- to 17-year-old high school adolescents about behaviors of which they either were or were not proud. For each proud or shameful act the high schoolers offered up, they were asked to explain the forces that they perceived as causing their conduct. Their causal explanations were subsequently coded as attributing either internal or external determinants to their actions. Internal attributions put the weight of responsibility on their own desires, beliefs, and choices, whereas external attributions turned to situational forces and made no explicit reference to personally held desires or commitments.

Before describing the results, it is important to briefly highlight two issues in the study: one having to do with pride and the other with unified self-concepts, or again, what Blasi would call, wholeheartedness. Regarding pride, it seems fair to say that inquiries concerning individuals' conduct of which they either are or are not proud is already like asking them to comment on aspects of themselves they see as "theirs" or "not theirs" – actions for which they do or do not feel ownership. Pride is generally the emotion we associate, to paraphrase the famous singer Frank Sinatra, with having "done it my way." So, to find, as this study did, that the majority of adolescents imagine that the actions they are proud of were internally motivated is not particularly surprising (Proud Conduct: 40 internal attributions vs. 5 external attributions). What is surprising, or at least more of a puzzle, is how these same adolescents explained their bad, or shameful, conduct. Here their causal attributions were split almost evenly between internal and external explanations (Shameful Conduct: 23 internal attributions vs. 22 external attributions). That is, approximately half of the high schoolers "owned up" to deeds they would otherwise prefer to hide by acknowledging that they, themselves, were the root cause of their conduct. The other half tried to actively avoid responsibility for their shameful conduct by attributing it to situational factors beyond their own control (or what social psychologists understand as a "self-serving" bias).

To make better sense of this split, Proulx and Chandler went on to inquire about these adolescents' views of their own self-concepts. This is where the second issue of self-unity or wholeheartedness enters the picture. The adolescents were asked to respond to interview materials that asked them to compare the classic split personality of Jekyll and Hyde with their own sometimes disjointed or fragmented conduct; the data showed that many young people frequently develop a "multiplicitous" conception of self that allows individuals to pull together a wide range of opposing attributes into their self structures. Like Blasi's (2005) more speculative claims regarding the rarity of wholeheartedness, then, Proulx and Chandler provide empirical evidence that multiple values are often seen to structure individuals' wills. Even though a number of the adolescents attempted to avoid blame, at least some of the sample could be seen as holding a more wholehearted, or, as they say, "singular" conception of self. Such a singular self-concept imposes order among competing self-attributes by unifying them within one "singular volition that underpins all of their seemingly diverse actions" (Proulx & Chandler, 2009, p. 270). As they describe, holders of singular self-concepts "abandon all passive or reactive conceptions of mental life, and count themselves instead as authors who plan and deliberate and are the owners of, and responsible for, all of their actions" (p. 270).

Returning now to the split in causal attributions for shameful conduct, Proulx and Chandler found that the majority of adolescents (14 of 20, or 70%) who regarded themselves as multiplicitous also understood their bad behavior as stemming from external causal factors. By contrast, the majority of adolescents holding singular conceptions of self (8 of 10, or 80%) ascribed internal causal attributes for their behavior. In short, the high schoolers who exhibited a singular or unified self-concept, while perhaps rare (just 10 of the 45 participants), nevertheless possessed the kind of wholehearted commitment suggested by Blasi (2005) that would lead them to claim ownership over even their own shameful acts.

CONCLUDING REMARKS

These findings not only speak to Blasi's contention about the rarity of wholehearted commitment in young people but also show how acts of self-appropriation in the formation of the will intersect with adolescents' developing conceptions of selfhood. The forms of agency found at later points along the developmental continuum draw heavily on processes of identity development. What, then, are we to take away from all our earlier talk about the front end of the agentive continuum involving the processes of perspective-taking? The trick here, as we see it, is to recognize, as many developmental psychologists already have, that the gap between perspective-taking and identity development is very narrow. Developmental models of perspective-taking, for good reason, commonly run these two processes together (e.g., Selman, 1980; see also Martin, Sokol, & Elfers, 2008).

In another paper, Sokol and Huerta (2010) have argued that we may preserve Piagetian and other similar conceptions of agency that emphasize perspective-taking only if we adopt a more nuanced view of what perspective-taking means. That is, not only does perspective-taking involve the ability to recognize and coordinate other points of view but it also means taking possession or ownership of some of these viewpoints, and not others. By emphasizing, in other words, the "taking" in perspective-taking, we see clearly how self-appropriation is part and parcel of the whole process. We hope that we have also made clear that the development of human agency, in the end, is similarly nuanced and complicated. We recognize that our views about agency are far from the definitive word. Still, as more and more social scientists (see, for example, Sugarman & Sokol, 2012) turn their own attention to this topic, or as James Russell might say, "alter [their] perceptual inputs," we are confident that the puzzle of "Constructing the Agent" will eventually come together.

REFERENCES

Baumeister, R. F., & Exline, J. J. (1999). Virtue, personality, and social relations: Self-control as the moral muscle. *Journal of Personality, 67*, 1165–1194.

Blair, C., & Ursache, A. (2011). A bidirectional model of executive functions and self-regulation. In K. D. Vohs & R. F. Baumeister (Eds.), *Handbook of self-regulation: Research, theory, and applications* (2nd ed., pp. 300–320). New York, NY: Guilford Press.

Blasi, A. (2004a). Neither personality nor cognition: An alternative approach to the nature of the self. In C. Lightfoot, C. Lalonde, & M. Chandler (Eds.), *Changing conceptions of psychological life* (pp. 3–25). Mahwah, NJ: Erlbaum.

Blasi, A. (2004b). Moral functioning: Moral understanding and personality. In D. K. Lapsley & D. Narvaez (Eds.), *Moral development, self, and identity* (pp. 335–347). Mahwah, NJ: Erlbaum.

Blasi, A. (2005). Moral character: A psychological approach. In D. K. Lapsley & F. Clark Power (Eds.), *Character psychology and character education* (pp. 67–100). Notre Dame, IN: University of Notre Dame Press.

Carver, C. C., & Scheier, M. F. (2011). Self-regulation of action and affect. In K. D. Vohs & R. F. Baumeister (Eds.), *Handbook of self-regulation: Research, theory, and applications* (2nd ed., pp. 3–21). New York, NY: Guilford Press.

Chandler, M. J., Lalonde, C. E., & Sokol, B. W. (2000). Continuities of selfhood in the face of radical developmental and cultural change. In L. P. Nucci, G. B. Saxe, & E. Turiel (Eds.), *Culture, thought, and development* (pp. 65–84). Mahwah, NJ: Erlbaum.

Chandler, M. J., & Sokol, B. W. (1999). Representation once removed: Children's developing conceptions of representational life. In I. Sigel (Ed.), *Development of mental representation: Theories and applications* (pp. 201–230). Mahwah, NJ: Erlbaum.

Frankfurt, H. (1988). *The importance of what we care about: Philosophical essays.* Cambridge. UK: Cambridge University Press.

Frie, R. (Ed.). (2008). *Psychological agency: Theory, practice, and culture.* Cambridge, MA: MIT Press.

Geertz, C. (1973). *The interpretation of cultures: Selected essays.* New York, NY: Basic Books.

Helwig, C. C. (2008). The moral judgment of the child reevaluated: Heteronomy, early morality, and reasoning about justice and inequalities. In C. Wainryb, J. G. Smetana, & E. Turiel (Eds.), *Social development, social inequalities, and social justice* (pp. 27–51). Mahwah, NJ: Erlbaum.

James, W. T. (1890). *The principles of psychology.* New York, NY: Holt, Rinehart, and Winston.

James, W. (1962). *Talks to teachers on psychology and to students on some of life's ideals.* New York, NY: Dover. (Original work published 1899.)

Janet, P. (1926–28). *De l'angoisse à l'extase. Études sur les croyances et les sentiments.* Paris: Felix Alcan.

Jurist, E. L. (2008). Becoming agents: Hegel, Nietzsche and psychoanalysis. In R. Frie (Ed.), *Psychological agency: Theory, practice, and culture.* (pp. 51–71) Cambridge, MA: MIT Press,

Kesselring, T. (2010). Die Rationalität der Emotionen. Eine Ergänzung zu Piagets Theorie. In R. L. Fetz, B. Seidenfuβ & S. Ullrich (Eds.), *Whitehead – Cassirer – Piaget. Unterwegs zu einem neuen Denken* (pp. 221–248). Freiburg: Alber.

Kesselring, T. (2010). Emotionale Entwicklung. Eine Erweiterung der Piagetschen Theorie (Teil 1). *Zeitschrift für Psychotraumatologie und Psychologische Medizin, 2.*

Kesselring, T. (2010). Emotionale Entwicklung. Eine Erweiterung der Piagetschen Theorie (Teil 2). *Zeitschrift für Psychotraumatologie und Psychologische Medizin, 4.*

Kesselring, T., & Müller, U. (2011). The concept of egocentrism in the context of Piaget's theory. *New Ideas in Psychology, 29*, 327–345.

Mackenzie, C., & Stoljar, N. (Eds.). (2000). *Relational autonomy: Feminist perspectives on autonomy, agency, and the social self.* Oxford, UK: Oxford University Press.

Martin, J., Sokol, B. W., & Elfers, T. (2008). Taking and coordinating perspectives: From pre-reflective interactivity, through reflective intersubjectivity, to metareflective sociality. *Human Development, 51*, 294–317.

Mays, W. (1997). *Piaget on social values.* Paper presented at the 27th Annual Symposium of the Jean Piaget Society, Santa Monica, CA.

McClelland, M., Ponitz, C. C., Messersmith, E. E., & Tominey, C. (2010). Self-regulation: Integration of cognition and emotion. In W. F. Overton (Vol. Ed.), R. M. Lerner (Editor-in-chief), *The handbook of life-span development: Vol. 1. Cognition, biology, and methods* (pp. 510–553). New York, NY: Wiley.

Modell, A. (1996). *The private self.* Cambridge, MA: Harvard University Press.

Moll, J., de Oliveira-Souza, R., & Zahn, R. (2009). Neuroscience and morality: Moral judgments, moral sentiments, and values. In D. Narvaez & D. K. Lapsley

(Eds.), *Personality, identity, and character: Explorations in moral psychology* (pp. 106–135). Cambridge, UK: Cambridge University Press.

Piaget, J. (1932/1965). *The moral judgment of the child.* London: Free Press.

Piaget, J. (1981). *Intelligence and affectivity.* (T. A. Brown & C. E. Kaegi, Trans.). Palo Alto, CA: Annual Reviews, Inc. (Original work published 1954.)

Proulx, T., & Chandler, M. J. (2009). Jekyll and Hyde and me: Age-graded differences in conceptions of self-unity. *Human Development, 52*, 261–286.

Russell, J. (1996). *Agency: Its role in mental development.* Oxford, UK: Taylor & Francis.

Russell, J. (1999). Cognitive development as an executive process – in part: A homeopathic dose of Piaget. *Developmental Science*, 2, 247–295.

Selman, R. L. (1980). *The growth of interpersonal understanding.* New York, NY: Academic Press.

Sokol, B. W. & Chandler, M. J. (2003). Taking agency seriously in the theories-of-mind enterprise: Exploring children's understanding of interpretation and intention. *British Journal of Educational Psychology Monograph Series II* (Number 2 – Development and Motivation), 125–136.

Sokol, B. W., & Hammond, S. I. (2009). Piaget and affectivity. In U. Müller, J. I. M. Carpendale, & L. Smith (Eds.), *The Cambridge companion to Piaget* (pp. 309–323). New York, NY: Cambridge University Press.

Sokol, B. W., & Huerta, S. (2010). Through thick and thin: Agency as "taking" perspectives. *Human Development*, 53, 46–52.

Sugarman, J. (2008). Understanding persons as relational agents: The philosophy of John Macmurray and its implications for psychology. In R. Frie (Ed.), *Psychological agency: Theory, practice, and culture* (pp. 73–93). Cambridge, MA: MIT Press.

Sugarman, J., & Sokol, B. (2012). Human agency and development: An introduction and theoretical sketch. *New Ideas in Psychology*, 30, 1–14.

Turiel, E. (2010). The development of morality: Reasoning, emotions, and resistance. In W. F. Overton (Vol. Ed.), R. M. Lerner (Editor-in-chief), *The handbook of life-span development: Vol. 1. Cognition, biology, and methods* (pp. 554–574). New York, NY: Wiley.

Turiel, E., & Killen, M. (2010). Taking emotions seriously: The role of emotions in moral development. In W. F. Arsenio & E. A. Lemerise (Eds.), *Emotions, aggression, and morality in children: Bridging development and psychopathology* (pp. 33–52). Washington, DC: American Psychological Association

Wright, D. (1982). Piaget's theory of moral development. In S. Modgil & C. Modgil (Eds.), *Jean Piaget: Consensus and controversy* (pp. 207–217). London: Holt, Rinehart & Winston.

Zelazo, P. D., & Müller, U. (2002). Executive function in typical and atypical development. In U. Goswami (Ed.), *Handbook of childhood cognitive development* (pp. 445–469). Oxford, UK: Blackwell.

Chapter 6

Revisiting the Moral Self-Construct: Developmental Perspectives on Moral Selfhood

TOBIAS KRETTENAUER
Wilfrid Laurier University

The year 2008 marked the 50th anniversary of Kohlberg's stage model. When celebrating this event, many scholars in the field of moral development and education stressed how much they owe to this theory. Inspired by Piaget's writings, Kohlberg was critical in establishing research on moral development as a self-reliant field in developmental psychology. In the 1970s and 1980s, his theory provided the most influential forum for lively and engaging debates around issues of moral and civic education. However, things have changed since then. In 1996, Lapsley proclaimed the "Post-Kohlbergian Era" in Moral Psychology (Lapsley, 1996). Lapsley did not define the term "Post-Kohlbergian" in its own right, but largely demarcated the new era negatively as not being Kohlbergian any more (as is the case with most "postisms"). At least part of this vagueness was finally lifted in 2008, when the MIT Press published a three-volume set entitled *Moral Psychology* (Sinnott-Amstrong, 2008). The titles for these three volumes specify the directions that "moral psychology" in the 21st century is assumed to take: Volume 1 – *Cognitive Science of Morality*; Volume 2 – *The Evolution of Morality*; Volume 3 – *The Neuroscience of Morality*. The Post-Kohlbergian Era in moral psychology turns out to be the era of a new synthesis of cognitive science, evolutionary theory, and neuroscience. It is commonly understood that Kohlberg's theory has little to offer to this enterprise as his theory focused on "conscious verbal reasoning" (Haidt, 2007, p. 998). Moreover, it is evident that a core concept of Kohlberg's theory, the idea of development as transformative change, plays at best a peripheral role in this theoretical context. Whereas in the 1970s and 1980s, developmental psychology was leading research on moral reasoning and action, this leadership status has been transferred to biology, neuroscience, and related disciplines.

The new synthesis of moral psychology (Haidt, 2007) is not without dissenters. Strong and thought-provoking arguments have been raised against a reductionistist understanding of morality (cf. Carpendale, Sokol, & Müller, 2010; Smetana & Killen, 2008). This chapter is not meant to repeat these arguments nor does it intend to discuss the three volumes that represent the new synthesis of moral psychology (for reviews, see Buchanan, 2008; Hammond, 2008; Wereha & Racine, 2008). Rather, it aims at highlighting one particular aspect of individual moral development that easily falls through the grid of current cognitive-neuro-biological theorizing: The fact that morality is intimately tied to individuals' sense of self. If moral actions were exclusively based on impersonal cognitive heuristics, evolutionary adaptations, or brain processes without any involvement of an agentic self, they would lack an important feature that renders moral actions truly moral: the fact that these actions are "ours."[1] People "own" their moral actions and therefore feel responsible for them. Without a self, moral emotions of guilt, shame, and pride would not exist (e.g., Tracy & Robins, 2007). Morality is imbued with selfhood (see also Frankfurt, 1988; Taylor, 1985).

Psychology as a discipline that is torn between biological reductionism, on the one hand, and social-constructionist contextualism, on the other (Martin, Sugarman, & Hickinbottom, 2010), has little room for the notion of (moral) self- or personhood. Still, the topic of the moral self has been the subject of some debate in the wake of Kohlbergian theorizing. In 1983, Blasi introduced his Self Model of Moral Functioning that aimed at accounting for observed (in)consistencies between an individual's moral judgment and action (Blasi, 1983). At that point in time, Blasi's self model could be understood as an extension of Kohlberg's stage model dealing with motivational issues that are not sufficiently addressed in his theory. In fact, many propositions made by Blasi (although not all) were later incorporated into Kohlberg's model to link the development of moral judgment with action (Candee & Kohlberg, 1987). However, in the 1990s the notion of the moral self gained increasing independence from Blasi's self model and its Kohlbergian heritage. Colby's and Damon's research on so-called moral exemplars, that is, individuals who are characterized by extraordinary and sustained moral commitment, was critical in this respect (Colby & Damon,

[1] To prevent possible misunderstandings, note at this point that cognitive-neuro-biological theorizing is not inherently reductionist but leaves ample room for the notions of self and agency. Using functional MRI techniques, Moll et al. (2007) demonstrated that agency and morality, in fact, share a large portion of a specific yet distributed neural system. This confirms the general claim made in this chapter, that self and morality are closely intertwined. At the same time, it provides an illustrative (albeit rare) example for nonreductionist neuropsychological research that takes the subjective experience of self and morality seriously.

1992). Colby and Damon attributed the moral commitment of moral exemplars to a particular fusion of self and morality. Once self and morality are fused, moral values are an integral part of a person's self-definition so that acting morally becomes an important mode of self-expression and part of one's identity. It is commonly assumed that this fusion or integration of self and morality takes place in adolescence when questions of identity are a key developmental issue (see Damon, 1996). It is, thus, the integration of moral values into the adolescent's sense of self that gives rise to a moral self, that is, a self that profoundly cares about matters of morality and ethical conduct. The idea of an integration of self and morality that constitutes the moral self runs through much of the literature on volunteerism and moral exemplars (see Hart, 2005).

The concept of the moral self as introduced by Blasi and elaborated by Damon, Hart, and others has not gone uncontested. In his presidential address to the 30th annual meeting of the Jean Piaget Society, Nucci formulated a poignant critique that was repeated and elaborated at various occasions (Nucci, 2001, 2004a, 2004b). In this critique, he pointed out three major flaws of the moral self-construct: First, the concept of the moral self as proposed by Blasi and others reduces moral motivation to one single motive, namely, the desire to be consistent with one's personal ideals and values. This motive in itself is not necessarily moral and seems to make moral actions contingent upon personal interests. Thus, the concept of the moral self runs into the danger of advocating ethical egoism. Second, research on the moral self mostly dealt with moral commitment of moral exemplars, with volunteerism and other forms of outstanding prosocial conduct. This hardly reflects the entire moral domain and leaves the concept of the moral self vulnerable to moral elitism, similar to Stage 5 or Stage 6 reasoning in Kohlberg's theory. If it is only moral exemplars who function on the basis of a moral self, how do we account for moral actions of ordinary people who, by implication, would not have a moral self? Finally, research on the moral self mostly operated on the assumption that adolescence is crucial for the integration of self and morality that gives rives to a moral self. Because of this focus on adolescence, other developmental periods that might have a bearing on the development of the moral self (notably childhood) were largely ignored. As a consequence, the literature on the moral self makes no connection between young children's morality and more mature forms of moral motivation in adolescence or adulthood. As Nucci (2004b) notes, there is a dearth of developmental theory in this field of research.

The notion of moral selfhood evidently has a hard time in psychology. It has been marginalized by contemporary moral psychology and fundamentally questioned from within the field of moral development. When taking up this notion we, thus, face challenges on many different fronts. Still, the topic appears to be too important to be discarded. As mentioned, morality is imbued with selfhood. But what does this connection of self and morality exactly entail? And how can we make sense of it from a developmental point of view? These are the leading questions of this chapter. In addressing these questions the chapter aims at clarifying some perennial issues around the notion of moral selfhood from the perspective of developmental psychology, with the hope of making the concept of the moral self more viable, and more respectable, again.

In the following, we first review research on the moral self that was not included in Nucci's critique on the moral self-construct (Nucci, 2004b) and that, implicitly or explicitly, responds to some of his criticism. Following this discussion, we present a model of moral self-development that distinguishes between three layers in the development of moral selfhood: the self as intentional, volitional, and identified agent. We explain how these different layers relate to each other from a developmental point of view, and how the model responds to Nucci's critique. Finally, we discuss implications for research on the moral self.

RESEARCH ON THE MORAL SELF: AN UPDATED REVIEW

In 2002 Bergman published a review article that summarized research on the moral self as it had evolved between the 1980s and 2000 (Bergman, 2002). The research described in this paper served as the basis for Nucci's critical evaluation of the moral self-construct (Nucci, 2004a). However, research on the moral self has been anything but inactive since then, as demonstrated by the most recent volume devoted to this topic: *Personality, Identity, and Character – Explorations in Moral Psychology* (Narvaez & Lapsley, 2009). Considering this research activity, the question arises of whether Nucci's earlier critique still applies to research on the moral self a decade later. This question is particularly pertinent since research on the moral self has diversified considerably over the past 10 years. Whereas Bergman's (2002) review discussed just a handful of authors who contributed to the literature on the moral self between 1980 and 2000 (notably Blasi, Damon, Rest, and Kohlberg), the volume edited by Narvaez and Lapsley contains 18 chapters that represent a broad range of different approaches to the topic. The present chapter is not meant to give an overview of all these approaches. Rather, it aims at providing an updated review by focusing on one particular aspect, namely, the extent to which a developmental perspective has been taken into consideration. Here, the approaches vary from elaborated developmental models to nondevelopmental ones, and even some in-between or hybrid perspectives. A full developmental model, for instance, has been presented by Blasi (2005) in which he traces the changes in the emergence of a moral will. By contrast, research on the moral self that is inspired by theories from outside developmental psychology (e.g., dual processing theories, social identity theory) typically does not put developmental issues at center stage. An example of this approach can be seen in Lapsley and Narvaez's (2004) work on moral expertise, in which developmental concerns are at best implicit. Between these two extremes is a third category of approaches that operate on the basis of certain developmental assumptions without necessarily fully clarifying the developmental nature of the moral self-construct. The most recent example for such an approach is the Reconciliation Model proposed by Frimer and Walker (2009).

Seven Steps in the Development of the Moral Will

When Blasi (1983) introduced his self model, its main purpose was to bridge the gap that separates moral judgment from moral action. The model itself consisted of seven theoretical propositions and 20 empirical questions, where the empirical questions mainly elaborated and substantiated the theoretical propositions. It would be beyond the scope of this chapter to discuss Blasi's original self model in detail (see Krettenauer, 2010). Nonetheless, a brief sketch of its core assumptions is in order to demarcate the common ground from which much of the research on the moral self started off. Stripped down to its core, Blasi's (1983) self model could be summarized in the following two propositions:

(1) Moral judgments, before leading to action, are at times processed through a second set of rules or criteria, the criteria of responsibility. The function of a responsibility judgment is to determine to what extent that which is morally good is also strictly necessary for the self. (Blasi, 1983, p. 198)
(2) The general criteria used to arrive at responsibility judgments differ from person to person and are related to one's self definition or to the organization of the self. (Blasi, 1983, p. 200)

Thus, individuals feel committed to their moral judgments to various degrees. This commitment is expressed in what Blasi called *judgment of responsibility*. The commitment itself is a function of the organization of the self. It depends on the extent to which the self has turned into a *moral* self.

Two aspects of self-organization were repeatedly identified as particularly relevant for conceptualizing the moral self (see Blasi, 1995, but also Lapsley, 1996): (a) moral centrality, that is the extent to which moral values are important for an individual's self-definition, and (b) self-integration, that is the extent to which moral values are integrated in the self-system. Moral actions can be performed for many different reasons. If moral rules are followed solely because of external considerations, the resulting moral motivation is external to the self. By contrast, if moral rules are observed because the person considers them as valid and important, or as part of what defines him or her as a person, the motivation is internal to the self (see also Deci & Ryan, this volume; Ryan & Deci, 2000). It is important to note that the two aspects, moral centrality and self-integration, are conceptually distinct even though they are empirically correlated (Krettenauer, 2011).

Blasi and Glodis (1995) pointed out that self-integration of moral values is a developmental process that is particularly pertinent in adolescence. In fact, Arnold (1993) reported a strong association between self-integration of moral values and adolescents' age, whereas moral centrality was unrelated to age in Arnold's study. However, it is exactly this restricted focus on adolescent development that instigated Nucci's critique, pointing out a lack of developmental continuity in the moral self-construct. In a later book chapter, Blasi (2005) made up for this limitation. In this publication, Blasi outlined seven steps in the development of the moral will, where "moral will" is defined as a person's desire toward the moral good in contradistinction to mere willpower. From Blasi's description, it follows that the moral will – and a fortiori the moral self – emerges well before adolescence. Step 1 in his sequence marks the absence of a moral will. Step 2 denotes an important transition, namely, the early formation of a moral will. Critical for the transition from Step 1 to Step 2 is the emergence of "second-order-desires," that is, the child's ability to form desires about desires. According to Blasi (2005), second-order desires establish an order of preferences, while second-order volitions are supposed to effectively translate these preferences into action. The following Steps 3 to 5 in the development of the moral will are characterized by extension (the child appropriates more and more desires by developing second-order volitions) and by reflective abstraction (the child develops an appreciation for general values that are abstracted from concrete desires). On Step 6, moral centrality becomes an important aspect of an individual's self-definition and, at the same time, a dimension of individual differences. The final Step 7 is marked by an acute sense of moral self-integration. Similar to Colby and Damon's description of moral exemplars (Colby & Damon, 1992), moral action becomes an important mode of self-expression.

Blasi (2005) emphasizes that these steps do not define a sequence in terms of Piagetian or Kohlbergian stages. Rather, Blasi assumes that the first steps leading to a set of stable values are common to many children whereas later steps reflect special experiences of those individuals who choose morality as the main source of values and core of their identity. Certainly, this assumption is speculative as is the whole sequence outlined by Blasi. Although Blasi referred to few empirical studies to support some of his claims, he did not attempt to empirically validate his theoretical model. Many questions around the model remain. Nevertheless, Blasi's contribution marks an important milestone in research on the moral self, as the self model, for the first time, was deliberately extended into childhood, addressing the lack of developmental perspectives Nucci had deplored.

Moral Centrality Development and the Reconciliation of Agency and Communion

Whereas Blasi's contributions to the literature on the moral self were mostly theoretical, others aimed at advancing the concept on empirical grounds. Inspired by Colby and Damon's interview study on moral exemplars, quite a few empirical studies were published in an attempt to identify distinctive features of outstanding moral commitment (e.g., Hart & Fegley, 1995; Matsuba & Walker, 2004; Walker & Frimer, 2007; Monroe, 1994). These studies confirmed a basic insight of Colby and Damon's study on moral exemplars, namely, that the moral actions of these individuals were associated with a high sense of certitude and spontaneity. Individuals reported little need to ponder moral decisions. In many instances, they instantly knew what to do. Colby and Damon (1992) attribute this high degree of certitude and spontaneity of moral actions to the fusion of self and morality described earlier. "These men and women have vigorously pursued their individual and moral goals simultaneously, viewing them in fact as one and the same.... They seamlessly integrate their commitments with their personal concerns so that the fulfillment of the one implies the fulfillment of the other" (Colby & Damon, 1992, p. 300).

As Frimer and Walker (2009) noted, many studies on moral exemplars were qualitative in nature, so that the central claim of a fusion of self and morality still "lacks a reliable empirical embodiment" (p. 1670). With this limitation in mind, Frimer and Walker (2009) developed a new measure designed to assess the degree of synergy of agency and communion in an individual's personality. Along with this measure, Frimer and Walker proposed the Reconciliation Model of moral centrality development. According to this model, agency and communion entail a fundamental motivational duality. Individuals either work toward achieving their own goals and projects (agency) or toward advancing those of others (communion). This duality exists by default and is supposed to be strongest in childhood. However, with development, individuals experience a growing tension between agency and communion as two opposing motivational systems, which eventually leads to an acute phase of disequilibrium. This disequilibrium can only be solved by either prioritizing one motivational system over the other or by reconciling the two. Reconciliation is supposed to lay the foundation for the extraordinary moral achievements that become evident in the lives of moral exemplars.

The reconciliation model proposed by Frimer and Walker (2009) makes strong developmental assumptions. Following these assumptions, morality and self are two fully separated motivational systems in childhood that become integrated in an Eriksonian-type crisis that typically occurs in adolescence (or at a later point in time as Frimer and Walker concede in a footnote). After reconciliation, stability is achieved. Since their empirical approach is new, they are not in the position yet to substantiate their developmental model by empirical data. Still, a developmental perspective is clearly present in their approach.

The Moral Self as Moral Expertise

The different types of moral self research described so far, even though highly variant in focus, have much in common. By stressing conflictual tendencies within the person that become integrated in a developmental process, which in turn constitutes a moral self that provides a sense of unity and purpose, research is highly indebted to Erikson's notions of ego-identity and integrity (see Erikson, 1959). Thus, much of the research on the moral self actually has developmental roots, even though these roots might not be very well articulated in all instances. However, this Eriksonian heritage is not common to all moral self models. Scholars might start from other theoretical premises and arrive at completely different developmental implications, as is the case with the moral self model proposed by Lapsley and Narvaez (see Lapsley & Narvaez, 2004; Narvaez, Lapsley, Hagele, & Lasky, 2005). Starting from a dual process view of human information processing, Lapsley and Narvaez shift the focus away from explicit-deliberate forms of self-related reasoning toward intuitive-heuristic processing. In their framework, the moral self is defined as having chronic accessibility of morally relevant schemes that influences information processing, decision making, and behavior. In other words, the moral self shows an automatic tendency to act and react in ways deemed moral by the self or by outside observers. According to Lapsley and Hill (2008), there are different types of automaticity. Preconscious automaticity is the involuntary activation of schemas, scripts, plans, and stereotypes outside conscious awareness. Preconscious is the kind of automaticity Haidt (2001) describes as the dominant process that triggers moral intuitions. A second form, called postconscious automaticity, operates on the nonconscious consequences of conscious thought. This type of automaticity is evident in the effects of priming – for instance, when activation of one social concept (e.g., honesty) in one context leads to utilization of this concept in another unrelated context. Finally, there is goal-dependent automaticity as a correlate of highly skilled or expert performance. It is well known that compared to novices, experts have a richer declarative and procedural knowledge base that allows automatic information processing and permits more efficient problem solving at higher levels of abstraction. In Lapsley and Hill's account, this goal-dependent automaticity is particularly relevant for the development of a moral self. The moral self, in terms of chronic accessibility of morally relevant schemes, is considered to be an outcome of repeated experience, direct instruction, coaching, practice, and routinization that creates moral expertise. Because these processes are functional at any time in the course of development, the development of the moral self is not limited to any specific age period, although expertise requires an experiential basis that probably develops over time.

Obviously, Lapsley and Narvaez draw a different picture of moral self-development. Development in their model depends on basic mechanisms of information processing. It is a function of schema activation and use.

A BOTTOM-UP MODEL FOR MORAL SELF-DEVELOPMENT

Thus far, the review suggests that research on the moral self has become more focused on developmental issues in the recent past than it had been in the 1980s and 1990s. In this respect, a major point of Nucci's critique of the moral self-construct can be considered outdated. However, research in this area seems to be far from providing a consolidated developmental model. The proposed models are tentative and rather speculative as they lack empirical validation. In this regard, Nucci's critique is still valid. In fact, it could be radicalized for two reasons. First, the various models were established largely in isolation from substantive bodies of literature on children's and adolescents' cognitive, emotional, and motivational development. Very few cross-references to research in these areas are made.

This appears to be problematic as the moral self certainly is not an isolated domain that develops separately from moral cognition, moral emotion, and moral action. Second, although the models arrive at fundamentally different developmental conclusions, they all have one feature in common: They start from a conception of a fully developed moral self that entails all those characteristics deemed to be important for describing a highly moral person. With this focus in mind, the authors employ a "top-down" logic of model construction by defining earlier forms of moral selfhood negatively as lack of these characteristics. As a consequence, the moral self in earlier developmental periods remains somewhat underdetermined and elusive.

In the following, a framework for studying the development of moral selfhood is proposed that starts from the opposite premises. In this framework, moral selfhood is not considered a separate domain of individual development that is to be described in isolation from cognitive, emotional, or personality development. The moral self crystallizes where various dimensions of cognitive, emotional, and motivational development intersect. Second, a bottom-up logic of model construction is employed. Rather than starting from a full-fledged account of mature moral selfhood the model starts from a minimalist conception and extends this conception into more inclusive forms. The question therefore is this: When does moral selfhood first emerge and what is added to this minimal moral self in the course of development? Approaching the moral self-concept from this perspective allows a fresh look at some perennial issues revolving around this concept.

The Moral Self as an Intentional, Volitional, and Identified Agent

Any discourse on the self starts with and returns to the notion of agency. Agency is the foundation of selfhood and provides the experiential basis for it. Certainly, the concept of agency is no less ambiguous, complex, and elusive than the concept of the self itself (for a thorough discussion of the concept of agency see Martin, Sugarman, & Thompson, 2003). According to Sokol and Huerta (2010), different conceptions of agency vary on a continuum from "thick" to "thin." In a thin sense, the term refers to overt goal-directed behavior. A thin view of agency offers a minimalist account of behavior as guided by mental states such as beliefs and desires. In a thick sense, agency refers to the self-conscious person who is able to reflect upon his or her own actions, put them in broader perspective, and imbue them with meaning derived from a sense of personal identity.

The moral self as intentional agent. Starting from a thin or minimalist account of agency, the definition of selfhood in infancy and childhood appears to be straightforward: The self is present once a child is capable of intentional actions. From a folk psychological perspective, an intention is a combination of desire and belief. Again, this is a minimalist understanding of intentions as argued, for instance, by Malle and Knobe (2001). Desires and intentions are not the same. Intentions are pro-attitudes with action content whereas desires may have any (and not just action) content (e.g., the desire to win a lottery even without buying a ticket). More important, intentions express a higher degree of commitment than mere desires (thus a person who intends to quit smoking is commonly understood as being more committed to following through than a person who merely expresses the desire to stop this behavior). There is no question that children around the age of 2.5 years understand subjective desires and the emotional implications of fulfilling a desire or frustrating it (Wellman & Phillips, 2001). However, an open question is what point in time children acquire more complex and subtle understandings of intentional action that include a clear differentiation between intentions and desires (Astington, 2001; Schult, 2002).

For instrumental actions, desires are about action outcomes and beliefs are about means-ends beliefs. For moral actions, however, things are more complex. Moral actions are inherently different from instrumental actions. Their success is not defined by attaining a goal but by conforming to a collectively shared standard or norm. Indeed, it is not an uncommon assumption in the literature on children's theory of mind that children's naive understanding of intentional action and their deontological reasoning (i.e., reasoning about obligatory and permissive acts) are two entirely separate domains. Similarly, domain theory proposes a personal domain that focuses on actions individuals are free to pursue as distinct from the moral and conventional domain (cf. Smetana, 2006). Wellman and Miller (2008) argued that even though the understanding of intentional actions and deontological reasoning are separate domains, they are connected. Deontological reasoning regulates the conditions under which belief-desire reasoning is activated. As Wellman and Miller (2008, p. 111) put it, permissions allow the actor to "engage in an action if I desire," whereas obligations require the actor to "engage in an action regardless of my desires." Even though Wellman and Miller (2008) argue for two mutually constitutive domains, the idea that moral obligations require an action "regardless of my desires" implies that moral actions cannot be desired. Within this framework, moral desires, by definition, cannot exist.

This implication of the theoretical framework developed by Wellman and Miller (2008) is in stark contrast with research on young children's capabilities to feel sympathy with others and the many observations of spontaneous acts of helping and sharing that were amassed in the literature on children's prosocial behavior (e.g., Dunfield, Kuhlmeier, O'Connell, & Kelley, 2011; Svetlova, Nichols, & Brownell, 2010; Warneken & Tomasello, 2009). Children around the age of 18 months do have a desire to help others in need, at least occasionally. They are able to effectively do so, once they understand that others' needs might be different from their own (see Hoffman, 2000). Certainly, prosocial behavior does not follow the logic of deontological reasoning applied by Wellman and Miller, as it is about socially desirable acts rather than strict obligations (cf. Kahn, 1992). However, even actions that are obligatory can be based on a spontaneous desire, namely, the desire *not* to inflict harm on others. Such a desire might be an outgrowth of spontaneous feelings of empathy or sympathy. It might be further informed by children's general understanding of moral rules that prohibit actions that are harmful to others. From this perspective, moral actions can be desired by young children. As desired action, they can be said to meet a minimal or thin requirement for moral selfhood.

The moral self as volitional agent. Young children around the age of 2 spontaneously engage in moral actions. At the same time, they regularly fail to act morally. Quite frequently, they are overpowered by emotions of anger or envy leading to acts of instrumental aggression. Very often, egoistic desires prevail over altruistic ones (Svetlova et al. 2010). From these behavioral observations, it becomes clear that moral actions involve more than a spontaneous desire to help others or not to inflict harm on them. Moral actions require the ability to regulate egoistic desires and to resist anti-social impulses. In other words, moral actions need a volitional self. It is important to note that in the context of moral action, the notion of a "volitional self" refers to two different processes (see Blasi, 2005). Volition may reflect willpower, that is, the ability to perform an action even when facing unanticipated obstacles, backlashes, or other adverse side effects (i.e., perseverance). Willpower is required after an intention has been formed. It is necessary for all goal-directed behavior including moral actions. In the context of moral actions, however, the volitional self is present not only when carrying out an action but also when forming an intention in the face of conflicting desires. The child may have the spontaneous desire to share his or her treats with other children and, at the same time, experience an equally strong desire to keep them all for himself or herself. In this case, choosing between one of the two opposing desires requires an act of volition. As described, in the context of charting the steps in the development of the moral will, Blasi (2005) relies on the concept of "second-order desires" to account for such an act. According to Blasi, children, at a certain age, develop desires about desires (e.g., the desire not to selfishly desire everything for oneself). In Blasi's view, the ability to form second-order desires constitutes the moral self as a volitional agent. However, the concept of second-order desires is rooted in Frankfurt's philosophy of the person rather than developmental psychology (Frankfurt, 1988). A direct empirical investigation into children's ability to form second-order desires so far does not exist.

A well-established empirical paradigm in developmental psychology that picks up the notion of the volitional self as described earlier is research on children's delay of gratification (for an overview, see Tobin & Graziano, 2010). In this research paradigm, children are given the opportunity to take a smaller reward immediately or to wait for a larger reward later. The ability to delay gratification, that is, to choose a temporally distant goal at the expense of an immediate goal, gradually increases with children's age (Mischel, 1974). At the same time, there are important individual differences in the ability to delay gratification that emerge early in development and have long-term implications (see Mischel, Shoda, & Peake, 1988; see Duckworth & Carlson, this volume). The empirical procedure for studying delay of gratification taps into two different processes: (a) the child's ability to make a delay choice and (b) his or her ability to carry out the decision. While the latter process reflects willpower, the former refers to the ability to form an intention in the face of two conflicting ways of action. As Lemmon and Moore (2007) note, children's ability to make a delay choice, on the one hand, and their ability to effectively wait for the superior reward, on the other, do not seem to be strongly correlated. While children's waiting times in the delay of gratification paradigm show a continuous increase with age, the ability to make delay choices has cognitive prerequisites that typically develop around the age of 4 years (Lemmon & Moore, 2001). Children need to be able to conceive of the self as extended over time in order to understand that the present desire will be better served in the future by waiting for the superior reward (Barresi, 2001). This concern for the future self needs to effectively inhibit the desire for the smaller reward. Accordingly, children's delay choices were shown to be associated with their understanding of the temporally extended self and other cognitive skills that reflect general changes in children's representational ability (Moore, 2010).

Strikingly, the understanding of a temporally extended self not only accounts for choosing future self-rewards but also for the ability to make future choices that benefit others (Thompson, Barresi, & Moore, 1997). Thus, understanding that the self is extended in time has implications for prosocial behavior as well. Still, it is obvious that the delay choice paradigm does not fully capture all requirements of the volitional self that are pertinent for moral actions. In the context of moral action, the child needs to understand that the presently dominant desire (e.g., the desire for a toy another child is playing with) might be less important in a future situation than the opposite moral desire (e.g., not to hurt the other child by taking away the toy). By contrast, in the delay choice paradigm, the child needs to project the present desire into the future and realize that this desire is better served by the larger reward. It is, thus, the ability to prioritize a moral desire over another temporarily stronger desire that constitutes the moral self as a volitional agent. Piaget (1954/1981), in his lectures on "Intelligence and Affectivity," described this ability as a "conservation of values" that makes it possible to subordinate a temporarily stronger impulse to a normative feeling (see Sokol & Hammond, 2009). According to Piaget (1954/1981), this conservation of values is tied to the development of concrete operations around the age of 7 to 8 years. Krettenauer, Malti, and Sokol (2008) noted a striking parallel between Piaget's notion and research on children's moral emotion expectancies, which demonstrates that children typically do not anticipate negative self-evaluative emotions when transgressing a moral rule to achieve a desired goal before the age of 7 to 8 years. The anticipation of moral emotions in such situations indicates the child's ability to uphold a moral desire even when an opposing immoral desire is presently dominant (see also Arsenio & Lover, 1995). Note that Piaget's notion of the "conservation of values" should not be confused with the concept of second-order desires as used by Blasi to describe the volitional self. Whereas second-order desires reflect upon first-order desires and thus operate on a meta-level, the conservation of values simply requires the ability to establish and maintain a stable relationship between conflicting desires (see also Barresi, 1999).

The moral self as identified agent. Once children have developed a volitional self, they are able to regulate egoistic desires and resist anti-social impulses by giving priority to moral desires. However, at this point in development they may still lack an integration of moral values into the self system such that moral actions reflect a form of self-expression, a point stressed in research on moral exemplars. In fact, at younger ages children's volitional acts might be fully based on considerations external to the self (such as fear of punishment), which implies moral heteronomy. In the context of moral action, a fully integrated (and autonomous) sense of self requires that the individual experience the act of prioritizing a moral desire over an immoral desire as a volition that emanates from the self rather than as a decision that is imposed by external factors.

Various models of self, ego, and identity development propose a general developmental trend toward higher levels of self-integration. These models generally assume that individuals' commitments to life goals, values, and ideals are increasingly experienced as self-chosen rather than imposed by external factors (e.g., Blasi & Glodis, 1995; Loevinger, 1976; Marcia, Waterman, Matteson, Archer, & Orlofsky, 1993). Even Kohlberg's stage model of moral development provides evidence of a decline of external regulation as teenagers move out of the preconventional Stages 1 and 2 (Colby, Kohlberg, Gibbs, & Lieberman, 1983). At the same time, standards of individual conscience become more salient at the conventional Stages 3–4 and 4. Colby and Kohlberg (1987) did not consider standards of individual conscience a defining feature of conventional stages, whereas Gibbs, Basinger, and Fuller (1992) incorporated them in their definition of moral maturity as it is achieved on the conventional level (see also Gibbs, Basinger, Grime, & Snarey, 2007).

While these developmental models tend to consider a high level of self-integration as an end point of development that, once achieved, is maintained across a broad range of domains, Self-Determination Theory as proposed by Deci, Ryan, and others considers it a more flexible attribute that is content- and context-dependent (see Deci & Ryan, this volume). According to Self-Determination Theory, individuals' motivation to act can be described along a continuum defined by the poles of extrinsic and intrinsic actions. Extrinsically motivated actions are instrumental to achieving standards set by others (e.g., meeting a deadline), whereas intrinsic motivation is inherent in the activity freely chosen by an individual (e.g., fun playing a musical instrument). Many actions can hardly be classified as being intrinsically motivated in this emphatic sense, either because there is little intrinsic gratification entailed in them (e.g., highly repetitive activities) or because these actions are demanded by others in the first place. However, individuals can integrate others' expectations to varying degrees (Ryan, 1993). In the context of moral action in particular, this process has often been described as rule internalization (Kochanska & Thompson, 1997). When rules are internalized they are experienced as binding regardless of others' reactions. Thus, evaluations of significant others are transformed into self-evaluative reactions (e.g., guilt feelings).

As pointed out by Self-Determination Theory, rule internalization refers to one form of internal motivation, which also includes introjected and identified motivation. Rule internalization leads to an introjected mode of self-regulation, where rule compliance becomes independent of explicit demands of others. Still, on the introjected level, norms are subjectively experienced as rules one is supposed to follow rather than as standards one wants to meet. This transformation of "shoulds" into "wants" takes place once individuals develop identified and integrated modes of self-regulation. On the identified level, individuals express a basic personal agreement with a norm or societal expectation, whereas on the integrated level norms are experienced as self-ideals the person does not want to betray. Ryan, Kuhl, and Deci (1997) propose a general organismic tendency to rely progressively on internal modes of self-regulation at the expense of external regulation. At the same time, actual development of self-regulation has been repeatedly shown to depend on social factors that support more integrated modes of self-regulation (see Grolnick, Deci, & Ryan, 1997; Grolnick & Raftery-Helmer, this volume). Such factors often are context specific. As a consequence, development of self-regulation is context dependent. For example, intrinsic academic motivation was shown to decrease with adolescents' age due to the prevalence of extrinsic contingencies in the school system, whereas environmental behavior tends to become more self-integrated during the same age period (see Renaud-Dube, Taylor, Lekes, Koestner, & Guay, 2010).

Once a child or teenager prioritizes moral desires over egoistic desires and feels that this prioritization reflects the way she or he wants to be, the volitional self has turned into an identified agent. This form of prioritization can be specific to particular contexts and situations. Thus, the notion of the moral self as an identified agent does not entail the concept of a consistent or steadfast moral identity. The moral self as an identified agent entails a sense of ownership of moral actions. Nevertheless, this sense of ownership does not imply that moral values provide a sense of unity and purpose in one's life.

Three Layers in the Development of Moral Selfhood

In the previous paragraph, three different notions of moral selfhood were outlined. It was argued that a comprehensive conception of moral selfhood requires a self as intentional, volitional, and identified agent. However, the question remains as to how the various notions of moral selfhood relate to each other from a developmental point of view. This question is addressed in the following. After discussing developmental issues we turn to implications of the proposed model.

The various notions of moral selfhood are hierarchically ordered. Thus, the self as intentional agent is foundational for developing a volitional self, and the volitional self is foundational for the self as identified agent. However, this hierarchical relationship does not imply stages in a Kohlbergian sense. The self as intentional agent is not replaced by the volitional self, nor is the volitional self superseded by the self as identified agent. All three forms of moral selfhood co-exist, and each form likely is subject to further change after first emerging in the course of development. It therefore is more appropriate to view the three notions of moral selfhood as layers, where each layer adds an important quality to the moral self (for a pictorial illustration see Figure 6.1). Layer I is defined by the self as intentional agent. Layer II constitutes the moral self as a volitional agent, and Layer III equips the moral self with a rudimentary sense of identity (note that a similar model of layers was used to describe the emergence of the self in infancy by Stern, 1993). As these layers are not stages, higher layers do not replace lower ones. As well, the developmental processes that constitute Layer I are likely different from those that constitute Layers II and III. Having stressed the foundational nature of the lower layers. it is important to note that higher layers influence lower ones. Thus, identification impacts volitional processes. Volitional processes, in turn, likely form and transform moral desires (i.e., impact the self as intentional agent). If this were not the case, the well-documented relevance of the moral identity for moral action (see Hardy & Carlo, 2011) would be difficult to explain.

Although the relationship between chronological age and development is complicated and age is not necessarily a good indicator of development (see Moshman, 2009), a legitimate question to be asked at this point is when

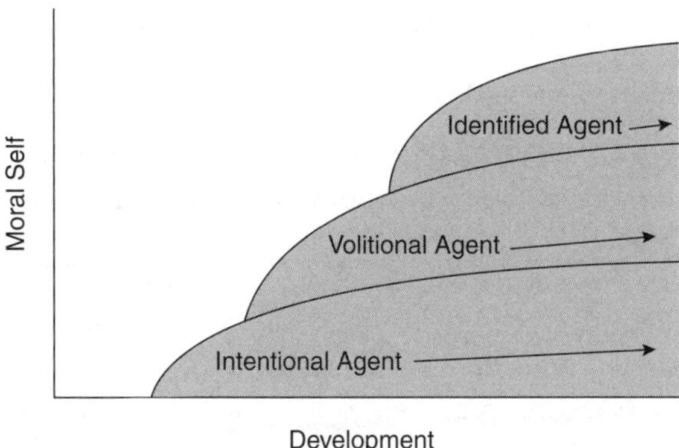

FIGURE 6.1 Three layers in the development of moral selfhood.

in the course of the development the three proposed layers of moral selfhood typically emerge. In our previous discussion of various developmental achievements in the cognitive, emotional, and motivational domain and their relations to the three different conceptions of the moral self we have already touched this issue. Basically, we suggest the following age-related changes in the development of the moral self (bearing in mind that age norms do not imply a fixed age of emergence of the different developmental layers). (1) Children's early moral desires are an outgrowth of their first sympathetic reactions that typically occur in the second half of the second year and are associated with children's mirror self-recognition (Bischof-Köhler, 1988). Thus, the moral self as intentional agent can be assumed to emerge around the age of 2 years. (2) In the delay of gratification choice paradigm, the emergence of a volitional self was related to children's understanding of the temporally extended self around the age of 4 years. However, as noted, the development of the volitional moral self requires more than extending just one desire into the future. If we take the ability to anticipate negatively charged self-evaluative emotions in the context of moral transgressions as an indicator of a "conservation of values" and hence a volitional moral self, we may assume that the volitional moral self normally develops between 6 and 8 years of age. (3) The association between age and the development of the moral self as identified agent is probably more variable. The moral self as identified agent requires a volitional self and therefore should not emerge before middle childhood. As noted at the beginning of this chapter, it is the age period of mid- to late adolescence that typically is considered crucial for the formation of a moral identity. However, the moral self as identified agent does not require a moral identity. The self as identified agent therefore might emerge well before middle adolescence, that is, in late childhood or the early teenage years.

IMPLICATIONS OF THE PROPOSED MODEL

A major goal of this chapter was to address important criticisms raised against the moral self-construct by Nucci (2004). Nucci argued that the moral self-construct is reductionistic in that it reduces moral actions to one single motive that by itself is not necessarily moral. Furthermore, Nucci criticized limitations in research on the moral self that mostly focused on prosocial engagement, and he noted its developmental narrowness.

It should be evident from the proposed model that the limitations pointed out by Nucci are not inherent to the moral self-construct but mostly reflect the shortcoming of previous research. By proposing three distinct but interrelated layers in the development of the moral self we avoid the pitfall of reductionism. Even if volitional processes depend on the desire to be consistent with the self, this by no means implies that a person acts out of an egoistic desire on the level of moral intentions. Second, the proposed framework does not in any way privilege prosocial actions over other moral behavior as being indicative of a moral self. Although it is assumed that sympathetic reactions form the basis for the first moral desires, these sympathetic reactions constitute both prosocial desires ("I want to help other") and moral desires ("I do not want to inflict harm on others"). Note that the proposed framework is anything but elitist. Even if it turns out that only a few moral exemplars have a steadfast or enduring moral identity, this is not to say that ordinary people lack a moral self. Moral selfhood is present on the intentional and volitional level. Finally, by tracing back the development of moral selfhood into the second year of children's life, we make clear that the moral self certainly is not limited to adolescence. In fact, the proposed framework points out that there is both continuity and discontinuity in the development of moral selfhood. There is continuity as the various layers of moral selfhood depend on each other, and there is discontinuity in that the developmental factors that constitute the three layers are not the same.

While it is essential to address criticisms that have plagued moral self research, it is also important to clarify the relations between the proposed model and other existing models. How does the proposed model connect to the models described earlier in this chapter, and in what way does it advance them? We argue that the bottom-up model of the development of the moral self proposed in this chapter provides a more comprehensive perspective and, at the same time, corrects some of the limitations inherent in previous research.

The seven steps in the development of the moral will outlined by Blasi (2005) share many commonalities with the proposed model. However, Blasi does not qualify the developmental nature of these steps. It remains open whether the steps are stages, levels, milestones, phases, or something else. The proposed model is more specific in this regard. Also, Blasi strongly relies on the notion of second-order desires to account for the volitional moral self. The proposed model does not assume that children need to develop second-order desires to establish a volitional moral self. They simply need to prioritize spontaneous moral desires over egoistic desires. Blasi probably would deny the moral significance of these spontaneous desires (see Blasi, 2000). As a consequence, there is no concept of the moral self as intentional agent in Blasi's model. At this point, the model proposed in this chapter connects well with Lapsley and Narveaz's idea of the moral self as an automatic way to act and react (Lapsley & Narvaez, 2004). As described, the moral self is present in spontaneous (i.e., automatic) desires and intentions that actually form the basis for higher-order volitional processing and for moral identifications. Thus, the proposed model for moral self-development is not limited to conscious and deliberate moral reasoning and decision making. At the same time, it does not restrict moral self-development to automatic responses as do Lapsley and Narvaez.

The assumption that children have spontaneous moral desires or intentions is incompatible with Frimer's and Walker's proposition of a fundamental duality of agency and communion that is predominant in childhood (Frimer & Walker, 2009). Frimer and Walker assume full separation of agency and communion at the onset of development. However, following Heinz Werner's *Orthogenetic Principle* (Werner & Kaplan, 1963/1984) one might argue that development typically does not begin with fully differentiated systems but with a lack of differentiation. Development proceeds through differentiation to hierarchical integration. The proposed model of moral self-development assumes a differentiation and integration of motivational processes pertinent for moral actions. The duality of agency and communion described by Frimer and Walker may exist at the level of value identifications but not at the level of children's spontaneous action tendencies. Thus, it appears that the Reconciliation Model of moral centrality development mostly is about the moral self as identified agent whereas it has little to say about volitional processes, intentions, and desires. In Frimer's and Walker's model, moral centrality development is essentially understood as the development of moral identity. This is somewhat puzzling given the fact Colby and Damon's (1992) landmark study on moral exemplars addresses not only issues of identification but also volitional and intentional processes. The seamless integration of personal concerns and moral commitments stressed by Colby and Damon (1992) as an outstanding feature of moral exemplariness actually suggests an ideal coordination of moral identifications with volitional processes leading to spontaneous moral intentions and actions. It might be an advantage of the proposed model of moral self-development that these three aspects of the moral self are considered simultaneously. From this perspective, moral centrality development is better understood as the coordination of different layers in the development of moral selfhood, rather than as a single dimension of individual differences in the self-importance of moral values.

CONCLUSION

This chapter argued for a conceptual differentiation of three different notions of moral selfhood: the moral self as intentional, volitional, and identified agent. At the same time, it introduced a developmental model that outlines how the three different conceptions of moral selfhood relate to each other from a developmental point of view. This developmental model is certainly no less speculative than other models on the development of the moral self discussed in this chapter, and as such, it awaits future empirical validation. It might turn out to be far too simplistic and in need of substantial revision. However, even if the developmental model as proposed in this chapter is refuted, this by no means disqualifies the conceptual distinction between the different notions of moral selfhood. These notions, on different levels and scales, describe what it means to take ownership of moral action (or conversely to deny it), and thus take up an important facet of moral autonomy. The idea of moral autonomy was crucial for Piaget's work on children's moral development, even though it was mostly understood in terms of a child's ability to critically evaluate social norms and to better understand the meaning of morality (for a critical assessment from the perspective of domain theory, see Helwig, 2008). However, moral autonomy is more than this. Moral actions need to originate freely and flow from the self to call them autonomous in the fullest sense of the word. Piaget (1932) assumed that this internal motivation is implied in children's autonomous reasoning capabilities, an assumption that is overly simplistic (cf. Wright, 1982). Kohlberg, in following up on Piaget, mostly focused on moral autonomy in terms of reasoning capabilities but neglected its motivational aspects. The proposed model of the development of the moral self aims at correcting this imbalance. It brings the concept of the moral self back to the theoretical context from where research on moral development started.

REFERENCES

Arnold, M. L. (1993). *The place of morality in the adolescent self* (Doctoral dissertation, Harvard University).

Arsenio, W., & Lover, A. (1995). Children's conceptions of sociomoral affect: Happy victimizers, mixed emotions, and other expectancies. In M. Killen & D. Hart (Eds.), *Morality in everyday life: Developmental perspectives* (pp. 87–128). New York, NY: Cambridge University Press.

Astington, J. W. (2001). The paradox of intention: Assessing children's metarepresentational understandings. In B. F. Malle, L. J. Moses, & D. A. Baldwin (Eds.), *Intentions and intentionality* (pp. 85–104). Cambridge, MA: MIT Press.

Barresi, J. (1999). On becoming a person. *Philosophical Psychology, 12*, 79–98.
Barresi, J. (2001). Extending self-consciousness into the future. In C. Moore & K. Lemmon (Eds.), *The self in time* (pp. 141–161). Mahwah, NJ: Erlbaum.
Bergman, R. (2002). Why be moral? A conceptual model from developmental psychology. *Human Development, 45*, 104–124.
Bischof-Köhler, D. (1988). Über den Zusammenhang von Empathie und der Fähigkeit, sich im Spiegel zu erkennen. *Schweizerische Zeitschrift für Psychologie, 47*, 147–159.
Blasi, A. (1983). Moral cognition and moral action: A theoretical perspective. *Developmental Review, 3*, 178–210.
Blasi, A. (1995). Moral understanding and the moral personality: The process of moral integration. In W. M. Kurtines & J. L. Gewirtz (Eds.), *Moral development: An introduction* (pp. 229–253). Boston, MA: Allyn and Bacon.
Blasi, A. (2000). Was sollte als moralisches Verhalten gelten? Das Wesen der 'frühen Moral' in der kindlichen Entwicklung. In W. Edelstein & G. Nunner-Winkler (Eds.), *Moral im sozialen Kontext* (pp. 116–145). Frankfurt/M.: Suhrkamp.
Blasi, A. (2005). Moral character: A psychological approach. In D. K. Lapsley & F. C. Power (Eds.), *Character psychology and character education* (pp. 67–100). Notre Dame, IN: University of Notre Dame Press.
Blasi, A., & Glodis, K. (1995). The development of identity. A critical analysis from the perspective of the self as subject. *Developmental Review, 15*, 404–433.
Buchanan, T. W. (2008). Review of moral psychology, Volume 3. *Journal of Research in Character Education, 6*, 105–112.
Candee, D., & Kohlberg, L. (1987). Moral judgment and moral action: A reanalysis of Haan, Smith, and Block's (1968) Free Speech Movement data. *Journal of Personality and Social Psychology*, 52, 554–564.
Carpendale, J. I. M., Sokol, B. W., & Müller, U. (2010). Is a neuroscience of morality possible? In P. D. Zelazo, M. J. Chandler, & E. Crone (Eds.), *Developmental social cognitive neuroscience* (pp. 289–311). Mahwah, NJ: Erlbaum.
Colby, A., & Damon, W. (1992). *Some do care*. New York, NY: Free Press.
Colby, A., & Kohlberg, L. (Eds.). (1987). *The measurement of moral judgment (Vol. I)*. Cambridge, UK: Cambridge University Press.
Colby, A., Kohlberg, L., Gibbs, J., & Lieberman, M. (1983). A longitudinal study of moral judgment. *Monographs of the Society for Research in Child Development, 48* Serial No. 200).
Damon, W. (1996). The lifelong transformation of moral goals through social influence. In P. B. Baltes & U. M. Staudinger (Eds.), *Interactive minds* (pp. 198–220). Cambridge, UK: Cambridge University Press.
Dunfield, K., Kuhlmeier, V. A., O'Connell, L., & Kelley, E. (2011). Examining the diversity of prosocial behavior: Helping, sharing, and comforting in infancy. *Infancy, 16*, 227–247.
Erikson, E. (1959). *Identity and the life cycle*. New York, NY: Norton.
Frankfurt, H. G. (1988). *The importance of what we care about*. Cambridge, UK: Cambridge University Press.
Frimer, J. A., & Walker, L. J. (2009). Reconciling the self and morality: An empirical model of moral centrality development. *Developmental Psychology, 45*, 1669–1681.

Gibbs, J. C., Basinger, K. S., & Fuller, D. (1992). *Moral maturity: Measuring the development of sociomoral reflection.* Hillsdale, NJ: Erlbaum.

Gibbs, J. C., Basinger, K. S., Grime, R. L., & Snarey, J. R. (2007). Moral judgment development across cultures: Revisiting Kohlberg's universality claims. *Developmental Review, 27*, 443–500.

Grolnick, W. S., Deci, E. L., & Ryan, R. M. (1997). Internalization within the family: The Self-Determination Theory perspective. In J. E. Grusec & L. Kuczynski (Eds.), *Parenting and children's internalization of values* (pp. 135–161). New York, NY: Wiley.

Hammond, S. I. (2008). Review of moral psychology, Volume 2. *Journal of Research in Character Education, 6*, 101–104.

Haidt, J. (2001). The emotional dog and its rational tail: A social intuitionist approach to moral judgment. *Psychological Review, 108*, 814–834.

Haidt, J. (2007). The new synthesis in moral psychology. *Science, 316*, 998–1002.

Hardy, S., & Carlo, G. (2005). Identity as a source of moral motivation. *Human Development, 48*, 232–256.

Hart, D. (2005). The development of moral identity. In G. Carlo & C. P. Edwards (Eds.), *Moral motivation through the life span* (pp. 165–196). Lincoln: University of Nebraska Press.

Hart, D., & Fegley, S. (1995). Prosocial behavior and caring in adolescence: Relations to self-understanding and social judgment. *Child Development, 66*, 1346–1359.

Helwig, C. C. (2008). The moral judgment of the child reevaluated: Heteronomy, early morality, and reasoning about social justice and inequalities. In C. Wainryb, J. G. Smetana & E. Turiel (Eds.), *Social development, social inequalities, and social justice* (pp. 27–52). Mahwah, NJ: Erlbaum.

Hoffman, M. L. (2000). *Empathy and moral development.* Cambridge, UK: Cambridge University Press.

Kahn, P. H. (1992). Children's obligatory and discretionary moral judgments. *Child Development, 63*, 416–430.

Kochanska, G., & Thompson, R. A. (1997). The emergence and development of conscience in toddlerhood and early childhood. In J. E. Grusec & L. Kuczynski (Eds.), *Parenting and children's internalization of values* (pp. 53–77). New York, NY: Wiley.

Krettenauer, T. (2010). Das moralische Selbst: Forschungsstand und Perspektiven. In B. Latzko & T. Malti (Eds.), *Moralische Entwicklung und Erziehung in Kindheit und Adoleszenz* (pp. 87–103). Göttingen: Hogrefe.

Krettenauer, T. (2011). The dual moral self: Moral centrality and intrinsic moral motivation. *Journal of Genetic Psychology, 172*, 309–328.

Krettenauer, T., Malti, T., & Sokol, B. W. (2008). Development of moral emotions and the happy-victimizer phenomenon: A critical review of theory and application. *European Journal of Developmental Science, 2*, 221–235.

Lapsley, D. K. (1996). *Moral psychology.* Boulder, CO: Westview.

Lapsley, D. K., & Hill, P. L. (2008). On dual processing and heuristic approaches to moral cognition. *Journal of Moral Education, 37*, 313–332.

Lapsley, D. K., & Hill, P. L. (2009). The development of moral personality. In D. Narvaez & D. K. Lapsley (Eds.), *Personality, identity, and character* (pp. 185–213). Cambridge, UK: Cambridge University Press.

Lapsley, D. K., & Narvaez, D. (2004). A social-cognitive approach to the moral personality. In D. K. Lapsley & D. Narvaez (Eds.), *Moral development, self, and identity* (pp. 189–212). Mahwah, NJ: Erlbaum.

Lapsley, D. K., & Thompson, J. (2003). *Psychology and the question of agency.* Albany: SUNY Press.

Lemmon, K., & Moore, C. (2001). Binding the self in time. In C. Moore & K. Lemmon (Eds.), *The self in time* (pp. 163–179). Mahwah, NJ: Erlbaum.

Lemmon, K., & Moore, C. (2007). The development of prudence in the face of varying future rewards. *Developmental Science, 2007*, 502–511.

Lerner, R. M. (2002). *Concepts and theories of human development.* Mahwah, NJ: Erlbaum.

Loevinger, J. (1976). *Ego development.* San Francisco, CA: Jossey-Bass.

Malle, B. F., & Knobe, J. (2001). The distinction between desire and intention: A folk-conceptual analysis. In B. F. Malle, L. J. Moses, & D. A. Baldwin (Eds.), *Intentions and intentionality* (pp. 45–68). Cambridge, MA: MIT Press.

Marcia, J. E., Waterman, A. S., Matteson, D. R., Archer, S. L., & Orlofsky, J. L. (1993). *Ego identity.* New York, NY: Springer-Verlag.

Martin, J., Sugarman, J. H., & Hickinbottom, S. (2010). *Persons: Understanding psychological selfhood and agency.* New York, NY: Springer.

Matsuba, M. K., & Walker, L. J. (2004). Extraordinary moral commitment: Young adults involved in social organizations. *Journal of Personality, 2004*, 413–436.

Mischel, W. (1974). Processes in delay of gratification. In L. Berkowitz (Ed.), *Advances in experimental social psychology* (Vol. 7, pp. 249–292). New York, NY: Academic Press.

Mischel, W., Shoda, Y., & Peake, P. K. (1988). The nature of adolescent competencies predicted by preschool delay of gratification. *Journal of Personality and Social Psychology, 54*, 687–696.

Moll, J., de Oliveira-Souza, R., Garrido, G. J., Bramati, I. E., Caparelli-Daquer, E. M. A., Paiva, M. L. M. F., et al. (2007). The self as moral agent: Linking the neural bases of social agency and moral sensitivity. *Social Neuroscience,* 2, 336–532.

Moore, C. (2010). The development of future-oriented decision-making. In B. W. Sokol, U. Müller, J. I. M. Carpendale, A. R. Young, & G. Iarocci (Eds.), *Self and social regulation* (pp. 270–286). Oxford, UK: Oxford University Press.

Moshman, D. (2009). Identity, morality, and adolescent development. *Human Development, 52*, 287–290.

Narvaez, D., & Lapsley, D. K. (Eds.). (2009). *Personality, identity, and character.* Cambridge, UK: Cambridge University Press.

Narvaez, D., Lapsley, D. K., Hagele, S., & Lasky, B. (2005). Moral chronicity and social information processing: Tests of a social cognitive approach to the moral personality. *Journal of Research in Personality, 40*, 966–985.

Nucci, L. (2001). *Education in the moral domain.* Cambridge, UK: Cambridge University Press.

Nucci, L. (2004a). Reflections on the moral self construct. In D. K. Lapsley & D. Narvaez (Eds.), *Moral development, self, and identity* (pp. 111–132). Mahwah, NJ: Erlbaum.

Nucci, L. (2004b). The promise and limitations of the moral self construct. In C. Lightfoot, C. E. Lalonde, & M. J. Chandler (Eds.), *Changing conceptions of psychological life* (pp. 49–70). Mahwah, NJ: Erlbaum.

Piaget, J. (1981). *Intelligence and affectivity: Their relationship during child development.* Palo Alto, CA: Annual Reviews Monograph. (Original work published in 1954).

Renaud-Dube, A., Taylor, G., Lekes, N., Koestner, R., & Guay, F. (2010). Adolescents' motivation toward the environment: Age-related trends and correlates. *Canadian Journal of Behavioral Science, 42*, 194–199.

Ryan, R. M. (1993). Agency and organization: Intrinsic motivation, autonomy, and the self in psychological development. In J. Jacobs (Ed.), *Nebraska Symposion on Motivation* (Vol. 40, pp. 1–56). Lincoln: University of Nebraska Press.

Ryan, R. M., & Deci, E. L. (2000). Self-determination theory and the facilitation of intrinsic motivation, social development and well-being. *American Psychologist, 55*, 68–78.

Ryan, R. M., Kuhl, J., & Deci, E. L. (1997). Nature and autonomy: An organizational view of social and neurobiological aspects of self-regulation in behavior and development. *Development and Psychopathology, 9*, 701–728.

Schult, C. A. (2002). Children's understanding of the distinction between intentions and desires. *Child Development, 73*, 1727–1747.

Sinnott-Amstrong, W. (Ed.). (2008). *Moral psychology.* Cambridge, MA: MIT Press.

Smetana, J. G. (2006). Social-cognitive domain theory: Consistencies and variations in children's moral and social judgments. In M. Killen & J. G. Smetana (Eds.), *Handbook of moral development* (pp. 119–153). Mahwah, NJ: Erlbaum.

Smetana, J. G., & Killen, M. (2008). Moral cognition, emotions and neuroscience: An integrative developmental view. *European Journal of Developmental Science, 2*, 324–339.

Sokol, B. W., & Hammond, S. I. (2009). Piaget and affectivity. In U. Müller, J. I. M. Carpendale, & L. Smith (Eds.), *The Cambridge Companion to Piaget* (pp. 309–323). Cambridge, UK: Cambridge University Press.

Sokol, B. W., & Huerta, S. (2010). Through thick and thin: Agency as 'taking' perspectives. *Human Development, 53*, 46–52.

Stern, D. (1993). *Die Lebenserfahrung des Säuglings.* Stuttgart: Klett-Cotta.

Svetlova, M., Nichols, S. R., & Brownell, C. A. (2010). Toddlers' prosocial behavior: From instrumental to empathic to altruistic helping. *Child Development, 81*, 1814–1827.

Taylor, C. (1985). *Human agency and language.* Cambridge, UK: Cambridge University Press.

Thompson, C., Barresi, J., & Moore, C. (1997). The development of future-oriented prudence and altruism in preschoolers. *Cognitive Development, 12*, 199–212.

Tobin, R. M., & Graziano, W. G. (2010). Delay of gratification: A review of fifty years of regulation research. In R. H. Hoyle (Ed.), *Handbook of personality and self-regulation* (pp. 47–63). New York, NY: Wiley-Blackwell.

Tracy, J., & Robins, R. W. (2007). The self in self-conscious emotions. In J. Tracy, R. W. Robins, & J. P. Tangney (Eds.), *The self-conscious emotions: Theory and research* (pp. 3–20). New York, NY: Guilford Press.

Walker, L. J., & Frimer, J. A. (2007). Moral personality of brave and caring exemplars. *Journal of Personality and Social Psychology, 93*, 845–860.
Warneken, F., & Tomasello, M. (2009). The roots of human altruism. *British Journal of Psychology, 100*, 455–471.
Wellman, H. M., & Miller, J. G. (2008). Including deontic reasoning as fundamental to theory of mind. *Human Development, 51*, 105–135.
Wellman, H. M., & Phillips, A. T. (2001). Developing intentional understandings. In B. F. Malle, L. J. Moses, & D. A. Baldwin (Eds.), *Intentions and intentionality* (pp. 125–148). Cambridge, MA: MIT Press.
Wereha, T. J. & Racine, T. P. (2008). Evolutionary psychology at the crossroads? A review of moral psychology, Volume 1. *Journal of Research in Character Education, 6*, 95–99.
Werner, H., & Kaplan, B. (1963/1984). *Symbol formation: An organismic-developmental approach to the psychology of language.* Hillsdale, NJ: Erlbaum.
Wright, D. (1982). Piaget's theory of practical morality. *British Journal of Psychology, 73*, 279–283.

Chapter 7

Facilitating Autonomy in the Family: Supporting Intrinsic Motivation and Self-Regulation

WENDY S. GROLNICK AND JACQUELYN N. RAFTERY-HELMER
Clark University

The goal of socialization is for children to acquire the attitudes, behaviors, and values important in society. Clearly this task falls largely on the shoulders of parents and other caregivers who live day-to-day with the children. However, beyond getting children to engage in desired behaviors and display knowledge of relevant beliefs and values, effective socialization involves children taking on and "owning" these values and behaviors – in effect, autonomously regulating them. For example, parents don't just want their children to clean their rooms because they won't be allowed to go out if they don't, but rather to do so because they themselves see the value in having a clean room.

For the student of child development (and for parents themselves!) the issue of socialization involves an interesting paradox. On the one hand, it is the role of socializers to introduce children to valued behaviors and ensure that they become competent at them so as to function effectively in society. On the other, if parents' goals are for their children to autonomously regulate these behaviors, introducing them externally and pressuring children to perform them may undermine children's engagement in these behaviors of their own accord. So how do parents socialize values and behaviors while facilitating autonomous functioning? In this chapter, we use a Self-Determination Theory (Deci & Ryan, 1985; see also Deci & Ryan, this volume) framework to understand this seeming paradox. Among the key questions we address are these: (1) What does autonomy look like in children? How do we know it when we see it? (2) How can parents facilitate autonomy while at the same time ensuring that children develop the attitudes and behaviors they need to be competent citizens? (3) Which parenting styles and behaviors are associated with children's movement toward greater autonomy?

AUTONOMY DEFINED

A first task in our foray into the paradox of socialization is to understand what autonomy is and what it isn't. To do this, we utilize Self-Determination Theory (SDT; Deci & Ryan, 1985; Ryan & Deci, 2000). From an SDT perspective, autonomy is one of three psychological needs that all people have (along with competence and relatedness). The need for autonomy involves a need to feel that one's actions are undertaken with a sense of volition rather than a sense of being coerced or pressured. Autonomous behaviors stem from one's personally endorsed values, beliefs, or decisions. Thus, when autonomous, individuals willingly engage in action without the experience of conflict or ambivalence. Because people see the action as valuable or able to move them toward personal goals, they do not feel controlled.

Within the literature there is controversy over the term autonomy. Some authors equate autonomy with independence – a lack of reliance on others. For these authors (e.g., Markus & Kitayama, 1991), autonomy is a quality that is valued and important only in Western societies. Autonomy defined in this way would not be a universal need for interdependent societies where reliance on others is emphasized (Oyserman, Coon, & Kemmelmeier, 2002). Autonomy as independence would also be problematic as a universal need for children who are, by definition, dependent on caregivers. Thus, it is important to clarify that from an SDT perspective, autonomy does not concern whether one is dependent on or independent of others but rather whether one is volitional with regard to one's behavior. For example, one can be autonomously dependent or independent with regard to others.

In addition, the need for autonomy within SDT is not a quality of a specific developmental stage, such as toddlerhood or adolescence. Within SDT, the need for autonomy is experienced across all developmental periods, albeit expressed in vastly different behaviors at different developmental phases. Thus, one can conceptualize the newborn's need to regulate the amount of stimulation during parent-child interaction as a need for autonomy. Similarly, one can conceptualize the child's need to play a role in determining when he or she studies spelling words as stemming from a need for autonomy. Thus, autonomy is a life span issue rather than a quality of a developmental period.

Autonomy can be seen in two types of behaviors. The first is in intrinsically motivated behaviors, or those that are motivated by the inherent interest or enjoyment one gets from them (Deci & Ryan, 1985). Intrinsically motivated behaviors do not have goals that are separable from the activity itself – they are undertaken because of the pleasure one gets from exercising one's abilities. In addition, autonomy can be seen in some extrinsically motivated behaviors. Extrinsically motivated behaviors are those in which individuals engage for some purpose that is separable from the activity itself. Yet these behaviors can vary in whether their goal is one that is experienced as controlled (e.g., to avoid punishment) or autonomous (i.e., stemming from personally endorsed values or beliefs). Thus, when a child practices piano because he wants to improve to qualify for a highly anticipated recital, this is an instance of autonomous regulation of behavior. Practicing may not be inherently fun, but it is moving him toward a valued goal and is thus experienced as autonomous. From an SDT perspective, children move toward greater autonomy for extrinsic behaviors through the process of internalization – the taking on of regulations into the self – which is, itself, an intrinsically motivated process. Thus, a need for autonomy underlies both intrinsically motivated and autonomously motivated extrinsic behaviors (see Deci & Ryan, this volume).

In our studies, we index intrinsically motivated behavior by looking at people's engagement in interesting activities in contexts where there are no external contingencies to do so. For example, in some studies (e.g., Grolnick, Frodi, & Bridges, 1984) we have examined factors that might undermine children's motivation to play with fun toys or puzzles on their own and without the presence of external prompts or rewards. We and our colleagues have examined the regulation of extrinsically motivated behaviors in several ways. One method is to ask children the reasons they engage in behaviors that may not be inherently interesting (Ryan & Connell, 1989). Reasons reflect several types of extrinsic motivation that vary along a continuum of autonomy and represent greater degrees of internalization. At the least self-determined end of the continuum, externally regulated activities are undertaken to obtain rewards, avoid punishments, or comply with environmentally imposed contingencies. Introjected behaviors are undertaken because of self-imposed pressures – because one would feel bad or guilty if one did not engage in them, and proud or self-aggrandized if one did. Both external and introjected regulation are nonautonomous forms of regulation since they lack a sense of volition to engage in behaviors. Instead, individuals undertake these behaviors out of a sense of pressure, which may be either self-imposed, in the case of introjected regulation, or other-imposed, in the case of external regulation. By contrast, identified regulation involves engaging in activities out of a sense of value or importance or for self-endorsed goals. This is an instance of autonomous regulation.

In addition, we have examined how children engage in various activities and tasks. For example, in one study (Leyva, Reese, Grolnick, & Price, 2008), which will be described in depth later, we examined children's engagement in a reminiscing task with an experimenter as a function of the way mothers reminisced with the child. We also look at the degree to which children use information or act consistently with guidelines in the absence of adult supervision or assistance.

Fulfillment of the need for autonomy, however, is not sufficient to ensure internalization. In addition to the need for autonomy, individuals need to experience themselves as competent or effective in interactions with the environment. In addition, from an SDT perspective, individuals have a third primary need –to feel connected or related to significant others. Thus, individuals are motivated to satisfy three needs: those for autonomy, competence, and relatedness in their interactions with their environments.

Self-Determination Theory also addresses *how* children move toward autonomy in the regulation of their behavior. SDT suggests that as part of the intrinsically motivated process of growth and development, children will naturally engage in intrinsically motivated activities and take on as their own behaviors and values presented by those around them (Deci & Ryan, 1985). However, since the process of internalization is presumed to be intrinsically motivated, they will only do so to the extent that the environment satisfies their needs for autonomy, competence, and relatedness. Thus, the context plays a key role in internalization. Specifically, the degree to which the context (1) supports autonomy by providing autonomy-supportive versus controlling behavior, (2) supports competence by providing structure, and (3) supports relatedness by providing warmth and involvement should be predictive of movement toward greater autonomy.

Autonomy support concerns the degree to which caregivers or others take children's perspectives and support their initiations and problem solving. Autonomy-supportive interventions include providing choice, encouraging initiation, and providing opportunities for children to provide input and express disagreement. On the other end of this continuum, controlling interventions pressure people toward specific outcomes. Controlling behaviors include taking the lead in interactions, solving children's problems for them, and prohibiting disagreement and discussion.

As with autonomy, there is confusion over the concept of autonomy support. To some, this would signify a hands-off approach whereby children are allowed to do whatever they want without guidance. This is not the case from an SDT perspective. Importantly, autonomy support is an active process whereby caregivers support and nurture children's volitional behavior. The issue of whether children are guided and provided boundaries and rules is captured in a second key dimension of parenting; structure.

Structure can be defined as the organization of the environment to facilitate competence. In particular, to effectively interact with the environment, individuals need to know the rules and expectations for their behavior and what will happen if they meet or do not meet these expectations. Thus, structured environments provide clear rules, expectations, and guidelines; predictable consequences for action; and feedback about how one is meeting them.

These two contextual dimensions; autonomy support and structure, are connected to dimensions in the parenting literature, namely, psychological and behavioral control (Barber, 1996; Schaefer, 1965). Psychological control is in evidence when parents or others intrude upon children's thoughts and feelings and use manipulative techniques, such as evoking guilt and withdrawing love. Behavioral control concerns parents' attempts to "regulate children" and typically includes monitoring and sometimes setting rules. However, Grolnick and Pomerantz (2009) argued that using the term "control" for these very different types of behaviors is confusing and potentially misleading. These authors suggest that the term control be reserved for actions that are pressuring and domineering. Further, Grolnick and Pomerantz (2009) suggested that the psychological versus behavioral distinction may be a false one as pressure may affect children both psychologically and behaviorally. Finally, behavioral control in many conceptualizations is not linked to children's needs and is often measured in a domain that is different from the other dimensions (e.g., autonomy support in general, monitoring during unsupervised time). Grolnick and Pomerantz (2009) suggest that making a clear distinction between two orthogonal dimensions, namely, (1) autonomy support versus control, and (2) structure, that, from an SDT perspective, are linked to children's needs (autonomy and competence, respectively) allows one to examine potential interactions within a domain. For example, one can look at the degree of structure in a home and whether this structure is implemented in a controlling or autonomy-supportive manner. This is a key part of an ongoing project (Grolnick et al., 2011a) described in detail later in the chapter.

A third social contextual dimension that meets the need for relatedness is involvement. Involvement concerns the resources provided to others – whether in the form of time, material resources, or love and affection (Grolnick & Slowiaczek, 1994). Again, involvement can be expressed in a manner that is controlling, e.g., as in the case of conditional love or parental conditional regard (Assor, Roth, & Deci, 2004), or in an autonomy-supportive manner, where time spent and warmth are noncontingent on the child's actions.

EMPIRICAL EVIDENCE – FACILITATING AUTONOMY

The empirical literature on intrinsic motivation began with studies demonstrating that when individuals received rewards for engaging in fun or interesting activities, these individuals spent less time engaging in the task when the experiment was concluded and they had a choice of activities to pursue (Deci, 1971). These results were interpreted as indicating that rewards change the motivation of the behavior from intrinsic (fun, interest) to extrinsic (to obtain the reward). This work was expanded to include other controls such as deadlines and surveillance. From these tangible controls, studies moved to considering the way individuals are treated – with pressure and coercion (i.e., control) or autonomy support. A number of studies have shown the positive effects of autonomy support in schools (e.g., Deci, Nezlek, & Sheinman, 1981; Vallerand, Fortier, & Guay, 1997), health care (e.g., Williams, 2002), work settings (e.g., Baard, Deci, & Ryan, 2004) and sports (e.g., Gillet, Vallerand, Amoura, & Valdes, 2010). This framework has been applied to parenting as well. In one such study, Grolnick, Frodi, and Bridges (1984) had parents and their one-year-olds play together. Mothers' styles of interacting with their children were coded for autonomy support versus control. In a separate session, children were introduced to fun and challenging tasks. Children whose parents were more controlling in interacting with them were less persistent in solving the problems presented by the tasks when on their own. Deci et al. (1993) reported a similar finding with 5–7 year olds; during a play session, children with mothers rated as relatively controlling showed subsequent intrinsic motivation (i.e., involvement with similar toys when given choices of several toys with which to play) that was lower than that of children whose mothers had been coded as more autonomy supportive. The evidence clearly suggests that being autonomy supportive around children's interesting and fun activities encourages their intrinsic motivation while controlling behavior can stifle it.

This chapter, however, focuses on tasks and activities that parents must introduce that are not necessarily fun or interesting. They are activities that necessitate parental guidance or assistance and which lead to important competencies that children need to function effectively in society. These can range from learning activities, to important conversations, to engagement in homework and studying. Motivating such activities is particularly challenging for parents if their goal is to have children engage in them autonomously.

In our program of research, we have addressed how parents can facilitate children's engagement in and internalization of the regulation of such activities. Though much of the work has focused on parents' interaction with their children around schoolwork and homework, we have done several studies addressing how parents interact with their children in other areas, such as chores and unsupervised time. We have also conducted studies of parents conversing with their children, and later in the chapter we review one such study of parents reminiscing with their preschoolers.

In the next part of the chapter, we provide evidence for the importance of autonomy support, structure, and involvement for children's motivation for behaviors important to parents, though not necessarily intrinsically motivated. We begin with studies that examine the three dimensions separately, and move to studies that integrate them.

In a first study examining the three dimensions of autonomy support, structure, and involvement, Grolnick and Ryan (1989) interviewed 114 parents (64 mothers and 50 fathers) of 66 children about their behavior in three domains: academics, chores, and bedtime. Parents were asked questions about how they motivated their child within the domain, how they responded to positive or negative behaviors in the domain, and whether there were rules and expectations in the domain. From the interview, coders rated the parents on three aspects of autonomy support, namely, how much the parent valued autonomy (versus compliance), whether they used autonomy-supportive motivational techniques such as setting limits and having discussions (versus controlling techniques such as rewards and threats), and whether the child was included in decision making (versus parents dictating decisions). Raters also coded the parents on three components of involvement; parents' knowledge of their child, including likes and dislikes; time spent with the child; and enjoyment of the child. Finally, there were two ratings of structure: information provided about rules and expectations, and consistency of follow through with rules and expectations.

The parenting dimensions were related to several indices of children's motivation, including their perceived competence, perceived control, self-regulation, grades, and achievement test scores. Results showed that the more autonomy supportive parents were, the more autonomously regulated children were in school (i.e., the less they did their work to avoid punishment and the more because of their own goals and values) and the higher was their school performance. Further, involvement was related to both children's perceived control and achievement. Finally, children whose parents were higher in structure felt more in control of their successes and failures in school and in general than did children of parents lower in structure. These findings held when all three parenting dimensions were examined simultaneously, showing independent effects of the three parenting dimensions.

The strong relations between parenting, especially autonomy support, and children's motivation suggest that when parents support children's autonomy, children are more likely to internalize the regulation of their own behavior. By contrast, control may keep children's regulation tied to external sources. Of course, this is a correlational study and thus the findings could easily be interpreted as child-to-parent effects (Bell, 1968). Clearly, it is easier to be autonomy supportive with a child who is taking responsibility for his or her own behavior. Thus, in our research program we felt it important to conduct laboratory studies where the direction of causality could be more clearly established. Further, in arguing for the effects of parent autonomy support on internalization, we are interested in whether children internalize the motives or information they are introduced to by their parents, as evidenced by their transferring them to new situations. Thus, we are interested in whether children engage in important activities when parents are not inducing them to do so or transfer information acquired to new settings. We now turn to laboratory studies that examine parenting on the dimension of autonomy support to control and include an outcome that is measured in a new setting in the absence of parents.

The first study examined children's learning in the context of parent-child interaction. This study involved parent-child interaction during homework-like tasks (Grolnick, Gurland, DeCourcey, & Jacob, 2002). Sixty mothers and their third grade children participated. Dyads visited the lab and mothers were given two tasks to do with their child. The first was a map task which involved learning how to give directions on a map (e.g., go south on Peach Street, cross over Grape Street). The second involved practicing and writing quatrain poems (four-line poems with a particular rhyming pattern). Parents and children were videotaped during the interaction. For each 5-second interval of interaction, parents were coded for the content of their interventions with the children as well as rated on a 5-point scale for the degree of autonomy support versus control of their behavior. Controlling behaviors were defined as those employed by the mother to change the ongoing course of the child's activity. Autonomy-supportive behaviors were those employed by the mother to help maintain the child's ongoing activity. These could be either verbal or nonverbal in form. Importantly, these ratings were always conducted considering the function of the mother's behavior, according to these definitions, with respect to the child's current behavior. Thus, the same verbalization might be coded as controlling or autonomy supportive depending on what the child was doing. If a child was stuck and asked for help and the mother said, "try looking near Grape Street," this verbalization would be considered provision of information and coded as autonomy supportive. If, on the other hand, the child was progressing well and moving on to the next item and the mother began with "try looking near Grape Street" it would be coded as a directive and thus controlling. Controlling content behaviors included giving directives, taking over, and giving answers. Autonomy-supportive interventions included providing feedback and information that the child needed. In order to examine relations between autonomy support versus control and children's learning, we asked children, after interacting with their mothers on these tasks, to solve similar problems on their own – giving directions on a map and writing a quatrain poem. We scored the accuracy of children's responses both with their mothers and on their own. In addition, using Amabile's (1983) coding system, we rated the creativity of the poems the children wrote on their own.

In examining relations between mothers' autonomy support and children's performance on their own, we felt it important to account for children's level of competence since parents are likely to be more autonomy supportive with children who are more able on the tasks (e.g., Pomerantz & Eaton, 2001). Thus, we controlled for children's grades in school as a proxy for academic competence. This was actually a conservative strategy since our coding system already took into account children's need for intervention since maternal behaviors would only be rated as controlling if they were above and beyond what children needed to succeed on the task. Partial correlations (controlling for grades) between mothers' behavior and children's performance indicated that the more nonverbal control mothers used in the dyadic interaction, the less accurate the children were on the poem task when working on their own. Conversely, the more mothers were rated autonomy supportive, the more accurate the children were. Further, the higher the mothers' verbal control during interaction, the less creative were the independently written poems. The more autonomy supportive the mother was in working with her child, the higher the creativity of the poems written by the children when on their own.

The next example involves studies of reminiscing in preschoolers (Cleveland, Reese, & Grolnick, 2007; Leyva, Reese, Grolnick, & Price, 2008). Autobiographical memory is a thriving research area focusing on the memories about oneself that an individual constructs (Fivush, 1994). These memories serve to give meaning to the self and build a sense of identity. Researchers in this area suggest that in young children these memories are socially constructed through conversations with caregivers about past events (e.g., Fivush & Fromhoff, 1988). Thus, when parents and children reminisce about past events, children build narratives about their lives that contribute to a sense of self.

Discussion of past events follows a developmental sequence, with children first only able to talk about the immediate past and unable to provide spontaneous details (Fivush & Fromhoff, 1988). Through their references to the past, parents introduce the idea of discussing the past and help their children to build narrative skills by scaffolding these conversations. Numerous studies have indicated that parents facilitate children's reminiscing by using an elaborative style (Fivush, 1994; Fivush & Fromhoff, 1988). An elaborative style includes open-ended "wh" questions such as "what," "where," and "when." An elaborative style can be contrasted with a repetitive style in which parents repeat questions and use closed ended questions. Several studies have shown that parents who reminisce with an elaborative style have children who demonstrate fuller memories in conversations both concurrently (Fivush & Fromhoff, 1988) and longitudinally (McCabe & Peterson, 1991). Particularly compelling is a study in which researchers trained parents to reminisce using an elaborative style (Peterson, Jesso, & McCabe, 1999). Two years later, children of parents who were trained displayed more memories of an event when reminiscing with an experimenter than those of parents who were not trained.

In several of these studies, a high elaborative style included both the use of "wh" questions and parents following up on children's verbalizations while a low elaborative style involved mothers dismissing children's perspectives when they did not line up with theirs. Thus, part of the elaborative style would be supporting children's autonomous contributions, while part of the repetitive style was controlling these contributions. However in these studies, following up was not separated from the use of open ended and "wh" questions, which could be conceptualized as parents setting up a framework for their children to participate in the conversation. Thus, the effects of providing a framework and the way the framework was conveyed (autonomy supportive versus controlling) could not be separated and it was not possible to decipher which aspect was facilitative of children's memory and motivation to reminisce. In a set of studies, we therefore examined separately the use of "wh" and open ended questions, conceptualized as structure, and the degree to which parents follow children's lead in these conversations and facilitate their own construction of memories, which we conceptualize as autonomy support.

In one study (Cleveland, Reese, & Grolnick, 2007), mothers and their preschoolers visited the "pretend zoo" in which an experimenter took children through a structured experience in which they had an opportunity to care for several animals and help find a baby elephant. Mothers were given a tape recorder and asked to have a conversation with their child about the pretend zoo at home that evening. Two weeks later, an experimenter visited the child's home and interviewed the child about his or her memories of the visit to the pretend zoo.

Mother-child conversations were coded for both elaborative style and for autonomy support. Each verbalization (turn) was coded for the degree to which it supported the child's autonomy or controlled his or her behavior. Autonomy-supportive vocalizations included information prompts following the child's focus or contribution, questions or prompts that helped to maintain the child's focus and helped him or her to elaborate, reflections of what the child said, and encouragement and praise to continue. Controlling ratings included the mother answering for the child without giving him or her an opportunity to respond, changing the topic or focus from what the child was talking about, and the mother giving her own version of the event.

Maternal elaborative style and autonomy support were relatively uncorrelated and predicted different aspects of children's behavior in the interview with the experimenter. In particular, the more parents displayed an elaborative style, the more memory the children displayed with the experimenter two weeks later. Thus, the elaborative style helped children to consolidate these memories. The more autonomy support parents displayed in conversing with the child, the more engaged the children were in the conversation with the experimenter. Thus, autonomy support appears to facilitate autonomous motivation to reminisce.

In a second study built on the first (Leyva, Reese, Grolnick, & Price, 2008), 61 mothers and their preschool children were visited in their homes. Mothers were asked to talk about four recent past events with their children; a shared event (mother and child were present), an unshared event (mother was not present), a good behavior, and a misbehavior. In addition, without their mothers present, children were asked by an experimenter to recount a past incident when they got injured. The experimenter provided minimal prompts to the child.

As in the previously described study, mothers' utterances were coded for elaborative style as well as the degree to which they supported versus controlled the child's autonomy. Narratives of the conversation with the experimenter about a past injury were transcribed and coded for amount of information provided by the child and the child's engagement in reminiscing.

A number of interesting findings emerged. First, there were mean differences in the degree of autonomy support provided in the four mother-child event conversations. Parents were rated as most autonomy supportive in the unshared event and most controlling in the conversations about the misbehavior. In fact, the misbehavior discussion for many parents became a lesson about what not to do rather than a reminiscing experience! We suggest that this indicates that when discussing a difficult situation like a misbehavior, parents may use this as an opportunity to teach the child or they may get invested in a way that prompts taking over. Not surprisingly, children were least engaged in these conversations. This finding is consistent with those of other studies showing that parents' high investment in an outcome, sometimes because of the high-stakes nature of the discussion, prompts controlling behavior. For example, Mauras, Grolnick, and Friendly (in press) found that mothers were more controlling in discussing sex-related topics with their young adolescent girls than in discussing an everyday topic (such as what to do during the summer). Gurland and Grolnick (2005) found that mothers who saw the world as a more threatening place were more controlling in interacting with their children than those who saw the world as less threatening. Clearly, concern and emotional investment make supporting children's autonomy more challenging.

Most relevant, however, were relations between autonomy support and children's engagement in the conversation. In all but the misbehavior event, higher maternal autonomy support was associated with higher levels of children's engagement in the conversation.. As in the Grolnick et al. (2002) study described earlier, these relations could easily be interpreted as parents' response to children, with parents of children who were more engaged in the conversation more able to provide autonomy support. Thus, relations between autonomy support in conversations with mothers and children's engagement and memory in the independent narratives with the experimenter were evaluated. Here, we also found significant relations. The more autonomy supportive mothers were in the unshared event, the more engaged the children were in discussing a past event with the experimenter. In addition, maternal elaborations during the shared and unshared events were associated with children's engagement in the independent narratives. Finally, maternal elaborations during shared conversations were associated with children's narrative recall.

The results of these three studies provide some consistent conclusions. Autonomy support appears to be associated with motivation to engage in mother-initiated activities and in positive learning. For example, Grolnick et al. (2002) showed better dyadic performance and Leyva et al. (2008) showed stronger engagement during mother-child conversations. In addition, both studies provide evidence that these effects generalize to other situations. Thus, Grolnick et al. (2002) showed that information obtained under conditions of control was less likely to be internalized and thus available for use than that presented under conditions of autonomy support. The Leyva et al. (2008) study showed that when mother-child reminiscing was more controlling, children were less active and engaged in reminiscing with an experimenter. Thus, these studies allow us to suggest that autonomy-supportive parenting leads to more autonomous regulation.

BALANCING AUTONOMY AND SOCIALIZATION GOALS – AUTONOMY SUPPORT AND STRUCTURE

Parents are most challenged by the paradox of socialization when they must help guide children in key areas of their lives that have real and serious consequences. Within these areas, parents' challenge is to ensure that children are introduced to the values inherent in these areas and the behaviors that will make them both safe and successful as they grow into adulthood. One of the ways that parents do this is by putting into place rules and expectations in the home. Thus, making sure that children are doing their schoolwork and homework is a key task for parents. Further, parents must assure the safety of their children by putting into place rules and expectations about where children can go and how they are to behave when unsupervised. However, they must do all these things keeping in mind that the ultimate goal is to have children internalize key values so that they continue the desired behaviors long after the parent has "control" over them.

The issue of how parents help children internalize the regulation of their behavior in various areas has been addressed in the literature on discipline (Grusec & Hastings, 2007). Grusec and her colleagues (e.g., Grusec & Goodnow, 1994), for example, suggest that the methods used to discipline influence its effectiveness. Their model suggests that the degree of internalization of values is dependent on both the accuracy of the child's perception of the message the parent is trying to convey as well as the child's acceptance of the message. Accuracy is influenced by the clarity, consistency, and understandability of what the parent is conveying as well as other features. Acceptance of the message, on the other hand, is influenced by whether the child feels the discipline is appropriate as well as the degree to which power assertion (i.e., physical punishment, displays of anger, disapproval, shame, and humiliation) is minimized. Threats and control should promote rejection of the parent's viewpoint and a desire to act in opposition.

We suggest that the first part of the model overlaps to a large extent with the concept of structure. Structure concerns whether the rules and expectations are clear and consistent and whether there is feedback provided.

In our conceptualization, this sets the stage for internalization because it facilitates a sense of competence, which is crucial for internalization. The second part of the model is congruent with the dimension of autonomy support versus control, although the model suggests what not to do (control, pressure) rather than what to do (i.e., support children's autonomy).

Though no previous research has examined these two aspects together, there are several studies linking power assertion to internalization. Hoffman (1960) showed that the more mothers used power assertion with children, the more those children were resistant to attempts by teachers and other children to influence them. In studies of younger children, Kochanska (1997, 2002) identified dyads with a "mutual positive orientation." In such dyads, mothers tended not to use physical or verbal power assertion and were high in perspective-taking. Such a mutual positive orientation was associated with higher levels of internalization, as assessed by children's willingness to comply with maternal prohibitions.

In order to address parents' rules and expectations about key areas and how these are linked to children's motivation, we conducted a first study (Farkas & Grolnick, 2010) in which we attempted to measure structure provided in the home. This study focused on one domain; academics. In this study, six components of structure were identified – clear and consistent rules and expectations, predictability of consequences, information feedback about how the child is doing in following the rules, opportunity to follow rules and expectations, provision of rationales for rules and expectations, and serving as an authority in the home. Seventy-five seventh and eighth grade children were interviewed about rules and expectations in the home, first with regard to homework and then grades. The interview included questions about rules and expectations their parents have for them about homework, what happens if they don't follow the rules about homework, whether parents provide information about how to do better next time if rules/expectations are not followed, whether there are things in the home that make it hard for them to follow rules and expectations about homework, and whether (and if so what) parents tell them about why they have the rules and expectations. These questions were repeated for children's grades. Children completed questionnaires about their perceived control (Skinner et al., 1990, 1998), perceived competence (Harter, 1982), and school engagement (Marchand & Skinner, 2007). Children's grades were also collected from their schools.

Interviews were coded by the interviewer and a second rater on six 7-point scales representing the six components of structure. Interrater reliabilities for the six components ranged from .83 to .99. With the exception of information feedback, the same structure components for homework and grades were correlated and thus combined. Structure components were examined separately as well as combined to form a structure composite.

Each of the structure components predicted children's motivational resources of perceived competence and control as well as their school performance. Clear and consistent guidelines showed the strongest prediction, with higher levels associated with children feeling in control of academic outcomes, their perceived competence in school, their engagement in school, and their grades. Predictability was associated with perceived competence and grades. Further, the structure composite was positively correlated with children's reports of belief in effort to control outcomes, perceived cognitive competence, academic engagement, and grades, and negatively correlated with children's maladaptive control beliefs such as in luck. Notably, the structure composite predicted perceived control, perceived competence, engagement, and grades above and beyond the effects of other parenting dimensions including involvement and autonomy support.

The results of our study suggest that structure in the home, especially clear and consistent rules and expectations and predictable consequences, may help children feel confident about and in control of their successes and failures and to perform competently. However, the results also left a number of issues unaddressed. First, SDT posits that not only must the need for competence be satisfied for children to take on the regulation of their own behavior but autonomy must be supported as well. Thus, we conducted a second study that examined, in addition to the level of structure, whether the structure was implemented in an autonomy-supportive versus controlling manner. Another issue was whether structure and its effects would differ across different domains since Farkas and Grolnick (2010) examined only the academic domain. This question is particularly pertinent to how structure is implemented, that is, in a more autonomy-supportive or controlling manner, given that the domain specificity model of social cognitive development (Turiel, 1983; Turiel & Davidson, 1986) suggests that the meaning of parents' imposition of authority may differ in different domains (Smetana, 1988; Smetana & Daddis, 2002). In particular, this model suggests that parents' and adolescents' conceptions of the legitimacy of parental authority differ according to conceptual domain (see Nucci, this volume). The theory differentiates moral issues (defined as acts that are wrong because they affect the welfare of others), conventional issues (defined as arbitrary consensually agreed upon behavioral uniformities), personal issues (acts that have consequences only to the actor), and prudential issues (pertaining to personal safety, harm to self, or health). Given hypothetical situations depicting potential parent intervention in these areas, adolescents and parents both perceived moral issues as more legitimately subject to parental authority than all other issues (Smetana & Asquith, 1994). Further, prudential issues were judged to be more legitimately subject to parental authority than personal and conventional issues, and personal issues were seen as the least legitimately subject to parental authority. Smetana and Daddis (2002) also found that children who believed that parents have less legitimate control in the personal domain rated their parents as more psychologically controlling. Thus, given the importance of children accepting the message in the Grusec and Goodnow (1994) model, we reasoned that the way rules and expectations are implemented, that is, either in a controlling versus an autonomy-supportive manner, would be most important for domains that contained more personal components (school and responsibilities) and less for unsupervised time, which concerned children's safety and well-being and thus had more prudential elements. The three domains chosen were academics (homework and studying), unsupervised time, and household responsibilities. The academic domain was chosen because academics are a central area for children and one that parents value and promote. Unsupervised time was chosen as much of the literature on dimensions related to structure (e.g., behavioral control) concerns unsupervised time and this is an emerging area of concern for parents as children transition into the tween years. A third domain was home responsibilities. Our pilot work with families suggested that a large proportion of the rules and expectations parents set (and a major source of conflict for families) centered around children completing their responsibilities. Interestingly, this is an area that has received limited research attention (Goodnow, 1988).

As indicated, in addition to adding two domains, the new study focused not only on level of structure but on the way structure was implemented, that is, in a more autonomy-supportive or controlling manner. Based on pilot work and the SDT literature, components of autonomy support were targeted in the interview and a coding system for rating interviews on the components was developed. The components included jointly established rules (i.e., whether the rules and expectations were jointly decided by the child and parent or parent dictated), open exchange (i.e., whether children could express disagreement with rules and whether parents and children engaged in dialogue about them), choice (i.e., whether parents provide choices about how children can follow the rule or expectation (not the choice of whether to follow the rule but rather when or how, for example, a child who can decide whether to clean his or her room during the week or on the weekend)), empathy (i.e., whether parents convey that they understand the child's perspective about the rules/expectations, for example, conveying understanding that the child didn't feel the rule was fair, or whether they discount the child's perspective).

Participants were 160 sixth grade students and their parents, oversampling European American, Latino, and low-income families. Children reported on their perceived control in the academic domain (Skinner et al., 1990, 1998), their perceived competence (Harter, 1982), and engagement (Marchand & Skinner, 2007). Parents completed a questionnaire assessing their perceptions of their children's competence in each domain. Structure ratings were combined to form a structure composite and autonomy support of structure ratings to form an autonomy support of structure composite.

A number of interesting findings emerged. First, consistent with Farkas and Grolnick (2010), structure around homework and studying predicted academic perceived control. In particular, children from higher structure homes reported greater perceived control over academic outcomes and lower levels of maladaptive control beliefs (i.e., believing they succeeded in school because of luck or powerful others). However, academic structure was not associated with either parents' or children's perceptions of academic competence. By contrast, autonomy support of structure was associated with all outcomes, with higher autonomy support positively related to parents' and children's perceptions of children's academic competence, academic engagement, perceptions of control, and grades.

There were similar findings within the responsibilities domain. While structure was associated with perceptions of control, autonomy support of structure positively predicted parents' perceptions of children's competence, children's reported engagement, and children's perceptions of control. Thus, similar to the academic domain, there were stronger relations between autonomy support of structure and outcomes for the responsibility domain.

Structure and the way it is implemented showed a different picture in the unsupervised time domain. In this domain, children from homes with higher levels of structure reported higher perceived competence and were more engaged in meeting expectations surrounding unsupervised time. In addition, there were positive correlations between structure during unsupervised time and children's general perceptions of control. By contrast, there was only one significant correlation between autonomy support of structure during unsupervised time and outcomes. Thus, there were stronger correlations between structure and outcomes than autonomy support of structure and outcomes in this domain.

These findings suggest some interesting conclusions about structure and the way it is implemented in various domains. As would be theoretically expected, home environments that provide children with rules, expectations, and guidelines that have consistent and predictable consequences allow children to differentiate who or what controls outcomes. Thus, it is not surprising that structure in each domain was associated with children's control perceptions.

However, the differential findings in the three domains also provide some support for the domain specificity model (Smetana, 1988). Structure was associated with competence perceptions only in the unsupervised domain. We suggest that this may be because the domain was relatively new for children. Many parents indicated that sixth grade was the first year that they were allowing their child to spend time unsupervised (whether outside playing, walking to school, or staying home alone). Thus, children may have been uncertain how to negotiate this domain, and clear rules, expectations, and consequences for action may have contributed to their feeling able in this domain. By contrast, sixth grade children have some experience with school and responsibilities. Thus, it seems that structure per se was not the factor that allowed for competence perceptions. The way that structure was implemented, that is, either in a controlling versus an autonomy-supportive manner, was most important for the academic and responsibilities domains. It appears that to feel competent or to be engaged in those two domains, children need to feel that they have ownership over what they do and feel like their behavior is volitional. This experience of volition would best be facilitated in autonomy-supportive contexts. Of course, because this was a correlational study, the findings could also be interpreted as child-to-parent effects. It may be that parents who perceive their child as being more competent, will in fact give their child more choices and allow their child to have a more active role in the implementation of structure. This interpretation is consistent with Pomerantz and Eaton's (2001) work in which parents were found to be more autonomy supportive with children who were more able on the tasks.

The way that structure was implemented may have been less important in the unsupervised domain because the adolescents judged this domain to be more legitimately subject to their parents' authority than in academics or responsibilities (Smetana & Daddis, 2002). Interestingly, we found some empirical support for this. When asked "how okay" they were with the rules and expectations in their homes, adolescents were more accepting of the rules and expectations in the unsupervised time domain than they were of the rules and expectations in the other two domains. The results thus suggest that the way structure is related to competence may depend on the domain. It is also likely that children's developmental level may play a role.

For example, when children are more accustomed to spending time unsupervised, autonomy support of structure may play a larger role in children's perceptions of competence.

One of the strengths of our structure project was its longitudinal nature. We were able to follow up with 136 of the participating families the following year when the children were in seventh grade (Grolnick et al., 2011b). Within the school district involved in our study, children transition from small elementary school classes with one teacher to large middle school classes with multiple teachers. Notably, the literature suggests that such transitions are a time of vulnerability with many (though not all) children showing declines in academic motivation and self-concept (e.g., Eccles, Wigfield, Midgley, Reuman, & Feldlaufer, 1993; Anderman & Midgley, 1997). We reasoned that the myriad of changes children experience at this transition might impact their sense of competence and control and that structure at home might help children weather the transition more effectively as it would help children to maintain a sense of connections between actions and outcomes. Further, we suggested that autonomy-supportive structure might help to buffer children from potential declines in autonomous regulation of school activities associated with the more controlling nature of middle schools (e.g., Anderman & Maehr, 1994).

Consistent with predictions, we found that higher structure at sixth grade was associated with increases (smaller declines) in perceived academic competence, intrinsic motivation, and English grades over the transition. In addition, more autonomy-supportive structure was associated with increases (smaller declines) in perceived competence, autonomous academic motivation, and grades over the transition. Further, there was some evidence that both structure and autonomy support of structure increased English grades by buffering children from declines in perceived competence over the transition. Thus, it appears that both structure and the way it is implemented are important facilitators of adjustment, particularly at the crucial transition to middle school which challenges children's need satisfaction.

CONCLUSIONS AND FUTURE DIRECTIONS

Parents have the challenging task of ensuring that their children acquire behaviors and attitudes important for successful functioning. In doing so, they must introduce these behaviors and attitudes and yet set the conditions within which the children are likely to volitionally engage in them. Our review of studies addressing children's tendency to engage in parent-initiated behaviors and skills suggests that when parents support children's autonomy – by supporting their initiations, involving them in problem solving and decisions, and taking their perspectives – they are most likely to engage in these behaviors when parents are not present and internalize information conveyed by their parents so that they can use it to solve problems on their own. In short, children will be most volitional or autonomous with regard to activities when they experience their parents as supporting their autonomy. Beyond this, however, when it comes to challenging, and often onerous, tasks, parents must also provide structure to facilitate children's sense of control and competence. Interestingly, the importance of structure and autonomy support appears to vary with domain. In areas in which parental authority is more easily accepted (e.g., unsupervised time) or which are difficult (reminiscing in young children) and which may be new or anxiety provoking (e.g., sex), it may be most crucial for parents to provide consistent structure, however it is administered, to facilitate competence in their children. However, in areas, such as doing homework and chores, in which children feel they should have more discretion, autonomy support is even more key.

Work on the interplay between structure and autonomy support has just begun and, as of yet, there are a number of unaddressed questions. First, what is the role of culture in the nature and effects of these two dimensions? A recent study with sixth graders from Ghana (Marbell & Grolnick, 2013) suggested that children's reports of parental structure were positively associated with children's competence, engagement in school, and lower levels of depression. Further, indices of parental control were negatively associated with children's adjustment. These results are quite similar to what we and others have found in Western countries (e.g., Grolnick et al., 1989; Pomerantz & Eaton, 2001). However, the results for autonomy support were more complex. In particular, children's reports of their parents "allowing them to make decisions" and "letting them do things their own way" did not factor with other autonomy support items as they do in our U.S. samples indicating that children in this interdependent, hierarchical society (Hofstede, 2001) interpreted these items quite differently from the way Western children did. In addition, parental provision of choice was not correlated with positive outcomes as in Western countries. However, two key aspects of autonomy support, valuing of the child's individuality and encouraging opinion exchange, were positively correlated with competence and autonomy outcomes. Thus, while there is evidence, consistent with that from other countries such as China (Wang, Pomerantz, & Chen, 2007), that parental control has negative effects and autonomy support positive effects on children, the meaning of autonomy support and the experience of specific practices may differ for children in different countries. Further research on how structure and autonomy support function in other cultures is clearly indicated.

A second issue concerns children's developmental level. It is certainly possible that structure and autonomy support will have a different salience or centrality for children at various developmental periods. For example, it is likely that children at younger ages will be more accepting of structure than older children within the same domain and this may have implications for the role of autonomy support. In any case, examining these issues at multiple age points will expand our understanding of these two parental resources.

Finally, it would be important to examine parents' autonomy support and structure in additional domains. Parents create rules in areas that they anticipate might create risk for their children. For example, Soenens, Vansteenkiste, and Niemiec (2009) examined parents' imposition of prohibitions around children's friendships and showed that parents' communication of prohibitions in an autonomy supportive (vs. controlling) style was related to greater internalization of parents' rules for friendships and less affiliation with deviant peers. Parents also create rules as new issues arise, for example, driving or dating for the first time. These are but two areas in which the balance of structure and autonomy support is of interest. The area is ripe for studies across cultures, domains, and ages to assist parents in helping their children become autonomous and effective members of their communities and societies.

REFERENCES

Amabile, T. (1983). *The social psychology of creativity*. New York, NY: Springer-Verlag.

Anderman, E. M., & Maehr, M. L. (1994). Motivation and schooling in the middle grades. *Review of Educational Research, 64*, 287–309.

Anderman, E. M., & Midgley, C. (1997). Changes in achievement goal orientations, perceived academic competence, and grades across the transition to middle-level schools. *Contemporary Educational Psychology, 22*, 269–298.

Assor, A., Roth, G., & Deci, E. L. (2004). The emotional costs of parents' conditional regard: A self-determination theory analysis. *Journal of Personality, 72*, 47–88.

Baard, P., Deci, E., & Ryan, R. (2004). Intrinsic need satisfaction: A motivational basis of performance and well-being in two work settings. *Journal of Applied Social Psychology, 34*, 2045–2068.

Barber, B. K. (1996). Parental psychological control: Revisiting a neglected construct. *Child Development, 67*, 3296–3319.

Bell, R. Q. (1968). A reinterpretation of the direction of effects in studies of socialization. *Psychological Review, 75*, 81–95.

Cleveland, E. S., Reese, E., & Grolnick, W. S. (2007). Children's engagement and competence in personal recollection: Effects of parents' reminiscing goals. *Journal of Experimental Child Psychology, 96*, 131–149.

Deci, E. L. (1971). Effects of externally mediated rewards on intrinsic motivation. *Journal of Personality and Social Psychology, 18*, 105–115.

Deci, E. L., Driver, R. E., Hotchkiss, L., Robbins, R. J., & Wilson, I. M. (1993). The relations of mothers' controlling vocalizations to children's intrinsic motivation. *Journal of Experimental Child Psychology, 55*, 151–162.

Deci, E. L., & Ryan, R. M. (1985). *Intrinsic motivation and self-determination in human behavior.* New York, NY: Plenum Press.

Deci, E., Nezlek, J., & Sheinman, L. (1981). Characteristics of the rewarder and intrinsic motivation of the rewardee. *Journal of Personality and Social Psychology, 40*, 1–10.

Eccles, J. S., Wigfield, A., Midgley, C. Reuman, D., Mac Iver, D., & Feldlaufer, J. (1993). Negative effects of traditional middle schools on students' motivation. *Elementary School Journal, 93*, 553–574.

Farkas, M. S., & Grolnick, W. S. (2010). Examining the components and concomitants of parental structure in the academic domain. *Motivation and Emotion, 34*, 266–279.

Fivush, R. (1994). Young children's event recall: Are memories constructed through discourse? *Consciousness and Cognition, 3*, 356–373.

Fivush, R., & Fromhoff, F. A. (1988). Style and structure in mother-child conversations about the past. *Discourse Processes, 11*, 337–355.

Gillet, N., Vallerand, R. J., Amoura, S., & Baldes, B. (2010). Influence of coaches' autonomy support on athletes' motivation and sport performance: A test of the hierarchical model of intrinsic and extrinsic motivation. *Psychology of Sport and Exercise, 11*, 155–161.

Goodnow, J. J. (1988). Children's household work: Its nature and functions. *Psychological Bulletin, 103*, 5–26.

Grolnick, W. S., Frodi, A., & Bridges, L. (1984). Maternal control style and the mastery motivation of one-year-olds. *Infant Mental Health Journal, 5*, 15–23.

Grolnick, W. S., Gurland, S. T., DeCourcey, W., & Jacob, K. (2002). Antecedents and consequences of mothers' autonomy support: An experimental investigation. *Developmental Psychology, 38*, 143–155.

Grolnick, W., & Pomerantz, E. (2009). Issues and challenges in studying parental control: Toward a new conceptualization. *Child Development Perspectives, 3*, 165–170.

Grolnick, W. S., Raftery-Helmer, J. N., Marbell, K. N., Flamm, E. S., Cardemil, E. V., & Sanchez, M. (2011a). *Parental provision of structure: Implementation, correlates, and outcomes in three domains.* Unpublished manuscript, Clark University.

Grolnick, W. S., Raftery-Helmer, J. N., Flamm, E. S., Marbell, K. M. & Cardemil, E. V. (2011b). *Parental provision of structure and the transition to middle school.* Unpublished manuscript, Clark University.

Grolnick, W. S., & Ryan, R. M. (1989). Parent styles associated with children's school-related self-regulation and competence. *Journal of Educational Psychology, 81*, 143–154.

Grolnick, W., & Slowiaczek, M. (1994). Parents' involvement in children's schooling: A multi-dimensional conceptualization and motivational model. *Child Development, 61*, 237–252.

Grusec, J., & Goodnow, J. (1994). Impact of parental discipline methods on the child's internalization of values: Reconceptualization of current points of view. *Developmental Psychology, 30*, 4–19.

Grusec, J. E., & Hastings, P. D. (Eds.) (2007). *Handbook of socialization*. New York, NY: Guilford.

Gurland, S. T., & Grolnick, W. S. (2005). Perceived threat, controlling parenting, and children's achievement orientations. *Motivation and Emotion, 29*, 103–121.

Harter, S. (1982). The perceived competence scale for children. *Child Development, 53*, 87–97.

Hoffman, M. L. (1960). Power assertion by the parent and its impact on the child. *Child Development, 31*, 129–143.

Hofstede, G. (2001). *Culture's consequences: Comparing values, behaviors, institutions, and organizations across nations* (2nd ed.). Thousand Oaks, CA: Sage.

Kochanska, G. (1997). Mutually responsive orientation between mothers and their young children: Implications for early socialization. *Child Development, 68*, 94–112.

Kochanska, G. (2002). Mutually responsive orientation between mothers and their young children: A context for the early development of conscience. *Current Directions in Psychological Science, 11*, 191–195.

Leyva, D., Reese, S., Grolnick, W. S., & Price, C. E. (2008). Elaboration and autonomy support in low-income mothers' reminiscing: Links to children's autobiographical memory. *Journal of Cognition and Development*, 9, 363–389.

Marbell, K. N., & Grolnick, W. S. (2013). The effects of parental control and autonomy support in an interdependent culture: A look at Ghanaian families. *Motivation and Emotion*, **37**, 79–92.

Marchand, G., & Skinner, E. (2007). Motivational dynamics of children's academic help- seeking and concealment. *Journal of Educational Psychology, 991*, 65–82.

Markus, H., & Kitayama, S. (1991). Culture and the self: Implications for cognition, emotion, and motivation. *Psychological Review, 98*, 224–253.

Mauras, C. E., Grolnick, W. S., & Friendly, R. W. (2013). Time for "The Talk" … Now what? The importance of structure in mother-daughter conversations about sex. *Journal of Early Adolescence*, **33**, 458–481.

McCabe, A., & Peterson, C. (1991). Getting the story: A longitudinal study of parental styles in eliciting narratives and developing narrative skill. In A. McCabe & C. Peterson (Eds.), *Developing narrative structure* (pp. 217–253). Hillsdale, NJ: Erlbaum.

Oyserman, D., Coon, H. M., & Kemmelmeier, M. (2002). Rethinking individualism and collectivism: Evaluations of theoretical assumptions and meta-analyses. *Psychological Bulletin, 128*, 3–72.

Peterson, Jesso, B., & McCabe, A. (1999). Encouraging narratives in preschoolers: An intervention study. *Journal of Child Language, 26*, 49–67.

Pomerantz, E. M., & Eaton, M. M. (2001). Maternal intrusive support in the academic context: Transactional socialization processes. *Developmental Psychology, 37*, 174–186.

Ryan, R. & Connell, J. (1989). Perceived locus of causality and internalization: Examining reasons for acting in two domains. *Journal of Personality and Social Psychology, 57*, 749–761

Ryan, R. M., & Deci, E.L. (2000). Self-determination theory and the facilitation of intrinsic motivation, social development, and well-being. *American Psychologist, 55*, 68–78.

Schaefer, E. S. (1965a). Children's reports of parental behavior: An inventory. *Child Development, 36*, 413–424.

Skinner, E. A., Wellborn, J. G., & Connell, J. P. (1990). What it takes to do well in school and whether I've got it: The role of perceived control in children's engagement and school achievement. *Journal of Educational Psychology, 82*, 22–32.

Skinner, E. A., Zimmer-Gembeck, M. J., & Connell, J. P. (1998). Individual differences and the development of perceived control. *Monographs of the Society for Research in Child Development, 63*, 1–220.

Smetana, J. G. (1988). Adolescents' and parents' conceptions of parental authority. *Child Development, 59*, 321–335.

Smetana, J. G., & Asquith, P. (1994). Adolescents' and parents' conceptions of parental authority and adolescent autonomy. *Child Development, 65*, 1147–1162.

Smetana, J. G., & Daddis, C. (2002). Domain-specific antecedents of parental psychological control and monitoring: The role of parenting beliefs and practices. *Child Development, 73*, 563–580.

Soenens, B., Vansteenkiste, M., & Niemiec, C.P. (2009). Should parental prohibition of adolescents' peer relationships be prohibited? *Personal Relationships, 16*, 507–530.

Turiel, E. (1983). *The development of social knowledge: Morality and convention.* Cambridge, UK: Cambridge University Press.

Turiel E., & Davidson, P. (1986). Heterogeneity, inconsistency, and asynchrony in the development of cognitive structures. In I. Levin (Ed.), *Stage and structure: Reopening the debate* (pp. 106–143). Norwood, NJ: Ablex.

Vallerand, R. J., Fortier, M. S., & Guay, F. (1997). Self-determination and persistence in a real-life setting: Toward a motivational model of high school dropout. *Journal of Personality and Social Psychology, 72*, 1161–1176.

Wang, Q., Pomerantz, E. M., & Chen, H. (2007). The role of parents' control in early adolescents' psychological functioning: A longitudinal investigation in the United States and China. *Child Development, 78*, 1592–1610.

Williams, G. (2002). Improving patients' health through supporting the autonomy of patients and providers. In E. L. Deci & R. M. Ryan (Eds.), *Handbook of self-determination research* (pp. 233-254). Rochester, NY: University of Rochester Press.

Chapter 8

"It's a Part of Life to Do What You Want": The Role of Personal Choice in Social Development

LARRY NUCCI
University of California

When psychologists discuss the relationship between self-regulation and socialization it is generally within a framework juxtaposing the desires and impulses of the child and the rules and norms of society (Grusec, 2011). Whether it is presented in psychoanalytic terms of the struggle between the id and the super-ego or in the more cognitive terms of recent theory of mind research focusing on deontic judgments (Lagattuta, 2005; Wellman & Miller 2008), the process of socialization is portrayed as involving the subordination of the child's desires toward compliance with social and moral norms. Beginning with Aronfreed (1968), socialization theorists have also acknowledged that children play an active role in evaluating the messages from socialization agents such as parents. From this cognitive perspective, children's evaluations of the reasonableness of parental directives form a core component of their acceptance of social norms and rules. Thus, most contemporary theorists afford the child with a degree of autonomy in the adoption of rules and norms of their immediate family and larger culture (Smetana, 2010).

As presented within self-determination theory, a key component of autonomy is the phenomenological experience of having elected to do a thing out of perceived choice (Deci & Ryan, this volume). Thus good parenting or healthy classroom management is less about exerting direct control or power over children than it is about the process of eliciting children's autonomous adoption of parental and societal standards (Grolnick & Raftery-Helmer, this volume). One reading of this work is that the goal of socialization is to get children to do what *we* adults want for *their* own reasons. Educators such as Marilyn Watson (2003) have combined this vision of childhood socialization with attachment theory and constructed an approach to classroom management known as *developmental discipline* in which the young child's emotional attachment to the teacher serves as the glue that engages the child in willingly (autonomously) adopting and internalizing the social norms and standards of the teacher. Grazyina Kochanska (2002) and her colleagues refer to this willing adoption of adult standards as "committed compliance."

What these perspectives on childhood socialization share is a view of social norms as forming a unified field. They are also concordant with the cross-cultural vision of agency offered by cultural psychology as the subjective experience of being the source of one's own actions (Geertz, 1984). A thesis that is developed in this chapter is that these are incomplete visions of personal autonomy and agency, and its relationship to social and moral development. What is missing is a theoretical and empirical account of what I refer to here as "justified" or "committed noncompliance." I am not referring here to noncompliance that arises in situations in which children or adolescents resist or disobey adult rules or commands that would result in harm to others (Perkins & Turiel, 2007), or to patterns of individual resistance to social inequalities (Nussbaum, 1999; Turiel, 2002). The focus of this chapter is upon the psychological and developmental significance of what children and adolescents define as their zone of personal discretion and privacy (Nucci, 1996). Over the past 15 years a wealth of studies have explored the extent to which children construct a conceptual framework around personal issues as distinct from matters of morality and social convention. This work has also examined the purported psychological functions served by the *personal.*

As described in previous sources (Nucci, 1981; 1996; Nucci & Turiel, 2000; Smetana, 2006), the *personal* refers to the conceptual framework individuals construct around actions and zones of decision making that they consider to be matters of individual prerogative and privacy. These are actions and choices interpreted as pertaining primarily to oneself and are therefore judged to be outside of the area of justifiable social regulation. Issues included within the *personal* are not matters of right and wrong, but of preference and choice. These would include decisions regarding one's own body, along with freedom of expression, communication, and association (Nucci, 1996). Examples of acts children and adolescents consider to be personal matters are the choice of friends; the content of personal diaries, phone calls, and letters; aspects of personal appearance; and the form of play during free time (Smetana, 2006).

Within social cognitive domain theory, concepts about personal issues are distinguished from conceptions of morality (fairness and human welfare) and social convention (consensually determined arbitrary norms for social organization) (Turiel, 1983). Understandings about personal issues are part of the *psychological domain* of conceptions about personhood, self, and identity (Nucci, 1996; Turiel, 1983). As I have argued elsewhere (Nucci, 1996), making choices about personal things allows us to create what is socially individual or unique about ourselves. It is control over the personal that serves to confirm a person's sense of agency not simply in the sense of originating one's own actions or of agreeing to parental goals, objective moral considerations, or preestablished social norms, but of having a direct hand in constructing oneself rather than being scripted by socially inherited roles and contexts. In sum, the personal is the zone of actions and social choices that permits the person to construct both a sense of the self as a unique social being and to have the subjective sense of agency and authorship that is fundamental to our sense of autonomy.

As stated, claims to a personal area co-exist with children's construction of morality and their understandings of the conventions of society. What this means at an individual level is that the boundaries of the personal are framed in relation to the person's understandings of interpersonal moral obligation and the bounds of convention and legal regulation. These dynamics provide for an ongoing dialectic throughout development and are purported to account for variations in particular content and expression of the personal (Miller, 2006; Nucci, 1996; Nucci & Turiel, 2000; Turiel, 2008).

This set of theoretical propositions leads to several implications and empirically testable hypotheses (Nucci, 1996). A basic premise of social cognitive domain theory is that distinct conceptual frameworks emerge out of efforts to account for qualitatively differing social interactions (Turiel, 1983). Extensive observational evidence in support of this proposition exists for the distinctions between morality and social convention (see Smetana, 2006, for a review). A conceptual framework purported to account for a zone of personal discretion and privacy should, therefore, be associated with patterns of childhood social interaction distinct from those associated with social conventional norms and morality.

Concepts about the *personal* are theorized to be grounded in the need to establish a sense of self, personal autonomy, and individuality (uniqueness) (Nucci, 1996). Thus, we should see evidence that individuals, including children and adolescents, link the maintenance of personal discretion and privacy to concepts about self and personhood. Establishing a personal zone of discretion and privacy serves a basic psychological function (psychological integrity). In contrast with regulation of moral or social conventional actions, individuals should display resistance to external control over the personal zone. Such resistance will be seen as "justified noncompliance." As a corollary, external constraints upon the personal, such as parental over-control or intrusion into the personal zones of children and adolescents, will be associated with psychological distress (i.e., symptoms of internalizing disorders).

The basic psychological functions served by the personal are theorized to apply to all human beings (Nucci, 1996). Thus, the basic elements of social interactions associated with the emergence of concepts about personal issues, claims to a personal area by children and acknowledgment by adults of children's needs for a personal zone, and the effects of external control on psychological well-being will be evidenced among individuals across cultures. Finally, the psychological requirements of the need for a zone of personal discretion and privacy will inform moral concepts of rights as personal freedoms (Nucci, 1996, 2000). Thus, the construction of a conceptual framework about the personal will be fundamental to the construction of a moral system that incorporates notions of rights (Helwig, 2006). As in the case of domain interactions between morality and convention (see Turiel, 1983, 2008), moral judgments will interact with matters of personal choice in some social contexts. Developmental changes in concepts within each domain will also impact the nature of social judgments in the context of those interactions. Additionally, development will be expected to impact the capacity of individuals to coordinate elements across domains.

The remainder of this chapter addresses these claims through findings from recent studies. This discussion builds from and extends an earlier exploration of these proposals (Nucci, 1996). This chapter will not reiterate in detail aspects of propositions that were fully addressed in that earlier piece. Instead the reader will be directed to it in those instances. In the process, the discussion will examine the more general issue of individual autonomy and the phenomenon of "committed noncompliance" in the course of children's socialization and moral development. The chapter concludes with a discussion of findings emerging from an ongoing study exploring the relationships between personal choice and moral judgments in context.

PARENT-CHILD INTERACTIONS AND CHILDREN'S NONCOMPLIANCE

A good place to begin is with a recent study that looked directly at young children's predictions of when children would comply and when they would resist maternal rules (Lagattuta, Nucci, & Bosacki, 2010). The study was done using Kristin Lagattuta's (2005) strategy for exploring young children's theory of mind applied to deontic judgments about social rules. Lagattuta has been interested in developmental changes in young children's predictions about hypothetical children's compliance with maternal moral rules, and predictions children make regarding the feelings associated with compliance or noncompliance. What she has found through a series of well-crafted studies is a shift from 4 to 7 years of age in children's predictions of compliance (Lagattuta, 2005, 2008). Older children are more likely to predict that a child would comply with a mother's moral rule than 4-year-olds. In addition, 7-year-olds are more likely than the 4-year-olds to predict that the child will feel good about compliance and bad about noncompliance with a maternal moral rule. Lagattuta (2005, 2008) has interpreted her results as evidence that between the ages of 4 and 7 years, young children subordinate their desires in favor of compliance with maternal moral rules, and that their reading of the mental states of others leads to predictions in line with those developmental trends. These findings are in line with the proposition that early childhood development is associated with children's increased committed compliance to moral norms.

In a subsequent study, Lagattuta and colleagues (2010) explored the predictions that children would make when mothers imposed a rule governing an action in the personal domain. More specifically, the study investigated children's predictions about compliance to maternal rules prohibiting engagement in personal activities or choices that were connected with the child's identity and sense of self. The procedure entailed providing children with hypothetical scenarios through line drawings depicting children engaged in actions that the mother then made a rule against. Personal domain actions included choices of friends, play activities, and clothing. These were presented in two conditions varying the centrality of the action to the child's self. Following the work of Gelman (2004), one condition presented the actions as essential elements of self, the other condition as general personal choices. For example, one of the personal scenarios depicts a girl named Gloria who likes to paint but also enjoys doing other things. The "essential personal" condition depicted the same child in the following way: "This is Gloria. Gloria likes to paint pictures. She paints pictures almost everyday. In fact, Gloria thinks of herself as 'Gloria the painter.' Gloria, the painter thinks she paints great pictures and that makes her feel happy about herself."

To determine whether any resistance to the mother's rule was simply a function of the high desirability of the personal actions, a third condition was added in which the child needed to engage in a moral transgression involving stealing or harm to another child in order to be able to achieve the *essential personal* domain action. Following the presentation of each story the child was asked to make a prediction about the story-child's behavior and her attendant feelings.

Findings for the moral situations in which the story-child must either steal from or harm the other child in order to engage in the desired activity were consistent with prior studies using moral stimuli. As the children increased in age from 4 to 7 years old, they were more likely to predict compliance with the maternal rule against the immoral action (stealing or hitting), and were also more likely with age to predict that the child in the story would be happy if she or he did comply and would feel negative emotions if the child disobeyed the mother's rule and engaged in the moral transgression. In addition, the children provided justifications for their predictions that were consistent with the moral nature of the transgressions. That is to say, their justifications focused upon the unfairness of the actions or harm that was caused as illustrated in the following examples of statements from the children in the study:

> *It wouldn't be very nice to take somebody else's clothes and just leave, because they're the other person's.*
>
> *Because if he hits the other boy, that would be really mean, and maybe hurt the other boy's feelings.*

In contrast with the findings from the moral scenarios there were no age-related changes in children's predictions about compliance with maternal rules to refrain from engagement in the behaviors that were personal matters and described activities central to the child's sense of self (essential personal). From ages 4 to 7 years, the children predicted greater levels of noncompliance to mothers' directives about these personal behaviors than they did to moral transgressions that would have allowed the children in the stories to engage in those same essential personal activities. Moreover, the children across ages predicted that the children in the stories would feel *good* about noncompliance, and would feel *bad* if they obeyed the mother's rule prohibiting the personal behavior. Predictions about peripheral personal behaviors were intermediate between the essential personal and moral, but also did not show a significant shift in compliance with age. As anticipated by the study's authors, the justifications that accompanied the predictions of noncompliance for maternal rules governing essential personal actions focused upon the impact of compliance upon the story-child's identity. This is illustrated in the following statement by a 5-year-old girl in the study: "Sue is her best friend, and it would really change her if she can't play with her [Sue]."

This set of findings from Lagattuta and colleagues (2010) provides evidence that young children have intuitions about the connection between control over a personal domain of actions and their sense of self and personal identity. It was the *essential personal* items that were associated with the most resistance to maternal regulation. That resistance was not supported by narcissistic arguments about appetitive desires and did not lead to an endorsement of moral transgressions that would yield the desired results. Instead, these young children connected their resistance to maternal rules to their goals of maintaining personhood and a particular identity. Other earlier work with older children had established that children can articulate this connection beginning in middle childhood, and that justifications for control over personal issues is associated with shifts in children's and adolescents' conceptions of selfhood and identity (Nucci, 1996).

Lagattuta and colleagues' (2010) study demonstrated that young children are able to articulate a psychological justification for noncompliance around personal issues. We see evidence in this study that children at very young ages are constructing a generalized view about personal actions as ones that should not be regulated. As a result, these young children make the predictions that children in general will not comply with such parental rules and are justified in their noncompliance. Findings from an earlier observational study with young children and their mothers (Nucci & Weber, 1995) provided evidence that these predictions offered by children of noncompliance around personal domain activities correspond to actual social interactions in the home. In this study (Nucci & Weber, 1995), extensive in-home observations were made of the interactions between working and middle-class White mothers and their 4-year-old children. Using social cognitive domain theory criteria, these mother-child interactions were coded into ones that focused upon issues of morality, social convention, prudential considerations, and personal issues. What was found is that the nature of the discourse shifts as a function of the domain of the interactions. With regard to personal issues, there were three distinctive interaction patterns. In the least common pattern, mothers explicitly labeled certain things as simply up to the child as in this mother's statement: "If you want, we can get your hair cut. It's your choice." About half of the time, however, the discourse around personal issues was more indirect and the mother tacitly conveyed the notion that the issue was a personal matter as in the following question posed by a mother to her daughter: "Have you decided what to wear today?" These first two discourse patterns indicate that working and middle-class American mothers overtly convey to children that there are areas of activity that are within the children's discretion. However, the idea that the personal domain is entirely defined for children by parents is belied by the finding that over one-fifth of the social interactions about personal issues involved resistance from the child and negotiation with the mother. What is also significant for the present discussion is that virtually all of the resistance to mothers was in the context of actions that the researchers had blind-coded as personal matters. Children objected to and resisted maternal rules or directives over personal issues (e.g., to wear a particular shirt rather than the one that the child had picked out) in roughly 90% of the observed incidents. In contrast, these very same children complied with 80% of maternal directives in response to children's transgressions of social conventions (e.g., table manners), and complied in 90% of the incidents involving a moral transgression (e.g., taking away a toy from a sibling).

This last observational study along with interview and survey research done with mothers indicates that middle-class mothers are generally sensitive to their children's needs for an area of personal discretion (Nucci & Smetana, 1996; Smetana, 2010). In the study referencing the youngest children, Smetana, Kochanska, and Chuang (2000) reported that American mothers begin to refer to justifications for allowing children personal discretion based on children's psychological needs for autonomy once children reach about 2 years of age. This would suggest that mothers who successfully engage children's committed compliance do so on the basis of justifications matching their children's social conceptual frameworks, and by acknowledging a sphere of personal discretion as important for autonomy.

IS THE PERSONAL A WESTERN PHENOMENON?

The studies reviewed up to this point have all involved children in North America. However, there is accumulating evidence from more than 20 published studies in support of a personal "domain" among children and adolescents in other countries and cultures. These include studies with children and adolescents in Latin America (Ardila-Rey & Killen, 2001; Darling, Cumsille, Pena-Alampay, & Coatsworth, 2009; Lins-Dyer & Nucci, 2007; Milnitsky-Sapiro, Turiel, & Nucci, 2006; Nucci, Camino, & Sapiro, 1996) and Asia (Darling, Cumsille, & Pen-Alampay, 2005; Hasebe, Nucci, & Nucci, 2004; Helwig, Yang, Nucci, Yun, & To, 2009; Nucci, Smetana, Araki, Nakaue, & Comer, 2012; Yau & Smetana, 1996, 2003; Yamada, 2004, 2009). To a surprising degree the results of these studies report similar dynamics both in terms of mother-child relations in early development and in the general trend toward an expansion in adolescence of issues considered to be personal matters as reported by Smetana and her colleagues (Smetana, 2011).

These cross-cultural studies have also detected a set of general trends in which parents and children in rural and lower-class families report somewhat higher levels of parental control than in urban and middle-class settings (e.g., Nucci et al., 1996). What is interesting is that higher levels of parental control have not translated into an across-the-board trend of greater acceptance of parental control over the personal area by rural and lower-class adolescents. For example, a study exploring mother-daughter relations in northeastern Brazil found that lower and middle-class daughters did not differ in their expectations over who should control or decide about their personal zones of activity (Lins-Dyer & Nucci, 2007). However, lower-class adolescent girls reported experiencing higher levels of control by their mothers and of engaging in higher rates of mother-daughter conflict than did their middle-class counterparts. Darling and her colleagues (2005) reported a similar phenomenon of social-class related levels of adolescent-parent conflict among adolescents in the Philippines. These findings challenge cultural psychology assumptions that social development is a steady process of children adopting and internalizing the social values of the adult culture (Shweder, Mahapatra, & Miller, 1987). More important for our discussion here is the finding of a general cross-national pattern of children's acceptance of parental rules around issues of morality, convention, and personal safety, and resistance or noncompliance around issues that children and adolescents interpret to be within their personal domain. As noted, these general patterns have held across social class and region.

This is not to say that there are no cultural variations in the content and scope of what gets included within the personal zones of individuals. Cultures differ in the extent to which particular forms of personal expression and behavior are up to the individual and which fall within the confines of the conventions of society (Miller, 2006). The field of developmental psychology, however, has moved away from the notion that the world's cultures can be divided up into those that are individualistic and rights-based (primarily Western), and those that are collectivist and duty-based (non-Western) (Shweder et al., 1987; Triandis, 1989) and presumably without room for a personal zone of privacy and personal choice. A comprehensive meta-analysis of the literature found no consistent associations between the individualism-collectivism dichotomy and culture (Oyserman, Coon, & Kemmelmeier, 2002). Indeed, the more accurate picture of cultures is that they are complex and heterogeneous with respect to the expression of individual and collectivist orientations (Turiel, 2008). Moreover, some of the original proponents of the distinction between individualist and collectivist societies have taken the position that a zone of personal choice is maintained by individuals across cultures (J. G. Miller, personal communication, March 21, 2011; Miller et al., 2011).

THE PERSONAL AND PSYCHOLOGICAL WELL-BEING

The implication of the cross-national findings just described is that the identification of a personal zone of privacy and discretion serves a fundamental psychological function (Nucci, 1996). We have attempted to explore this hypothesis by examining the impact of perceived parental control upon the psychological well-being of adolescents. The basic premise of this research was that if the establishment of the *personal* is an essential element in the construction of personhood and a sense of personal identity, then disruptions or impediments to this process would have negative psychological consequences. It has also been well-established that parental over-control is associated with internalizing disorders such as anxiety and depression among adolescents (Dornbusch, Carlsmith, Bushwall, Ritter, Leiderman et al., 1985). It was our hypothesis that the negative impact of parental control is not the result of a generalized across-the-board exertion of control but is limited to the over-exertion of control and parental interference in the personal. Put another way, parental control exerted in relation to moral, conventional, and safety norms should be associated with normative development whereas perceived parental control over personal issues would result in an increased likelihood of expression of internalizing disorders.

The first study led by Yuki Hasebe (Hasebe et al., 2004) involved 170 suburban middle-class Midwestern American adolescents between the ages of 14 and 16 years and 125 adolescents from a Japanese high school in a middle-class community located in a semi-rural town. These adolescents responded to a survey that asked them to indicate on a 5-point scale who they thought should control or decide a number of behaviors, including prudential, conventional, and personal items along with items that comprised an overlap between personal and either conventional or prudential considerations. In the second version, subjects responded to the same items but indicated who in their own situations, in their perceptions, actually does or *would* control the behavior. Each participant also filled out the Brief Symptom Inventory, which is a checklist of symptoms asking for self-reports of feeling or being distressed by each symptom within the past seven days from *Not at all* to *Extremely*.

We found that adolescent perceptions of idealized control, who they thought should control their behaviors, was not associated with self-reports of psychological symptoms in either country. However, there was a positive correlation between perceptions of control over personal issues and self-reports of symptoms indicative of internalizing disorders such as anxiety, depression, and somatization for adolescents in both countries. For the Japanese, there was also a significant positive correlation between perceived parental control of overlapping domain issues and internalizing disorders. There was no significant relationship between parental control over conventional and prudential issues and self-reports of internalizing disorders in either country.

These findings were recently replicated in a study with urban and rural adolescents in mainland China (Helwig et al., 2009). The study involved 318 high school students from the city of Guangzhou and a rural village in the northern region of Guandong province. The research followed the same general procedure as in the study conducted in Japan with some modifications only to specific items to make them suitable for use in China. When these Chinese adolescents were asked to indicate who should control or decide about their behaviors or associations they claimed greater control over items describing personal issues such as friendship choices and matters of privacy such as control over who would read their diary, and granted parents relatively higher levels of control over the conventional and prudential items. These researchers also found that adolescents in the rural areas tended to cede greater authority to parents over conventional and prudential activities than did the urban adolescents, but did not differ in their claims to control over the personal.

The analyses of the relations between perceived parental control and the adolescents' self-reports of internalizing disorders followed a pattern quite similar to what we had observed in Japan (Hasebe et al., 2004). There were no associations between perceived parental control over prudential and conventional issues and psychological symptoms, but significant correlations between parental control over personal issues and self-reports of internalizing disorders. This held for both the urban and rural samples. One surprising finding from this study is the impact of gender on these correlations. The observed correlations between control over the personal and internalizing disorders were considerably higher for the boys, especially those in the urban setting where the correlation for adolescent males was nearly double that observed with females and considerably higher than correlations obtained with Japanese and American samples. A definitive answer for these gender effects will await additional research.

The findings from China (Helwig et al., 2009) stand as powerful evidence that the construction of a personal area of discretion and privacy is a fundamental element of human development and not simply the outcome of Western liberal ideology. However, the outcomes regarding gender also caution against any interpretation that would discount cultural and social-contextual factors in the ways in which these dynamics play out in individual development. Judith Smetana's (2010) work with middle-class African American adolescents and families has shown that the ages at which parents cede control over overlapping issues that contain both personal elements of choice and privacy and prudential elements of safety – such as how late a teenage child can stay out on a weekend night, or how far a teen can venture from home – differ from and are later than the ages that middle-class White parents allow their teenage children to handle such decisions. When middle-class White parents continue to control such behavioral choices to the ages at which African American parents modally allow their children control, the White American adolescents self-report higher levels of depression than their peers. Conversely, when African American parents cede control to their teens at the younger ages modal for White middle-class teens, the African American adolescents report higher levels of internalizing disorders and higher rates of engagement in at-risk behaviors than when parents delay such freedoms.

THE PERSONAL AND THE MORAL

The argument that has been laid out thus far is that children and adolescents stake claim to a personal zone of privacy and choice that is critical to their construction of personal identity and sense of themselves as having personal agency. There is emerging evidence as described that establishing this personal zone is a fundamental aspect of development that will receive expression cross-culturally, and that its suppression will result in psychological consequences for the individual. This section explores the link between the construction of concepts about the personal sphere and moral development and moral judgment. What has been argued in the past is that these experiences of laying claim to a personal domain, and the interactions children and adolescents have around these claims provide the psychological experiential information that leads to the generation of a rights component of morality as freedoms (Nucci, 1996, 2000). Children's and adolescents' concepts about personal issues, and their understandings of the psychological function served by control over the personal, are not an aspect of moral reasoning. They constitute a distinct conceptual framework within the *psychological domain* of social cognitive development (Nucci, 1977, 1996; Turiel, 1983). The connection to morality is through the role that these psychological concepts and underlying social experiences have for the generation of children's privacy, expression, association, and similar moral conceptions of rights as freedoms (Dworkin, 1978; Helwig, 2006; Nucci, 2000). Thus, moral development is not simply about children's committed compliance to social and moral rules but is also dependent upon their committed noncompliance in this personal sphere.

It has long been recognized that rights claims can be conflated with the language of privilege (Turiel, 2008) and the language of choice as self-determination (Shweder et al., 1987). Turiel and Wainryb (2000) and others (Neff, 2001) have elegantly shown how cultural hierarchy in gendered societies can lead men to use the language of rights in reference to their privileged status in relation to women. Claims to personal freedom as unfettered choice have also been over-applied in ideological visions of individuality. One of the most egregious examples illustrating this over-application of rights comes from the writings of the political libertarian, Ayn Rand (1943). Rand's ideology maintained that morality is defined through "bold" pursuit of self-interest and a complete disregard for social convention (Burns, 2009). An excellent and broadly familiar example of this overextension of personal choice is captured by the self–interested and exploitive nature of the main character Howard Roark in Rand's (1943) most famous book, the "Fountainhead." This well-known character was presaged by a male figure appearing in a much earlier play called "Night of January 16th." According to Rand's biographer, Jennifer Burns (2009), the main character of the play, Bjorn Faulkner, was intended by Rand to embody heroic individualism through his penchant to disregard all of society's rules and moral restrictions. In the play, Faulkner rapes his secretary on her first day of work. Thereupon, she falls immediately in love with him and becomes his eventual business partner. The two of them then proceed to engage in unscrupulous business practices that would have made the now bankrupt Wall Street firm, Lehman Brothers, proud.

Fortunately, children are not blinded by political ideology, and their concepts of personal privacy and zones of behavioral freedom co-exist with moral conceptions of justice and human welfare. This chapter closes with a discussion of some of the ways in which children's and adolescents' concepts about personal choice intersect with their concepts of morality. In the study discussed next, children and adolescents were asked in some instances to weigh personal self-interest against the needs of others and to determine when they have a right to engage in a given behavioral choice. Readers interested in a related discussion of the research on children's moral concepts of rights should consult Helwig (2006).

NEW RESEARCH ON MORAL REASONING

The discussion that follows comes from a recently completed study of moral development conducted with Elliot Turiel for which the data analyses are still ongoing. Thus, the findings presented here are preliminary. In this study we explored age-related changes in reasoning about three basic moral issues: direct harm in the form of hitting; indirect harm stemming from whether to return money that the story protagonist sees someone lose; and helping. Each of these three basic situations was presented within three conditions. In the *unconflicted* situations the protagonist must make a moral decision without any obvious personal needs or the needs of any third party coming into play. There were two conflict conditions. In the *conflicted-self* condition the story protagonist has personal needs or wants that are in conflict with causing harm or providing help to another person. In the *conflicted-other* condition the moral choice of whether to cause harm or help someone is in conflict with the needs of a third party. Finally, these basic situations were varied in terms of the characteristics of the person who is the object of the moral decision: a generic other, a vulnerable other, or an antagonistic other. The other child was described simply as a "girl" or "boy," or as someone who had antagonized the child the previous day by teasing and making fun of him or her, or as a vulnerable child who falls or drops money because of a handicapping condition or engages in hitting because of an inability to control emotions. These characteristics of the other were intended to impact the degree of empathy for the other child in the moral conflict situations. Participants in the study were in four age groups: early elementary (7–8 years), middle elementary (10–11 years), middle school (13–14 years), and high school (16–17 years). Children were heterogeneous in terms of race and ethnicity and were drawn from urban and suburban settings in two regions of the country.

Patterns of moral reasoning. Three basic findings are emerging from this study. The first is that there are general age-related changes in moral reasoning that take place over the 9-year age span investigated in this research. Each pattern reflects a shift in the ways that individuals address the various (sometimes competing) elements of a given moral situation. The pattern we have labeled *Simple/Straightforward* is one in which evaluation of the right or wrong of an action is based on the most salient moral elements of harm or welfare presented in the situation. The decisions made using this pattern appear nonwavering and unambiguous. Individuals may recognize or mention other elements, or they can recognize other elements if these are brought to their attention. However, these elements are not incorporated into the moral decision process. Reasoning we have labeled *Uncoordinated/Conflicted* is characterized by attention to competing elements of a moral situation, and an appreciation of moral ambiguity, but without resolution or evidence of coordinating the moral and nonmoral concerns in a systematic, generalized, and consistent way. This reasoning is manifested by inconsistency and ambivalence that sometimes results in the altering of a moral principle to fit the situation, or a reading of moral ambiguity as allowing for selection of an action that fits the needs and desires of the actor. In contrast, *Coordinated* reasoning, which is the third form that emerged from our data, is characterized by consideration and weighing of multiple (moral and nonmoral) aspects or concerns with a clear resolution. Individuals who employ *Coordinated* reasoning will often demonstrate an awareness of moral ambiguity and the arguments that can be made for acting in self-interest in such situations. However, they engage in reasoning that leads to a resolution of moral ambiguity and the integration of nonmoral concerns in a consistent and systematic way. As discussed later, these patterns of reasoning are strongly associated with moral decision making, with the *Straightforward* and *Coordinated* forms generally associated with decisions that prioritize morality and the *Uncoordinated/Conflicted* pattern resulting in less consistency in the direction of moral choice.

The second basic finding from our study is that the age of emergence or expression of the forms of reasoning uncovered in this research is impacted by context. More complex moral situations tend to generate more complex forms of moral reasoning, and the ages at which individuals demonstrate complex moral reasoning is impacted by the salience of the moral issue or action. The third finding, related to the previous one, is that many of the moral situations depicted in this research did not generate or seem to require moral reasoning beyond the most basic form evidenced by our youngest participants. Another way of putting this is that for many moral situations investigated in this study, there were no age-related changes either in the judgment of the right thing to do or in the reasoning employed to sustain that judgment.

Age-related findings and illustrative examples. Following is a sampling of the findings from the situations used in the study that illustrate the general developmental patterns obtained in our results. Because of the complexity of the study, this discussion focuses on outcomes from the hitting and indirect stealing (returning the money) scenarios. We begin by referencing the findings regarding direct harm as they present the most straightforward moral situations. The direct harm scenarios all revolved around the act of hitting another person. In the unconflicted scenarios the protagonist was described as being in a bad mood and hitting another child without provocation. In these direct harm situations, virtually all respondents across ages indicated that the protagonist in the *Unconflicted* situation would be wrong to engage in hitting, and that the protagonist would have no right to engage in the behavior. In generating these judgments, 90% to 100% of participants across ages employed *Straightforward* reasoning invariably focusing upon the harm that the hitting would cause. These outcomes regarding judgments of wrongness are not surprising given that a 3-year-old would treat unprovoked hitting as wrong (Smetana & Braeges, 1990). What is interesting in terms theories of moral development is that there were no age shifts in the forms of moral reasoning employed to generate these decisions. Virtually all of the participants employed the least complex reasoning to justify their decisions. This situation is the moral analogy to solving the math problem of how much is 2 plus 2.

Findings from the indirect stealing situation, however, were quite different. In this situation a child is described as boarding an empty bus. Soon afterward a second person boards the bus and drops $10 while reaching for the money to pay the bus fare. Neither the driver nor the passenger is aware of the $10 bill on the floor. The protagonist has to decide whether to tell the passenger that he or she dropped the money or keep silent and pick up the bill and keep it. If we examine these two situations we can see that they contain different elements with respect to their moral implications. In the case of hitting, the harm is a direct consequence of the action. The moral evaluation would involve drawing inferences and conclusions directly from experiences surrounding the harm caused by the act. In the case of not returning the money, the harm can be viewed as both indirect and as involving a number of potentially complicating factors. Among these are the following considerations. Theft is involved whenever one person knowingly acquires the property of another without the other person's permission. A case of direct theft would be to place your hand in someone else's pocket and take money from it. In this case, the protagonist is aware that the $10 bill that was dropped was the property of the person who dropped it. The protagonist is also aware that the person who dropped the money has not given permission for anyone else to take it and keep it. So, to not tell the person who dropped the money and to pick it up and keep it is a case of theft. On the other hand, the protagonist did not actively cause the money to fall from the other person's pocket. In addition, if the protagonist had not been on the scene, and the protagonist would therefore not have seen that the other child dropped the $10 bill, it would have been lost. Moreover, if the protagonist had been walking along a street and had seen a $10 bill he would have been within his rights to keep it. Thus, given the nature of this situation, there is some potential for moral ambiguity that does not exist in the case of direct theft.

Table 8.1 summarizes the forms of reasoning produced by children at different ages when responding to the scenarios involving a generalized other child. If we look first at the reasoning produced by the 8-year-olds, we see that it is predominantly in the form of straightforward judgments based on the salient moral features of the situation. The youngest children did not refer to the ambiguous aspects of this scenario and read it as a clear-cut case of stealing. In essence, for an 8-year-old, there is no moral difference between indirect and direct theft. As children get older, however, there is

TABLE 8.1 *Percentage of Reasoning Pattern by Age and Context: Reasoning About Returning Money – (Unconflicted)*

	Simple	**Uncoordinated**	**Coordinated**
8 years	94	6	0
11 years	86	14	0
14 years	73	27	0
17 years	56	12	31

Reasoning About Returning Money – (Conflicted With Needs of Self)

	Simple	**Uncoordinated**	**Coordinated**
8 years	100	0	0
11 years	87	13	0
14 years	58	33	9
17 years	7	7	86

Reasoning About Returning Money – (Conflicted With Needs of Another)

	Simple	**Uncoordinated**	**Coordinated**
8 years	92	8	0
11 years	75	25	0
14 years	45	36	18
17 years	13	33	53

evidence that they take into account the elements of this situation that differentiate it from a simple case of direct theft, but without coordination. This is particularly the case with the 14-year-olds. A third of their reasoning was categorized as Uncoordinated. Finally, the oldest adolescents in our study provided Coordinated reasoning in which the ambiguous aspects of the "indirect" stealing situation are recognized and resolved. The use of the more complex forms of reasoning are more evident in the two conflict situations where the moral decision requires weighing the needs of the self or of a friend against returning the $10 to its owner. These results provide evidence for the confluence of development and context on moral judgment.

Our findings with regard to reasoning were mirrored in the judgments that our study participants made regarding whether it would be wrong or right for the story protagonist to keep the money. What we observed was a U-shaped curve in which the decisions made by the 8-year-olds and 17-year-olds were similar and overwhelmingly in support of the evaluation that it would be wrong to keep the money, while the 10- to 14-year-olds were more likely to endorse keeping the money. These differences in moral thinking are illustrated in the following interview excerpts. The following excerpts from an 8-year-old boy and girl nicely illustrate what we labeled Straightforward reasoning.

> *Would it be wrong or all right for (protagonist) to keep the money instead of giving it back to the other girl/boy?*
>
> GIRL: No, because it's someone else's $10 bill, she shouldn't keep it because it's not hers.
>
> BOY: He's stealing, and you don't want to, it's not good to steal.

For an 8-year-old, the situation poses little ambiguity and is responded to in the same way as if the protagonist had put his hand into the person's pocket and taken the money. For a 14-year-old, however, the situation is much more complex:

> GIRL: … he's not doing anything wrong. He's not necessarily doing something wrong, but the right thing to do would be to give it back, but he's not necessarily, he doesn't necessarily have any wrongdoing.
>
> BOY: He's got every right to keep the $10, like I said, because it's in nowhere land. And it's his, he found it. It's not in the kid's house or anything.

What can be seen in these excerpts and especially in the statements from the budding female attorney is the inconsistency and ambivalence that can result in the altering of a moral principle to fit the situation, or the reading of moral ambiguity allowing for selection of an action that fits the needs and desires of the actor. By the age of 16 to 17 years, the majority of adolescents in the study had resolved the ambiguity of the situation as entailing a form of theft. This can be seen in the following excerpt. One interesting thing to note in the statements of this 17-year-old is the recognition of the arguments from the younger participants, such as the 14-year-olds quoted earlier.

> GIRL: Well, in reality, would it be all right or not all right? You should always give the money back. But, I can understand the thought process for not giving the money back. Well in reality, if something, I don't know how to say that, if someone loses money, it's theirs and if you know that, she should give it back. But, if you just saw $10 on the street and you have no idea who it belongs to, keep it, but if you know who it belongs to, it's your duty to give it back. But I can understand the thought process.

Conflating rights and personal choice. The U-shaped developmental trends described became readily apparent when the children were asked to judge whether the protagonist would have a right to keep the money if that is what she or he wanted to do. Figure 8.1 presents the proportions of participants at each age who argued that you would have a "right" to keep the money. As can be seen in Figure 8.1, young children generally stated that the protagonist would *not* have a right to keep the money. More than half of the 14-year-olds, however, were of the opinion that one would have a "right" to keep the money. By 16 to 17 years, the vast majority of respondents again took the position that one would not have a right to keep the money.

A position developed early in this chapter is that claims to a personal domain are integral to the construction of moral concepts about rights (Nucci, 1996). Any notion of rights, however, is also delimited by moral considerations regarding the rights and welfare of others (Dworkin, 1978; Helwig, 2006; Nucci, 2000). The references to rights made by the adolescents in our study, who also exhibited uncoordinated moral reasoning, appeared to conflate an agent's capacity to elect to act on a personal choice with the right to engage in that action. The following excerpts from the statements provided by 14-year-old participants discussing whether to keep the money or whether to help someone in need nicely illustrate the conflation of personal choice with "rights."

> BOY: I think she has a right to do what she wants to. Because it is once again, his decision to do what he wants.
>
> GIRL: He has the right to do anything he doesn't want to, so like, if he didn't want to help he didn't have to help.
>
> BOY: It's his choice. It is a free country.

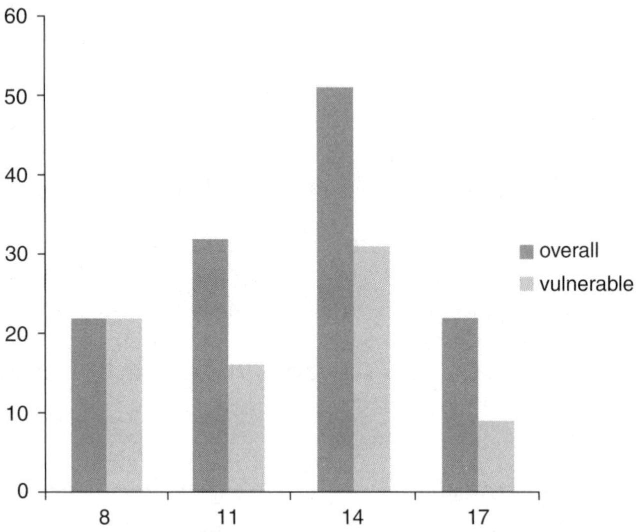

FIGURE 8.1 Percentage at each age saying would have a right to steal "overall" and from a vulnerable other child.

It is important to point out that the reasoning of these early adolescents should not be characterized as operating solely from self-interest or instrumentalism as depicted in Kohlberg's (1984) proposed second stage of his global stage theory. For one thing, nearly all of these same adolescents did not maintain that one would have a right to engage in unprovoked hitting of another person even if the protagonist in the scenario was described as wanting to engage in the action. Second, as can be seen in Figure 8.1, the decisions to keep the money were quite different when the other person in the situation was described as vulnerable. In this context, less than one-third of the 14-year-olds provided uncoordinated reasoning in response to the rights question, and two-thirds of them rejected the notion that the protagonist would have a right to keep the money dropped by a handicapped person. That is, once the salience of the moral elements of a situation are elevated and situational ambiguity minimized as in the case of unprovoked harm, or keeping the money dropped by a handicapped person, the appeal to personal choice and rights was diminished.

CONCLUSIONS

The main thesis of this chapter is that agency is not reducible to a subjective sense of being the source of one's decisions. It includes establishing a personal zone of behavioral choice and privacy. This aspect of children's social development is critical to the construction of identity and personhood, and constitutes a fundamental category of social knowledge (Nucci, 1996). What we have learned from the past decade-and-a-half of research is that individuals across cultures establish a personal zone, and that parental suppression or over-involvement in the personal and private areas of their adolescent children has negative consequences for their psychological well-being. We have also learned that children and adolescents actively pursue control over this zone of privacy and personal choice, and that their resistance to external authority is often systematically associated with children's and adolescents' interpretations of their disputed actions as matters of personal choice.

Moral development, as Piaget (1932) taught us long ago, is not simply a matter of acquiring the norms and standards of society. It entails the construction of conceptions of fairness that reflect moral concerns for human welfare. What we have learned over the past four decades is that children's basic concepts of morality emerge very early in life and are distinct from concepts about society's conventions (Turiel, 2006). In more recent work described in this chapter, we have confirmed that many basic moral concepts about clear-cut moral issues such as unprovoked harm do not change with age. However, moral reasoning around more complex moral situations appears to undergo a U-shaped developmental progression in the capacity to coordinate the elements of moral situations such that the moral decisions of young children and older adolescents are more similar and more frequently in the moral direction than are those of older children and young adolescents. An aspect of that transition is the capacity of children and adolescents to coordinate moral considerations of welfare and fairness with individual claims to personal choice and rights.

The research on children's and adolescents' reasoning about their personal growth and recent findings about their moral growth points toward an account of social development that calls into question positions that define children's socialization in terms of "committed compliance" to adult standards (Grolnick & Raftery-Helmer, this volume; Kochanska, 2002). There is no question that adults play an integral role in children's social development (Smetana, 2010), but the preponderance of evidence is that children and adolescents also engage in what has been referred to in this chapter as *committed noncompliance* around personal issues that is a normative and necessary component of social development. A comprehensive constructivist account of social development cannot rest solely on descriptions of children's adoption of social standards, or their rational commitment to moral principles of fairness and human welfare. It must include an account of children's rational and systematic claims for areas of behavioral discretion and privacy.

As one 7-year-old girl once said in the context of one of our interviews, "It's a part of life to do what you want."

REFERENCES

Aronfreed, J. (1968). *Conduct and conscience: The socialization of internalized control over behavior.* New York, NY: Academic Press.

Ardila-Rey, A., & Killen, M. (2001). Middle-class Colombian children's evaluations of moral, social-conventional and personal events in the classroom. *International Journal of Behavioral Development*, 25, 246–255.

Burns, J. (2009). *Goddess of the market: Ayn Rand and the American Right.* Oxford, UK: Oxford University Press.

Darling, N., Cumsille, P., & Pena-Alampay, L. (2005). Rules, legitimacy, and parental authority, and obligation to obey in Chile, Philippines, and the United States. In J. Smetana (Ed.), *Changing boundaries of parental authority* (pp. 47–60). San Francisco, CA: Jossey-Bass.

Darling, N., Cumsille, P., Pena-Alampay, L., & Coatsworth, D. (2009). Individual and issue-specific differences in parental knowledge and adolescent disclosure in Chile, the Philippines, and the United States. *Journal of Research on Adolescence*, 19, 715–740.

Dornbusch, S. M., Carlsmith, J. M., Bushwall, S. J., Ritter, P. L., Leiderman, H., Hastorf, A. H., et al. (1985). Single parents, extended households, and control of adolescents. *Child Development*, 56, 326–341.

Dworkin, R. (1978). *Taking rights seriously.* Cambridge, MA: Harvard University Press.

Geertz, C. (1984). From the natives' point of view: On the nature of anthropological understanding. In R. A. Shweder & R. Levine (Eds.), *Culture theory* (pp. 125–136). Cambridge, UK: Cambridge University Press.

Gelman, S. (2004). *The essential child: Origins of essentialism in everyday thought.* Oxford, UK: Oxford University Press.

Grusec, J. (2011). Socialization processes in the family: Social and emotional development. *Annual Review of Psychology*, 62, 243–269.

Hasebe, Y., Nucci, L., & Nucci, M. (2004). Parental control of the personal domain and adolescent symptoms of psychopathology: A cross-national study in the U.S. and Japan. *Child Development*, 75, 815–828.

Helwig, C. (2006). Rights, civil liberties, and democracy across cultures. In M. Killen & J. Smetana (Eds.), *Handbook of moral development* (pp. 185–210). Mahwah, NJ: Erlbaum.

Helwig, C., Yang, S., Nucci, L., Yun, K., & To, S. (2009). Parental control of the personal domain and adolescent symptoms of psychopathology in urban and rural China. Paper presented at the biennial meeting of the Society for Research in Child Development, Denver, CO.

Kochanska, G. (2002). Committed compliance, moral self, and internalization: A mediational model. *Developmental Psychology, 38*, 339–351.

Kohlberg, L. (1984). *Essays on moral development: Vol 2. The psychology of moral development.* San Francisco, CA: Harper and Row.

Lagattuta, K.H. (2005). When you shouldn't do what you want to do: Young children's understanding of desires, rules, and emotions. *Child Development, 76*, 713–733.

Lagattuta, K.H . (2008). Young children's understanding of the influence of thoughts on emotions in rule situations, *Developmental Science. 11*, 809–818.

Lagattuta, K. H., Nucci, L., & Bosacki, S. (2010). Bridging theory of mind and the personal domain: Children's reasoning about resistance to parental control. *Child Development, 81*, 616–635.

Lins-Dyer, T., & Nucci, L. (2007). The impact of social class and social cognitive domain on northeastern Brazilian mothers' and daughters' conceptions of parental control. *International Journal of Behavioral Development, 31*, 105–114.

Miller, J. G. (2006). Insights into moral development from cultural psychology. In M. Killen and J. Smetana (Eds.)., *Handbook of moral development* (pp. 375–398). Mahwah, NJ: Erlbaum.

Miller, J. G., Das, R., & Chakravarthy, S. (2011). Culture and the role of choice in agency. *Journal of Personality and Social Psychology, 101*, 46–61.

Milnitsky-Sapiro, C., Turiel, E., & Nucci, L. (2006). Brazilian adolescents' concepts of autonomy and parental authority. *Cognitive Development, 21*, 317–331.

Neff, K. D. (2001). Judgments of personal autonomy and interpersonal responsibility in the context of Indian spousal relationships: An examination of young people's reasoning in Mysore, India. *British Journal of Developmental Psychology, 19*, 233–257.

Nucci, L. (1981). Conceptions of personal issues: A domain distinct from moral or societal concepts. *Child Development, 52*, 114–121.

Nucci, L. (1996). Morality and the personal sphere of actions. In E. Reed, E. Turiel, & T. Brown (Eds.), *Knowledge and values.* Hillsdale, NJ: Erlbaum.

Nucci, L. (2000). Culture, context and the psychological sources of human rights concepts. In W. Edelstein and G. Nunner-Winkler (Eds.), *Morality in context.* Frankfurt am Main: Suhrkamp.

Nucci, L., Camino, C., & Milnitsky-Sapiro, C. (1996). Social class effects on Northeastern Brazilian children's conceptions of areas of personal choice and social regulation. *Child Development, 67*, 1223–1242.

Nucci, L., & Smetana, J. G. (1996). Mothers' concepts of young childrens' areas of personal freedom. *Child Development, 67*, 1870–1886.

Nucci, L., Smetana, J. G., Araki, N., Nakaue, M., & Comer, J. (Manuscript submitted for publication). Japanese adolescents' disclosure to parents and well-being: The role of family decision-making and domain of activity.

Nucci, L. & Turiel, E. (1996). The moral and personal sources of conflicts. In L. Nucci, G. Saxe, & E. Turiel (Eds.), *Culture, thought, and development.* Mahwah, NJ: Erlbaum.

Nucci, L., & Weber, E. K. (1995). Social interactions in the home and the development of young children's conceptions within the personal domain. *Child Development, 66*, 1438–1452.

Nussbaum, M. (1999). *Sex and social justice.* Oxford, UK: Oxford University Press.
Oyserman, D., Coon, H. M., & Kemmelmeier, M. (2002). Rethinking individualism and collectivism: Evaluation of theoretical assumptions and meta-analysis. *Psychological Bulletin, 128*, 3–72.
Perkins, S. A., & Turiel, E. (2007). To lie or not to lie: To whom and under what circumstances. *Child Development, 78*, 609–621.
Piaget, J. (1932). *The moral judgment of the child.* New York: Free Press.
Rand, A. (1943). *The fountainhead.* New York: Bobbs-Merrill.
Shweder, R., Mahapatra, M., & Miller, J. (1987). Culture and moral development. In J. Kagan & S. Lamb (Eds.)., *The emergence of morality in young children.* Chicago, IL: University of Chicago Press.
Smetana, J. G. (2002). Culture, autonomy, and personal jurisdiction in adolescent-parent relationships. In H. W. Reese & R. Kail (Eds.), *Advances in child development and behavior (Vol. 29*, pp. 51–87). New York, NY: Academic Press.
Smetana, J. G. (2006). Social-cognitive domain theory. In M. Killen and J. Smetana (Eds.)., *Handbook of moral development* (pp. 119–154). Mahwah, NJ: Erlbaum.
Smetana, J. G. (2011). *Adolescents, families and social development: How teens construct their worlds.* Sussex, UK: Wiley-Blackwell.
Smetana, J. G., & Braeges, J. (1990). The development of toddlers' moral and conventional judgments. *Merrill-Palmer Quarterly 36*, 329–346.
Smetana, J., Kochanska, G., & Chuang, S. (2000). Mothers' conceptions of everyday rules for young toddlers: A longitudinal investigation of the effects of maternal reasoning and child temperament. *Merrill-Palmer, 46*, 391–416.
Triandis, H. (1989). The self and social behavior in differing cultural contexts. *Psychological Review, 96*, 506–520.
Turiel, E. (1983). *The development of social knowledge: Morality and convention.* Cambridge, UK: Cambridge University Press.
Turiel, E. (2002). *The culture of morality: Social development, context, and conflict.* Cambridge, UK: Cambridge University Press.
Turiel, E., & Wainryb, C. (2000). Social life in cultures: Judgments, conflicts, and rights in hierarchically organized society. *British Journal of Developmental Psychology, 16*, 375–395.
Watson, M. (2003). *Learning to trust: Transforming difficult elementary classrooms through developmental discipline.* San Francisco, CA: Jossey-Bass.
Wellman, H., & Miller, J. G. (2008). Including deontic reasoning as fundamental to theory of mind. *Human Development, 51*, 105–135.
Yamada, H. (2004). Japanese mothers' views of young children's areas of personal discretion. *Child Development, 75*, 164–179.
Yamada, H. (2009). Japanese children's reasoning about conflict with parents. *Social Development, 18*, 962–977.
Yau, J., & Smetana, J. G. (1996). Adolescent-parent conflict among Chinese adolescents in Hong Kong. *Child Development, 67*, 1262–1275.

PART III

SELF-REGULATION AND AUTONOMY AT SCHOOL

Chapter 9

Toward a Social Psychology of Assimilation: Self-Determination Theory in Cognitive Development and Education

RICHARD M. RYAN AND EDWARD L. DECI
University of Rochester

But what is the true type of education?
It is like the art of the gardener under whose care
a thousand trees blossom and grow.
He contributes nothing to their actual growth;
the principle of growth lies in the trees themselves.
He plants and waters....
(Pestalozzi, 1818)

Humans are curious, interested creatures, who naturally seek out novelty and challenge, enjoy learning, and actively internalize new practices and cultural values from others around them. These evolved tendencies to be curious (Silvia, 2008) and to assimilate (Piaget, 1971) would seem to be primary resources in the social promotion of learning and development (Niemiec & Ryan, 2009). Yet, it is increasingly frequent in contemporary societies for parents and educators not to rely on these inherent propensities, but rather to try to ensure learning through external incentives and controls, often interfering with or crowding out intrinsic epistemic processes. Externally controlling motivators have been systemically extended to teachers as well. For example, in many nations policies link rewards and sanctions contingently on raising specific test scores (Ryan & Brown, 2005; Ryan & Weinstein, 2009). Under such controlling conditions, predictable changes in teaching practices occur that attempt to supplant active learning by assimilation with learning by externally controlled directives and goals.

It is particularly interesting in this regard that this chapter is occasioned by a common focus of Jean Piaget Society members and a few of us representatives of self-determination theory on autonomy and self-regulation in cognitive and socioemotional development. Piagetian theory has long been focused on the development of cognitive structures through the inherent processes of organization. *Self-Determination Theory* (SDT; Deci & Ryan, 2000; Ryan & Deci, 2000b) in turn is an organismic theory focused on factors that facilitate or derail organizational or integrative processes across domains of development (Deci & Ryan, this volume; Ryan, 1993).

The dialectic between an active assimilative human nature and social contexts is of course nowhere more apparent and nowhere more important to understand than in the domain of education (Guay, Ratelle, & Chanal, 2008). This is a domain in which students' inherent propensities to learn represent perhaps the greatest resource an educator can tap, and yet it is also a domain where external controls, evaluations, and pressures are regularly imposed, often with the intent of "making" students learn, and in the process unwittingly undermining that very outcome (Ryan & Brown, 2005).

In what follows we describe some important elements of SDT as they apply to both learning as a natural developmental process and learning within the contexts of modern educational settings. We begin by examining the concept of *intrinsic motivation* – arguing that much of early cognitive and motor development is dependent on intrinsic motivation. Further intrinsic motivation can, and optimally does, play an important role in structured classroom environments, and we discuss factors that support or undermine it in classrooms.

Beyond intrinsic motivation we discuss *extrinsic motivation* and the process of its *internalization* as a critical element for learning and achievement. We argue that the process of internalization and integration of ambient social norms, values, and practices is itself natural, but like intrinsically motivated assimilation, it is highly dependent on supports for learners' psychological needs for autonomy, competence, and relatedness. When supports for these needs are afforded, greater intrinsic motivation and internalization follow; when these needs are thwarted, greater controlled motivation and more impoverished learning results. In this regard, we discuss the systemic conditions affecting teachers and learners that support or thwart their needs, and the consequences for motivational and assimilative processes. We conclude with a discussion of the interplay between motivation and cognitive development in theory and practice.

INTRINSIC MOTIVATION AND LEARNING

All work on the part of intelligence rests on interest. Interest is nothing other, in effect, than the dynamic aspect of assimilation. (Piaget, 1970, p. 158)

Intrinsic motivation refers to behaviors that are done because they are inherently interesting and enjoyable and that do not depend on external controls for their occurrence (Ryan & Deci, 2000a). When children play, explore, examine objects, and engage in new activities they are frequently intrinsically motivated – these actions emanate from the child and are sustained by the satisfactions of acting. In such behaviors the child is displaying what Piaget (1971) would have described as the inherent tendency of structures, once existing, to function, and thereby to extend themselves. But as Piaget (1981) also recognized, a phenomenological perspective supplements and enriches this structural account. He noted that the affective and experiential aspect of assimilation is *interest*. The child volitionally engages in such actions, finding them immersive, interesting, and fun.

Intrinsically motivated activities are in turn critical to the unfolding and refinement of cognitive structures and to the integration of knowledge (Deci & Ryan, 1985). As Flavell, Miller, and Miller (2002) stated, "a great deal of mentation, at all developmental levels, is intrinsically rather than extrinsically motivated" (p. 66). Indeed, much new learning in early childhood is intrinsically motivated, whereas to repeat previously assimilated skills one needs extrinsic motivation – some external incentive.

Here we see the importance of the inbuilt engine of growth for expanding organismic capacities. Through play and curiosity, both brain and intellectual development proceed. In fact, play is particularly prevalent during the most rapid periods of neurological development, promoting neural connections and differentiation. Accordingly, many educational theorists, from Montessori to Dewey to modern constructivists, have recognized the power of curiosity, interest, and playful activities in advancing educational aims. Yet contemporary test-focused approaches to educating seem largely to have forgotten this inner resource. We are indeed far from the original meanings associated with the word *school*, a concept that etymologically derived from the idea of *leisure* – a place for the employment of the playful, assimilating mind.

Intrinsic Motivation and SDT

We begin with a foundational point that is often forgotten by educational policy makers – namely, that humans are endowed by evolution with a strong propensity to learn. It is not a motivation that must necessarily be taught or prodded – indeed, it seems that curiosity and desire to learn are often fountains that, unfortunately, get turned off in school settings (Guay et al., 2008; Ryan & Brown, 2005).

The existence of intrinsic motivation is evident from birth. As Bronson (2000) noted, from early infancy, children show delight in controlling their own activity and producing effects on the environment. This fact was also frequently noted by Piaget (e.g., 1967; 1970) in discussing the unfolding of the child's cognitive capacities and understanding. Yet this robust interest in developing mastery and understanding of one's physical and social environments is significantly impacted by caregiver supports, a fact that has been a major focus of SDT. Specifically, adults' mirroring, interest, and responsiveness to children's initiative support this motivated activity, whereas anxious, controlling behaviors can diminish it (e.g., Grolnick, Kurowski, McMenamy, Rivkin, & Bridges, 1998; Landry et al., 2008). That is to say, right from the beginning, the tendency to explore and assimilate is either facilitated or thwarted by factors in the social context related to caregiver pressure, control, and anxieties.

Much of the early research within SDT focused on identifying those factors that enhance or derail intrinsic motivation. Deci and Ryan (1980), for example, argued that intrinsic motivation, although a natural tendency, is sustained by satisfaction of *psychological needs for autonomy and competence*. The need for autonomy refers to the experience of behavior as self-organized and volitional; it is disrupted when activity is impinged upon, or controlled externally, even through rewards. The need for competence refers to the experience of effectiveness or capability in action. It is undermined when feedback is negative or challenges are nonoptimal. Thus by either enhancing or diminishing satisfaction of these basic needs, social contexts either support or thwart the active developmental processes underpinned by intrinsic motivation, including many that Piaget examined. To date, hundreds of experimental studies have supported the SDT postulate that both autonomy and competence are necessary for the maintenance of intrinsic motivation (e.g., see Deci, Koestner, & Ryan, 1999; Ryan & Deci, 2000a).

Given the sensitivity of intrinsic motivation to social contextual influences it is no wonder that schools variously succeed in tapping into this rich inner resource. The SDT approach to intrinsic motivation has been studied in multiple school contexts, across varied countries and cultures. For example, Deci, Schwartz, Sheinman, and Ryan (1981) assessed U.S. elementary teachers' self-reports of their orientations toward supporting students' autonomy versus controlling their behavior. Subsequently, children assigned to more autonomy-supportive teachers, relative to those assigned to controlling teachers, reported increased intrinsic motivation, perceived competence, and self-esteem over time. Ryan and Grolnick (1986) obtained similar findings using students' self-reported and projective assessments of teacher autonomy support and control. Students experiencing more autonomy-supportive teachers reported both more intrinsic motivation to learn and greater feelings of competence. In research with over 4,000 Canadian students, Vallerand, Fortier, and Guay (1997) showed that persistence (versus dropout) in schools was associated with greater intrinsic motivation and the overall relative autonomy of motives.

Since such early work, research on classroom climate and motivation has continued and is extensive. Recently, for example, Jang, Reeve, Ryan, and Kim (2009) examined the intrinsic motivation of South Korean high school students and found that perceived classroom autonomy support predicted greater autonomy and competence need satisfactions, which in turn predicted intrinsic motivation and positive engagement. Standage, Duda, and Ntoumanis (2003) showed that in British physical education classes, perceived autonomy support was associated with greater self-determination, including intrinsic motivation, within classrooms, which in turn was associated with greater intentions for leisure time physical activity.

Finally, we turn to multi-level modeling strategies. Tsai, Kunter, Ludtke, Trautwein, and Ryan (2008) examined variations in interest for classroom lessons across three subject areas on multiple days in a sample of German seventh graders. They found that, even controlling for individual differences in subject interest, variations in teacher autonomy support versus control predicted students' proximal interest experienced in the classroom on any given day. Mouratidis, Vansteenkiste, Lens, and Sideridis (2011) reported similar findings in their research within Belgian classrooms. Such within-person variation in interest as a function of ambient autonomy support bespeaks the dynamic nature of interest and active learning in school contexts.

Self-Determination Theory and Learning

Sparking intrinsic motivation and interest through autonomy support also enhances learning outcomes. Grolnick and Ryan (1987) showed that autonomy-supportive versus controlling evaluative conditions fostered more interest and more conceptual learning for text material in elementary schoolchildren. Kage and Namiki (1990) similarly found that in Japanese school contexts, evaluative pressures undermined, and support for autonomy facilitated, not only intrinsic motivation toward classroom materials but also performance. Benware and Deci (1984) exposed college students to a neuroscience lesson, allowing them to expect that they would either teach it to another student (active condition) or be tested on it (passive condition). Results revealed that students who learned in order to use the material actively were more intrinsically motivated than those who learned in order to take a test, and they showed better conceptual learning. Koestner, Ryan, Bernieri, and Holt (1984) performed an in-school experiment examining the effect of setting limits on behaviors. Limit setting is important to educational contexts, as limits facilitate students' effective functioning within the structures of the classroom environments. Yet teachers can set limits in different ways. Koestner et al. found that students who were given limits in controlling ways showed significantly less intrinsic motivation than those given limits in a more autonomy-supportive manner. Important too was the finding that the work of those children given autonomy-supportive limits was rated as significantly more creative than that of children given limits in a controlling way.

A number of conclusions can be drawn from these findings, and from those in the larger literature from which they are drawn, concerning intrinsic motivation and classroom contexts. First, both teachers' orientations and specific aspects of learning tasks that are perceived as autonomy supportive are conducive to students' intrinsic motivation, whereas controlling educational climates undermine intrinsic motivation. Second, students tend to learn better and are more creative when intrinsically motivated, particularly on tasks requiring conceptual understanding. Tasks that involve active engagement as opposed to passive intake are more likely to be intrinsically motivated, and this promotes deeper processing and more reciprocal assimilation as active engagement entails more coordination and organization than compartmentalized, externally directed learning. Third, how teachers introduce and communicate learning tasks affects students' psychological needs for autonomy and competence, thus either enhancing or thwarting their intrinsic motivation and the high-quality engagement and deep learning that can stem from it.

EXTRINSIC MOTIVATION, INTERNALIZATION, AND LEARNING

Intrinsic motivation provides an important natural basis for learning that can be harnessed by educators to enhance development. Nonetheless, many of the daily tasks and goals that educators ask students to do are not inherently satisfying or fun activities. Elementary school students may not find learning multiplication tables fun; high school teens may not want to memorize the periodic elements table. In such cases, students often need other reasons such as incentives to learn. *Extrinsic motivation* refers to behaviors performed to obtain some outcome separable from the activity itself (Ryan & Deci, 2000a). SDT holds, however, that extrinsic motivation is not a unitary phenomenon. Instead, according to SDT there are several subtypes of extrinsic motivation that vary along a continuum of relative autonomy, and are therefore more or less volitional. These different types of extrinsic motivation are also associated with different classroom practices.

Four different types of extrinsic motivation have been specified within SDT, and these differ in terms of the degree to which they represent controlled versus autonomous functioning. The most controlled is *external regulation*, which refers to behaviors that are undertaken in order to obtain a reward or avoid a punishment. External regulators can often produce immediate compliance, but such behaviors are poorly maintained once the controlling contingencies (e.g., grades, threats, etc.) are removed. For example, a student might do a science project to avoid sanctions, but that student would likely not seek out additional information on the topic once the project is complete and graded. The second type of extrinsic motivation, which is also relatively controlled, is *introjected regulation*. Behaviors regulated by introjects are enacted to satisfy internal contingencies, such as gaining self-aggrandizement or avoiding self-derogation. For example, a student may study for exams to feel like a worthy son or daughter, or to avoid feeling a loss of self-esteem for poor performance. Indeed, an important and widely studied subtype of introjected motivation is *ego-involvement* (Ryan, 1982; Niemiec, Ryan, & Brown, 2008) in which one's self-esteem is contingent on performance. Introjection can be viewed as a partial internalization, in which the regulation has been "taken in" by the person but not really accepted as his or her own. Both external regulation and introjected regulation are phenomenologically characterized by an *external perceived locus of causality* (de Charms, 1968) – that is, these forms of behavioral regulation are not experienced as emanating from one's true sense of self. Accordingly, SDT views both external and introjected regulations as relatively impoverished methods of inspiring learning motivation, and it predicts that these lead to shallower learning, less reciprocal assimilation, and less transfer, among other indicators of learning quality.

Proceeding toward greater autonomy, behaviors that are enacted because they are considered personally valuable or important are said to exemplify *identified regulation*. For example, a teenaged girl might study some difficult topics because mastery of such information is important for her future career goals or can help her accomplish some valued task. Finally, even more autonomous is *integrated regulation*, whereby identified regulations have been synthesized with other aspects of the self, and thus are experienced as harmonious. For example, a young woman might study law because doing so enables her to enter a profession in which she can help those in need, which is consistent with her abiding values and interests. Both identified regulation and integrated regulation are characterized by an *internal perceived locus of causality* (de Charms, 1968) – that is, these forms of behavioral regulation are experienced as reflecting one's true self and thus as volitional and autonomous.

A large number of empirical studies have examined the psychological and academic outcomes associated with more internalized or autonomous regulation for learning, of which we shall review only a few examples. Grolnick, Ryan, and Deci (1991) found that elementary students reporting more autonomous regulation for learning (i.e., identified and intrinsic motivation, rather than introjected and externally regulated) were rated by teachers as better adjusted in the classroom and as more academically achieving. Miserandino (1996) found that more autonomous learners had better classroom attitudes and affects and more enhanced learning outcomes across subject matters compared to less autonomous learners, even when prior achievement levels were controlled. Ratelle, Guay, Larose, and Senecal (2004) studied developmental trajectories of students' motivation in the transition to college. They found for many an increase in intrinsic motivation, but for others a loss of identification. They also reported that more positive motivational trajectories during change were associated with students who experienced parents as more autonomy supportive and involved. Black and Deci (2000) found that college students who reported higher autonomous self-regulation for learning organic chemistry reported higher perceived competence and interest/enjoyment for the course material, as well as lower anxiety. Moreover, this autonomous motivation predicted better performance even after controlling for prior grades and achievement test scores. Williams and Deci (1996) found that medical students who reported higher autonomous self-regulation for a course on medical interviewing were subsequently rated as more autonomy-supportive when interviewing standardized patients. Such evidence suggests that internalization of extrinsic motivation is critical to effective academic functioning at all levels of education. Through internalization, students can autonomously self-regulate those behaviors that are not inherently satisfying, which is important for continued engagement in important academic activities.

FACILITATING ENVIRONMENTS

Given that intrinsic motivation and more autonomous forms of extrinsic motivation are associated with enhanced learning and adjustment in schools, SDT has focused considerable attention on how schools can enhance autonomous motivations. As with intrinsic motivation, SDT maintains that supporting students' basic needs for autonomy and competence is likely to lead them to internalize motivations to learn and to stay in school (Hardre & Reeve, 2003).

Autonomy-supportive teachers first and foremost consider their students' frame of reference in designing and motivating learning tasks. They minimize the sense of coercion, evaluative pressure, and control, and they maximize a sense of choice and volitional engagement. One important part of promoting autonomy is providing a meaningful rationale for why a task is important or useful. For example, Reeve, Jang, Hardre, and Omura (2002) found that autonomy-supportive rationales led students to more fully internalize regulations and to put more effort into the learning. More generally, Chirkov and Ryan (2001) showed that in both Russian and U.S. classrooms, students' perceptions of teacher and parental autonomy support were associated with greater internalization of academic motivation.

To support feelings of competence, educators introduce tasks that students can succeed at but that are not too easy, and they provide students with tools and feedback to help their feelings of efficacy emerge. Within SDT this concerns both positive feedback for effective efforts and *structure* that allows an active learner to know how to progress (Farkas & Grolnick, 2010; Grolnick & Ryan, 1989; Jang, Reeve, & Deci, 2010). Structure concerns the scaffolding that clarifies tasks, strategies, goals, and feedback and enhances the learners' feelings of efficacy as they engage in new tasks.

Finally, SDT posits that internalization depends on a sense of relatedness (Baumeister & Leary, 1995; Ryan & Powelson, 1991). People only adopt and internalize values and practices coming from others either to whom they feel attached or to whom they would like to be connected. That is, individuals internalize ambient practices and beliefs not only because they are in their environment but also as a way of connecting and feeling belongingness within that environment. Students' feelings of relatedness in classrooms is associated with the perception that the teachers like, value, and respect them. A student who reports such perceptions is more likely to exhibit identification and integration with respect to achievement-related tasks (e.g., Bao & Lam, 2008; Jang et al., 2009).

Numerous studies support the critical role of all three of these need-related supports for student motivation (Reeve, 2006; Reeve & Halusic, 2009). Classroom contexts where students experience autonomy, competence, and relatedness tend not only to foster more intrinsic motivation but also more willing engagement in less interesting academic activities.

Along with this increased learner autonomy come better quality learning outcomes, enhanced wellness, and a greater value for sustained learning.

AUTONOMY AND LEARNING ACROSS CULTURES

The strong experimental and field evidence concerning the relations of autonomy-support and control to basic processes of learning, interest-taking, and valuing has strong implications for educational practice. Yet even though the evidence is clear, and derived from studies of learners from around the globe, there remains resistance to the view that autonomy-support is universally beneficial. For example, authors such as Markus and Kitayama (1991) and Heinrich, Heine, and Zorenzayan (2010) suggest that autonomy has little significance outside the West.

This kind of cultural relativism, however, provides an excellent contrast with organismic thinking. Without denying that cultures impact the style and content of behavioral regulations, an organismic view understands that our active, assimilative human nature involves autonomy and self-organization, and that this is a natural rather than acquired human tendency. Suppression of autonomy will therefore detract from volitional motivation and vitality everywhere. Accordingly, much new research supports the SDT view of the functional importance of autonomy within schools across cultural contexts, only a small portion of which we have cited (see also Guay et al., 2008; Helwig & McNiel, 2012; Reeve & Assor, 2012). Whereas some deny that autonomy is meaningful to Asian individuals, research shows, to the contrary, that choice was associated with increased intrinsic motivation and performance in Chinese children (Bao & Lam, 2008); that autonomy mattered to school engagement in Korean high school pupils (e.g., Jang et al., 2009); and that functional magnetic resonance imaging data from Japanese students demonstrated the expected undermining effect of rewards on intrinsic motivation (Murayama, Matsumoto, Izuma, & Matsumoto, 2010). These and dozens of additional studies, using diverse methods and examining multiple outcomes, suggest strongly that there are no national or cultural boundaries on the most fundamental aspects of human growth and development.

TEACHERS' AUTONOMY AND CLASSROOM PRACTICE

Teaching practices do not occur in a vacuum. According to SDT, one major reason teachers use controlling rather than autonomy-supportive strategies in classrooms is because of the external pressures placed on them (Niemiec

& Ryan, 2009; Ryan & Brown, 2005). This basic idea has been supported in a growing number of studies. For example, Roth, Assor, Kanat-Maymon, and Kaplan (2007) found that among Israeli teachers, those who felt more controlled in their own professional activities were less autonomy supportive toward students. Pelletier, Séguin-Lévesque, and Legault (2002) found that to the extent that Canadian teachers (grades 1 through 12) perceived pressure from above (e.g., toward test performances or curriculum coverage), the less autonomous they felt in teaching. Moreover, they were less autonomy supportive and more controlling in teaching and interacting with students, showing the negative cascading effect of controlling policies. This suggests that as teachers' own needs for autonomy are undermined, they will bring less enthusiasm and vitality to their teaching. Furthermore, the pressure placed on teachers to achieve specified outcomes leads them to use teaching strategies that tend to be more controlling and that crowd out effective and inspiring teaching practices that might otherwise be in place.

Policy makers are increasingly relying on controlling methods in an attempt to motivate teachers, with the hope that these in turn will pressure students to learn. Yet employing controlling contingencies to produce "accountability" ironically leads all partners in the learning process to suffer in regard to motivation, performance, and wellness (Ryan & Weinstein, 2009).

SDT research has shown that linking performance outcomes to rewards or sanctions is likely to be experienced as controlling. Predictably, it leads to narrow, goal-directed behaviors as well as reduced personal interest and investment in teachers and students alike (Deci & Ryan, 2002). In fact, empirical evidence suggests that such a linkage probably undermines complex learning as well as students' interest. This is because, typically, facts that have been predetermined as important are transmitted passively, supplanting significant learning through discovery. This kind of teaching lacks "ownership" or an internal perceived locus of causality among students and teachers alike, which is what sparks integrative interest and reciprocal assimilations. This lack of empowerment and latitude is also reflected in lower teacher morale and educational innovation (Ryan & Brown, 2005). In addition, because high-stakes assessments are uniform, or "one size fits all," usually they will not be optimally challenging for most individuals or school populations; they are not likely to support mastery and competence experiences, and can readily have an amotivating impact, undermining all motivation.

Policy makers who champion high-stakes testing techniques claim that these sanction-and-reward contingencies that are being attached to test scores simply represent the use of reinforcements, in accord with behaviorist theories (see, e.g., Finn, 1991). Yet, classical behaviorist methods of reinforcement do not target outcomes; they target the behaviors themselves. For example, Skinner (1953) advocated applying reinforcement contingencies to *specific targeted behaviors*. Policies involving rewards and sanctions for test scores, in contrast, apply contingent consequences to *cognitive outcomes* rather than behaviors. Ryan and Brown (2005) suggested that a danger with this outcome focus is that all kinds of behaviors, both desirable (e.g., clearer lesson plans) and undesirable (e.g., teaching to the test, narrowing of curriculum) can be equally "reinforced" insofar as they are expected to produce desired outcomes. Even worse, practices such as outright cheating can be "reinforced" and supplant the improved instructional practices that policy makers may have intended to foster.

Moreover, policy makers focused on rewards for performance outcomes seem to implicitly assume an absence of inner motivation among teachers, a deficit they believe they are rectifying with rewards and punishments. That is, they are assuming the problem has been lack of incentives for teachers, rather than, for example, concentrations of poverty or inadequate numbers of adults in the classroom. We would dispute that assumption and, moreover, point out that these policies fail to consider the incompatibility of their motivational approaches and the motivation known to underlie quality learning.

Learning is a cultural resource that itself requires cultivation. It is more than facts – it is also about a way of engaging information that involves interest and value, and the coordinating, synthesizing, and integrating processes associated with these. There are identifiable methods by which these inner tendencies to be interested in or to value a domain of inquiry are best nurtured and fostered. But what is being applied instead is a factory model, not of nurturance, but of force-feeding. What is taken in is, in turn, predictably poorly digested.

CONCLUDING COMMENTS

Self-determination theory is a contemporary, empirically based approach to motivation and development. Its focus is on social contexts as facilitators of and barriers to the intrinsic motivational processes associated with intellectual and socioemotional growth and integration. There is an easily congruent interface between SDT and Piagetian theories, especially as applied to classroom practices. Classroom practices that support autonomy, competence, and relatedness are associated with both greater intrinsic motivation and autonomous forms of extrinsic motivation. Facilitative practices for enhancing autonomy include providing choice and meaningful rationales for learning tasks, acknowledging students' feelings about the learning topics, and minimizing pressure and control. Strategies for enhancing competence include providing adequate and clear structure, effectance relevant feedback, and optimally engaging tasks. Facilitating relatedness entails the conveyance of warmth, respect, and a caring involvement.

Learning is assimilation, and attending not just to the structural transformations that occur but also to the contextual grounds in which active assimilation most readily occurs is critical to effective education. Piagetian theory demonstrates how innate functional tendencies toward growth, coherence, and integration of knowledge supply the mechanisms through which active engagement and true assimilation occur. This interest is in turn complemented by SDT and its focus on what facilitates or diminishes these developmentally critical human propensities.

Yet despite the common focus of these theories, contemporary educational policies around the world too often fail to recognize the importance of organismic principles for educational practice. Unlike many activities, learning is one that requires the active and willing participation of the learner (and teacher), which in turn means creating an atmosphere that supports that willing engagement. Not only does a psychological-need-supportive environment enhance learning outcomes, but it also facilitates holistic health development, and the overall well-being of the growing person. Nurturing such developmental flourishing should, after all, be the central goal of education.

REFERENCES

Bao, X., & Lam, S. (2008). Who makes the choice? Rethinking the role of autonomy and relatedness in Chinese children's motivation. *Child Development*, *79*, 269–283. doi: 10.1111/j.1467-8624.2007.01125.x

Baumeister, R. F., & Leary, M. R . (1995). The need to belong: Desire for interpersonal attachments as a fundamental human motivation. *Psychological Bulletin*, *117*, 497–529. doi: 10.1037/0033-2909.117.3.497

Benware, C. A., & Deci, E. L. (1984). Quality of learning with an active versus passive motivational set. *American Educational Research Journal*, *21*, 755–765. doi: 10.2307/1162999

Black, A. E., & Deci, E. L. (2000). The effects of instructors' autonomy support and students' autonomous motivation on learning organic chemistry: A self-determination theory perspective. *Science Education*, *84*, 740–756. doi: 10.1002/1098-237X(200011)84:6<740::AID-SCE4>3.0.CO;2-3

Bronson, M. B. (2000). *Self-regulation in early childhood: Nature and nurture*. New York, NY: Guilford Press.

Chirkov, V. I., & Ryan, R. M. (2001). Parent and teacher autonomy-support in Russian and U.S. adolescents: Common effects on well-being and academic motivation. *Journal of Cross Cultural Psychology, 32*, 618–635. doi: 10.1177/0022022101032005006

de Charms, R. (1968). *Personal causation*. New York, NY: Academic Press.

Deci, E. L., Koestner, R., & Ryan, R. M. (1999). A meta-analytic review of experiments examining the effects of extrinsic rewards on intrinsic motivation. *Psychological Bulletin, 125*, 627–668. doi: 10.1037/0033-2909.125.6.627

Deci, E. L., & Ryan, R. M. (1980). The empirical exploration of intrinsic motivational processes. In L. Berkowitz (Ed.), *Advances in experimental social psychology* (pp. 39–80). New York, NY: Academic Press.

Deci, E. L., & Ryan, R. M. (1985). *Intrinsic motivation and self-determination in human behavior*. New York, NY: Plenum Press.

Deci, E. L., & Ryan, R. M. (2000). The "what" and "why" of goal pursuits: Human needs and the self-determination of behavior. *Psychological Inquiry, 11*, 227–268. doi: 10.1207/S15327965PLI1104_01

Deci, E.L., & Ryan, R. M. (2002). The paradox of achievement: The harder you push, the worse it gets. In J. Aronson (Ed.), *Improving academic achievement: Contributions of social psychology* (pp. 59–85). New York, NY: Academic Press. doi: 10.1016/B978-012064455-1/50007-5

Deci, E. L., Schwartz, A. J., Sheinman, L., & Ryan, R. M. (1981). An instrument to assess adults' orientations toward control versus autonomy with children: Reflections on intrinsic motivation and perceived competence. *Journal of Educational Psychology, 73*, 642–650. doi: 10.1037/0022-0663.73.5.642

Farkas, M. S., & Grolnick, W. S. (2010). Examining the components and concomitants of parental structure in the academic domain. *Motivation and Emotion, 34*, 266–279. doi: 10.1007/s11031-010-9176-7

Finn, C. (1991). *We must take charge: Our schools and our future*. New York, NY: Free Press.

Flavell, J. H., Miler, P. H., & Miller, S. A. (2002). *Cognitive development* (4th ed.). Upper Saddle River, NJ: Prentice Hall.

Grolnick, W. S., Kurowski, C. O., McMenamy, J. M., Rivkin, I., & Bridges, L. J. (1998). Mothers' strategies for regulating their toddlers' distress. *Infant Behavior and Development, 21*, 437–450. doi: 10.1016/S0163-6383(98)90018-2

Grolnick, W. S., & Ryan, R. M. (1987). Autonomy in children's learning: An experimental and individual difference investigation. *Journal of Personality and Social Psychology*, 52, 890–898. doi: 10.1037/0022-3514.52.5.890

Grolnick, W. S., & Ryan, R. M. (1989). Parent styles associated with children's self-regulation and competence in school. *Journal of Educational Psychology, 81*, 143–154. doi: 10.1037/0022-0663.81.2.143

Grolnick, W. S., Ryan, R. M., & Deci, E. L. (1991). Inner resources for school achievement: Motivational mediators of children's perceptions of their parents. *Journal of Educational Psychology*, 83, 508–517. doi: 10.1037/0022-0663.83.4.508

Guay, F., Ratelle, C. F., & Chanal, J. (2008). Optimal learning in optimal contexts: The role of self-determination in education. *Canadian Psychology*, 49, 233–240. doi: 10.1037/a0012758

Hardre, P. L., & Reeve, J. (2003). A motivational model of rural students' intentions to persist in, versus drop out of, high school. *Journal of Educational Psychology*, *95*, 347–356. doi: 10.1037/0022-0663.95.2.347

Heinrich, J., Heine, S.J., & Norenzayan, A. (2010). The weirdest people in the world? *Behavioral and Brain Sciences*, *33*, 61–83. doi: 10.1017/S0140525X0999152X

Helwig, C.C., & McNiel, J. (2012). The development of conceptions of personal autonomy, rights, and democracy and their relation to psychological well-being. In V. I. Chirkov . R. M. Ryan, & K.M. Sheldon (Eds.), *Human autonomy in cross-cultural context* (pp. 241–256). New York, NY: Springer.

Jang, H., Reeve, J., & Deci, E. L. (2010). Engaging students in learning activities: It's not autonomy support or structure, but autonomy support and structure. *Journal of Educational Psychology*, *102*, 588–600. doi: 10.1037/a0019682

Jang, H., Reeve, J., Ryan, R. M., & Kim, A. (2009). Can self-determination theory explain what underlies the productive, satisfying learning experiences of collectivistically oriented Korean students? *Journal of Educational Psychology*, *101*, 644–661. doi: 10.1037/a0014241

Kage, M., & Namiki, H. (1990). The effects of evaluation structure on children's intrinsic motivation and learning. *Japanese Journal of Educational Psychology*, *38*, 36–45.

Koestner, R., Ryan, R. M., Bernieri, F., & Holt, K. (1984). Setting limits on children's behavior: The differential effects of controlling versus informational styles on intrinsic motivation and creativity. *Journal of Personality*, *52*, 233–248. doi: 10.1111/j.1467-6494.1984.tb00879.x

Landry, R., Whipple, N., Mageau, G. A., Joussemet, M., Gingras, I., Didio, L., & Koestner, R. (2008). Trust in organismic development, autonomy support, and adaptation among mothers and their children: A self-determination theory approach to parenting. *Motivation & Emotion*, *32*, 173–188. doi: 10.1007/s11031-008-9092-2

Markus, H., & Kitayama, S. (1991). Culture and self: Implications for cognition emotion and motivation. *Psychological Review*, *98*, 224–253. doi: 10.1037/0033-295X.98.2.224

Miserandino, M. (1996). Children who do well in school: Individual differences in perceived competence and autonomy in above average children. *Journal of Educational Psychology*, *88*, 203–214. doi: 10.1037/0022-0663.88.2.203

Mouratidis, A. A., Vansteenkiste, M., Lens, W., Sideridis, G. (2011). Vitality and interest–enjoyment as a function of class-to-class variation in need-supportive teaching and pupils' autonomous motivation. *Journal of Educational Psychology*, *103*, 353–366. doi: 10.1037/a0022773

Murayama, K., Matsumoto, M., Izuma, K., & Matsumoto, K. (2010). Neural basis of the undermining effect of monetary reward on intrinsic motivation. *Proceedings of the National Academy of Science*, *107*, 20911–20916. doi: 10.1073/pnas.1013305107

Niemiec, C. P., & Ryan, R. M. (2009). Autonomy, competence, and relatedness in the classroom: Applying self-determination theory to educational practice. *Theory and Research in Education*, *7*, 133–144. doi: 10.1177/1477878509104318

Niemiec, C. P., Ryan, R. M., & Brown, K. W. (2008). The role of awareness and autonomy in quieting the ego: A self-determination theory perspective.

In H. A. Wayment & J. J. Bauer (Eds.), *Transcending self-interest: Psychological explorations of the quiet ego* (pp. 107–115). Washington, DC: APA Books. doi: 10.1037/11771-010

Pelletier, L. G., Séguin-Lévesque, C., & Legault L. (2002). Pressure from above and pressure from below as determinants of teachers' motivation and teaching behavior. *Journal of Educational Psychology, 94*, 186–196. doi: 10.1037/0022-0663.94.1.186

Pestalozzi, J. H. (1818). Address to my house, 1818. In J. A. Green & F. A. Collie (Eds.), *Pestalozzi's educational writings*. London: Edward Arnold, 1912.

Piaget, J. (1967). *The child's conception of the world* (J . & A. Tomlinson, Trans.). London, UK: Routledge & Kegan Paul.

Piaget, J. (1970). *Science of education and the psychology of the child* (D. Coltman, Trans.). New York. NY: Orion Press.

Piaget, J. (1971). *Biology and knowledge* (B. Walsh, Trans.). Chicago, IL: University of Chicago Press.

Piaget, J. (1981). *Intelligence and affectivity: Their relationship during child development* (T. A. Brown & C. E. Kaeg, Trans.). Palo Alto, CA: Annual Reviews.

Ratelle, C. F., Guay, F., Larose, S., & Senecal, C. (2004). Family correlates of trajectories of academic motivation during a school transition: A semiparametric group-based approach. *Journal of Educational Psychology, 96*, 743–754.

Reeve, J. (2006). Teachers as facilitators: What autonomy-supportive teachers do and why their students benefit. *Elementary School Journal, 106*, 225–236. doi: 10.1086/501484

Reeve, J., & Assor, A. (2012). Do social institutions necessarily suppress individuals' need for autonomy: The possibility of schools as autonomy-promoting contexts across the globe. In V. I. Chirkov, R. M. Ryan, & K. M. Sheldon (Eds.), *Human autonomy in cross-cultural context* (pp. 111–132). New York, NY: Springer.

Reeve, J., & Halusic, M. (2009). How k–12 teachers can put self-determination theory principles into practice. *Theory and Research in Education, 7*, 145–154. doi: 10.1177/1477878509104319

Reeve, J., Jang, H., Hardre, P., & Omura, M. (2002). Providing a rationale in an autonomy-supportive way as a strategy to motivate others during an uninteresting activity. *Motivation and Emotion, 26*, 183–207. doi: 10.1023/A:1021711629417

Roth, G., Assor, A., Kanat-Maymon, Y., & Kaplan, H. (2007). Autonomous motivation for teaching: How self-determined teaching may lead to self-determined learning. *Journal of Educational Psychology, 99*, 761–774. doi: 10.1037/0022-0663.99.4.761

Ryan, R. M. (1982). Control and information in the intrapersonal sphere: An extension of cognitive evaluation theory. *Journal of Personality and Social Psychology, 43*, 450–461. doi: 10.1037/0022-3514.43.3.450

Ryan, R. M. (1993). Agency and organization: Intrinsic motivation, autonomy, and the self in psychological development. In J. Jacobs (Ed.), *Nebraska symposium on motivation: Developmental perspectives on motivation* (Vol. 40, pp. 1–56). Lincoln: University of Nebraska Press.

Ryan, R. M., & Brown, K. W. (2005). Legislating competence: The motivational impact of high stakes testing as an educational reform. In A. E. Elliot & C. Dweck (Eds.), *Handbook of competence* (pp. 354–374). New York, NY: Guilford Press.

Ryan, R. M. & Deci, E. L. (2000a). Intrinsic and extrinsic motivations: Classic definitions and new directions. *Contemporary Educational Psychology*, 25, 54–67. doi: 10.1006/ceps.1999.1020

Ryan, R. M. & Deci, E. L . (2000b). Self-determination theory and the facilitation of intrinsic motivation, social development, and well-being. *American Psychologist*, 55, 68–78. doi: 10.1037/0003-066X.55.1.68

Ryan, R. M. & Grolnick, W. S . (1986). Origins and pawns in the classroom: Self-report and projective assessments of individual differences in children's perceptions. *Journal of Personality and Social Psychology*, 50, 550–558. doi: 10.1037/0022-3514.50.3.550

Ryan, R. M. & Powelson, C. L. (1991). Autonomy and relatedness as fundamental to motivation in education. *Journal of Experimental Education*, 60, 49–66.

Ryan, R. M. & Weinstein, N. (2009). Undermining quality teaching and learning: A self-determination theory perspective on high-stakes testing. *Theory and Research in Education*, 7, 224–233. doi: 10.1177/1477878509104327

Silvia, P. J. (2008). Interest – the curious emotion. *Current Directions in Psychological Science*, 17, 57–60. doi: 10.1111/j.1467-8721.2008.00548.x

Skinner, B. F. (1953). *Science and human behavior*. New York, NY: Macmillan.

Standage, M., Duda, J. L., & Ntoumanis, N. (2003). A model of contextual motivation in physical education: Using constructs and tenets from self-determination and goal perspective theories to predict leisure-time exercise intentions. *Journal of Educational Psychology*, 95, 97–110. doi: 10.1037/0022-0663.95.1.97

Tsai, Y., Kunter, M., Lüdtke, O., Trautwein, U., & Ryan, R. M. (2008). What makes lessons interesting? The role of situational and individual factors in three school subjects. *Journal of Educational Psychology*, 100, 460–472. doi: 10.1037/0022-0663.100.2.460

Vallerand, R. J., Fortier, M. S., & Guay, F. (1997). Self-determination and persistence in a real-life setting: Toward a motivational model of high-school drop out. *Journal of Personality and Social Psychology*, 72, 1161–1176. doi: 10.1037/0022-3514.72.5.1161

Williams, G. C., & Deci, E. L. (1996). Internalization of biopsychosocial values by medical students: A test of self-determination theory. *Journal of Personality and Social Psychology*, 70, 767–779. doi: 10.1037/0022-3514.70.4.767

Chapter 10

Self-Regulation and School Success

ANGELA LEE DUCKWORTH
University of Pennsylvania
STEPHANIE M. CARLSON
University of Minnesota

Some children fare better academically than others, even when family background and school and teacher quality are controlled for (Rivkin, Hanushek, & Kain, 2005). Variance in performance that persists when situational variables are held constant suggests that individual differences play an important role in determining whether children thrive or fail in school. In this chapter, we review research on individual differences in self-regulation and their relation to school success.

Historically, research on individual differences that bear on school success has focused on general intelligence. A century of empirical evidence has now unequivocally established that intelligence, defined as the "ability to understand complex ideas, to adapt effectively to the environment, to learn from experience, to engage in various forms of reasoning, to overcome obstacles by taking thought" (Neisser et al., 1996, p. 77) has a monotonic, positive relationship with school success (Gottfredson, 2004; Kuncel, Ones, & Sackett, 2010; Lubinski, 2009). In contrast, the relation between school success and temperamental differences among children has only recently attracted serious attention from researchers. Temperament is typically defined as "constitutionally based individual differences in reactivity and self-regulation, in the domains of affect, activity, and attention" (Rothbart & Bates, 2006, p. 100). While assumed to have a substantial genetic basis, temperament is also influenced by experience and demonstrates both stability and change over time.

This chapter focuses on self-regulation because it is the dimension of temperament most reliably related to school success. We address several related questions: What is the relation between self-regulation and both educational *attainment* (e.g., years of education, high school completion) and *achievement* (e.g., teacher-assigned course grades, standardized achievement test scores)? Does self-regulation also predict job performance, health, and other dimensions of success in life? Finally, what progress has been made in deliberately cultivating self-regulatory competence in children?

NAMING, DEFINING, AND MEASURING SELF-REGULATION

We define self-regulation as the voluntary control of attentional, emotional, and behavioral impulses in the service of personally valued goals and standards. By specifying that goals and standards are personally valued, we do not mean that they are necessarily selfish. On the contrary, self-regulation is required to adhere to goals and standards that are altruistic in nature (e.g., sharing a prize rather than keeping it all for oneself) as well as those that are not (e.g., receiving a larger treat for oneself rather than a smaller one). For clarity's sake, we point out that we use the term "self-regulation" interchangeably with the terms self-control, self-discipline, and willpower – and suggest that the terms impulsiveness and impulsivity connote deficits in self-regulatory competence. Of particular relevance to this chapter, we consider self-regulation to be coextensive with effortful control, a well-recognized aspect of temperament in children that has been defined as "the ability to inhibit a dominant response to perform a subdominant response, to detect errors, and to engage in planning" (Rothbart & Rueda, 2005, p. 169). Crucially, in situations that tax self-regulation, at least two mutually exclusive responses are possible, and the weaker (i.e., subdominant) response is preferred to the stronger (i.e., dominant) impulse. While self-regulation is most certainly multi-dimensional in the sense of involving more than one distinct psychological process (Duckworth & Kern, 2011; Whiteside & Lynam, 2001; Zimmerman & Kitsantas, 2005), we suggest it is nevertheless a coherent higher-order construct (de Ridder, Lensvelt-Mulders, Finkenauer, Stok, & Baumeister, 2012; Heatherton & Wagner, 2011) and a profitable target of study alongside its component processes.

In taxonomies of childhood temperament, self-regulation is typically distinguished from two factors that are more reactive and less voluntary in nature: negative emotionality (shyness, fear, sadness, etc.) and surgency (activity level, sensation seeking, positive emotion) (Rothbart & Rueda, 2005). The location of self-regulation in omnibus taxonomies of adult personality is debatable (Revelle, 1997). At present, the most widely accepted organization for adult personality distinguishes five families of traits (the Big Five): Conscientiousness, Agreeableness, Extraversion, Emotional Stability, and Openness to Experience. Many psychologists consider self-regulation to be identical – or nearly so – with Big Five Conscientiousness (Caspi & Shiner, 2006; Moffitt et al., 2011). Others have proposed that self-regulation relates to other Big Five factors as well. For instance, Whiteside and Lynam (2001) suggest that the tendency to think and plan before acting and the regulation of behavior in the face of frustration are both aspects of Big Five Conscientiousness, whereas the regulation of urgent, negative emotions corresponds to Big Five Emotional Stability, and the tendency to have strong impulses toward risky, exciting activities (which makes self-regulation more difficult) relates to Big Five Extraversion. Additionally, in children, the regulation of impulses in the context of interactions with peers and adults has clear conceptual links to Big Five Agreeableness (Tsukayama, Duckworth, & Kim, 2011).

Executive functioning overlaps conceptually with the temperament trait of effortful control, though the scientific investigation of these two constructs tends to be segregated, with neuroscientists primarily interested in executive functioning and temperament researchers primarily concerned with effortful control (Rothbart & Rueda, 2005). Rueda, Posner, and Rothbart (2005) have argued that executive function (and in particular, the executive attention network, which monitors and resolves conflict between other brain networks) and effortful control are concepts representing different methodological approaches to studying self-regulation of behavior (see also Checa, Rodriguez-Bailon, & Rueda, 2008). Children who do better on direct tasks of executive function tend to be rated significantly higher in effortful control by their parents (Chang & Burns, 2005; Gerardi-Caulton, 2000; Gonzalez, Fuentes, Carranza, & Estevez, 2001; Rothbart, Ellis, Rueda, & Posner, 2003; Simonds, 2007). However, a recent meta-analysis suggests that in general, correlations between individual executive function tasks and questionnaire measures of self-control are small in size (e.g., $r = .14$ with informant-report ratings; Duckworth & Kern, 2011). Even when batteries of executive function tasks are used to improve reliability and validity (Carlson, Faja, & Beck, in press), associates with informant ratings are only moderate in magnitude, suggesting that executive function is not the only contributing factor to self-controlled behavior.

HISTORICAL INTEREST IN SELF-REGULATION AND SCHOOL SUCCESS

The idea that self-regulation plays an important role in the classroom is not new. In a series of lectures addressed to Boston schoolteachers, William James (1899) stated that in "schoolroom work" there is inevitably "a large mass of material that must be dull and unexciting" (pp. 104–105). Further, "there is unquestionably a great native variety among individuals in the type of their attention. Some of us are naturally scatter-brained, and others follow easily a train of connected thoughts without temptation to swerve aside to other subjects" (p. 112). It follows, James argued, that a dispositional advantage in the capacity for sustained attention is tremendously beneficial in the classroom.

Improbably, pioneers of intelligence testing were among the first to recognize the importance of self-regulation to academic performance. Binet and Simon (1916), architect of the first modern intelligence test, noted that performance in school:

> admits of *other things* than intelligence; to succeed in his studies, one must have qualities which depend on attention, will, and character; for example a certain docility, a regularity of habits, and especially *continuity of effort*. A child, even if intelligent, will learn little in class if he never listens, if he spends his time in playing tricks, in giggling, in playing truant. (p. 254, italics added)

David Wechsler (1943), who several decades later helped usher intelligence testing into widespread clinical and educational practice, made similar observations about the unfortunate neglect of "non-intellective" factors which, in conjunction with general intelligence, determine intelligent behavior:

> When our scales measure the non-intellective as well as the intellectual factors in intelligence, they will more nearly measure what in actual life corresponds to intelligent behavior. Under these circumstances they might not be so efficient in selecting individuals likely to succeed in Latin and geometry, but they should do a much better job in selecting those destined to succeed in life (p. 103).

Despite these exhortations of intelligence testing pioneers, the study of temperament and its role in academic achievement languished for much of the 20th century. Happily, there has been a renaissance of theoretical and empirical interest in the role of temperament, and particularly in self-regulation, in determining success in and beyond school (Borghans, Duckworth, Heckman, & ter Weel, 2008; Duckworth, 2009; Duckworth & Seligman, 2005; Roberts, Kuncel, Shiner, Caspi, & Goldberg, 2007). Notably, the proportion of scientific publications on self-regulation has accelerated in recent years, with a nearly threefold increase in relevant publications in the child development literature (Carlson, 2011; Duckworth & Kern, 2011).

We now turn to the empirical findings on self-regulation as it relates to three dimensions of success in school: high school completion, report card grades, and standardized achievement tests.

HIGH SCHOOL COMPLETION

About one in four American students drops out of formal schooling before receiving a high school diploma, and in recent decades this dropout rate has increased slightly (Heckman & LaFontaine, 2007). Research on the General Educational Development (GED) testing program suggests that many high school dropouts are sufficiently intelligent to graduate with their classmates and that aspects of temperament may contribute to their failure to complete high school training. The GED was originally designed to certify veterans who interrupted their high school education to serve in World War II. Since its inception, the GED has evolved into a second-chance program for high school dropouts to certify they have mastered the same skills and knowledge as typical high school graduates. GED recipients have the same measured intelligence as high school graduates who do not attend college, but when measured ability is controlled, GED recipients have lower hourly wages and annual earnings and attain fewer years of education, suggesting they may "lack the abilities to think ahead, to persist in tasks, or to adapt to their environments" (Heckman & Rubinstein, 2001, p. 146).

Several prospective studies have confirmed that self-regulation predicts successful graduation from high school (Kelly & Veldman, 1964). A relatively separate literature has specifically examined the importance of early attention and aggression in determining graduation from high school. Duncan and Magnuson (2010) analyzed a sample of 1,433 individuals in the NLSY-C study, which includes children born to women in the National Longitudinal Study of Youth study initiated in 1979. When child and mother background characteristics, including intelligence and demographic variables, were controlled, anti-social behavior, but not attention measured in childhood, predicted high school completion. Likewise, Fergusson and Horwood (1998) analyzed a sample of 969 individuals in a birth cohort of New Zealand children and found that teacher and parent ratings of conduct problems at age 8 inversely predicted high school completion at age 18. In contrast, Vitaro, Brendgen, Larose, and Tremblay (2005) examined 4,340 individuals in a population-based sample of Quebec children and found that kindergarten teacher ratings of hyperactivity-inattention inversely predicted completion of high school better than did aggressiveness-opposition. In sum, there is evidence that self-regulation of attention, as well as interpersonal behavior, positively predicts high school completion, although there is not enough evidence at this point to suggest whether control of attention or of aggressive impulses is more prognostic of school completion.

COURSE GRADES

Binet's (1916) supposition that success in the classroom depends not only on general intelligence, but also on "attention, will, and character; for example a certain docility, a regularity of habits, and especially continuity of effort" augured Poropat's (2009) meta-analysis of Big Five personality traits and course grades in primary, secondary, and post-secondary education. In an aggregate sample of over 70,000 students, Poropat found that the correlation between grades and Conscientiousness ($r = .19$) was almost as large as that between grades and cognitive ability ($r = .23$). Associations with grades were substantially smaller for other Big Five factors, the largest of which was Openness to Experience ($r = .10$). This pattern remained when cognitive ability was controlled and correlations were corrected for scale reliability (see Figure 10.1).

Complementing Poropat's (2009) analyses, several studies examining more narrowly defined traits and course grades support the conclusion that at all levels of schooling, self-regulatory competence robustly predicts the grades students earn from their teachers. Of particular note are prospective, longitudinal studies that have estimated the effect of self-regulation on course grades when baseline levels of grades are controlled. These studies help isolate the effects of temperament by reducing the likelihood that third variable confounds (e.g., socioeconomic status) and halo effects (e.g., inflated ratings of self-regulation based on perceptions of strong academic performance at baseline) account for the observed associations. For instance, self-regulation measured with parent, teacher, and self-report ratings, in addition to performance on delay of gratification tasks, was found to predict report card grades, with both general intelligence and baseline report card grades controlled, in a sample of American middle school students (Duckworth & Seligman, 2005). Likewise, Duckworth, Tsukayama, and May (2010) have used longitudinal hierarchical linear modeling to show that changes in self-regulation, measured with self-report, parent, and teacher ratings, prospectively predict subsequent changes in report card grades, whereas neither changes in report card grades nor in self-reported self-esteem prospectively predict changes in self-regulation. There is some evidence that the importance of self-regulation to school success generalizes to non-U.S. students. For instance, in a sample of Chinese primary

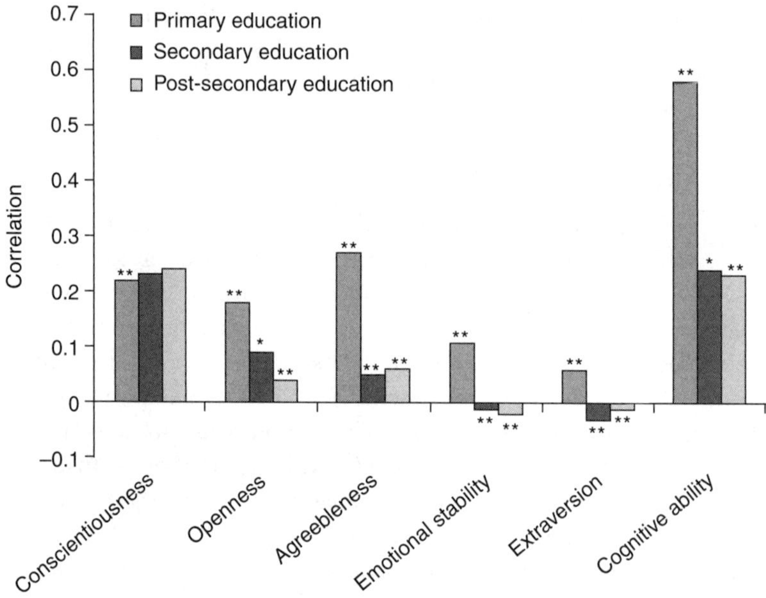

FIGURE 10.1 Associations with course grades by level of education.

Note. Associations were reported in a meta-analysis by Poropat (2009). Estimated correlations with Big Five personality factors control for cognitive ability and are corrected for scale reliability.

schoolchildren, effortful control measured with parent and teacher ratings predicted report card grades, when baseline grades were controlled for (Zhou, Main, & Wang, 2010).

Why might the capacity to regulate emotion, attention, and behavior in the service of valued goals and standards help students earn higher grades? The adage summarizing Aristotle's view of education holds a clue: "The roots of education are bitter, but the fruit is sweet." Indeed, even high-ability students do not generally enjoy completing homework assignments and studying for tests (Wong & Csikszentmihalyi, 1991). To a large degree, the many tasks required of a student to earn high course grades (e.g., concentrating on difficult new concepts, attending to the teacher rather than joking with classmates, practicing skills repeatedly to the point of fluency, working on homework alone rather than socializing with friends) all yield long-term rewards at the expense of short-term comfort and pleasure. Indeed, there is evidence that the association between self-regulation and course grades is mediated by effective study habits, effort, and prosocial behavior in the classroom (Credé & Kuncel, 2008; Duckworth & Seligman, 2005; Lubbers,

Van Der Werf, Kuyper, & Hendriks, 2010; Noftle & Robins, 2007; Valiente, Lemery-Chalfant, & Castro, 2007; Valiente, Lemery-Chalfant, Swanson, & Reiser, 2008).

There is increasing evidence to suggest that the path of school success is set at a tender age. For example, self-regulation measured during the preschool years predicts school readiness and academic achievement (e.g., Blair & Razza, 2007; Mazzocco & Kover, 2007; Morrison, Ponitz, & McClelland, 2010), and teachers often report that the most important determinant of classroom success in kindergarten and early school grades is the extent to which children can sit still, pay attention, and follow rules (e.g., Rimm-Kaufman, Pianta, & Cox, 2000). In fact, self-regulation is often a better predictor of academic outcomes than is IQ or grades. In an especially impressive report, with school achievement levels controlled, children who were rated one standard deviation above the mean on attention span/persistence at age 4 years had 39% greater odds of completing college by age 25 (McClelland, Piccinin, Acock, & Stallings, 2011).

STANDARDIZED ACHIEVEMENT TEST SCORES

Like course grades, standardized achievement test scores reflect a student's acquired skills and knowledge. However, psychological research studies using standardized achievement tests to index academic performance are somewhat less common than those using course grades. There is nevertheless sufficient empirical evidence to suggest that more self-regulated learners surpass their more impulsive peers on these measures of performance as well.

Martin and colleagues were among the first to demonstrate, in a series of small-sample studies, that teacher and parent ratings of early childhood persistence, (low) distractibility, and (low) activity prospectively predict both course grades and standardized achievement test scores (see Martin, 1989, for a summary). Likewise, in a representative sample of 790 Baltimore first graders, teacher ratings of attention span-restlessness in first grade predicted both course grades and standardized achievement test scores four years later (Alexander, Entwisle, & Dauber, 1993).

More recently, in a sample of 143 preschool children from low-income homes, a peg-tapping executive function task (in which children were instructed to tap twice with a wooden dowel when the experimenter tapped once, and once when the experimenter tapped twice) accounted for unique variance in standardized assessments of math knowledge, phonemic awareness, and letter knowledge in kindergarten, even after controlling for general intelligence (Blair & Razza, 2007). Similarly, in a sample of 291 kindergarteners, teacher and parent ratings of effortful control predicted performance on standardized achievement tests six months later, and this association held when controlling for both verbal intelligence and family socioeconomic status (Valiente, Lemery-Chalfant, & Swanson, 2010). Likewise, Finn, Pannozzo, and Voelkl (1995) found that teacher ratings of inattention at the beginning of the school year predicted standardized achievement test scores at the end of the school year in a sample of 1,103 fourth graders.

Task measures of effortful control and related traits in the Conscientiousness family have also been shown to predict performance on standardized achievement tests. For instance, the number of seconds a child waits for a more preferred treat in the preschool delay of gratification paradigm has been shown to predict performance on the SAT college admission test more than a decade later (Mischel, Shoda, & Rodriguez, 1989). The Head-to-Toes and Head-Toes-Knees-Shoulders tasks require young children to inhibit automatic responses, pay attention, and keep instructions in working memory (e.g., to touch their heads when the experimenter says "touch your toes") (Ponitz et al., 2008; Ponitz, McClelland, Matthews, & Morrison, 2009). Performance on this brief task predicts later performance on standardized achievement tests (McClelland et al., 2007).

Perhaps most conclusively, Duncan and colleagues (2007) analyzed six large, longitudinal datasets whose collective sample size exceeded 34,000 and found that school-entry attention skills, measured variously by task and questionnaire measures, prospectively predict standardized achievement test scores, even with school-entry academic skills controlled. In contrast, internalizing and externalizing behaviors at school entry do not reliably predict standardized achievement test scores.

Where Course Grades and Standardized Achievement Test Scores Diverge

While course grades and standardized achievement tests are highly correlated and are both designed to assess academic skills and knowledge, they are not equally predicted by individual differences in self-regulation. For instance, Duckworth, Quinn, and Tsukayama (2012) found in two samples of middle school students followed longitudinally that self-control predicted changes in report card grades over time better than did IQ, an effect that was mediated by homework completion and classroom conduct. In contrast, IQ predicted changes in standardized achievement test scores over time better than did self-control. These findings are consistent with those of

Willingham, Pollack, and Lewis (2002), who examined data from 8,454 high school seniors in the National Education Longitudinal Study (NELS). Self-regulated behaviors such as attending class regularly and promptly, participating in class activities, completing work on time, and avoiding drug and gang activity were more strongly associated with grade point average (GPA) than with standardized achievement test scores. Likewise, Oliver, Guerin, and Gottfried (2007) found that parent and self-report ratings of distractibility and persistence at age 16 predicted high school and college GPA but not SAT test scores. Similarly, several cross-sectional studies of college students have shown that aspects of self-regulation are more strongly associated with GPA than with SAT scores (Conard, 2005; Noftle & Robins, 2007; Wolfe & Johnson, 1995).

Why does self-regulation predict course grades better than standardized achievement test scores? Course grades and standardized test scores are generally highly correlated (Willingham et al., 2002). Not surprisingly, therefore, standardized achievement tests and grades are often wrongly assumed to be "mutual surrogates; that is, measuring much the same thing, even in the face of obvious differences" (Willingham et al., 2002, p. 2). Table 10.1 compares these two indices of achievement on several dimensions, including content, format, and the relevance of homework and classroom conduct. Many of the design features of standardized achievement tests can be understood as facilitating apples-to-apples comparisons of students from diverse contexts (e.g., different schools). The design features of course grades, on the other hand, reflect a distinct function – the communication of a classroom "teacher's judgment as to how well a student has fulfilled the implicit local contract between teacher and student" (Willingham et al., 2002, p. 28).

The power of standardized achievement tests to predict later academic and occupational outcomes is well established (Kuncel & Hezlett, 2007; Sackett, Borneman, & Connelly, 2008; Willingham, 1985). Nevertheless, Bowen, Chingos and McPherson (2009) found that cumulative high school GPA predicts graduation from college dramatically better than SAT/ACT scores do, even without adjusting for differences in high school quality. Bowen and colleagues also found high school GPA to more powerfully predict college rank-in-class. In an analysis of about 80,000 University of California students followed over four years, Geiser and Santelices (2007) reached the same conclusion.

In sum, standardized achievement tests and teacher-assigned course grades both reflect students' accumulated knowledge and skill, but they differ in important ways. The benefits of dispositional self-regulation, which

TABLE 10.1 *A Comparison of Standardized Achievement Tests and Teacher-Assigned Course Grades*

Dimension	Standardized Achievement Tests	Teacher-Assigned Course Grades
Format	Typically multiple-choice questions, with fewer essay and short-answer questions	Eclectic, including multiple-choice questions, essays and short-answer questions
Authorship	Centralized testing company or government agency	Classroom teacher
Time limitations	Strictly time-limited, with the expectation that at least some students may not finish all questions in the allotted time	Typically less stringent in terms of time limits
Academic content	Skills and knowledge expected to be covered by all students at a given grade level in a particular region (e.g., content that is aligned to school district, state, or national standards).	Specific skills and knowledge taught in the classroom that year to those students
Effort and conduct	Not directly considered	Considered by most teachers, at least to some degree
Homework and long-term projects	Not considered	Considered by most teachers, at least to some degree
Grading standards	Objective and uniform across all test-takers	Subjectively determined by individual teachers
Frequency of assessment	Typically administered once annually during one or two testing sessions	Assessments that contribute to course grades can be daily or weekly

predicts better conduct in the classroom (Duckworth, Quinn, & Tsukayama, 2012), more hours of homework and studying (Duckworth & Seligman, 2005), and fewer hours of television watching (Duckworth & Seligman, 2005), seem more relevant to accomplishing the work teachers have prescribed. In part for this reason, girls, who often are higher than boys in self-regulation, reliably earn higher course grades than boys in every subject from primary school through college (U.S. Department of Education, 2004) and take equally difficult courses (Buchmann, DiPrete, & McDaniel, 2008) – but do not reliably outperform boys on intelligence tests (Duckworth & Seligman, 2006; Fergusson & Horwood, 1997; Matthews, Ponitz, & Morrison, 2009; Stricker, Rock, & Burton, 1993) or standardized achievement tests (Duckworth &

Seligman, 2006). It is worth noting that across all racial groups in the United States, girls now graduate from high school and college at higher rates than boys, a reversal of the historic trend favoring boys (Buchmann et al., 2008).

SCHOOL-BASED INTERVENTIONS

Despite this overwhelming evidence for a positive association between self-regulation and school success, one might be concerned about taking a proactive approach through intervention on the grounds that there can be too much of a good thing. Indeed, it has been argued that the extremes of any trait, even those demonstrated to be salutary in most contexts, have deleterious consequences (Grant & Schwartz, 2011). Despite theoretical concerns that "overcontrol" could manifest itself in pathological behavior (Kohn, 2008), there is scant evidence that very many children suffer from being overly capable of regulating their attention and behavior in the service of their personally valued goals and standards (Baumeister, Schmeichel, & Vohs, 2007; de Ridder et al., 2012; Moffitt et al., 2011).

So then, what can schools do to encourage the development of self-control in children? One perspective is that temperament is entirely immutable; the opposite view is that behavior is entirely determined by context and situation. Empirical evidence supports neither of these extreme positions. On the contrary, generally, the rank-order stability of traits is moderate in childhood (Hampson & Goldberg, 2006; Roberts & DelVecchio, 2000). Thus, while there is enough stability to make it sensible to talk about individual differences in self-regulation, there is enough rank-order shuffling to consider means of intentionally accelerating self-control development. Indeed, several recent studies indicate that executive function is malleable (see Diamond & Lee, 2011). Next we summarize research on school-based interventions, though we should note that there are fewer rigorous empirical studies than one might imagine. Taking a broader view, the U.S. Institute of Education Sciences examined 93 studies of 41 programs aimed at improving aspects of character including self-control, and only 7 of these met their criteria for evidence standards without reservation.

Tools of the Mind, a Vygotskian preschool and early primary school curriculum, has demonstrated in random-assignment studies that it can improve classroom behavior as well as executive functioning (Barnett, Yarosz, Thomas, Hornbeck, Stechuk, & Burns, 2006; Barnett et al., 2008; Bodrova & Leong, 2001; Bodrova & Leong, 2007; Diamond, Barnett, Thomas, & Munro, 2007). *Tools of the Mind* is a multi-faceted curriculum in which teachers receive detailed curriculum materials and extensive training and support throughout the school year. Key principles of the program's approach include scaffolding student development from regulation by others to self-regulation, mental tools (i.e., strategies) to help children gain control of their behavior, reflective and meta-cognitive thinking, practice of self-regulation via developmentally appropriate games and activities, and increasingly complex and extended social, imaginary play (Bodrova & Leong, 2001). For example, one of the activities in the *Tools* curriculum is "buddy reading" in which one student is the speaker, symbolized by holding up a sign illustrating a mouth, while the peer is the listener, symbolized by a drawing of an ear. In keeping with Vygotsky's (1978) law of development in which regulation shifts from inter- to intra-personal, these cultural tools are gradually shed as children learn to self-regulate during story time.

Likewise, children who attended a Montessori school have been shown to perform better on tasks of executive function than children assigned by lottery to non-Montessori schools (Lillard, 2012; Lillard & Else-Quest, 2006). As with *Tools of the Mind*, the Montessori approach is multi-faceted. Characteristics of Montessori schools include multi-age classrooms, student-chosen learning activities carried out with minimal instruction from teachers, and long periods of time designated for uninterrupted pursuit of these activities. Both *Tools of the Mind* and the Montessori approach have been shown in random-assignment studies to improve performance on standardized achievement tests (Barnett et al., 2008; Lillard & Else-Quest, 2006).

In another example, the Promoting Alternative Thinking Strategies (PATHS) curriculum teaches self-control, emotional awareness, and social problem-solving skills and is aimed at elementary school children (Bierman et al., 2010). Like *Tools of the Mind* and the Montessori approach, the PATHS curriculum is multi-faceted, with an explicit commitment to fostering skills that support each other. For instance, emotional awareness (e.g., recognizing the internal and external cues of affect) is understood as essential to social problem solving (e.g., sustaining friendships, peacefully resolving conflicts with classmates). Teachers trained to deliver the PATHS curriculum guide students through skill-building activities and also reinforce the same lessons throughout the school day. A recent random-assignment, longitudinal study demonstrated that the PATHS curriculum reduces teacher and peer ratings of aggression, improves teacher and peer ratings of prosocial behavior, and improves teacher ratings of academic engagement (Bierman et al., 2010). PATHS is an exemplar of school-based social and emotional learning (SEL) programs, whose impact on both course grades

($d = .33$) and standardized achievement tests scores ($d = .27$) was recently documented in a meta-analysis of controlled studies involving over 270,000 children in kindergarten through college (Durlak, Weissberg, Dymnicki, Taylor, & Schellinger, 2011). Note, however, that not all random-assignment studies of SEL programs have yielded positive results (Social and Character Development Research Consortium, 2010), underscoring the need for research on the active ingredients of multi-faceted SEL interventions.

More generally, classrooms offering strong instructional and emotional support can boost academic performance as measured by standardized achievement test scores. Children identified as at-risk on the basis of prior attention and behavior problems, in particular, benefit from being in classrooms whose general climate is warm, relaxed, and well-managed, with teachers who respond flexibly and appropriately to children's needs while also encouraging children to take responsibility for their own actions (Hamre & Pianta, 2005; Rudasill, Gallagher, & White, 2010). Similar results were reported in the Chicago School Readiness Project, in which teachers who received support and training in classroom management had students who were better self-regulated and, in turn, had higher performance on academic outcomes (Raver et al., 2011). Therefore, interventions and professional development opportunities that help teachers create positive classroom environments should yield downstream benefits for their students (Jennings & Greenberg, 2009; Zins, Elias, & Greenberg, 2007).

Interventions that teach children meta-cognitive strategies, such as goal setting and planning, can also improve self-regulatory competence and academic outcomes. The technique of mental contrasting with implementation intentions (MCII), for example, first developed as a self-regulatory strategy for adults, has also been shown to help children and adolescents. For instance, in a random-assignment study of high school students preparing for college entrance examinations, students were instructed to mentally contrast the positive benefits of studying (e.g., "I'll have a better chance of getting into my top-choice college") with obstacles that stood in the way of this study goal (e.g., "My little sister bothers me when I try to study"), and then to make a plan to obviate these obstacles (e.g., "If my little sister bothers me, then I will study in my bedroom with the door closed") (Duckworth, Grant, Loew, Oettingen, & Gollwitzer, 2010). Compared to students in a placebo-control condition who wrote a practice essay for the entrance exam, students who learned MCII completed over 60% more questions in study materials provided to students in both conditions. Likewise, in a random-assignment study at an urban middle school, fifth grade students taught MCII improved their report card grades and school attendance relative to students in a placebo-control condition (Duckworth, Gollwitzer, Kirby, & Oettingen, 2010). Children as young as preschool age demonstrate superior self-control when using plans to avoid distraction and temptation (Mischel & Patterson, 1976, 1978; Patterson & Mischel, 1975, 1976), suggesting that this meta-cognitive strategy might be introduced to children in the earliest years of formal education.

Any review of school-based interventions to foster positive dimensions of temperament would be incomplete without mention of exercise and play. Aerobic exercise has been shown to improve executive function and performance on standardized achievement tests in preadolescent children (Best, 2010; Hillman et al., 2009). The robust findings linking physical activity to attention and other aspects of self-control suggest that eliminating gym class to make room for formal academic instruction may, paradoxically, reduce self-control (Hillman, Erickson, & Kramer, 2008). Play, and in particular pretend (i.e., imaginary) play with others, facilitates the development of a wide array of self-regulation skills (Berk, Mann, & Ogan, 2006; Saltz, Dixon, & Johnson, 1977; Singer & Singer, 1990, 2006). Like gym class, recess is often considered of secondary importance to academic objectives, but reducing opportunities for children to make up stories, exercise their imaginations and their bodies, and resolve conflicts without help from adults may ultimately impair normative development of attention and other aspects of Conscientiousness (Panksepp, 2007).

CONCLUSION

Early psychologists speculated that differences in temperament can help or hinder performance in – and beyond – the classroom. This conjecture has since been confirmed. Substantial empirical evidence suggests that children's ability to regulate attentional, behavioral, and emotional impulses paves the way for success in school. That is, learning, applying skills and knowledge, staying in school, and graduating from high school and college depend in large part on the capacity to inhibit dominant impulses in order to execute subdominant but superior actions, which overlaps substantially with the temperament/personality trait of Conscientiousness. Growing evidence of the benefits of self-regulation for success in school has motivated several school-based interventions targeting school culture, classroom curriculum and environment, metacognitive strategies, and aerobic exercise. Several of these efforts have now been shown in rigorous random-assignment studies to have measurable effects on behavior and academic performance, collectively providing proof that a child's temperament, while strongly influenced by genetic factors, is nevertheless amenable to environmental influence. Self-regulation can be cultivated.

REFERENCES

Alexander, K. L., Entwisle, D. R., & Dauber, S. L. (1993). First-grade classroom behavior: Its short-and long-term consequences for school performance. *Child Development, 64*, 801–814.

Barnett, W. S., Yarosz, D., Thomas, J., Hornbeck, A., Stechuk, R., & Burns, M. S. (2006). *Educational effectiveness of a Vygotskian approach to preschool education: A randomized trial.* Rutgers, NJ: National Institute for Early Education Research.

Barnett, W. S., Jung, K., Yarosz, D. J., Thomas, J., Hornbeck, A., Stechuk, R., & Burns, S. (2008). Educational effects of the Tools of the Mind curriculum: A randomized trial. *Early Childhood Research Quarterly, 23*, 299–313.

Baumeister, R. F., Schmeichel, B. J., & Vohs, K. D. (2007). Self-regulation and the executive function: The self as controlling agent. In A. W. Kruglanski & E. T. Higgins (Eds.), *Social psychology: Handbook of basic principles* (pp. 516–539). New York, NY: Guilford Press.

Berk, L. E., Mann, T. D., & Ogan, A. T. (2006). *Make-believe play: Wellspring for development of self-regulation.* New York, NY: Oxford University Press.

Best, J. R. (2010). Effects of physical activity on children's executive function: Contributions of experimental research on aerobic exercise. *Developmental Review, 30*, 331–351.

Bierman, K. L., Coie, J. D., Dodge, K. A., Greenberg, M. T., Lochman, J. E., McMahon, R. J., & Pinderhughes, E. (2010). The effects of a multiyear universal social-emotional learning program: The role of student and school characteristics. *Journal of Consulting and Clinical Psychology, 78*, 156–168.

Binet, A., & Simon, T. (1916). *The development of intelligence in children (The Binet-Simon Scale).* Baltimore, MD: Williams & Wilkins.

Blair, C., & Razza, R. P. (2007). Relating effortful control, executive function, and false belief understanding to emerging math and literacy ability in kindergarten. *Child Development, 78*, 647–663.

Bodrova, E., & Leong, D. J. (2001). Tools of the mind: A case study of implementing the Vygotskian approach in American early childhood and primary classrooms. *Innodata Monographs 7*. Geneva, Switzerland: International Bureau of Education.

Bodrova, E., & Leong, D. J. (2007). *Tools of the mind: The Vygotskian approach to early childhood education* (2nd ed.). Upper Saddle River, NJ: Pearson Education.

Borghans, L., Duckworth, A. L., Heckman, J. J., & ter Weel, B. (2008). The economics and psychology of personality traits. *Journal of Human Resources, 43*, 972–1059.

Bowen, W. G., Chingos, M. M., & McPherson, M. S. (2009). Test scores and high school grades as predictors. *Crossing the finish line: Completing college at America's public universities* (pp. 112–133). Princeton, NJ: Princeton University Press.

Buchmann, C., DiPrete, T. A., & McDaniel, A. (2008). Gender inequalities in education. *Annual Review of Sociology, 34*, 319–337.

Carlson, S. M. (2011). Introduction to the special issue: Executive function. *Journal of Experimental Child Psychology, 108*, 411–413.

Carlson, S. M., Faja, S., & Beck, D. M. (in press). Incorporating early development into measurement approaches: The need for a continuum of measures across development. In J. A. Griffin, L. S. Freund, & P. McCardle (Eds.), *Executive function in preschool age children: Integrating measurement, neurodevelopment, and translational research.* Washington, DC: American Psychological Association.

Caspi, A., & Shiner, R. L. (2006). Personality development. In W. Damon, R. Lerner, & N. Eisenberg (Eds.), *Handbook of child psychology* (6th ed., Vol. 3, pp. 300–365). New York, NY: Wiley.

Chang, F., & Burns, B. M. (2005). Attention in preschoolers: Associations with effortful control and motivation. *Child Development, 76*, 247–263.

Checa, P., Rodriguez-Bailon, R., & Rueda, M. R. (2008). Neurocognitive and temperamental systems of self-regulation and early adolescents' social and academic outcomes. *Mind, Brain, and Education, 2*, 177–187.

Conard, M. A. (2005). Aptitude is not enough: How personality and behavior predict academic performance. *Journal of Research in Personality, 40*, 339–346.

Credé, M., & Kuncel, N. R. (2008). Study habits, skills, and attitudes: The third pillar supporting collegiate academic performance. *Perspectives on Psychological Science, 3*, 425–453.

de Ridder, D. T. D., Lensvelt- Mulders, G., Finkenauer, C., Stok, F. M., & Baumeister, R. F. (2012). Taking stock of self-control: A meta-analysis of how trait self-control relates to a wide range of behaviors. *Personality and Social Psychology Review, 16*, 76–99.

Diamond, A., Barnett, W. S., Thomas, J., & Munro, S. (2007). Preschool program improves cognitive control. *Science, 318*(5855), 1387–1388.

Diamond, A., & Lee, K. (2011). Interventions shown to aid executive function development in children 4 to 12 years old. *Science, 333*(6045), 959–964.

Duckworth, A. L. (2009). (Over and) beyond high-stakes testing. *American Psychologist, 64*, 279–280.

Duckworth, A. L., Gollwitzer, A., Kirby, T., & Oettingen, G. (2010). From fantasy to action: Mental Contrasting with Implementation Intentions (MCII) improves report card grades and school attendance among disadvantaged children. Manuscript in preparation.

Duckworth, A. L., Grant, H., Loew, B., Oettingen, G., & Gollwitzer, P. M. (2010). Self-regulation strategies improve self-discipline in adolescents: Benefits of mental contrasting and implementation intentions. *Educational Psychology, 31*, 17–26. doi: 10.1080/01443410.2010.506003

Duckworth, A. L., & Kern, M. (2011). A meta-analysis of the convergent validity of self-control measures. *Journal of Research in Personality, 45*, 259–268.

Duckworth, A. L., Quinn, P. D., & Tsukayama, E. (2012). What *No Child Left Behind* leaves behind: The roles of IQ and self-control in predicting standardized achievement test scores and report card grades. *Journal of Educational Psychology*, 104, 439–451.

Duckworth, A. L., & Seligman, M. E. P. (2005). Self-discipline outdoes IQ in predicting academic performance of adolescents. *Psychological Science, 16*, 939–944.

Duckworth, A. L., & Seligman, M. E. P. (2006). Self-discipline gives girls the edge: Gender in self-discipline, grades, and achievement test scores. *Journal of Educational Psychology, 98*, 198–208.

Duckworth, A. L., Tsukayama, E., & May, H. (2010). Establishing causality using longitudinal hierarchical linear modeling: An illustration predicting achievement from self-control. *Social Psychological and Personality Science, 1*, 311–317.

Duncan, G. J., Dowsett, C. J., Claessens, A., Mugnuson, K., Huston, A. C., Klebanov, P., … Japel, C. (2007). School readiness and later achievement. *Developmental Psychology, 43*, 1428–1446.

Duncan, G. J., & Magnuson, K. (2010). The nature and impact of early achievement skills, attention skills, and behavior problems. In G. Duncan & R. Murnane (Eds.), *Whither opportunity? Rising inequality and the uncertain life changes of low-income children*. New York, NY: Russell Sage Press.

Durlak, J. A., Weissberg, R. P., Dymnicki, A. B., Taylor, R. D., & Schellinger, K. B. (2011). The impact of enhancing students' social and emotional learning: A meta-analysis of school-based universal interventions. *Child Development, 82*, 405–432. doi: 10.1111/j.1467–8624.2010.01564.x

Fergusson, D. M., & Horwood, L. J. (1997). Gender differences in educational achievement in a New Zealand birth cohort. *New Zealand Journal of Educational Studies, 32*, 83–96.

Fergusson, D. M., & Horwood, L. J. (1998). Early conduct problems and later life opportunities. *Journal of Child Psychology and Psychiatry, 39*, 1097–1108.

Finn, J. D., Pannozzo, G. M., & Voelkl, K. E. (1995). Disruptive and inattentive-withdrawn behavior and achievement among fourth graders. *Elementary School Journal, 95*, 421–434.

Geiser, S., & Santelices, M. V. (2007). Validity of high school grades in predicting student success beyond the freshman year: High-school record vs. standardized tests as indicators of four-year college outcomes. *Research and Occasional Paper Series from the Center for Studies in Higher Education at the University of California, Berkeley, CSHE 2007* (CSHE.6.07). Retrieved from http://cshe.berkeley.edu/publications/publications.php?id=265.

Gerardi-Caulton, G. (2000). Sensitivity to spatial conflict and the development of self-regulation in children 24–36 months of age. *Developmental Science, 3*, 397–404.

Gonzalez, C., Fuentes, L. J., Carranza, J. A., & Estevez, A. F. (2001). Temperament and attention in the self-regulation of 7-year-old children. *Personality and Individual Differences, 30*, 931–946.

Gottfredson, L. S. (2004). Schools and the g factor. *Wilson Quarterly, 28*, 34–35.

Grant, A. M., & Schwartz, B. (2011). Too much of a good thing: The challenge and opportunity of the inverted-U. *Perspectives on Psychological Science, 6*, 61–76.

Hampson, S. E., & Goldberg, L. R. (2006). A first large-cohort study of personality-trait stability over the 40 years between elementary school and midlife. *Journal of Personality and Social Psychology, 91*, 763–779.

Hamre, B. K., & Pianta, R. C. (2005). Can instructional and emotional support in the first-grade classroom make a difference for children at risk of school failure? *Child Development, 76*, 949–967.

Heatherton, T. F., & Wagner, D. D. (2011). Cognitive neuroscience of self-regulation failure. *Trends in Cognitive Science, 15*, 132–139.

Heckman, J. J., & LaFontaine, P. A. (2007). The American high school graduation rate: Trends and levels. *Discussion Paper IZA DP No. 3216* (pp. 1–62). Bonn, Germany: Forschungsinstitut zur Zukunft der Arbeit Institute for the Study of Labor.

Heckman, J. J., & Rubinstein, Y. (2001). The importance of noncognitive skills: Lessons from the GED testing program. *American Economic Review, 91*, 145–149.

Hillman, C. H., Erickson, K. I., & Kramer, A. F. (2008). Be smart, exercise your heart: Exercise effects on brain and cognition. *Nature Reviews Neuroscience, 9*, 58–65.

Hillman, C. H., Pontifex, M. B., Raine, L. B., Castelli, D. M., Hall, E. E., & Kramer, A. F. (2009). The effect of acute treadmill walking on cognitive control and academic achievement in preadolescent children. *Neuroscience, 159*, 1044–1054.

James, W. (1899). *Talks to teachers on psychology and to students on some of life's ideals*. New York, NY: Holt.

Jennings, P. A., & Greenberg, M. T. (2009). The prosocial classroom: Teacher social and emotional competence in relation to student and classroom outcomes. *Review of Educational Research, 79*, 491–525.

Kelly, F. J., & Veldman, D. J. (1964). Delinquency and school dropout behavior as a function of impulsivity and nondominant values. *Journal of Abnormal and Social Psychology, 69*, 190–194.

Kohn, A. (2008). Why self-discipline is overrated: The (troubling) theory and practice of control from within. *Phi Delta Kappan, 90*, 168–176.

Kuncel, N. R., & Hezlett, S. A. (2007). Standardized tests predict graduate students' success. *Science, 315*, 1080–1081.

Kuncel, N. R., Ones, D. S., & Sackett, P. R. (2010). Individual differences as predictors of work, educational, and broad life outcomes. *Personality and Individual Differences, 49*, 331–336.

Lillard, A. (2012). Preschool children's development in classic Montessori, supplemented Montessori, and conventional programs. *Journal of School Psychology, 50*, 379–401.

Lillard, A., & Else-Quest, N. (2006). Evaluating Montessori education. *Science, 313*, 1893–1894.

Lubbers, M. J., Van Der Werf, M. P. C., Kuyper, H., & Hendriks, A. A. J. (2010). Does homework behavior mediate the relation between personality and academic performance? *Learning and Individual Differences, 20*, 203–208.

Lubinski, D. (2009). Exceptional cognitive ability: The phenotype. *Behavior Genetics, 39*, 350–358.

Martin, R. P. (1989). Activity level, distractibility, and persistence: Critical characteristics in early schooling. In G. A. Kohnstamm, J. E. Bates, & M. K. Rothbart (Eds.), *Temperament in childhood* (pp. 451–461). Chichester, England: Wiley.

Matthews, J. S., Ponitz, C. C., & Morrison, F. J. (2009). Early gender differences in self-regulation and academic achievement. *Journal of Educational Psychology, 101*, 689–704.

Mazzocco, M. M., & Kover, S. T. (2007). A longitudinal assessment of executive function skills and their association with math performance. *Child Neuropsychology, 13*, 18–45.

McClelland, M. M., Cameron, C. E., Connor, C. M., Farris, C. L., Jewkes, A. M., & Morrison, F. J. (2007). Links between behavioral regulation and preschoolers' literacy, vocabulary, and math skills. *Developmental Psychology, 43*, 947–959.

McClelland, M. M., Piccinin, A., Acock, A. C., & Stallings, M. C. (2011). *Relations between preschool attention and later school achievement and educational outcomes*. Manuscript submitted for publication.

Mischel, W., & Patterson, C. J. (1976). Substantive and structural elements of effective plans for self-control. *Journal of Personality and Social Psychology, 34*, 942–950.

Mischel, W., & Patterson, C. J. (1978). Effective plans for self-control in children. In W. A. Collins (Ed.), *Minnesota symposia on child psychology* (Vol. 11, pp.199–230). Hillsdale, NJ: Erlbaum.

Mischel, W., Shoda, Y., & Rodriguez, M. L. (1989). Delay of gratification in children. *Science, 244*, 933–938.

Moffitt, T. E., Arseneault, L., Belsky, D., Dickson, N., Hancox, R. J., Harrington, H. L., … Caspi, A. (2011). A gradient of childhood self-control predicts health, wealth, and public safety. *Proceedings of the National Academy of Sciences, 108*, 2693–2698.

Morrison, F. J., Ponitz, C. C., & McClelland, M. M. (2010). Self-regulation and academic achievement in the transition to school. In S. D. Calkins & M. A. Bell (Eds.), *Child development at the intersection of emotion and cognition*. Washington, DC: American Psychological Association.

Neisser, U., Boodoo, G., Bouchard, T. J., Jr., Boykin, A. W., Brody, N., Ceci, S. J., … Urbina, S. (1996). Intelligence: Knowns and unknowns. *American Psychologist, 51*, 77–101.

Noftle, E. E., & Robins, R. W. (2007). Personality predictors of academic outcomes: Big five correlates of GPA and SAT scores. *Journal of Personality and Social Psychology, 93*, 116–130.

Oliver, P. H., Guerin, D. W., & Gottfried, A. W. (2007). Temperamental task orientation: Relation to high school and college educational accomplishments. *Learning and Individual Differences, 17*, 220–230.

Panksepp, J. (2007). Can play diminish ADHD and facilitate the construction of the social brain? *Journal of the Canadian Academy of Child and Adolescent Psychiatry, 16*, 57–66.

Patterson, C. J., & Mischel, W. (1975). Plans to resist distraction. *Developmental Psychology, 11*, 369–378.

Patterson, C. J., & Mischel, W. (1976). Effects of temptation-inhibiting and task-facilitating plans on self-control. *Journal of Personality and Social Psychology, 33*, 209–217.

Ponitz, C. C., McClelland, M. M., Jewkes, A. M., Connor, C. M., Farris, C. L., & Morrison, F. J. (2008). Touch your toes! Developing a direct measure of behavioral regulation in early childhood. *Early Childhood Research Quarterly, 23*, 141–158.

Ponitz, C. C., McClelland, M. M., Matthews, J. S., & Morrison, F. J. (2009). A structured observation of behavioral self-regulation and its contribution to kindergarten outcomes. *Developmental Psychology, 45*, 605–619.

Poropat, A. E. (2009). A meta-analysis of the five-factor model of personality and academic performance. *Psychological Bulletin, 135*, 322–338.

Raver, C. C., Jones, S. M., Li- Grining, C. P., Zhai, F., Bub, K., & Pressler, E. (2011). CSRP's impact on low-income preschoolers' preacademic skills: Self-regulation as a mediating mechanism. *Child Development, 82*, 362–378.

Revelle, W. (1997). Extraversion and impulsivity: The lost dimension? In H. Nyborg (Ed.), *The scientific study of human nature: Tribute to Hans J. Eysenck at eighty* (pp. 189–212). Oxford, UK: Pergamon/Elsevier Science.

Rimm-Kaufman, S. E., Pianta, R. C., & Cox, M. J. (2000). Teachers' judgments of problems in the transition to kindergarten. *Early Childhood Research Quarterly, 15*, 147–166.

Rivkin, S. G., Hanushek, E. A., & Kain, J. F. (2005). Teachers, schools, and academic achievement. *Econometrica, 73*, 417–458. doi: 10.1111/j.1468–0262.2005.00584.x

Roberts, B. W., & DelVecchio, W. F. (2000). The rank-order consistency of personality traits from childhood to old age: A quantitative review of longitudinal studies. *Psychological Bulletin, 126*, 3–25.

Roberts, B. W., Kuncel, N. R., Shiner, R., Caspi, A., & Goldberg, L. R. (2007). The power of personality: The comparative validity of personality traits, socioeconomic status, and cognitive ability for predicting important life outcomes. *Perspectives on Psychological Science, 2, 313*–345.

Rothbart, M. K., & Bates, J. E. (2006). Temperament. In N. Eisenberg (Vol. Ed.), W. Damon, & R. M. Lerner (Series Eds.), *Handbook of child psychology: Social, emotional, and personality development* (6th ed., Vol. 3, pp. 99–166). New York, NY: Wiley.

Rothbart, M. K., Ellis, L. K., Rueda, M. R., & Posner, M. I. (2003). Developing mechanisms of temperamental effortful control. *Journal of Personality, 71*, 1113–1143.

Rothbart, M. K., & Rueda, M. R. (2005). The development of effortful control. In U. Mayr, E. Awh, & S. W. Keele (Eds.), *Developing individuality in the human brain* (pp. 167–188). Washington, DC: American Psychological Association.

Rudasill, K. M., Gallagher, K. C., & White, J. M. (2010). Temperamental attention and activity, classroom emotional support, and academic achievement in third grade. *Journal of School Psychology, 48*, 113–134.

Rueda, M. R., Posner, M. I., & Rothbart, M. K. (2005). The development of executive attention: Contributions to the emergence of self-regulation. *Developmental Neuropsychology, 28*, 573–594.

Sackett, P. R., Borneman, M. J., & Connelly, B. S. (2008). High stakes testing in higher education and employment: Appraising the evidence for validity and fairness. *American Psychologist, 63*, 215–227.

Saltz, E., Dixon, D., & Johnson, J. (1977). Training disadvantaged preschoolers on various fantasy activities: Effects on cognitive functioning and impulse control. *Child Development, 48*, 367–380.

Simonds, J. (2007). The role of reward sensitivity and response execution in childhood extraversion. *Dissertation Abstracts International: Section B: Sciences and Engineering, 67*, 6099.

Singer, D. G., & Singer, J. L. (1990). Cognitive and emotional growth through play. *The house of make-believe: Children's play and the developing imagination* (pp. 117–152). Cambridge, MA: Harvard University Press.

Singer, J. L., & Singer, D. G. (2006). Preschoolers' imaginative play as precursor of narrative consciousness. *Imagination, Cognition and Personality, 25*, 97–117.

Social and Character Development Research Consortium (2010). *Efficacy of schoolwide programs to promote social and character development and reduce problem behavior in elementary school children.* Retrieved from http://ies.ed.gov/ncer/pubs/20112001/pdf/20112001.pdf.

Stricker, L. J., Rock, D. A., & Burton, N. W. (1993). Sex differences in predictions of college grades from scholastic aptitude test scores. *Journal of Educational Psychology, 85*, 710–718.

Tsukayama, E., Duckworth, A. L., & Kim, B. E. (2011). *Domain-specific impulsivity in school-age children.* Manuscript submitted for publication.

U.S. Department of Education, Institute of Education Sciences (2004). *The high school transcript study: A decade of change in curricula and achievement, 1990–2000 (NCES 2004–455).* Retrieved from http://nces.ed.gov/pubs2004/2004455.pdf.

U.S. Department of Education (2007). *What Works Clearinghouse topic report: Character education.* What Works Clearinghouse, Institute of Education Sciences.

Valiente, C., Lemery-Chalfant, K., & Castro, K. S. (2007). Children's effortful control and academic competence. *Merrill-Palmer Quarterly, 53*, 1–25.

Valiente, C., Lemery-Chalfant, K., & Swanson, J. (2010). Prediction of kindergartners' academic achievement from their effortful control and emotionality: Evidence for direct and moderated relations. *Journal of Educational Psychology, 102*, 550–560.

Valiente, C., Lemery-Chalfant, K., Swanson, J., & Reiser, M. (2008). Prediction of children's academic competence from their effortful control, relationships, and classroom participation. *Journal of Educational Psychology, 100*, 67–77.

Vitaro, F., Brendgen, M., Larose, S., & Tremblay, R. E. (2005). Kindergarten disruptive behaviors, protective factors, and educational achievement by early adulthood. *Journal of Educational Psychology, 97*, 617–629.

Wechsler, D. (1943). Non-intellective factors in general intelligence. *Journal of Abnormal & Social Psychology, 38*, 101–103.

Whiteside, S. P., & Lynam, D. R. (2001). The Five Factor Model and impulsivity: Using a structural model of personality to understand impulsivity. *Personality and Individual Differences, 30*, 669–689.

Willingham, W. W. (1985). *Success in college: The role of personal qualities and academic ability.* New York, NY: College Entrance Examination Board.

Willingham, W. W., Pollack, J. M., & Lewis, C. (2002). Grades and test scores: Accounting for observed differences. *Journal of Educational Measurement, 39*, 1–37.

Wolfe, R. N., & Johnson, S. D. (1995). Personality as a predictor of college performance. *Educational and Psychological Measurement, 55*, 177–185.

Wong, M. M., & Csikszentmihalyi, M. (1991). Motivation and academic achievement: The effects of personality traits and the duality of experience. *Journal of Personality, 59*, 539–574.

Zhou, Q., Main, A., & Wang, Y. (2010). The relations of temperamental effortful control and anger/frustration to Chinese children's academic achievement and social adjustment: A longitudinal study. *Journal of Educational Psychology, 102*, 180–196.

Zimmerman, B. J., & Kitsantas, A. (2005). The hidden dimension of personal competence. In A. J. Elliot & C. S. Dweck (Eds.), *Handbook of competence and motivation* (pp. 509–526). New York, NY: Guilford Press.

Zins, J. E., Elias, M. J., & Greenberg, M. T. (2007). School practices to build social-emotional competence as the foundation of academic and life success. In R. Bar-On, J. G. Maree, & M. J. Elias (Eds.), *Educating people to be emotionally intelligent* (pp. 79–94). Westport, CT: Praeger.

Chapter 11

Understanding Explanatory Talk Through Vygotsky's Theory of Self-Regulation

CHALLIS J. E. KINNUCAN AND JANET E. KUEBLI
Saint Louis University

It is important for developmental and cognitive psychologists to study explanatory competence because of the centrality of explanations in everyday cognition and learning (Gopnik, 1998; Keil, 2006, Keil & Wilson, 1998; Lombrozo, 2006; Wilson & Keil, 1998). Indeed, it has been said that individuals' everyday cognitive functioning might be impossible without explanations (Keil & Wilson, 1998). As guides to reasoning and constraints on inference making and generalization (Chi, 2000; Lombrozo, 2006; Wellman, 2011), explanations serve potentially important regulatory functions. Keil also noted the "transactional nature of explanations" (2006, p. 229). People, including children and their caregivers, communicate and exchange explanations. In the course of daily life, we are often called upon to explain the world around us, explain ourselves and others, or seek out explanations from others. Explanations also figure largely in children's schooling as teachers routinely proffer explanations as answers to various academic questions (e.g., *Why is the sky blue? What did Shakespeare mean? What makes us human?*), as well as prompt students to generate their own explanations as evidence of their growing capacities to know the world. Thus, explanations may be considered socially regulated and regulating, as well as self-regulatory phenomena.

Arguing that explanatory skills are important in their own right, Wellman (2011) issued a call to "re-invigorate" developmental investigation of children's explanations. In this chapter, we consider explanatory talk as one aspect of children's developing capacities for self-regulation. We rely upon a broad definition of self-regulation as the ability to "modulate behavior according to cognitive, emotional, and social demands of a particular situation" (Calkins & Fox, 2002, p. 479). Different theoretical perspectives have framed researchers' study of self-regulation (see Bronson, 2000, for a discussion), but we will ground our discussion of self-regulation and explanatory skills in a sociocultural perspective. Here we address two general questions: How might social regulatory processes contribute to children's developing explanatory skills? How may explanatory skills contribute to children's ability to further regulate their own thinking and learning?

We begin our chapter by reviewing basic insights from Lev Vygotsky (1896–1934), for whom social experiences served as the "prime catalysts of development" (Berk, Mann, & Ogan, 2006, p. 74). Our viewpoint is that Vygotsky's sociocultural theory can be mined to inform new investigations of both self-regulatory development in general and of explanatory skills in particular. Diaz, Neal, and Amaya-Williams (1990) provided an early Vygotskian account that highlighted the facilitation of self-regulation that occurs in the course of children's social interactions with others. A more recent elaboration of sociocultural theory related to development of regulatory ability is provided by Fernyhough (2010). Our second aim is to selectively review studies on explanatory talk to illustrate how aspects of Vygotsky's sociocultural framework can inform and expand our understanding of children's regulatory development. We conclude our discussion by posing several new questions that arise from adopting a Vygotskian perspective.

VYGOTSKIAN FOUNDATIONS OF SELF-REGULATION

As originally described by Vygotsky (1979), we conceptualize the development of self-regulation as an outcome of both social and individual processes. Notably, Diaz and colleagues (1990) considered self-regulation the over-arching consequence of the development. The unfinished status of Vygotsky's theory of self-regulation, due to the brevity of his life, has inspired new interpretation and extension by others (e.g., Daniels, Cole, & Wertsch, 2007; Fernyhough, 2008). In a recent review, for example, Fernyhough identified five key Vygotskian ideas as frames for research on children's social understanding. In a similar vein, we believe that reexamining Vygotsky's writings can be fruitful for research on the processes that underlie the development of children's regulatory capacities such as their explanatory competence. Thus, in this section, we review two of Vygotsky's well-known themes that have implications for the study of self-regulatory development: higher mental processes and mediation.

Self-Regulatory Processes as Higher Mental Processes

Higher mental processes serve, in Vygotsky's theory, as problem-solving tools, practices, and strategies. Despite the centrality of higher mental function in Vygotsky's thinking, he "never provided a rigorous definition of [this] basic concept" (Meshcheryakov, 2007, p. 160). The fundamentally regulatory nature of higher mental processes was noted more explicitly by Luria, a close collaborator of Vygotsky's and "founding father of modern neuropsychology" (Fernyhough, 2010, p. 57). In Luria's words, higher mental processes are "complex and self-regulating, and are social in origin, mediated in their structure, and conscious and voluntary in their mode of functioning" (Luria, 1980, p. 31, as cited by Meshcheryakov, 2007; see also Diaz et al., 1990). Vygotsky and Luria concurred that higher mental processes guided and controlled both action and thought and distanced humans from the control of environmental stimuli. Ultimately, the operation of higher mental processes yielded self-regulated action and adaptation. In Vygotsky's theory, the key process that produces higher mental functioning, or regulatory skill, is internalization. Internalization is both a developmental outcome and the primary mechanism by which interpersonal activity (e.g., dialogue, shared practices and strategies) is transformed into inner, self-regulating thought processes.

Vygotsky contrasted higher mental functions with more elementary mental processes. Elementary or *lower* mental processes "developed" along a strong biologically based trajectory and included what cognitive scientists today classify as basic sensory, perceptual, attentional, and memory processes. In Vygotsky's theory, lower mental processes correspond to unconscious, unlearned, fairly automatic behaviors that are immediate responses to either internal physiological or external environmental stimuli.

Alternatively, the higher mental (psychological) processes were the "uniquely human aspects of behavior" (Vygotsky, 1978, p. 19). Vygotsky claimed that such processes were of a higher order due to their greater complexity, and also because they developed through reorganizations of lower mental processes during children's social and cultural interactions with others, particularly while children participated in interactions rich in language. Among higher mental processes, Vygotsky included voluntary attention and sustained concentration, concept formation, planning, and problem solving. In Fernyhough's (2010) view, components of executive function and forms of regulatory behavior are contemporary examples of what Vygotsky categorized as higher mental processes.

Diaz et al. outlined a preliminary model of regulatory development in which earlier forms of control and regulation arising from elementary processes and the social environment were transformed into a higher level of independent *self*-regulation. Before children are genuinely self-regulating, they demonstrate capacities for action and self-control that reflect a qualitatively different level of behavioral organization. By Diaz et al.'s account, neither the self-soothing behaviors of infants nor the toddler's externally directed compliance with caregivers' requests rises to the level of true self-regulation. Self-regulation, as a later developing level of behavioral organization, is demonstrated when children have "taken over effectively the caregiver's regulating role" (p. 130) in order to plan, monitor, guide, and adjust their thoughts and actions to obtain their own goals. Only after self-control capacities first acquired from others are internalized do they "become a vehicle of [the child's own] activity" (Bakhurst, 2007, p. 72) and thereby transformed into self-regulating higher mental functions.

Among Vygotsky's most powerful insights was that sociocultural processes forged new *intermental* or *interfunctional* links among higher mental functions. Vygotsky wrote:

> In other words, with a change in developmental level there occurs a change not so much in the structure of a single function (which, for example, we may call memory) as in the character of those functions with the aid of which remembering takes place; what changes is the *interfunctional* relations that connect memory with other functions. (1978, p. 49)

Fernyhough (2010) offered compelling reasons that the interfunctionality asserted by Vygotsky and Luria should continue to guide research. One implication of Fernyhough's discussion for self-regulatory development is that researchers should focus on the "interfunctional relations" between both individual and social factors that contribute to regulatory skills, instead of studying each component separately (see also Conway & Stifter, 2012). Further, according to Vygotsky, interfunctionality itself is dynamic, such that connections among mental functions change over time and with experience. Thus, researchers ought to anticipate that the relations among components that constitute self-regulatory skill may differ over the course of development and in different developmental contexts. Understanding both individual factors and social conditions that alter interfunctional relations is therefore critical to advancing the understanding of self-regulatory development.

The Mediation of Self-Regulated Thinking and Behavior

As noted, the mechanism in Vygotsky's theory that produces higher mental functioning, and thereby self-regulation, is internalization. Despite his interpreters' efforts, internalization remains a less than fully articulated process since Vygotsky did not explicitly delineate the cognitive processes that constitute internalization. Critically, however, Wertsch concluded that "understanding the emergence and the definition of higher mental processes must be grounded in the notion of mediation" (2007, p. 178). In this section, we address central features of Vygotsky's view of mediation as a component of the internalization process that may underlie self-regulatory development.

At various times, Vygotsky described different meanings and forms of mediation (Wertsch, 2007) which merit study as potential factors contributing to self-regulatory development. For example, Wertsch addressed Vygotsky's views regarding *explicit* meditation. To Vygotsky, human-made objects (e.g., the abacus, dice, clocks, and computers) exemplify cultural tools that do the work of explicit mediation. Such concrete objects are injected "into an ongoing stream of activity" (Wertsch 2007, p. 180) as a deliberate and obvious strategy that transforms basic mental functions into higher level mental function (e.g., remember, compute) in order to solve problems and accomplish goals. Questions can be posed regarding how children employ concrete objects, and which objects, in ways that enable them to self-regulate their thoughts and actions. Additionally, researchers should not overlook the possibility that differential access to objects may help account for individual and group differences in self-regulatory capacities

Vygotsky also discussed human or social manifestations of explicit mediation. This idea is most evident in the *Law of Cultural Development* which states: "Every function in the child's cultural development appears twice.... First it appears on the social level, and later, on the individual level" (1978, p. 57). Everyday interactions with parents and others embed children in social interactions where more expert others, instead of objects, function as mediating agents. During these interactions, adults who scaffold (i.e., externally control, organize, and regulate) children's actions and behaviors facilitate children's gradual internalization of the learning processes and topics at hand. A caregiver who explains how to receive an undesirable gift graciously or who demonstrates a "count to ten" strategy for cooling anger is providing explicit social mediation that fosters emotional regulation. Only once these explicit forms of social mediation are internalized can a child be said to be emotionally self-regulating. Diaz et al. observed that higher mental functions generally "can be understood as the internalization of social regulating interactions" (1990, p. 128).

Human mediation may be especially critical early in development since children must be supported in their mastery of particular cultural strategies for thinking and doing before they can use them to accomplish self-regulated actions. An example of explicit social mediation was given by Wertsch:

> A 6-year-old child has lost a toy and asks her father for help. The father asks where she last saw the toy; the child says, "I can't remember." He asks a series of questions: "Did you have it in your room? Outside? Next door?" To each question the child answers, "No." When he says, "In the car?" she says "I think so" and goes to retrieve the toy. (Wertsch, 1991, p. 27, quotation from Tharp & Gallimore, 1988, p. 14)

Wertsch continues:

> In such cases, we cannot answer the question "Who did the remembering ... ?" Instead, it is the dyad as a system that carried out the function of remembering on the intermental plane. By prompting the child to consider possible solutions, the father has guided the child to remember the location of the lost object. In addition, the child may also begin to internalize the process of such self questioning or prompts and may use this process in the future when a similar situation arises. (Wertsch, 1991, p. 28)

The question could be restated: Who did the regulating? In Wertsch's terms, the answer once again is the dyad which jointly regulated the child's response to the situation. The father's questions and prompts also may have enabled his child to inhibit other activity (e.g., blaming someone else for moving the toy, worrying that it will be lost forever, or giving up entirely). The dyad's dialogue may have also mediated the child's immediate ability to regulate feelings of frustration, sadness, or anger about the absent toy. Over time, self-questioning and self-prompting may become internalized strategies the child can use independently to achieve self-formulated aims. From a sociocultural perspective, therefore, joint or co-constructed social activity early in development, in its role as explicit mediation, is a crucial subject for investigation since such social interactions may figure importantly in young children's ability to focus attention, inhibit other behaviors, control emotions, and support future mastery of culturally normative styles of thinking and acting (e.g., Conway & Stifter, 2012; Landry, Miller-Loncar, Smith, & Swank, 2002).

Kozulin (2002) warned that the full range of meditational social interactions is still not fully grasped. He attributed researchers' lack of consensus concerning classification of social mediation partly to its necessarily context-specific nature. To address this issue, he proposed distinguishing between *type* of social mediation and the particular mediating *techniques* used by adults with children. To illustrate, *scaffolding* is one *type* or category of social mediation that serves to help children organize tasks. Scaffolding can be contrasted with other types of mediation, such as approval or encouragement, which serve to motivate children. Kozulin referred to *techniques* as the more "localized," concrete and contextually constrained mediating behaviors of adults that reflect task demands, individual differences, and other situational factors. By example, suppose a parent uses scaffolding while helping a child to assemble a puzzle. In the specific situation, the parent may rely on a sequence of different *scaffolding techniques* each of which serve to organize the task, such as prompting the child to wait (i.e., inhibition) before putting pieces together and instead to first turn puzzle pieces right side up; then to look for (i.e., attention) and set aside corner pieces; and finally to group pieces with similar colors and patterns together (i.e., working memory). Notably, the adult who sustains the child's attention to the puzzle task despite frustration when pieces do not interlock quickly is providing a different *type* of socially mediated self-regulation, but not scaffolding. The array of techniques parents use to scaffold activity, sustain children's attention, and manage their emotions may all contribute to internalized self-regulatory abilities and merit investigation. Kozulin further speculated that mediation *type* and *technique* may, on occasion, serve distinct functions.

Most provocative is Kozulin's contention that different techniques of the same type may not provide equally effective social mediation of children's functioning in a given situation. Indeed, Kozulin cautioned that "not every type of parent-child interaction has a mediational effect" (2002, p. 17). Thus, a given type of social mediation may facilitate development of self-regulating higher mental processes only when a particular *technique* subsumed under that same type falls within the child's zone of proximal development (ZPD). Social mediation, for example, might be insufficient or ineffective in mediating some children's executive functions (i.e., higher-order conscious control processes including working memory, inhibition, and shifting) or emotional regulation if a specific technique is pitched too low within the child's zone of actual development or too high beyond the child's ZPD. Consider again the parent and child co-constructing a puzzle. The child may be entirely capable of independently turning the pieces upright and finding the corner pieces. However, a parent who is not fully attuned to the child's current self-regulatory level may scaffold the task by turning all the puzzle pieces over for the child and pointing to the corner pieces. This parent's scaffolding is not facilitating the child's development of self-regulatory skills since the parent's technique does not provide sufficient autonomy support to engage the child in more advanced self-regulatory strategies that he or she has yet to master or internalize. Although some research has been conducted on a variety of techniques and specific practices that facilitate children's problem solving and other activities (e.g., Bernier, Carlson & Whipple, 2010; Conway & Stifter, 2012; Hammond, Müller, Carpendale, Bibok, & Liebermann-Finestone, 2012; Landry et al., 2002), further research is required to more fully understand which forms of social mediation best support self-regulatory development for which children and under what conditions.

Vygotsky also described forms of mediation that were *implicit* (Wertsch, 2007). Wertsch explained implicit mediators as "involving signs, especially natural language" and nonmaterial meaning (2007, p. 181). Implicit mediators tend to be more transparent as "objects" than explicit mediators and less subject to deliberate "conscious reflection or manipulation" (Wertsch, 2007, p. 180). Certainly, developmental researchers have focused their attention more directly on explicit than implicit mediation, perhaps because meaning and sense-making are, in Wertsch's own words, more "ephemeral and fleeting" (Wertsch, 2007, p. 180) and less readily apparent.

Symbols or signs (e.g., alphabet letters, numbers, formulas, diagrams) are examples in Vygotsky's theory of "higher order symbolic mediators" (Kozulin, 2002, p. 19). It is important to note that symbolic or semiotic mediators can be implicit or explicit. Like tools and human forms of explicit mediation, explicit symbolic mediators can be used consciously to organize and regulate thinking and problem solving. Explicit social mediation is in fact often essential to children's initial ability to use semiotic mediators to regulate their own behaviors: "Symbols may remain useless unless their meaning as cognitive tools is properly mediated to the child" (Kozulin, 2002, p. 19).

In development, language operates initially as an explicit symbolic mediator when it is used by adults to regulate children's actions and behaviors and by children to verbally communicate with others. The father's questions and prompts in Wertsch's example relied upon language to explicitly mediate the child's ability to remember the location of the lost toy. Explicit signs, in this sense, are external stimuli that are deliberately and consciously introduced into the flow of children's thought and activity first by parents, teachers, and others, and only in time independently by children themselves. However, children's internalization of social speech via private speech provides further insights into the self-regulatory functions of implicit mediation, to which we turn next.

In development, according to Vygotsky (1978, 1986), the social and communicative functions of language develop first. He identified speech for and with others as social or external speech. Inner speech, or speech for self, developed later from social speech with others. However, self-regulative uses of external speech were, in Vygotsky's view, the earliest manifestations of inner speech. For Vygotsky, this egocentric or private speech was a transitional stage that shared more features with inner speech (e.g., its form and function) than with social speech. Research has since demonstrated that private speech gradually "takes on a planning and guiding function" (Diaz et al., 1990, p. 135) of activity, serving to organize and regulate practical activity and cognitive thought. Moreover, Vygotsky asserted that private speech was an *individual* activity for the self. He wrote: "It does not merely accompany the child's activity; it serves mental orientation, conscious understanding; it helps in overcoming difficulties; it is speech for oneself, intimately and usefully connected with the child's thinking.... In the end, it becomes inner speech" (Vygotsky, 1986, p. 228). Therefore, internalization of social speech was accomplished first through private speech that diminished, becoming more interior and yielding to increasingly implicit mediation of thought.

Serving as the "bridge that linked social and individual functioning" (Diaz et al., 1990, p. 147), private speech paves the way for silent, inner speech that Vygotsky (1986) argued is more than simply subvocal: "Inner speech is speech almost without words" (p. 244), but with "meaning ... more than ever in the forefront" (p. 244). Compared to external speech, inner speech is more condensed and abbreviated, with its own "peculiar syntax" (Vygotsky, 1986, p. 235). With development, therefore, social speech and other explicit sign forms are appropriated and internalized by children and begin to regulate their thinking more automatically or implicitly. Vygotsky regarded implicit mediation via inner speech as becoming "built into mental functioning" (Wertsch, 2007, p. 184). One would expect then, from this account, that successively higher levels of self-regulation would become less deliberate and perhaps even less immediately accessible to consciousness.

Thus, Vygotsky's theory suggests that the explicit mediating and regulatory aspects of language are observed first during social speech and then private speech, but that language becomes an implicit mediator when private speech goes underground and becomes inner speech. Thus, the planning, guiding, and monitoring functions of language with which adults initially regulate children's behaviors during social interactions are internalized eventually and transformed into the self-regulating functions of inner speech that constitute thought itself. However, the specific mental processes underlying self-regulation via inner speech remain a "tantalizing gap" (Fernyhough, 2009, p. 43) in Vygotsky's theory. Fernyhough's (2008, 2009) discussion of the dialogic nature of inner speech provides an intriguing starting point for posing new questions about the nature of implicitly mediated forms of self-regulation. Based upon Fernyhough's model, for example, self-regulation might entail increasingly internalized social dialogue representing multiple perspectives or problem-solving orientations for responding to situations confronting children. Although the challenges of studying internal dialogue cannot be dismissed, new theory and research are needed to test the idea that implicit semiotic mediation results in "fundamental restructuring of children's cognition" (Fernyhough, 2008, p. 244), as manifested in the development of an array of higher-order self-regulatory capacities.

In the next section, we turn to children's explanations and most specifically to children's self-explanations. We maintain that self-explanation is a particular form of self-talk that may, like private speech, support later development of higher forms of self-regulated thought and action. We first very briefly review research suggestive of the important role that social interaction plays in the emergence of children's earliest explanatory skills. We will suggest that family explanatory talk provides a socially mediated foundation for children's use of self-explanations later in development. This is followed by a brief discussion of several studies on self-explanation with the aim of illustrating Vygotsky's ideas about the gradual shift from externally to internally mediated forms of self-regulated thought.

DEVELOPING EXPLANATORY COMPETENCE

Explanations are a means for understanding and adapting to the world. Researchers have only begun to describe the origins of and developmental changes in children's capacities to seek and formulate explanations. Exposure to explanatory talk (e.g., questions and answers pertaining to *why, how,* and *what for*) probably begins at birth when parents provide explanations to their own questions while in the company of their children. Naturalistic samplings of family talk indicate that by age 3 children themselves regularly participate in explanatory talk with their parents (e.g., Callanan & Oakes, 1992; Callanan, Shrager, & Moore, 1995; Dunn, Brown, Slomkowski, Tesla, and Youngblade, 1991; Frazier, Gelman, & Wellman, 2009; Hood and Bloom, 1979). Across studies of spontaneous family conversations, researchers report that family members explained one another's actions, discussed cause-and-effect connections, and explained the functions and purposes of objects and events and the meaning of words (e.g., Beals, 2001; Callanan & Oakes, 1992; Kelemen Callanan, Casler, & Perez-Granados, 2005). Converging evidence for the ubiquity of family explanatory talk comes from studies using parent diaries (Callanan & Jipson, 2001; Callanan & Oakes, 1992), parent interviews (Kelemen, Callanan, Casler, & Perez-Granados, 2005), and conversational analyses collected during family museum trips (Callanan & Jipson, 2001). As early as 2.5 years, children start asking *why* questions, and by age 4 they generate causal explanations more often than they pose causal questions (Hickling & Wellman, 2001). In another study (Chouinard, 2007), the relative frequency of children's requests for explanations increased from 4% of questions at age 2 to 30% at age 5. Consistent with the sociocultural approach, the evidence overall strongly suggests that the seeds of explanatory competence are at least partly social, as Vygotsky hypothesized. However, these descriptive accounts of children's early explanatory dialogue with others have not typically invoked Vygotsky's constructs, such as mediation or internalization.

Questions remain about the nature and development of children's independent explanatory skills. A well-established literature demonstrates preschoolers' developing capacities to independently explain psychological, biological, and physical events (e.g., Gelman, 2002; Hickling & Wellman, 2001; Inagaki & Hatano, 2002). However, the processes that underlie children's ability to generate such explanations are not well understood (Keil, 2006). What specific mechanisms, for example, account for children's capacities to become autonomous, self-regulated explainers? Moreover, to what degree and in what ways are language and explanatory skills linked? Viewed through a Vygotskian lens, explanatory skill functions as a semiotic, meaning-making tool, which first explicitly and then implicitly serves to mediate and regulate problem solving. Children who have internalized when and how to ask questions and who also are independently able to formulate their own explanations may be more able to succeed in school, in relationships, and in the world. To self-regulate one's thoughts and actions via explanatory skill, for example, may be a critical regulatory wedge that permits children to put psychological distance between themselves and the immediate situation (Giesbrecht, Müller, & Miller, 2010; Sigel, 1993), thereby increasing the chance for better solutions. We believe that Vygotsky's sociocultural framework can be used profitably to further study the social and individual processes that in concert result in the emergence, growth, and internalization of explanatory skills and their contribution to self-regulated thinking and acting. To paraphrase Callanan and Jipson (2001), an advantage of sociocultural theory is that it can direct inquiry into *how* social activities and interactions of everyday life may provide an essential foundation for children to autonomously create, convey, and receive explanations that in time enable them to independently construct understandings of the world around them.

The Self-Regulatory Potential of Self-Explanations

Both educators and researchers advocate self-explanation as a strategy whereby students may self-regulate during problem solving or while learning academic concepts. Diaz et al.'s (1990) review of attempts to train children to employ self-talk predated most research on self-explanation. At the time, Diaz et al. found little evidence of children's internalization of a new level of self-regulated behavioral organization when children simply imitated adults' self-verbalizations. However, newer research on self-explanation, highlights of which we discuss next, indicates that self-explanation (and prompts for self-explanations) may enhance development of higher mental functions. In this section, we describe several studies on self-explanation in children, noting how findings may be interpreted and further explored using Vygotsky's ideas.

Chi and colleagues' studies with adults and older children are recognized as having set the standards for self-explanation research. The term "self-explanation" initially referred to explanations directed to and provided by the self in order to facilitate one's own knowledge on a subject (Chi et al., 1989; Chi, de Leeuw, Chiu, & LaVancher, 1994; VanLehn, Jones, & Chi, 1992). The "self-explanation effect" describes the learning facilitation that occurs when people generate explanations about studied material (e.g., Calin-Jageman & Ratner, 2005; Chi et al., 1994; Lombrozo, 2006; Schworm & Renkl, 2007; Siegler, 2002; VanLehn, Jones, & Chi, 1992; Wong, Lawson, & Keeves, 2002). Spontaneous generation of explanations, using talking aloud protocols, characterized many of the earlier studies with adults and adolescents (e.g., Chi et al., 1989). By contrast, *prompted* self-explanations usually have been employed in studies with children (e.g., Siegler, 1995). Study protocols often involve children in conversations with a researcher who *instructs* children to generate explanations (e.g., Calin-Jageman & Ratner, 2005; Rittle-Johnson, Saylor, & Swygert, 2008; Siegler, 1995) either for themselves or for others.

Prompted self-explanations, in our view, may be an important precursor of children's internalization of self-explanation as an unprompted, spontaneous self-regulatory skill. In the context of Vygotsky's theory, self-explanations may be considered a product of social and individual processes interwoven over time that result in higher self-regulated levels of explanatory competence. Given the important role in early development that Vygotsky attributed to explicit forms of human (social) and semiotic mediation, we propose that initially practicing self-explanation as a means for problem solving on the social plane (i.e., *prompted* self-generated explanations for self and others) would in time facilitate children's internalization of self-explanation skills (i.e., *spontaneously* self-generated explanations) on the individual plane of mental functioning.

Thus, before self-explanations facilitate children's learning or problem solving, children first need to acquire knowledge of when and how to generate accurate self-explanations and knowledge about what information to explain, all of which may be learned through dialogue with expert others. Essentially, in keeping with Vygotsky's theory, self-regulated forms of self-explanation can be considered a higher mental function that initially relies upon prior explicit social mediation by others and then later begins to implicitly mediate thinking and action. Notably, Diaz et al. (1990) identified teaching strategies other than modeling whereby mothers of 3-year-olds effectively fostered their children's spontaneous verbalizations for self-regulated problem solving. Among the techniques that correlated with children's increased self-regulation was asking children conceptual questions "that could not be answered by simply attending to the immediate perceptual field but rather required a mental representation of the rules or goals of the task" (Diaz et al., 1990, p. 148). More direct observation of everyday explanatory conversations between children and adults would help to identify both the types and techniques of social mediation that facilitate children's acquisition of self-explanations at different ages and in different contexts.

Research on self-explanation with children is mostly laboratory-based with children interacting with researchers. Siegler (1995) pioneered an approach in which researchers prompted children to produce self-explanations, usually identified as "other-directed self-explanations." Crowley and Siegler (1999), for example, investigated children's (grades K–2) learning of a tic-tac-toe strategy (i.e., the fork strategy) and their explanations for why the strategy was desirable. During a learning phase, children either first heard the researcher's explanation for an upcoming "good" move (i.e., use of the fork strategy) or did not hear any explanation. After the move was demonstrated, children were prompted to explain to the researcher why it was chosen. Following each game (4 games total) that they observed, children replicated the moves they had just witnessed and explained their own moves. Subsequently, all children played additional tic-tac-toe games to assess strategy replication and transfer.

Perhaps not surprisingly, children who had heard the researcher's explanation referenced the fork strategy more often during the learning observation games than did those who had not heard the researcher's explanation. In the replication games, there was no group difference in children's use of explanations referencing this strategy. However, collapsing across conditions, Crowley and Siegler compared performance on the posttest transfer games of children who learned the fork strategy and were prompted to give an explanation for its effectiveness with the performance of those who neither learned about nor explained the fork strategy, and those who only learned one or the other of these aspects of the strategy. They found that children who both learned the strategy and provided an overt explanation of the strategy performed better on the posttest transfer games than did children in the other three groups.

Although the laboratory situation is not natural for children, in this instance it may have simulated variations in children's experiences at home and at school when adults may or may not use explicit social mediation to prompt children to formulate a jointly constructed explanation or cue them to produce explanations for their own thoughts and actions. Crowley and Siegler speculated that the other-directed self-explanations also may have helped children to "resist the temptation of abandoning the new approach in favor of defensive moves or simpler offensive approaches" (1995, p. 313). In effect, explaining the experimenter's strategy aloud may have enhanced children's inhibition and helped them attend to the goals of the activity. Or, put another way, such explanations may have facilitated children's ability to regulate their own behavior.

Prompted self-explanations were also examined by Calin-Jageman and Ratner (2005) in a study with 5-year-olds. Children alternated solving sets of addition problems themselves and watching a researcher solve problems. Children then either (a) described the researcher's reasoning ("explain-expert"), (b) described their own reasoning ("explain-novice"), or (c) did neither (control). Results indicated that the explain-expert group showed the most improved performance across sessions as compared to the other two groups who did not differ in improved performance. Since all groups *saw* the expert's solutions, the results reinforce the conclusion that verbalizing one's own explanations may enhance young children's problem solving. The authors reasoned that by prompting children to explain the expert's solutions, they were directing children's attention to the expert solutions, which was not the case in the explain-novice condition. These prompts may again qualify as a form of explicit social mediation that served to direct attention to pertinent problem-solving information, thereby enhancing children's attention, inhibition, and other executive functioning skills that contribute to self-regulation.

The use of prompts for self-explanations has only recently been introduced in studies with preschoolers. Honomichl and Chen (2006) administered relational reasoning tasks to 3- to 5-year-olds and then told the children the correct answers. Importantly, only children in a "re-explain" group were prompted to explain why the researcher's answer was correct. Analyses for older preschoolers (ages 4.5–5.9 years) demonstrated improved performance only for those who were prompted to re-explain. Follow-up analyses were not conducted with the younger preschoolers (ages 3.0–4.4 years) who showed "very low" relational reasoning regardless of condition. Results overall suggest a potential lower age limit (under 4.5 years of age) for the effectiveness of self-explanations to promote learning. This fits with Kozulin's point that mediation techniques are context-specific and must be developmentally attuned to children's ZPD. However, more research is clearly warranted to understand at what ages and under what circumstances mediated self-explanations promote learning and internalization.

A few studies with older children (e.g., 8th graders studying biology concepts, Chi et al., 1994), but not younger children, have investigated processes that may promote the full internalization of the self-explanation strategy. Nor does the literature with children examine possible interfunctional links between self-explanation and executive functions or other regulatory capacities (but see Bielaczyc, Pirolli, & Brown, 1995, for a discussion of self-explanation and self-regulation with adults). An interesting question raised in this literature is whether the learning facilitation that results from self-explanation requires conscious awareness of the strategy itself coupled with the active intention to use it (Chi et al., 1989). A similar question has been raised regarding the importance of conscious awareness of private speech (e.g., Winsler & Naglieri, 2003). Lack of such awareness might explain why younger children in Honomichl and Chen (2006) did not seem to profit from prompted self-explanation.

From our perspective, the answer to this question is neither simple nor straightforward. First, Vygotsky's theory leads us to view internalization as a gradual and progressive transformation that arises from dynamic reorganizations of unconscious lower mental processes into successively higher self-regulating levels of mental functioning. Vygotsky likened development to a spiral, "passing through the same point at each new revolution while advancing to a higher level" (1978, p. 56). Self-conscious, deliberate utilization of self-explanation in the service of learning and problem-solving perhaps reflects a point in the "spiral" indicating explicit semiotic mediation of a higher mental function. Studies employing talk aloud protocols, for example, showed that college students (especially *good* students) used self-explanations spontaneously (or at least when not prompted to do so) while studying, suggesting that at some point individuals may become consciously aware of this process as a tool for learning (e.g., Chi et al., 1989; Renkl, 1997).

Even when self-explanation would appear to be "internalized," however, children and adults may on occasion actually speak aloud and engage in overt, self-directed speech when alone or faced with difficult concepts or processes (e.g., scientific or mathematical procedures for solving problems) (e.g., Duncan & Tarulli, 2010; Winsler & Naglieri, 2003). Additionally, 50% of individuals do not spontaneously engage in adequate or appropriate self-explanation when a talk aloud protocol is used (Renkl, 1997). Why these individual differences exist is still unclear; additionally it is difficult to determine whether self-explanations have been internalized fully and therefore are simply covert, inner speech or whether they are actually absent. Indeed, Vygotsky's notion of implicit mediation would imply that neither overt self-talk nor conscious reflection nor intentionality are always essential once cognitive processing shifts from being explicitly to implicitly mediated. In this sense, we would anticipate that full mastery of self-explanation as a self-regulating tool for thought and problem solving may in time become "built into mental functioning" (Wertsch, 2007, p. 184) via implicit semiotic mediation; therefore conscious awareness of employing this strategy might not be necessary.

Thus, it is possible that children, including those in the primary grades, may not yet have internalized the process of effectively generating explanations directed toward the self to facilitate their own learning. Critically, they may still rely upon the social context in order to utilize and develop these skills. This view is consistent with the results of the only study (Rittle-Johnson, Saylor, & Swygert, 2008) that has investigated whether self-explanations directed at the self versus those directed at another person are more effective for facilitating children's learning. Specifically, Rittle-Johnson et al. asked children (ages 4.5–5.9 years) to study and explain patterns. After the children had provided their own answers, experimenter feedback was given about the correct answers. Two experimental groups consisted of (a) children who were then asked to explain the solutions to their mothers and (b) children who were then prompted to generate self-directed self-explanations (into an audio recorder for later use). A control group repeated the answer provided by the researcher but did not generate any further explanations.

Rittle-Johnson et al. found that children who were prompted to give explanations performed better than did controls on posttest measures that included familiar problems and transfer problems. Importantly, performance on the transfer problems by those asked to explain to their mothers was also superior to that of those asked to explain into an audio recorder. Interestingly, this finding suggests that problem type may interact with the effectiveness of self-explanations. It is also possible that children at these ages were motivated to generate more complete mother-directed explanations than self-directed explanations, underscoring Kozulin's attention to the context- and age-specific nature of mediation. At younger ages, prompted other-directed explanations may in fact promote greater understanding and internalization of material than prompted self-directed explanations. More studies are needed that directly compare social and individual contexts for the use of prompts for self-explanation as a self-regulatory process to facilitate learning. Given that not all adult-child interactions are apt to yield identical mediational effects, future investigations should also address how different types and techniques of social mediation may contribute to the self-explanation effect.

CONCLUSION

In sum, we believe explanatory competence is an important dimension of regulatory development that developmental scientists should not overlook. We have briefly suggested how understanding of the development of explanatory skills, along with other regulatory skills, may be elaborated and amplified through application of key themes in Vygotsky's sociocultural theory. Using Vygotsky's theory, we proposed that explanatory skill and other self-regulatory processes may be conceptualized as forms of higher mental function. In turn, sociocultural approaches, derived from Vygotsky's emphasis on the social origins of higher mental functions, direct attention to how explanatory skills may initially unfold during children's daily social interactions, and particularly during their conversations with others. A few studies have begun to describe family talk directed at explanations; however, this work has not typically viewed these family interactions in terms of self-regulatory development. Deliberate application of Vygotsky's ideas could focus investigation on the full range of mediational processes that may underlie explanatory dialogue in families and provide a better understanding of individual and group differences in children's explanatory competence.

Integration of the research on family explanatory talk and the laboratory research on self-explanations is under-developed. In this case, Vygotsky's description of the progression from social to inner speech, via private speech, may be informative. Thus, we contend that adults (at home or in the lab) who prompt children to engage in self-explanation may be providing explicit social mediation that enables children to focus their attention on pertinent information and inhibit automatic reactions and competing behaviors. By prompting self-explanations, expert others may also promote children's use of language, spoken aloud, during problem solving. Children's reliance on private speech, in turn, ought to facilitate their internalization of the explanations of expert others, as well as the internalization of the self-explanation strategy itself. In this way, self-explanation may in time become a means of implicit semiotic mediation employed by individuals in order to independently regulate their thinking, problem solving, and action. Longitudinal research offers opportunities to examine these processes as well as Vygotsky's assumption that internalization is dynamic and gradual.

Finally, viewing explanatory skills and other self-regulatory skills, through the filter of Vygotsky's writings may lead to productive new lines of inquiry. For example, what might be the implications of viewing transfer effects in self-explanation research as internalization via implicit semiotic mediation? Vygotsky's notion of interfunctionality presents additional questions about how explanatory skill and other self-regulatory skills may be related. Gaps in Vygotsky's theory also provide new opportunities for study. Thus, based on Fernyhough's (2008) thoughtful proposal about the dialogic basis of internalization and inner speech, we might expect that children's initial explanatory dialogues with others would "survive the transition" (p. 46) from prompted to unprompted verbalized explanations to fully internalized mental dialogue. Fernyhough and colleagues (Al-Namlah, Fernyhough, & Meins, 2006; Fernyhough, 2009) also have raised broader issues about the domain-specificity/generality of semiotic mediation in private and inner speech that merit consideration in the context of children's self-explanations. In conclusion, if one measure of a good theory is its generativity, we would argue that Vygotsky's theory satisfies this criterion and should continue to inform our understanding of self-regulation in all of its manifestations.

REFERENCES

Al-Namlah, A. S., Fernyhough, C., & Meins, E. (2006). Sociocultural influences on the development of verbal mediation: Private speech and phonological recoding in Saudi Arabian and British samples *Developmental Psychology, 42*, 117–131.

Bakhurst, D. (2007). Vygotsky's demons. In H. Daniels, M. Cole, & J.V. Wertsch (Eds.), *The Cambridge Companion to Vygotsky* (pp. 50–76). New York, NY: Cambridge University Press.

Beals, D. E. (2001). Eating and reading: Links between family conversations with preschoolers and later language and literacy. In D. K. Dickinson & P. O. Tabors (Eds.), *Beginning literacy with language* (pp. 75–92). Baltimore, MD: Paul H. Brookes.

Berk, L.E., Mann, T. D., & Ogan, A. T. (2006). Make-believe play: Wellspring for development of self-regulation. In D. G. Singer, R. M. Golinkoff, & K. Hirsch-Pasek (Eds.), *Play = learning: How play motivates and enhances children's cognitive and social-emotional growth* (pp. 74–100). New York, NY: Oxford University Press.

Bernier, A., Carlson, S. M., & Whipple, N. (2010). From external regulation to self-regulation: Early parenting precursors of young children's executive functioning. *Child Development, 81*, 326–339.

Bielaczyc, K., Pirolli, P. L., & Brown, A. L., (1995). Training in self-explanation and self-regulation strategies: Investigating the effects of knowledge acquisition activities on problem solving. *Cognition and Instruction, 13*, 221–252.

Bronson, M. B. (2000). *Self-regulation in early childhood: Nature and nurture.* New York, NY: Guilford Press.

Calin-Jageman, R. J., & Ratner, H. H. (2005). The role of encoding in the self-explanation effect. *Cognition and Instruction, 23*, 523–543.

Calkins, S. D., & Fox, N. A. (2002). Self-regulatory processes in early personality development: A multilevel approach to the study of childhood social withdrawal and aggression. *Development and Psychopathology, 14*, 477–498. doi: 10.1017.S095479402000305X

Callanan, M. A., & Jipson, J. L. (2001). Explanatory conversations and young children's developing scientific literacy. In K. Crowley, C. D. Schunn, & T. Okada (Eds.), *Designing for science: Implications from everyday, classroom, and professional settings* (pp. 21–49). Mahwah, NJ: Erlbaum.

Callanan, M. A., & Oakes, L. M. (1992). Preschoolers' questions and parents' explanations: Causal thinking in everyday activity. *Cognitive Development, 72*, 213–233.

Callanan, M. A., Shrager, J., & Moore, J. L. (1995). Parent-child collaborative explanations: Methods of identification and analysis. *Journal of the Learning Sciences, 4*, 105–129.

Chi, M. T. H. (2000). Self-explaining: The dual process of generating inference and repairing mental models. In R. Glaser (Ed.), *Advances in instructional psychology: Educational design and cognitive science: Vol. 5. Education design and cognitive science.* Mahawa, NJ: Erlbaum.

Chi, M. T. H., Bassok, M., Lewis, M., Riemann, P., & Glaser, R. (1989). Self-explanations: How students study and use examples in learning to solve problems. *Cognitive Science, 13*, 145–182.

Chi, M. T. H., De Leeuw, N., Chiu, M-H., & LaVancher, C. (1994). Eliciting self-explanation improves understanding. *Cognitive Science, 18*, 439–477.

Chouinard, M. M. (2007). Children's questions: A mechanism for cognitive development. Monographs of the Society for Research in Child Development, *72*, (Serial No. 286).

Conway, A., & Stifter, C. A. (2012). Longitudinal antecedents of executive function in preschoolers. *Child Development, 83*, 1022–1036. doi: 10.1111/j.1467-8624.2012.01756.x

Crowley, K., & Siegler, R. S. (1999). Explanation and generalization in young children's strategy learning. *Child Development, 70*, 304–316.

Daniels, H., Cole, M., & Wertsch, J. V. (2007). *The Cambridge companion to Vygotsky*. New York, NY: Cambridge University Press.

Diaz, R. M., Neal, C. J., & Amaya-Williams, M. (1990). The social origins of self-regulation. In L. C. Moll (Ed.), *Vygotsky and education: Instructional implications and applications of sociohistorical psychology* (pp. 127–154). New York, NY: Cambridge University Press.

Duncan, R., & Tarulli, D. (2010). On the persistence of private speech: Empirical and theoretical considerations. In A. Winsler, C. Fernyhough, & I. Montero (Eds.), *Private speech, executive functioning, and the development of verbal self-regulation* (pp. 176–187). New York, NY: Cambridge University Press.

Dunn, J., Brown, J., Slomkowski, C., Tesla, C., and Youngblade, L. (1991). Young children's understanding of other people's feelings and beliefs: Individual differences and their antecedents. *Child Development, 62*, 1352–1366.

Fernyhough, C. (2008). Getting Vygotskian about theory of mind: Mediation, dialogue, and the development of social understanding. *Developmental Review, 28*, 225–262.

Fernyhough, C. (2009). Dialogic thinking. In A. Winsler, C. Fernyhough, & I. Montero (Eds.) *Private speech, executive functioning, and the development of verbal self-regulation* (pp. 42–52). New York, NY: Cambridge University Press.

Fernyhough, C.(2010). Vygotsky, Luria, and the social brain. In B. W. Sokol, U. Müller, J. I. M. Carpendale, A. R. Young, & G. Iarocci (Eds.), *Self and social regulation: Social interaction and the development of social understanding and executive functions* (pp. 56–79). New York, NY: Oxford University Press.

Frazier, B. N., Gelman, S. A., & Wellman, H. M. (2009). Preschoolers' search for explanatory information within adult-child conversation. *Child Development, 80*, 1592–1611.

Gelman, R. (2002). *Cognitive development.* In H. Pashler, D. L. Medin, R. Gallistel, & J. Wixted (Eds.), *Stevens' handbook of experimental psychology* (3rd ed., pp. 396–443). New York, NY: Wiley.

Giesbrecht, G. F., Müller, U., & Miller, M. R. (2010). Psychological distancing in the development of executive function and emotion regulation. In B. W. Sokol, U. Müller, J. I. M. Carpendale, A. R. Young, & G. Iarocci (Eds.), *Self and social regulation: Social interaction and the development of social understanding and executive functions* (pp. 337–357). New York, NY: Oxford University Press.

Gopnik, A. (1998). Explanation as orgasm. *Minds and Machines, 8*, 101–118.

Hammond, S. I., Müller, U., Carpendale, J. I. M., Bibok, M. B., & Liebermann-Finestone, D. P. (2012). The effects of parental scaffolding on preschoolers' executive function. *Developmental Psychology, 48*, 271–281.

Hickling, A. K., & Wellman, H. M. (2001). The emergence of children's causal explanations and theories: Evidence from everyday conversation. *Developmental Psychology, 37*, 668–683. doi: 10.1037//0012-1649.37.5.668

Honomichl, R. D., & Chen, Z. (2006). Learning to align relations: The effects of feedback and self-explanation. *Journal of Cognition and Development, 7*, 527–550.

Hood, L., & Bloom, L. (1979). What, when, and how about why: A longitudinal study of early expressions of causality. *Monographs of the Society for Research in Child Development, 44* (Serial No. 118).

Inagaki, K., & Hatano, G. (2002). *Young children's naive thinking about the biological world*. New York, NY: Psychology Press.

Keil, F. (2006). Explanation and understanding. *Annual Review of Psychology, 57*, 227–254. doi: 10.1146/annurev.psych.57.102904.190100

Keil, F., & Wilson, R. (1998). Cognition and explanation. *Mind and Machines, 8*, 1–5.

Kelemen, D., Callanan, M. A., Casler, K., & Perez-Granados, D. R. (2005). Why things happen: Teleological explanation in parent-child conversations. *Developmental Psychology, 41*, 251–264. doi: 10.1037/0012-1649.41.1.251

Kozulin, A. (2002). Sociocultural theory and the mediated learning experience. *School Psychology International, 23*, 7–35.

Landry, S. H., Miller-Loncar, C. L., Smith, K. E., & Swank, P. R. (2002). The role of early parenting in children's development of executive processes. *Developmental Neuropsychology, 21*, 15–41.

Lombrozo, T. (2006). The structure and function of explanations. *TRENDS in Cognitive Sciences, 10*, 464–470. doi: 10.1016/j.tics.2006.08.004

Meshcheryakov, B. G. (2007). Terminology in L. S. Vygotsky's writings. In H. Daniels, M. Cole, & J. V. Wertsch (Eds.), *The Cambridge Companion to Vygotsky* (pp. 155–177). New York, NY: Cambridge University Press.

Renkl, A. (1997). Learning from worked-out examples: A study of individual differences. *Cognitive Science, 21*, 1–29.

Rittle-Johnson, B., Saylor, M., & Swygert, K. E. (2008). Learning from explaining: Does it matter if mom is listening? *Journal of Experimental Child Psychology, 100*, 215–224. doi: 10.1016/jrcp.200.10.002

Schworm, S., & Renkl, A. (2007). Learning argumentation skills through the use of prompts for self-explaining examples. *Journal of Educational Psychology, 2007, 99*, 285–296. doi: 10.1037/0022-0663.99.2.285

Siegler, R. S. (1995). How does change occur: A microgenetic study of number conservation. *Cognitive Psychology, 28*, 225–273.

Siegler, R. S. (2002). Microgenetic studies of self-explanation. In N. Granott & J. Parziale (Eds.), *Microdevelopment: Transition processes in development and learning* (pp. 31–58). Cambridge, England: Cambridge University Press.

Sigel, I. E. (1993). The centrality of a distancing model for the development of representational competence. In R. R. Cocking, & K. A. Renninger (Eds.), *The development and meaning of psychological distance* (pp. 141–158). Hillsdale, NJ: Erlbaum.

VanLehn, K., Jones, R. M., & Chi, M. T. H. (1992). A model of the self-explanation effect. *Journal of the Learning Sciences*, 2, 1–59.

Vygotsky, L. S. (1978). *Mind in society: The development of higher psychological processes*. In M. Cole, V. John- steiner, S. Scribner, & E. Souberman (Eds. and Trans.). Cambridge, MA: Harvard University Press. (Original work published 1930–1935.)

Vygotsky, L. (1986). *Thought and language*. In A. Kozulin (Ed. and Trans.). Cambridge, MA: MIT Press. (Original work published 1934.)

Wellman, H. M. (2011). Reinvigorating explanations for the study of early cognitive development. *Child Development Perspectives*, 5, 33–38.

Wertsch, J. V. (2007). Mediation. In H. Daniels, M. Cole, & J.V. Wertsch (Eds.), *The Cambridge Companion to Vygotsky* (pp. 178–192). New York, NY: Cambridge University Press.

Wilson, R. A., & Keil, F. (1998). The shadows and shallows of explanation. *Minds and Machines*, *8*, 137–159.

Winsler, A., & Naglieri, J. (2003). Overt and covert verbal problem-solving strategies: Developmental trends in use, awareness, and relations with task performance in children aged 5 to 17. *Child Development*, *74*, 659–678.

Wong, R. M. F., Lawson, M. J., & Keeves, J. (2002). The effects of self-explanation training on students' problem solving in high-school mathematics. *Learning and Instruction*, *12*, 233–262.

PART IV

NEUROLOGICAL PERSPECTIVE

Chapter 12

Two-Mode Models of Self-Regulation and Serotonergic Functioning: Divergent Manifestations of Impulse and Constraint

CHARLES S. CARVER
University of Miami
SHERI L. JOHNSON
University of California, Berkeley
JUTTA JOORMANN
University of Miami

The term "self-regulation" sometimes is used to refer to the process of carrying out an intended behavior by monitoring its consequences to keep it on track (Carver & Scheier, 1998). Sometimes it is used more narrowly to refer to exerting self-control when under the pressure of competing demands (Vohs & Baumeister, 2011). It will be used in both ways in various parts of this chapter. The three of us have been interested in manifestations of self-regulation for some time. One of us is a personality psychologist (CSC); the others are clinical psychologists, with particular interest in mood disorders. This chapter derives from our developing curiosity about a self-regulatory puzzle in personality psychology, which quite unexpectedly led us to different puzzles in neurobiology and genetics, and eventually turned to issues in clinical psychology.

The focus of this chapter is on issues of impulse or reactivity versus constraint or deliberative control of action. This distinction is a key aspect of self-regulation. We begin by describing two psychological views on it. We then turn to evidence that serotonergic function helps to promote constraint. In that context we also give some attention to how this system might operate to constrain rather different forms of impulses. More specifically, we consider the idea that serotonergically innervated areas of the brain help modulate the effects of both over-activity and under-activity of underlying systems for approach and avoidance. This idea helps to explain how serotonergic deficits could be involved in a broad set of problems, ranging from antisocial behavior to depression.

IMPULSE AND CONSTRAINT

We begin our journey in personality psychology. The field of personality has been characterized for over a century by great conceptual diversity. Textbook authors have generally dealt with the diversity by describing a range of theoretical perspectives as alternative viewpoints on personality and its functions (e.g., Carver & Scheier, 2012). Sometimes the textbook authors also try to synthesize across theoretical boundaries, pointing to themes that seem to rise to the surface in one theory after another. Often enough, it turns out, similar themes are addressed by different theories but are handled differently by them.

One such theme is the tension in life between impulsiveness and constraint. From Freud onward, this issue has been important to personality theories, whether framed in terms of delay of gratification, planfulness, or socialization. Despite the fact that the concept of impulsiveness has been used in diverse ways (Carver, 2005), the core of the issue is relatively straightforward. People often face situations in which they can immediately follow an impulse or desire, or they can overrule that impulse and evaluate more fully before acting.

Both impulse and constraint as qualities of behavior have useful and valuable characteristics in the appropriate contexts (Block & Block, 1980). When manifested as spontaneity, impulsiveness brings a sense of vigor and freedom to the human experience (e.g., Dickman, 1990; Hansen & Breivik, 2001). There are also cases in which survival literally may depend on impulsive action – when a threat or an opportunity must be reacted to quickly (cf. Langewiesche, 2004).

However, unfettered impulses can also create problems. Impulsiveness can yield physical danger (e.g., impulsively chasing a ball into the street without looking for traffic). Impulses can interfere with attainment of longer-term goals (e.g., spending for the moment rather than saving for the future). Impulses can lead to violation of social norms (Cooper, Wood, Orcutt, & Albino, 2003; Lynam, 1996) and thereby to interpersonal conflict and legal problems. Other potential effects of impulsiveness including marital instability (Kelly & Conley, 1987), employment problems (Hogan & Holland, 2003), and disruption of health-maintaining behaviors (Bogg & Roberts, 2004; Hampson, Andrews, Barckley, Lichtenstein, & Lee, 2000;

Hampson, Severson, Burns, Slovic, & Fisher, 2001; Skinner, Hampson, Fife-Schaw, 2002). Being able to control impulsive reactivity thus is crucial to successful self-management (Vohs & Baumeister, 2011).

What influences the balance between impulse and constraint? What prevents impulses from always having free rein? Different theorists have posed different answers to these questions. Here we consider two of them (for broader review, see Carver, 2005).

Approach and Avoidance

One answer stems from the general view that incentives draw behavior toward them and threats inhibit those actions (e.g., Cloninger, 1987; Davidson, 1984, 1998; Fowles, 1993; Gray, 1994a, 1994b; Lang, 1995). The incentive system is often called a behavioral approach system (BAS; Gray, 1972, 1982, 1994a) or an activation or facilitation system (Depue & Collins, 1999; Fowles, 1980, 1987). When engaged by incentive cues, it yields approach behavior and positive affect (Gray, 1994a, 1994b). The threat system is often called a behavioral inhibition system (BIS; Gray, 1972, 1982, 1994a) or a withdrawal system (Davidson, 1992, 1998). When activated by cues of threat, it produces behavioral inhibition or withdrawal (Fowles, 1993; Gray, 1994a) and emotions such as anxiety or fear (Carver & White, 1994; Davidson, 1992; Gray, 1982).

In principle, it might be argued that nothing more is needed to account for variability in impulsiveness than these approach and avoidance processes. The weaker the approach tendency, the lower is the likelihood of impulsive action; the stronger the approach tendency, the greater is the likelihood of impulsive action. Indeed, Gray (1994a) chose *impulsivity* as his label for the personality dimension deriving from approach. In the presence of threat cues, however, the BIS becomes active, creating anxiety and behavioral inhibition – stifling ongoing approach. A very reactive BIS presumably permits little impulsive behavior. Low BIS sensitivity, in contrast, allows more frequent expression of impulsive approach.

There are a number of reasons, however, for believing that this is not the entire story regarding impulse and constraint. One reason is that in comprehensive trait models of personality, the trait that coalesces around approach and positive emotions and the trait that coalesces around avoidance and negative emotions, respectively, are distinct from the trait that coalesces around constraint (Clark & Watson, 1999; Depue & Collins, 1999; Zelenski & Larsen, 1999). That is, constraint and threat sensitivity are separate dimensions.

Another reason for believing that approach and avoidance are not the entire story is that it is relatively easy to point to situations in which constraint seems to be unrelated to anxiety. An example is delay of gratification: foregoing a small reward now in order to obtain a larger one later (Mischel, 1974). Constraint in that situation does not seem to be based on avoidance of any threat but rather about using time and planning to create more desirable overall outcomes.

Dual-Process Models

A different view derives from the idea that people process information in two somewhat distinct ways simultaneously, one more primitive than the other. The two processing modes appear to use different aspects of available information (Rudman, Phelan, & Heppen, 2007). There is also evidence that the two modes learn in different ways, and that the two patterns of learning create parallel and competing paths to action, which require continuous arbitration (Daw, Niv, & Dayan, 2005). The more primitive mode operates largely outside consciousness. The other is the familiar symbolic processor of the rational mind.

This idea helped deal with a clash between two viewpoints in cognitive psychology. One view treats cognition as sequential symbol processing; another assumes simultaneous parallel processing (e.g., Bechtel & Abrahamsen, 1991; Dawson, 2005; McClelland, 1999). Many cognitive psychologists now believe that both views are partly correct, that cognition (broadly conceived) uses two kinds of processes. One process – effortful, top-down, symbolic, and reflective – is used for planning and strategic behavior. The other – automatic, reflexive, bottom-up, and associationist – is used for acts that are heuristic, skilled, or urgent (e.g., Sloman, 1996; Smolensky & Legendre, 2006).

The literature of personality psychology also contains two-mode models (or dual-process models). Epstein's (1973, 1985, 1990, 1994) cognitive-experiential self theory was based on the premise that humans experience reality via a symbolic processor (the rational mind) and also an associative and intuitive processor that functions automatically and quickly. Epstein argued that both systems are always at work and that they jointly determine behavior. Metcalfe and Mischel (1999), drawing on several decades' work on delay of gratification, proposed a similar model. They proposed that the relative strength of two systems determines whether one is able to restrain oneself: a "hot" system (emotional, impulsive, reflexive, and connectionist) and a "cool" system (strategic, flexible, slower, and unemotional). How a

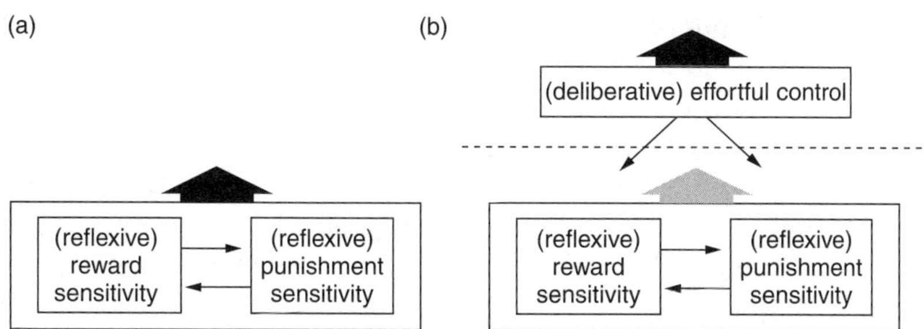

FIGURE 12.1 Three temperamental influences on behavior. (a) A reactive system for approaching rewards and a reactive system for avoiding threats or punishment compete for ascendance; in the absence of effortful control, the resultant of that competition is expressed in behavior. (b) The engagement of an effortful control system permits the resultant arising from the competition of the reactive systems to be overridden, thus dampening the role of the reactive systems in determining behavior. From Carver, Johnson, and Joormann (2008), adapted from various statements by Rothbart, Eisenberg, and others.

person responds to a situation with competing pressures depends on which system presently dominates.

The two-mode idea also has an important presence in developmental psychology. For example, Rothbart and her colleagues (e.g., Rothbart, Ahadi, & Evans, 2000; Rothbart, Ahadi, Hershey, & Fisher, 2001; Rothbart & Bates, 1998; Rothbart, Ellis, Rueda, & Posner, 2003; Rothbart & Posner, 1985) have argued for the existence of basic temperament systems for approach and avoidance and a third temperament, termed effortful control, which is slower to emerge (see also Kochanska & Knaack, 2003; MacDonald, 2008; Marcovitch & Zelazo, 2009; Nigg, 2000, 2003, 2006). Before the emergence of effortful control, behavior is a result of the influences of approach and avoidance temperaments (Figure 12.1). Greater sensitivity of the approach temperament makes impulsive action more likely; greater sensitivity of the avoidance temperament makes reflexive restraint more likely.

Effortful control is superordinate to approach and avoidance temperaments (e.g., Ahadi & Rothbart, 1994; see also Clark, 2005). Its emergence permits control over reactive behavior: suppressing tendencies that are triggered by the approach or avoidance temperament, when doing so is situationally appropriate. If effortful control capacity is available, the grabbing of incentives that arises from a sensitive approach system can be restrained (Kochanska & Knaack, 2003; Murray & Kochanska, 2002). This child (or adult) can delay gratification.

Importantly, this child (or adult) can also do other things. It can override a reflexive tendency toward avoidance, in situations where the avoidance temperament is more active than the approach temperament. It can also override a reflexive tendency toward *inaction*, if the approach temperament is weak. Thus, exerting effortful control can move a person toward either restraint or action, depending on what reflexive response is being overcome. This puts a rather different light on the concept of impulsivity. In this view, what is impulsive is what is *reactive*, whether its outward display is of action or inaction. This idea becomes more important later on.

The label "effortful" conveys the sense that this is an executive, planful activity, entailing the use of cognitive resources to deter the tendency to react impulsively. Rothbart (e.g., Rothbart & Bates, 1998), Eisenberg (e.g., Eisenberg et al., 2004), and Kochanska (e.g., Kochanska & Knaack, 2003) see effortful control as being dependent on certain prefrontal brain areas (see also Nigg, 2001, 2003), and evidence from neuroimaging studies of both adults and children supports that argument (e.g., Durston, Thomas, Worden, Yang, & Casey, 2002; Durston, Thomas, Yang, Ulug, Zimmerman, & Casey, 2002).

Characterizations of the two processing modes by various writers share many elements. The more primitive mode is typically described by such terms as impulsive, reflexive, reactive, implicit, heuristic, and associative. This mode is said to be responsive to situational cues of the moment, schematic associations, and especially to strong emotions. Its strengths are its quickness and its low demand on processing resources. It spontaneously creates action when its schemas are sufficiently activated. It thus can act even with little available information and high time urgency. The other mode is typically described by such terms as reflective, explicit, strategic, deliberative, and logical. Its strength is its ability to take into account circumstances that go beyond the immediate present. This mode requires substantial processing resources and thus loses efficiency when cognitive capacity is limited.

This two-mode model of the determination of action seems to resolve the issues that are not well handled by the viewpoint that considered only approach and avoidance. In the two-mode model, behavior is restrained sometimes because anxiety is stronger than desire (thus creating a kind of reflexive restraint), and sometimes because the reflective mode is acting to optimize longer-term outcomes. This is the viewpoint on self-regulation that we will assume as we continue.

SEROTONERGIC FUNCTION

We now turn to a very different viewpoint on personality, one that is guided heavily by neurobiological considerations. A number of theorists have begun to consider the possible role played by different neurotransmitter systems in the management of behavior, and thus in the variations that emerge among people's personalities. One of the neurotransmitter systems that has been the subject of much investigation is the serotonin system. In this section we consider the possible role of serotonergic function in impulse and constraint.

Serotonin has been studied for some time, in both humans and other animals (for greater detail, see Manuck, Kaplan, & Lotrich, 2006). The processes by which it operates are complex and not fully understood (Hensler, 2006; Lesch & Canli, 2006). To think only in terms of level of serotonin per se can be misleading, because a good deal more is involved than that (e.g., Neumeister et al., 2006). On the other hand, some experimental manipulations do influence how much serotonin is available during a definable window of time. This is the reasoning behind a procedure called acute tryptophan depletion. Tryptophan, an amino acid that is a precursor to serotonin, can be depleted by administering a drink (or capsules) containing high levels of other amino acids but no tryptophan. Several hours later, behavioral effects of artificially lowered serotonin can be studied. The question of interest in this paradigm is the nature and extent of the response (behavioral, affective, or cognitive) to the lowering of available serotonin.

Another methodological strategy is to relate behavior to genetic polymorphisms that have independently been linked to serotonergic function (Manuck et al., 2006). Most of this research has examined the gene that codes the serotonin transporter. Transcriptional activity of this gene is believed to be influenced by (or at least associated with) a repetitive sequence in a region called 5-HTTLPR, which has a short version and a long version (i.e., has more repetitions). A variety of indirect evidence links this polymorphism to variation in serotonergic function (reviewed in Carver, Johnson, & Joormann, 2008). It is now widely believed that the short allele is a marker of low serotonergic function (e.g., Canli & Lesch, 2007). The question of interest using this genetic paradigm is what kinds of characteristics (behavioral, affective, cognitive, or personality) differ between persons with the short allele and those with the long allele.

The sections that follow provide a flavor of some of the research that has been done using these methods and others. We argue that this research suggests that the serotonergic system functions to decrease reactive behavior and to increase constraint.

Correlates of Serotonergic Markers in the Laboratory

Some of the evidence on manifestations of serotonergic function comes from laboratory studies. Tryptophan depletion affects performance on a range of behavioral and cognitive tasks that have emotional components. More specifically, tryptophan depletion appears to impair constraint over automatic emotional responses. As an example, consider a task in which specific cues are rewarded and for which the response thus becomes habitual. Then the rules change and this response is no longer rewarded. Tryptophan depletion impairs the ability to inhibit those responses after the rule changes (Cools, Blackwell, et al., 2005; Park et al., 1994; Rogers et al., 2003). Tryptophan depletion has also led persons to report more sadness during exposure to uncontrollable stress (aversive noise), whereas the effect was only minor when the noise was controllable (Richell, Deakin, & Anderson, 2005). These types of studies suggest that the serotonin system can help inhibit responses to both rewarding and aversive stimuli.

Several studies have examined effects of tryptophan depletion on aggression. An important conceptual point was made in a study by Cleare and Bond (1995). Participants were pre-assessed as being either high or low in aggressive tendencies. Those high in aggressive tendencies became more aggressive, hostile, and quarrelsome after tryptophan depletion, but there was no effect for those low in aggressive tendencies. Similar results were reported by Finn, Young, Pihl, and Ervin (1998). This pattern suggests that effects of low serotonergic function on aggression are less about aggression and more about the release of existing habitual tendencies to be aggressive (see also Manuck et al., 2006; Spoont, 1992). A later study (Bjork et al., 2000) further reinforced this point: tryptophan depletion in this case led to greater aggressive response to provocation among men high in aggressiveness but had an opposite effect among those low in aggressiveness.

Correlates of Serotonergic Markers with Personality

Another set of studies has examined relationships of serotonergic function to personality as measured by self-report, using several different procedures to assess serotonergic function. Some of this work focused on qualities pertaining to aggression and impulsiveness; other studies have examined a broader spectrum of personality qualities. Hostility as a trait has been related to low serotonergic function in nonclinical samples (Cleare & Bond, 1997; Depue, 1995; Netter, Hennig, & Rohrmann, 1999). Depue (1995) related low serotonergic function as well to the Control-impulsivity facet scale from the Constraint factor of the Multidimensional Personality Questionnaire (MPQ; Tellegen, 1985), the Aggression facet of the MPQ's Negative emotionality factor (but not other facets), two sensation-seeking subscales, and several indices of impulsiveness.

There is also a substantial literature on the serotonin polymorphism and personality as assessed by broad-ranging self-report inventories. These studies permit investigation of diverse possible associations, if facets as well as factors are examined. This work began with several large-scale studies in which the data were examined thoroughly. Lesch et al. (1996) found that the short allele (linked to low serotonergic function) related positively to neuroticism (by NEO-PI-R) and inversely to agreeableness. In facet analyses, the neuroticism facets most closely associated with the short allele were Angry hostility, Depression, and Impulsiveness. Greenberg et al. (2000) also related the short allele to both neuroticism and agreeableness, with an additional weaker but significant association for conscientiousness. Analysis of neuroticism facets again revealed the strongest relations for Angry hostility and Depression.

Many other studies have since been done, and even several meta-analyses (for review, see Carver et al., 2008). Interestingly, however, the meta-analyses have all focused on neuroticism, as has most of the developing literature. The consistent association with agreeableness has generally been disregarded.

Correlates of Serotonergic Markers With Impulsive Disorders

A good deal of research has also examined serotonergic function in adults with clinical conditions reflecting impulsive aggression (for more extensive review, see Manuck et al., 2006). Lower serotonergic function has long been linked to history of fighting and assault (Coccaro, Kavoussi, Cooper, & Hauger, 1997), domestic violence (George et al., 2001), and impulsive aggression more generally, particularly among men (Coccaro, Kavoussi, Hauger, Cooper, & Ferris, 1998; Cleare and Bond, 1997).

Genetic evidence also connects serotonergic function to violent and antisocial behavior. For example, Dolan, Anderson, and Deakin (2001) linked low serotonergic function to higher impulsivity and higher aggression in male aggressive offenders. Interestingly, both impulsivity and aggression also related to higher anxiety in this sample. This argues against a path in which impulsive aggression is a product of low anxiety.

Characterizing the Pattern

The pattern of these findings (and others) appears consistent with the view that serotonergic pathways are involved in impulse control (Depue, 1995; Depue & Collins, 1999; Depue & Spoont, 1986; Manuck, Flory, Muldoon, & Ferrell, 2003; Soubrié, 1986; Spoont, 1992; Zuckerman, 2005), particularly impulses that reflect strong emotions. On the other side, high serotonergic function appears to relate to consideration of the future consequences of one's behavior (promoting conscientiousness) and to positive social connection (promoting agreeableness).

We have characterized this pattern in terms of the dual-process model described in the preceding section of the chapter (Carver et al., 2008). We said there that the basic, reactive mode of functioning is impulsive and is highly responsive to strong emotions. The reflective mode is planful and less reactive to immediate emotional cues. Taking these descriptions together with the findings described in this section, we suggest that serotonergic function may shift the balance of influence between these two modes of functioning. That is, it appears that lower serotonergic function may increase the influence of the reactive system or decrease the influence of the reflective system.

DEPRESSION AND SEROTONERGIC FUNCTION

We now turn to depression. As mentioned in the previous section, depression as a facet scale of neuroticism has been linked repeatedly to the serotonin transporter gene, the short allele being associated with higher depression scores. There is also an accumulation of evidence from other studies linking serotonergic function (operationalized in various ways) to more clinically meaningful depression (for review, see Carver et al., 2008).

Early studies looked for a direct link from the serotonin transporter polymorphism to depression vulnerability, but more recent work has tended to focus on the possibility of a gene by environment interaction. Caspi et al. (2003) first reported that this polymorphism interacted with early maltreatment to predict depression diagnosis by early adulthood: negative life events had an adverse effect on those carrying at least one short allele, but not among those with two long alleles. A number of other studies followed, and by now there have been several meta-analyses of this literature (Risch, et al.,

2009; Uher & McGuffin, 2008, 2010). The outcomes of the meta-analyses have varied as a function of selection criteria. However, Uher and McGuffin (2010) determined that the serotonin transporter polymorphism interacted with early maltreatment to predict vulnerability to depression in each of the 11 studies that used objective or interview measures of maltreatment (see also Caspi, Hariri, Holmes, Uher, & Moffitt, 2010).

Impulsivity and Depression

Previous sections linked low serotonergic function to impulse expression, particularly impulsive reactions to emotional cues. Research has also linked low serotonergic function to behavioral problems in which a salient feature was poor impulse control. Now we are saying that low serotonergic function also relates to vulnerability to depression. Although depression has sometimes been linked to what would be widely recognized as impulsive qualities (Peluso et al., 2007), it is more often associated with lethargy, an absence of behavioral engagement (Sobin & Sackeim, 1997). This seems very confusing. How can we account for this very substantial difference in presentation?

In addressing this question we return to the dual-process models of self-regulation. We have said that the reactive mode is characterized as acting impulsively (reflexively) and as being highly responsive to emotions. But these are "operating characteristics" of that mode of function. How these operating characteristics are manifested depends on what reactive impulse exists in the person and what emotions the person is experiencing. In depression, the impulse is different and the emotion is different. Sadness (the affective core of depression) differs from other emotions in a very important way. Sadness is a deactivating emotion (Frijda, 1986).

Thus, to address the fact that low serotonergic function and the resulting deficits in effortful control have divergent effects in different groups of people requires hypothesizing an interaction (see also Depue & Lenzenweger, 2005). People who are sensation seekers and people who are vulnerable to depression must differ systematically from each other in some way other than low serotonergic function.

What other systematic variation among people might interact with serotonin function to yield such a divergence? A plausible candidate is variation in the degree of sensitivity, or engagement, of the incentive approach system. When poor executive oversight is combined with moderately high incentive sensitivity (a fairly reactive approach system), the result is overt impulsiveness. When poor executive oversight is combined with low incentive sensitivity (a nonreactive approach system), the result is inaction: lack of effort toward potential rewards. In both cases, the effects of variation in level of incentive sensitivity (high and low, respectively) are amplified by the absence of effortful override (Figure 12.1).

In the case of depression vulnerability, a lack of incentive sensitivity means that the person is not strongly motivated to approach potentially rewarding contexts. A relative deficit in effortful control amplifies this problem, such that the person has greater difficulty overcoming this lack of motivations. This combination thus should yield apathy, passivity, and fatigue, which characterize many cases of depression.

There are several sources of evidence that depression is associated with a blunted approach system. Electroencephalogram (EEG) laterality has been used as a way to measure activity of the approach system. Several studies have suggested that behavioral and personality measures of approach motivation are correlated with higher activation in left than right anterior cortical areas (e.g., Coan & Allen, 2003; Harmon-Jones & Allen, 1997; Sutton & Davidson, 1997).Previously depressed (Henriques & Davidson, 1990) and clinically depressed persons (Henriques & Davidson, 1991) have been found to have lower activation in left anterior cortical areas than nondepressed persons, with no difference in right anterior activation.

Behavioral research also suggests that depression relates to blunted incentive sensitivity. For example, depressed persons have been found to be less responsive to reward than nondepressed persons (Henriques, Glowacki, & Davidson, 1994; Henriques & Davidson, 2000). Other evidence relates self-reports of low incentive sensitivity to depression (Campbell-Sills, Liverant, & Brown, 2004; Pinto-Meza, Caseras, Soler, Puigdemont, Perez, & Torrubia, 2006). Indeed, three separate studies have found that self-reports of low incentive sensitivity predicted a worse course of depression over time (Campbell-Sills et al., 2004; Kasch, Rottenberg, Arnow, & Gotlib, 2002; McFarland, Shankman, Tenke, Bruder, & Klein, 2006).

Blunted approach motivation may also be reflected in low dopaminergic function. Dopaminergic pathways are believed to be critical in the engagement of goal-directed effort (Farrar, Pereira, Velasco, Hockemeyer, Müller, & Salamone, 2007; Salamone, Correa, Farrar, & Mingote, 2007; Salamone, Correa, Mingote, & Weber, 2005; Salamone, Correa, Mingote, Weber, & Farrar, 2006). A weakly functioning dopaminergic incentive system yields less "wanting" for appetitive outcomes (Berridge, 2007) and less engagement of effort in pursuit of them (Salamone et al., 2005, 2006, 2007). A recent review reported a range of evidence for deficits in the function of dopamine among depressed persons, drawing from pharmacological studies, genetic studies, and dopamine challenge studies (Dunlop & Nemeroff, 2007).

Impulsive Passivity

It may seem counterintuitive to characterize vulnerability to depression as reflecting impulsiveness, but in effect that is what we are saying. As noted earlier, impulsiveness is manifested in many different ways. It may be most intuitive to think about impulsiveness in terms of leaping quickly toward positive events or experiences, as in sensation seeking. But the term impulsiveness also suggests being easily distracted, leaping to conclusions, not persisting in task-directed efforts, and being easily overwhelmed by emotions. It seems quite likely that some of these characterizations do fit with depression. If the labels impulsiveness versus control are taken to refer to the reactive versus deliberative nature of the response, rather than to its behavioral content (action vs. inaction), then depression may represent impulsive passivity. The serotonergic system, then, would be seen as exerting effortful control over an underactive approach system, just as it does over an overactive approach system.

To explore this idea, we have recently collected data from a sample of college students using a variety of questionnaires, some developed explicitly for the study and others preexisting. A subsample completed a diagnostic interview for lifetime episodes of major depression. Of interest is whether the self-reports differentiated those who had positive diagnoses from the others. Results showed that self-reports reflecting strong reactions to emotions (both cognitive and behavioral reactions, to both negative and positive emotions) were endorsed more by persons with diagnoses of having had an episode of major depressive disorder than those who had not (Carver, Johnson, & Joormann, in press).

ISSUES

We close by briefly considering several issues that are raised by the work described here. We begin with a recapitulation of the main points. The serotonin system doubtlessly has many effects in the body. But one reflection of serotonergic function seems to be in the dimension of reactivity versus oversight and self-control, the degree to which a person can exert cognitive control over emotions (Spoont, 1992).

Interactive Model

As noted previously, however, these are abstract functional properties that can be manifested in many ways. The fact that low serotonergic function has been linked both to problems of impulse control (e.g., impulsive violence) and to problems with strong overtones of passivity (depression) implies an interaction. We suggested in the preceding section that a variable that may be interacting with variations in serotonergic function is the level of engagement of the system responsible for eager, effortful approach. Impulsive aggression was characterized as reflecting low serotonergic function and relatively high approach motivation (perhaps true of other impulse-related problems as well; cf. Depue & Lenzenweger, 2005). Depression was characterized as reflecting low serotonergic function and blunted approach motivation.

A broad question for the future is whether other interactions should also be explored more fully (Depue & Lenzenweger, 2005; Nigg, 2006). For example, it has been argued that overt expression of a vulnerability to anxiety disorders may also depend on poor executive control (Lonigan et al., 2004). Consistent with this idea, serotonin has been implicated in the development of anxiety disorders (Leonardo & Hen, 2006). These findings suggest an interactive combination of a highly sensitive threat system and low serotonergic functioning.

Many observers have noted that the attempt to link any given neurotransmitter to the operation of a single behavioral system is likely to be a great oversimplification. Nonetheless, it does not seem too far an extrapolation from the evidence to suggest that low serotonergic function promotes a stronger manifestation of whatever tendencies the person has at the reflexive or implicit level of functioning (for similar conclusions, see Depue, 1995; Nigg, 2006; Spoont, 1992). In an incentive-sensitive person, low serotonergic function amplifies the pursuit of incentives. In an incentive-*in*sensitive person, low serotonergic function exaggerates the lack of effortful engagement. In a threat-sensitive person, low serotonergic function may enhance vigilance to threat.

The specific cases of depression, impulsive disorders, and anxiety disorders are only three possibilities, reflecting interactions of a serotonergic system with two other systems. A more complete understanding of the role of serotonin in behavior will require a more elaborated understanding of how serotonergic function interacts with effects of other neurotransmitters. The idea that diverse disorders follow from diverse combinations of system sensitivities (Depue & Lenzenweger, 2005; Fowles & Dindo, 2009;

Lenzenweger & Willett, 2007) is very intriguing and seems worthy of much more examination.

Two-Mode Models

Recent years have seen an explosion of interest in neurobiological processes underlying behavior. Psychologists are now routinely collecting genetic data and they are very often, if not quite routinely yet, collecting imaging data to indicate what areas of the brain are especially active in varying experimental conditions. The involvement of different neurotransmitters – such as serotonin – in psychological phenomena is also an active area of exploration.

We have argued that it is useful to conceptualize the functions of the serotonergic system in terms of two-mode models of self-regulation. Viewed through this lens, the evidence suggests that serotonergic function can be linked to impulsivity versus constraint in the personality literature, effortful control processes in the cognitive and developmental literatures, and (not addressed here, but discussed by Carver et al., 2008) executive control over the amygdala and other subcortical areas in the neurobiological literature. This two-mode picture helps organize what is known about the experience of depression, and it may also be useful in suggesting new areas of investigation.

The serotonergic system is a biological system. Yet ideas and evidence from literatures that are psychological in nature appear to foster a deeper understanding of the role of this system. It is frequently said that biological concepts and methods should be taken as key resources to inform psychological theory. We would hold, however (along with Posner and Rothbart, 2007), that the path of influence goes both ways, that interpretation of neurobiological evidence also benefits from considering the findings through the lens of psychological principles.

Two Modes of Functioning: Historical Resonances

Dual-process models of self-regulation are enjoying a surge in popularity in today's psychology. We would be remiss if we failed to note at least briefly that there are resonances of these ideas far back in the history of psychology. The most obvious is the structural model of psychoanalysis (Freud, 1962/1923). In that model, the id is the starting point for personality. It is the source of impulses, and it follows a principle of immediately expressing any impulse that is triggered. The slower-developing ego restrains those impulses. Indeed, the ego was said to evolve as a mode of functioning precisely because of the need for a mechanism to take the pressures and restrictions of social and physical reality into account. That is, the ego acts to restrain the id's impulses until an appropriate time and place is found to express them. This taking into account of pressures beyond one's immediate impulses greatly resembles what is described as the reflective mode of functioning.

Another broad resonance we wish to note is with the ideas of Piaget (e.g., 1971). Early child development is a time of building simple schemas, associations among experiences, both perceptual and motor. The young child is certainly capable of developing habits of considerable complexity, but this child is not yet capable of developing rules. The development of a system of rules requires a cognitive capacity that is not just broader, but different from what is required to form habits. It is more reflective, deliberative, extracting different kinds of information from experiences than are required to form habits. It may well be that the reflective, deliberative mode of processing that represents the second layer in dual-process models is the same set of mental structures as were identified by Piaget as the substrate that permits the development of concrete operational thought.

CONCLUSION

This chapter addressed the broad theme of behavioral self-regulation from the perspective of contemporary dual-process models. In the dual-process view, two distinguishable parts of the mind and brain can lead to behavior. One is a relatively primitive set of structures that learns about the world in associationist, essentially actuarial ways. This part of the mind specifies behaviors relatively reflexively, when situations are identified by the schemas it has developed over time. The other influence on behavior is a slower developing but more advanced set of structures that learn about the world in a somewhat different way. It gradually learns rules and principles. It can reason. When deciding how to act, it can take into account considerations that are broader in scope than the present stimulus situation. These systems can come to different conclusions about the appropriate action to engage in. What action emerges depends on which mode has the greater influence at that moment.

Many forces influence the balance of influence between these two kinds of self-regulatory systems. We have suggested that the balance depends partly on serotonergic portions of the nervous system. When central serotonergic function is low (as indicated by one of several indices), behavior appears to be very responsive to situational (and especially emotional) cues.

This is as would be expected from dominance of the reactive, associationist system. When serotonergic function is high, behavior appears to be more deliberative, taking into account issues that transcend the immediate context and the immediate moment. This is as would be expected from dominance of the reflective system.

As we said in the opening of the chapter, the term self-regulation has more than one meaning. In some contexts it means nothing more than monitoring the consequences of an action so as to keep it on track. Used in this way, both of these modes of function engage in self-regulatory activities. Even the more basic mode incorporates the simple feedback processes required to ensure that the act stipulated by the context is the act that is executed. When we talk about the two systems in competition, however, we are almost always talking about situations in which the alternative meaning of self-regulation is invoked. That is, the deliberative system engages a broader sort of self-control, which otherwise seems not to be part of our behavioral repertoire.

REFERENCES

Ahadi, S. A., & Rothbart, M. K. (1994). Temperament, development and the big five. In C. F. Halverson, Jr., G. A. Kohnstamm, & R. P. Martin (Eds.), *The developing structure of temperament and personality from infancy to adulthood* (pp. 189–207). Hillsdale, NJ: Erlbaum.

Bechtel, W., & Abrahamsen, A. (1991). *Connectionism and the mind: An introduction to parallel processing in networks*. Cambridge, UK: Basil Blackwell.

Berridge, K. C. (2007). The debate over dopamine's role in reward: The case for incentive salience. *Psychopharmacology, 191*, 391–431.

Bjork, J. M., Dougherty, D. M., Moeller, F. G., & Swann, A. C. (2000). Differential behavioral effects of plasma tryptophan depletion and loading in aggressive and nonaggressive men. *Neuropsychopharmacology, 22*, 357–369.

Block, J. H., & Block, J. (1980). The role of ego-control and ego-resiliency in the organization of behavior. In W. A. Collins (Ed.), *Development of cognition, affect, and social relations* (Minnesota Symposia on Child Psychology, Vol. 13, pp. 39–101). Hillsdale, NJ: Erlbaum.

Bogg, T., & Roberts, B. W. (2004). Conscientiousness and health-related behaviors: A meta-analysis of the leading behavioral contributors to mortality. *Psychological Bulletin, 130*, 887–919.

Campbell-Sills, L., Liverant, G. I., & Brown, T. A. (2004). Psychometric evaluation of the Behavioral Inhibition/Behavioral Activation Scales in a large sample of outpatients with anxiety and mood disorders. *Psychological Assessment, 16*, 244–254.

Canli, T., & Lesch, K. (2007). Long story short: The serotonin transporter in emotion regulation and social cognition. *Nature Neuroscience, 10*, 1103–1109.

Carver, C. S. (2005). Impulse and constraint: Perspectives from personality psychology, convergence with theory in other areas, and potential for integration. *Personality and Social Psychology Review, 9*, 312–333.

Carver, C. S., Johnson, S. L., & Joormann, J. (2008). Serotonergic function, two-mode models of self-regulation, and vulnerability to depression: What depression has in common with impulsive aggression. *Psychological Bulletin, 134*, 912–943.

Carver, C. S., Johnson, S. L., & Joormann, J. (in press). Major depressive disorder and impulsive reactivity to emotion: Toward a dual process view of depression. *British Journal of Clinical Psychology.*

Carver, C. S., & Scheier, M. F. (1998). *On the self-regulation of behavior.* New York, NY: Cambridge University Press.

Carver, C. S., & Scheier, M. F. (2012). *Perspectives on personality* (7th ed.). Upper Saddle River, NJ: Pearson Education.

Carver, C. S., & White, T. L. (1994). Behavioral inhibition, behavioral activation, and affective responses to impending reward and punishment: The BIS/BAS scales. *Journal of Personality and Social Psychology, 67*, 319–333.

Caspi, A., Hariri, A. R., Holmes, A., Uher, R., & Moffitt, T. E. (2010). Genetic sensitivity to the environment: The case of the serotonin transporter gene and its implications for studying complex diseases and traits. *American Journal of Psychiatry, 167*, 509–527.

Caspi, A., Sugden, K., Moffitt, T. E., Taylor, A., Craig, I. W., Harrington, H., et al. (2003). Influence of life stress on depression: Moderation by a polymorphism in the 5-HTT gene. *Science, 301*, 386–389.

Clark, L. A. (2005). Temperament as a unifying basis for personality and psychopathology. *Journal of Abnormal Psychology, 114*, 505–521.

Clark, L. A., & Watson, D. (1999). Temperament: A new paradigm for trait psychology. In L. A. Pervin & O. P. John (Eds.), *Handbook of personality: Theory and research* (2nd ed., pp. 399–423). New York: Guilford Press.

Cleare, A. J., & Bond, A. J. (1995). The effect of tryptophan depletion and enhancement on subjective and behavioural aggression in normal male subjects. *Psychopharmacology, 118*, 72–81.

Cleare, A. J., & Bond, A. J. (1997). Does central serotonergic function correlate inversely with aggression? A study using D-fenfluramine in healthy subjects. *Psychiatry Research, 69*, 89–95.

Cloninger, C. R. (1987). A systematic method for clinical description and classification of personality variants: A proposal. *Archives of General Psychiatry, 44*, 573–588.

Coan, J. A., & Allen, J. J. B. (2003). Frontal EEG asymmetry and the behavioral activation and inhibition systems. *Psychophysiology, 40*, 106–114.

Coccaro, E. F., Kavoussi, R. J., Cooper, T. B., & Hauger, R. L. (1997). Central serotonin activity and aggression: Inverse relationship with prolactin response to d-fenfluramine, but not CSF 5-HIAA concentration, in human subjects. *American Journal of Psychiatry, 154*, 1430–1435.

Coccaro, E. F., Kavoussi, R. J., Hauger, R. L., Cooper, T. B., & Ferris, C. F. (1998). Cerebrospinal fluid vasopressin levels: Correlates with aggression and serotonin function in personality-disordered subjects. *Archives of General Psychiatry, 55*, 708–714.

Cools, R., Blackwell, A., Clark, L., Menzies, L., Cox, S., & Robbins, T. W. (2005). Tryptophan depletion disrupts the motivational guidance of goal-directed behavior as a function of trait impulsivity. *Neuropsychopharmacology, 30*, 1362–1373.

Cooper, M. L., Wood, P. K., Orcutt, H. K., & Albino, A. (2003). Personality and the predisposition to engage in risky or problem behaviors during adolescence. *Journal of Personality and Social Psychology, 84*, 390–410.

Dawson, M. R. W. (2005). *Connectionism: A hands-on approach.* Malden, MA: Blackwell.

Davidson, R. J. (1984). Affect, cognition, and hemispheric specialization. In C. E. Izard, J. Kagan, & R. Zajonc (Eds.), *Emotion, cognition, and behavior* (pp. 320–365). New York. NY: Cambridge University Press.

Davidson, R. J. (1992). Prolegomenon to the structure of emotion: Gleanings from neuropsychology. *Cognition and Emotion, 6*, 245–268.

Davidson, R. J. (1998). Anterior electrophysiological asymmetries, emotion, and depression: Conceptual and methodological conundrums. *Psychophysiology, 35*, 607–614.

Daw, N. D., Niv, Y., & Dayan, P. (2005). Uncertainty-based competition between prefrontal and dorsolateral striatal systems for behavioral control. *Nature Neuroscience, 8*, 1704–1711.

Depue, R. A. (1995). Neurobiological factors in personality and depression. *European Journal of Personality, 9*, 413–439.

Depue, R. A., & Collins, P. F. (1999). Neurobiology of the structure of personality: Dopamine, facilitation of incentive motivation, and extraversion. *Behavioral and Brain Sciences, 22*, 491–517.

Depue, R. A., & Lenzenweger, M. F. (2005). A neurobiological dimensional model of personality disturbance. In M. F. Lenzenweger & J. F. Clarkin (Eds.), *Major theories of personality disorder* (2nd ed.). New York, NY: Guilford Press.

Depue, R. A., & Spoont, M. R. (1986). Conceptualizing a serotonin trait: A behavioral dimension of constraint. *Annals of the New York Academy of Sciences, 487*, 47–62.

Dickman, S. J. (1990). Functional and dysfunctional impulsivity: Personality and cognitive correlates. *Journal of Personality and Social Psychology, 58*, 95–102.

Dolan, M. C., Anderson, I. M., & Deakin, J. F. W. (2001). Relationship between 5-HT function and impulsivity and aggression in male offenders with personality disorders. *British Journal of Psychiatry, 178*, 352–359.

Dunlop, B. W., & Nemeroff, C. B. (2007). The role of dopamine in the pathophysiology of depression. *Archives of General Psychiatry, 64*, 327–337.

Durston, S., Thomas, K. M., Worden, M. S., Yang, Y., & Casey, B. J. (2002). The effect of preceding context on inhibition: An event-related fMRI study. *NeuroImage, 16*, 449–453.

Durston, S., Thomas, K. M., Yang, Y., Ulug, A. M., Zimmerman, R. D., & Casey, B. J. (2002). A neural basis for the development of inhibitory control. *Developmental Science, 5*, F9–F16.

Eisenberg, N., Spinrad, T. L., Fabes, R. A., Reiser, M., Cumberland, A., Shepard, S. A., et al. (2004). The relations of effortful control and impulsivity to children's resiliency and adjustment. *Child Development, 75*, 25–46.

Epstein, S. (1973). The self-concept revisited: Or a theory of a theory. *American Psychologist, 28*, 404–416.
Epstein, S. (1985). The implications of cognitive–experiential self theory for research in social psychology and personality. *Journal for the Theory of Social Behavior, 15*, 283–310.
Epstein, S. (1990). Cognitive–experiential self-theory. In L. Pervin (Ed.), *Handbook of personality: Theory and research* (pp. 165–192). New York, NY: Guilford Press.
Epstein, S. (1994). Integration of the cognitive and the psychodynamic unconscious. *American Psychologist, 49*, 709–724.
Farrar, A. M., Pereira, M., Velasco, F., Hockemeyer, J., Müller, C. E., & Salamone, J. D. (2007). Adenosine A2A receptor antagonism reverses the effects of dopamine receptor antagonism on instrumental output and effort-related choice in the rat: Implications for studies of psychomotor slowing. *Psychopharmacology, 191*, 579–586.
Finn, P. R., Young, S. N., Pihl, R. O., & Ervin, F. R. (1998). The effects of acute plasma tryptophan manipulation on hostile mood: The influence of trait hostility. *Aggressive Behavior, 24*, 173–185.
Fowles, D. C. (1980). The three arousal model: Implications of Gray's two-factor learning theory for heart rate, electrodermal activity, and psychopathy. *Psychophysiology, 17*, 87–104.
Fowles, D. C. (1987). Application of a behavioral theory of motivation to the concepts of anxiety and impulsivity. *Journal of Research in Personality, 21*, 417–435.
Fowles, D. C. (1993). Biological variables in psychopathology: A psychobiological perspective. In P. B. Sutker & H. E. Adams (Eds.), *Comprehensive handbook of psychopathology* (2nd ed., pp. 57–82). New York, NY: Plenum Press.
Fowles, D. C., & Dindo, L. (2009). Temperament and psychopathy: A dual-pathway model. *Current Directions in Psychological Science, 18*, 179–183.
Freud, S. (1962). *The ego and the id*. New York, NY: Norton. (Originally published, 1923.)
Frijda, N. H. (1986). *The emotions*. Cambridge, UK: Cambridge University Press.
George, D. T., Umhau, J. C., Phillips, M. J., Emmela, D., Ragan, P. W., Shoaf, S. E., et al. (2001). Serotonin, testosterone, and alcohol in the etiology of domestic violence. *Psychiatry Research, 104*, 27–37.
Gray, J. A. (1972). The psychophysiological basis of introversion-extraversion: A modification of Eysenck's theory. In V. D. Nebylitsyn and J. A. Gray (Eds.), *The biological bases of individual behaviour* (pp. 182–205). New York, NY: Academic Press.
Gray, J. A. (1982). *The neuropsychology of anxiety: An enquiry into the functions of the septo-hippocampal system*. New York, NY: Oxford University Press.
Gray, J. A. (1994a). Personality dimensions and emotion systems. In P. Ekman & R. J. Davidson (Eds.), *The nature of emotion: Fundamental questions* (pp. 329–331). New York, NY: Oxford University Press.
Gray, J. A. (1994b). Three fundamental emotion systems. In P. Ekman & R. J. Davidson (Eds.), *The nature of emotion: Fundamental questions* (pp. 243–247). New York, NY: Oxford University Press.
Greenberg, B. D., Li, Q., Lucas, F. R., Hu, S., Sirota, L. A., Benjamin, J., et al. (2000). Association between the serotonin transporter promoter polymorphism and

personality traits in a primarily female population sample. *American Journal of Medical Genetics (Neuropsychiatric Genetics)*, *96*, 202–216.

Hampson, S. E., Andrews, J. A., Barckley, M., Lichtenstein, E., & Lee, M. E. (2000). Conscientiousness, perceived risk, and risk-reduction behaviors: A preliminary study. *Health Psychology*, *19*, 496–500.

Hampson, S. E., Severson, H. H., Burns, W. J., Slovic, P., & Fisher, K. J. (2001). Risk perception, personality factors and alcohol use among adolescents. *Personality and Individual Differences*, *30*, 167–181.

Hansen, E. B., & Breivik, G. (2001). Sensation seeking as a predictor of positive and negative risk behaviour among adolescents. *Personality and Individual Differences*, *30*, 627–640.

Harmon-Jones, E., & Allen, J. J. B. (1997). Behavioral activation sensitivity and resting frontal EEG asymmetry: Covariation of putative indicators related to risk for mood disorders. *Journal of Abnormal Psychology*, *106*, 159–163.

Hensler, J. G. (2006). Serotonergic modulation of the limbic system. *Neuroscience Biobehavioral Review*, *30*, 203–214.

Henriques, J. B., & Davidson, R. J. (1990). Regional brain electrical asymmetries discriminate between previously depressed and healthy control subjects. *Journal of Abnormal Psychology*, *99*, 22–31.

Henriques, J. B., & Davidson, R. J. (1991). Left frontal hypoactivation in depression. *Journal of Abnormal Psychology*, *100*, 535–545.

Henriques, J. B., & Davidson, R. J. (2000). Decreased responsiveness to reward in depression. *Cognition and Emotion*, *14*, 711–724.

Henriques, J. B., Glowacki, J. M., & Davidson, R. J. (1994). Reward fails to alter response bias in depression. *Journal of Abnormal Psychology*, *103*, 460–466.

Hogan, J., & Holland, B. (2003). Using theory to evaluate personality and job performance relations: A socioanalytic perspective. *Journal of Applied Psychology*, *88*, 100–112.

Kasch, K. L., Rottenberg, J., Arnow, B. A., & Gotlib, I. H. (2002). Behavioral activation and inhibition systems and the severity and course of depression. *Journal of Abnormal Psychology*, *111*, 589–597.

Kochanska, G., & Knaack, A. (2003). Effortful control as a personality characteristic of young children: Antecedents, correlates, and consequences. *Journal of Personality*, *71*, 1087–1112.

Kelly, E. L., & Conley, J. J. (1987). Personality and compatibility: A prospective analysis of marital stability and marital satisfaction. *Journal of Personality and Social Psychology*, *52*, 27–40.

Lang, P. J. (1995). The emotion probe: Studies of motivation and attention. *American Psychologist*, *50*, 372–385.

Langewiesche, W. (2004). A sea story. *Atlantic Monthly*, *293*, 85–95.

Lenzenweger, M. F., & Willett, J. B. (2007). Predicting individual change in personality disorder features by simultaneous individual change in personality dimensions linked to neurobehavioral systems: The longitudinal study of personality disorders. *Journal of Abnormal Psychology*, *116*, 684–700.

Leonardo, E. D., & Hen, R. (2006). Genetics of affective and anxiety disorders. *Annual Review of Psychology*, *57*, 117–137.

Lesch, K-P., Bengel, D., Heils, A., Sabol, S. Z., Greenberg, B. D., Petri, S., et al. (1996). Association of anxiety-related traits with a polymorphism in the serotonin transporter gene regulatory region. *Science, 274*, 1527–1531.

Lesch, K-P., & Canli, T. (2006). 5-HT_{1A} receptor and anxiety-related traits. In T. Canli (Ed.), *Biology of personality and individual differences* (pp. 273–294). New York, NY: Guilford Press.

Lonigan, C. J., Vasey, M. W., Phillips, B. M., & Hazen, R. A. (2004). Temperament, anxiety, and the processing of threat-relevant stimuli. *Journal of Clinical Child and Adolescent Psychology, 33*, 8–20.

Lynam, D. R. (1996). Early identification of chronic offenders: Who is the fledgling psychopath? *Psychological Bulletin, 120*, 209–234.

MacDonald, K. B. (2008). Effortful control, explicit processing, and the regulation of human evolved dispositions. *Psychological Review, 115*, 1012–1031.

Manuck, S. B., Flory, J. D., Muldoon, M. F., & Ferrell, R .E. (2003). A neurobiology of intertemporal choice. In G. Loewenstein, D. Read, & R. F. Baumeister (Eds.), *Time and decision: Economic and psychological perspectives on intertemporal choice* (pp. 139–172). New York, NY: Russell Sage Foundation.

Manuck, S. B., Kaplan, J. R., & Lotrich, F. E. (2006). Brain serotonin and aggressive disposition in humans and nonhuman primates. In R. J. Nelson (Ed.), *Biology of aggression* (pp. 65–102). New York, NY: Oxford University Press.

Marcovitch, S., & Zelazo, P. D. (2009). A hierarchical competing systems model of the emergence and early development of executive function. *Developmental Science, 12*, 1–25.

McClelland, J. L. (1999). Cognitive modeling, connectionist. In R. W. Wilson & F. C. Keil (Eds.), *The MIT encyclopedia of the cognitive sciences* (pp.137–139). Cambridge, MA: MIT Press.

McFarland, B. R., Shankman, S. A., Tenke, C. E., Bruder, G. E., & Klein, D. N. (2006). Behavioral activation system deficits predict the six-month course of depression. *Journal of Affective Disorders, 91*, 229–234.

Metcalfe, J., & Mischel, W. (1999). A hot/cool-system analysis of delay of gratification: Dynamics of willpower. *Psychological Review, 106*, 3–19.

Mischel, W. (1974). Processes in delay of gratification. In L. Berkowitz (Ed.), *Advances in experimental social psychology* (vol. 7, pp. 249–292). New York, NY: Academic Press.

Murray, K. T., & Kochanska, G. (2002). Effortful control: Factor structure and relation to externalizing and internalizing behaviors. *Journal of Abnormal Child Psychology, 30*, 503–514.

Netter, P., Hennig, J., & Rohrmann, S. (1999). Psychobiological differences between the aggression and psychoticism dimension. *Pharmacopsychiatry, 32*, 5–12.

Neumeister, A., Hu, X., Luckenbaugh, D. A., Schwarz, M., Nugent, A. C., Bonne, O., et al. (2006). Differential effects of 5-HTTLPR genotypes on the behavioral and neural responses to tryptophan depletion in patients with major depression and controls. *Archives of General Psychiatry, 63*, 978–986.

Nigg, J. T. (2000). On inhibition/disinhibition in developmental pychopathology: Views from cognitive and personality psychology as a working inhibition taxonomy. *Psychological Bulletin, 126*, 220–246.

Nigg, J. T. (2001). Is ADHD a disinhibitory disorder? *Psychological Bulletin, 2001, 127*, 571–598.

Nigg, J. T. (2003). Response inhibition and disruptive behaviors: Toward a multiprocess conception of etiological heterogeneity for ADHD combined type and conduct disorder early-onset type. *Annuals of the New York Academy of Sciences, 1008*, 170–182.

Nigg, J. T. (2006). Temperament and developmental psychopathology. *Journal of Child Psychology and Psychiatry, 47*, 395–422.

Park, S. B., Coull, J. T., McShane, R. H., Young, A. H., Sahakian, B. J., Robbins, T. W., et al. (1994). Tryptophan depletion in normal volunteers produces selective impairments in learning and memory. *Neuropharmacology, 33*, 575–588.

Peluso, M. A. M., Hatch, J. P., Glahn, D. C., Monkul, E. S., Sanches, M., Najt, P., et al. (2007). Trait impulsivity in patients with mood disorders. *Journal of Affective Disorders, 100*, 227–231.

Piaget, J. (1971). *Biology and knowledge*. Chicago, IL: University of Chicago Press.

Pinto-Meza, A., Caseras, X., Soler, J., Puigdemont, D., Perez, V., Torrubia, R. (2006). Behavioural inhibition and behavioural activation systems in current and recovered major depression participants. *Personality and Individual Differences, 40*, 215–226.

Posner, M. I., & Rothbart, M. K. (2007). Research on attention networks as a model for the integration of psychological science. *Annual Review of Psychology, 58*, 1–23.

Richell, R. A., Deakin, J. F. W., & Anderson, I. M. (2005). Effect of acute tryptophan depletion on the response to controllable and uncontrollable noise stress. *Biological Psychiatry, 57*, 295–300.

Risch, N., Herrell, R., Lehner, T., Liang, K.-Y., Eaves, L., Hoh, J., et al. (2009) Interaction between the serotonin transporter gene (5-HTTLPR), stressful life events, and risk of depression: A meta-analysis. *Journal of the American Medical Association, 301*, 2462–2471.

Rogers, R. D., Tunbridge, E. M., Bhagwagar, Z., Drevets, W. C., Sahakian, B. J., & Carter, C. S. (2003). Tryptophan depletion alters the decision-making of healthy volunteers through altered processing of reward cues. *Neuropsychopharmacology, 28*, 153–162.

Rothbart, M. K., Ahadi, S. A., & Evans, D. E. (2000). Temperament and personality: Origins and outcomes. *Journal of Personality and Social Psychology, 78*, 122–135.

Rothbart, M. K., Ahadi, S. A., Hershey, K., & Fisher, P. (2001). Investigations of temperament at three to seven years: The Children's Behavior Questionnaire. *Child Development, 72*, 1394–1408.

Rothbart, M. K., & Bates, J. E. (1998). Temperament. In W. Damon (Series Ed.) and N. Eisenberg (Vol. Ed.), *Handbook of child psychology: Vol 3. Social, emotional and personality development* (5th ed., pp. 105–176). New York, NY: Wiley.

Rothbart, M. K., Ellis, L. K., Rueda M. R., & Posner, M. I. (2003). Developing mechanisms of temperamental effortful control. *Journal of Personality, 71*, 1113–1143.

Rothbart, M. K., & Posner, M. (1985). Temperament and the development of self-regulation. In L. C. Hartlage & C. F . Telzrow, C. F. (Eds.), *The neuropsychology of individual differences: A developmental perspective* (pp. 93–123). New York, NY: Plenum Press.

Rudman, L. A., Phelan, J. E., & Heppen, J. B. (2007). Developmental sources of implicit attitudes. *Personality and Social Psychology Bulletin, 33*, 1700–1713.

Salamone, J. D., Correa, M., Mingote, S. M., & Weber, S. M. (2005). Beyond the reward hypothesis: Alternative functions of nucleus accumbens dopamine. *Current Opinion in Pharmacology*, *5*, 34–41.

Salamone, J. D., Correa, M., Mingote, S. M., Weber, S. M., & Farrar, A. M. (2006). Nucleus accumbens dopamine and the forebrain circuitry involved in behavioral activation and effort-related decision making: Implications for understanding anergia and psychomotor slowing in depression. *Current Psychiatry Reviews*, *2*, 267–280.

Salamone, J. D., Correa, M., Farrar, A., & Mingote, S. M. (2007). Effort-related functions of nucleus accumbens dopamine and associated forebrain circuits. *Psychopharmacology*, *191*, 461–482.

Skinner, T. C., Hampson, S. E., & Fife-Schaw, C. (2002). Personality, personal model beliefs, and self-care in adolescents and young adults with Type 1 diabetes. *Health Psychology*, *21*, 61–70.

Sloman, S. A. (1996). The empirical case for two forms of reasoning. *Psychological Bulletin*, *119*, 3–22.

Smolensky, P., & Legendre, G. (2006). *The harmonic mind: From neural computation to optimality-theoretic grammar* (Vols. 1 and 2). Cambridge, MA: MIT Press.

Sobin, C., & Sackeim, H. A. (1997). Psychomotor symptoms of depression. *American Journal of Psychiatry*, *154*, 4–17.

Soubrié, P. (1986). Reconciling the role of central serotonin neurons in human and animal behavior. *Behavioral and Brain Sciences*, *9*, 319–364.

Spoont, M. R. (1992). Modulatory role of serotonin in neural information processing: Implications for human psychopathology. *Psychological Bulletin*, *112*, 330–350.

Sutton, S. K., & Davidson, R. J. (1997). Prefrontal brain asymmetry: A biological substrate of the behavioral approach and inhibition systems. *Psychological Science*, *8*, 204–210.

Tellegen, A. (1985). Structure of mood and personality and their relevance to assessing anxiety, with an emphasis on self-report. In A. H. Tuma & J. D. Maser (Eds.), *Anxiety and the anxiety disorders* (pp. 681–706). Hillsdale, NJ: Erlbaum.

Uher, R., & McGuffin, P. (2008). The moderation by the serotonin transporter gene of environmental adversity in the aetiology of mental illness: Review and methodological analysis. *Molecular Psychiatry*, *13*, 131–146.

Uher, R., & McGuffin, P. (2010). The moderation by the serotonin transporter gene of environmental adversity in the aetiology of depression: 2009 update. *Molecular Psychiatry*, *15*, 18–22.

Vohs, K. D., & Baumeister, R. F. (Eds.). (2011). *Handbook of self-regulation: Research, theory, and applications* (2nd ed., pp. 3–21). New York, NY: Guilford Press.

Zelenski, J. M., & Larsen, R. J. (1999). Susceptibility to affect: A comparison of three personality taxonomies. *Journal of Personality*, *67*, 761–791.

Zuckerman, M. (2005). *Psychobiology of personality* (2nd ed.). New York, NY: Cambridge University Press.

Chapter 13

Self-Regulation of Neural Development

ALLISON C. WATERS AND DON M. TUCKER
University of Oregon
Electrical Geodesics, Inc.

An evolutionary-developmental perspective utilizes characteristics of neuroanatomy to construct models of brain function. An understanding of brain function founded in this way also provides evidence that complex human psychology results from neurodevelopmental processes. This includes features of cognitive development described by Jean Piaget. The process of *assimilation*, we suggest, is related to functions of the dorsal cortex, while *accommodation* is related more to functions of the ventral cortex. We also consider the implications of this neural duality in the interplay of autonomy and attachment in childhood and adolescence.

From the perspective of the brain, self-regulation is an ongoing negotiation between internal needs and the constraints of the environmental context. Consistent with Piaget's reasoning, we find it helpful to describe the process of self-regulation in *cybernetic* terms. A cybernetic system establishes a predictive model and then adjusts behavior according to any detected discrepancy from what was expected. We elaborate on this dual-system model of brain function by emphasizing the role of internal drives (the visceral brain) and interface with the environment (the somatic brain). We also provide evidence to suggest that dorsal and ventral self-regulatory processes are each motivated by unique affective biases (i.e., positive and negative affect, respectively). We propose that cognitive ability emerges from the dynamic interaction of these various functional and affective divisions.

It follows that complex phenomena we identify in psychological terms (e.g., autonomy) are also developed and maintained by the interaction of emotional, self-regulatory mechanisms in the human brain. After Tucker and Luu (2012), we characterize these dual processes as the *impetus* (impulse) and the *artus* (constraint). As recognized by psychoanalytic developmental theorists, cognitive development proceeds within the context of social relations. Self-regulation, or the process by which an organism functions in response to internal drives and environmental demands, is both neurocybernetic and inherently interpersonal. Once situated in self-regulatory brain function, the learning processes conceptualized by Piaget (accommodation, assimilation) can be understood as the neurodevelopmental process of synaptic growth and modification. Cognition, in general, may be viewed as an emergent property of brain evolution and brain development in a social context.

We further suggest that cognition *is* neural development continued in the present moment. Thus, our presentation is aligned with theories of mind-brain duality that imply causality between the biological construct (i.e., the brain) and the emergent psychological phenomenon. Taking this functionalist perspective, we acknowledge only a narrow context in which it is productive to differentiate psychological phenomena from dynamic neural processes. Neurodevelopment may be viewed as the integration of dynamic, self-regulatory neural processes across the life span, and these processes are isomorphic with features of human psychology (e.g., cognition).

We conclude by revisiting concepts of autonomy and attachment from a neurodevelopmental perspective. Autonomy may represent a shift in the effect of the parent-child relationship from one aspect of the neurocybernetic moiety to the other (i.e., from impetus to artus). The attachment-relation is retained as a necessary component of effective self-regulation. It may, however become ever-more aligned with environmental demands and removed from internal motives and self-schema. Perhaps more than Piaget recognized, neurocognitive development thus proceeds within the context of negotiating between attachment and autonomy.

BRAIN STRUCTURE AND FUNCTION: MECHANISMS OF NEURAL PLASTICITY AND SELF-REGULATION

The vertebrate brain has evolved through a process of punctuated elaboration. Each major genetic mutation can be seen to give way to the emergence of "new" brain regions (e.g., cerebral cortex) atop the phylogenetically "old" foundations of the neuraxis. Brain development (neuroembryology) recapitulates phylogenetic progression to a surprising extent. Patterns of neural development, from fetus to adult, also provide insight into the general functionality of complex brains. An evolutionary developmental framework provides unique opportunities to relate theories of human behavior to brain function. Piaget's work is particularly amenable to this because of his methodical developmental analysis of cognitive behavior.

Even a rough sketch of brain evolution (and development) – from the simplest to the most complex brains – provides a great deal of insight into how the most complicated brains work. For both anatomy and function, it is important to recognize that evolved additions to brain structure are not modular. Instead, newer structures adopt and change the functionality of older parts, and thus alter the functioning of the system as a whole. These newest additions (e.g., neocortex) largely inhibit or control older parts. In many cases, they subsume the functionality of more primitive regions entirely. This can bring about radical changes in the properties of the system as a whole, including the emergence of novel capacities, such as self-awareness. Importantly, these novel capacities retain primitive characteristics associated with their evolutionary and developmental origin (e.g., association with bodily needs).

In neuroscience, complex human psychology (e.g., cognition) is most often associated with recently evolved aspects of vertebrate brain structure (i.e., neocortex). Much insight is gained, however, by acknowledging the function of primitive characteristics retained by these newest features. In the section that follows, we briefly review such evidence from brain evolution and development that is relevant to the neurocircuitry of self-regulation. We then expand this self-regulatory neural framework to related psychological constructs (e.g., assimilation).

Reflecting his appreciation of evolutionary developmental reasoning, Piaget also characterized stages of development (i.e., cognitive) as a radical reconstruction of preceding ability. Piaget was careful to note that emergent functionality is not additive but that the structure of intelligence is entirely altered by experience, or personal evolution (Piaget, 1971). He rightly suggests, for example, that although a worm's brain contains primitive components of the human brain, the worm's capacity for intellect is not equivalent to a subcomponent of ours. It is both functionally and phenotypically different, but it is nonetheless the primitive core of our neural apparatus (Boden, 1994).

An evolutionary developmental approach to understanding human brain function elaborates on Piaget's work in several ways. First, as we show, it reveals primitive, affective constraints inherent to functional brain architecture. Second, it suggests that cognition itself is a form of neural development that occurs across the human life span. Following this observation, we suggest that two of Piaget's key theoretical constructs (*assimilation* and *accommodation*) can be applied to child development and can serve as a general model of brain function. This general model implicates the cybernetic action of self-regulatory neural processes. Finally, with these cognitive constructs identified in functional neuroanatomy, the model is used to investigate concepts important to developmental psychology, such as the integral role of attachment in cognition and the individuation of an autonomous self in childhood.

The Visceral Brain and the Somatic Brain

A key insight to the evolution of human intelligence may be that as the brain evolved through vertebrate phylogeny, there emerged an increased capacity to delay between stimulus and response (Herrick, 1948; Tucker, Derryberry, & Luu, 2000). The human talent for cognition is supported in large part by this superior memory capacity. It is exquisite memory that allows humans to learn, to retain symbolic concepts, or to inhibit immediate drives to achieve future goals. Importantly, within the dynamic neural circuits associated with memory, we retain vestigial appetitive and defensive drives of our more limited vertebrate ancestors. We now review the origin and implication of these primitive drives that are integrated in our most highly evolved neural system.

Even in the earliest vertebrates, the functional organization of the nervous system can be divided into two broad domains – *visceral* and *somatic*. Visceral functions concern the maintenance of internal homeostasis (e.g., temperature, thirst, hunger, pain, organ function). The somatic brain, in contrast, interfaces with the environment. As the vertebrate brain evolved, phylogenetically newer structures (mutations) continued to elaborate the essential visceral and somatic functions. For example, the hypothalamus and thalamus (*diencephalon*; Figure 13.1) are primarily associated with visceral and somatic concerns, respectively. The thalamus is a hub point for sensory and motor traffic oriented toward, and received from, the outside world. The hypothalamus, in contrast, maintains endocrine and autonomic control of internal bodily processes. In complex vertebrate brains, of course, binary frames rarely tell the whole story. Functional brain circuits affect a great deal of integration between these structures. Still, the hypothalamus and thalamus of the interbrain in humans continue to reflect an important division between visceral and somatic processes that extend influence vertically up and down the neuraxis.

In concert with more primitive brainstem and hindbrain aspects, the visceral brain is concerned with what goes on inside of us, providing the motive basis for somatic behavior. As brain complexity increases over the vertebrate phylogeny, visceral functioning is also elaborated. The influence of visceral structures extends from basic bodily homeostasis to more value-laden desires and needs. In the most recently evolved vertebrates, visceral functioning extends into the neocortex (*telencephalon;* Figure 13.1). The limbic cortices are the innermost regions of the neocortex (Figure 13.2). They receive considerable projections from the hypothalamus. In humans, it is visceral control exerted by limbic cortices that provides motivation

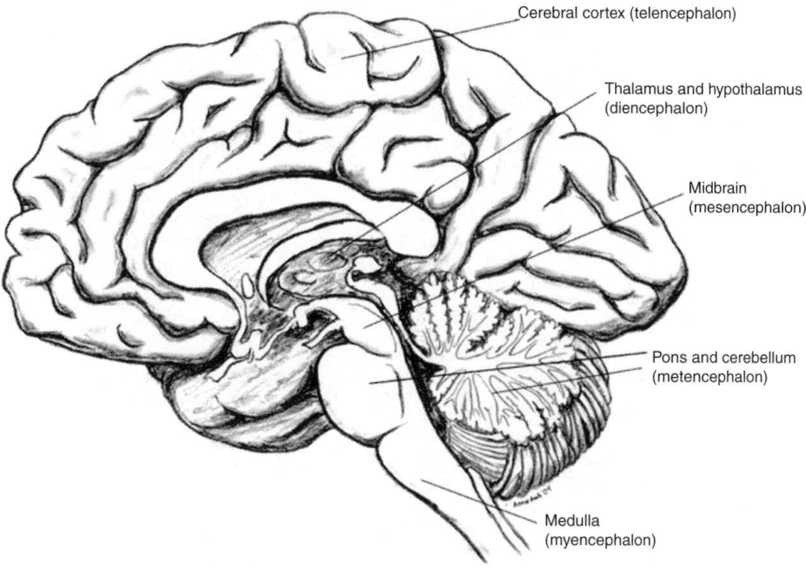

FIGURE 13.1 Gross anatomy of the brain.

(From Tucker & Luu, 2012) In the human brain, the telencephalon is composed of the cerebral cortex, basal ganglia and limbic system. The diencephalon or interbrain is situated at the top of the brain stem and includes the thalamus and hypothalamus.

(impulse and constraint) for most behaviors. Not surprisingly, these cortical regions are implicated in evaluative cognition and the interpretation of information relative to internal significance. The limbic networks are essential for regulating the consolidation of memory (retention of information relevant to internal needs). It is perhaps our remarkable success in this regard that allows for such complexity in human cognition.

In contrast to the visceral, inner cortices, the somatic brain is well represented in the outmost regions of the human neocortex: the primary sensory and association cortices (Figure 13.2). Ironically, it is this phylogenetically newest aspect that is often associated with the basic processing of sensory and motor data that is received from or oriented toward the environment. It appears that over the course of recent evolution, this cortical area (where some of our most uniquely human features reside) has taken over and elaborated upon these somatic processes that are almost entirely located in the midbrain of more primitive vertebrates. In humans this system is also implicated in higher order psychological constructs also related to interfacing with the environment, such as attention, executive control, and conscious awareness.

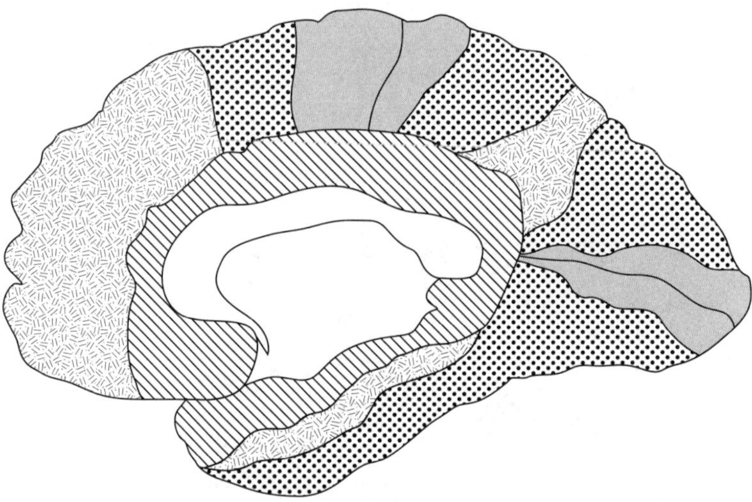

FIGURE 13.2 Somatic and visceral neocortex.

(From Tucker & Luu, 2012) Medial wall of the right hemisphere, showing approximate positions of limbic (striped), heteromodal (dashed), unimodal (stippled), and primary sensory or motor cortex (shaded). Adapted from Mesulam (2000).

Dorsal and Ventral Cortico-Limbic Circuitry of Self-Regulation

There is something of a controversy over how the mammalian neocortex evolved (Butler & Hodos, 2005; Tucker & Luu, 2012). But in addition to these visceral and somatic aspects, we understand there to be a second level of neocortical complexity relevant to neural self-regulation. This level is delineated roughly along a dorsal (upper) and ventral (lower) axis (Table 13.1). Limbic cortices emerged from visceral origins along these dorsal and ventral routes. Preferential connections to dorsal and ventral somatic cortices developed concurrently, as did specialized cell types and tissue organization. These features of the dorsal and ventral duality hinge on limbic cortices and affect all cortical functioning in important ways. Indeed, it is the self-regulatory push and pull between these two limbic-cortical systems that gives rise to memory consolidation, to learning and to the cognitive capacity that emerges from those abilities.

To begin, we briefly review the work of Sanides, which provides evidence of cortical evolution from two different points of origin in primitive limbic cortices (Sanides, 1970).Comparative vertebrate neuroanatomy, especially among primates, supports this hypothesis (Barbas & Pandya, 1986, 1989; Pandya & Seltzer, 1982; Pandya & Barnes, 1987; Pandya & Yeterian, 1984).

TABLE 13.1 *Properties of Dorsal and Ventral Limbic-Cortical Divisions*

Dorsal	Ventral
Projectional	Reactive
Feed-forward	Feed-back
Impetus	Artus
Internality	Externality
Intention	Attention
Pragmatic	Semantic
Limbifugal	Limbipetal
Egocentric	Allocentric
Visceromotor	Viscerosensory
Assimilation	Accommodation
Habituation	Redundancy

A schematic of the reptilian brain (Figure 13.3) shows progenitor regions in the dorsal and ventral cortices in the pallium and the external striatum, features of which we now discuss in more detail.

A simplified account of neocortical evolution would suggest that the dorsal limbic cortex (e.g., hippocampus and cingulate cortex) evolved from one point of origin – identifiable in extant reptiles as a cortical region called the pallium. In reptiles, the pallium contains pyramidal neurons and a broadly integrated neural architecture. In mammalian neocortex, these tissues, including the hippocampus, have been drawn laterally from a dorsal position into the temporal lobe. One interpretation is that this tissue retains holistic specialization of its primitive roots. Indeed, in the human brain, the dorsal stream has been associated with holistic representation of context (Tucker & Luu, 2012). Neurotransmitter systems that support this dorsal functionality (e.g., serotonin) combined with clinical and behavioral evidence suggest that motivational properties of the dorsal stream are related to positive affect (Tucker & Luu, 2007). Indeed, the absence of positive emotion in depression, for example, is related to pathology in the dorsal limbic-cortices (e.g., Mayber et al., 1999).

The ventral limbic-cortical aspect of the mammalian telencephalon (e.g., insula, pyriform, and amygdalar cortices) appears to have evolved from a different point of origin. In extant reptiles, this region is known as the subpallium (*shaded region*; Figure 13.3) and is important to sensory-motor integration, among other functions. In humans, the ventral route includes both somatic and visceral origins: the basal ganglia and the amygdala. As the ventral neocortex evolved, primitive functions of these neural structures

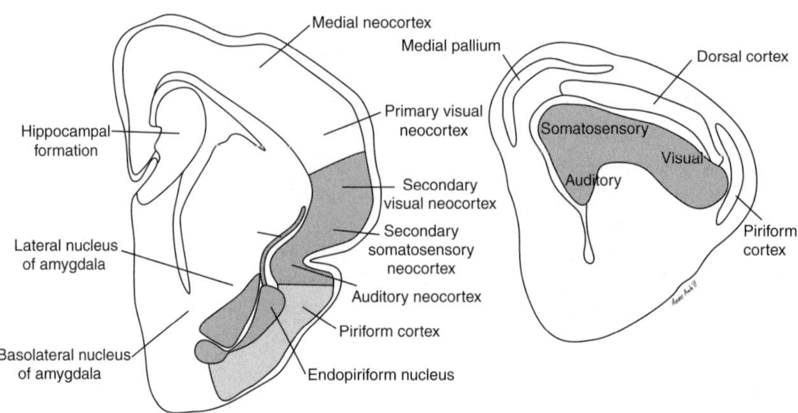

FIGURE 13.3 Origins of mammalian neocortex in the reptilian brain.

(From Tucker & Luu, 2012) Dorsal cortex (pallium) and hippocampal formation in reptilian brain represent progenitors of the medial-dorsal limbic-cortex in mammals. Ventral structures (shaded), including the amygdala represent progenitors of the ventral-lateral limbic-cortex in mammals.

expanded from control of sensory-motor behavior to include object-oriented cognitive capacities such as object specification and control of attention (Tucker & Luu, 2012). Amygdalar influence over this functionality is reflected in a negative affective bias. Ventral stream functionality is inherently anxious. Indeed, hyperactivity in these ventral aspects of the mammalian brain are associated with hyper-vigilant behavior and pathological anxiety (reviewed in Tucker & Luu, 2007).

In summary, the human cortex has extended the functionality of more primitive brain systems but has done so in a way that reflects themes inherent to visceral (limbic cortex) and somatic (unimodal, heteromodal, and association cortices) divisions (Figure 13.2). Emotion and motivation are key aspects of evolved cognitive capacity, including adaptive memory consolidation. In a highly cognitive creature, this duality is key to understanding most cognitive concepts.

Embryonic Roots of Dorsal and Ventral Corticolimbic Circuitry

Though we can extract important information about brain function by examining the path of mammalian brain evolution generally, it is an incomplete picture. Fortunately, neuroembryology (i.e., ontogeny) recapitulates the evolutionary progression to such an extent that additional insight can be derived from studying the embryonic patterns of change. In several interesting ways, the pattern of dorsal and ventral cortico-limbic differentiation suggested by Sanides also appears in human neuroembryology. Dorsal and ventral divisions of the cortico-limbic architecture are initially defined by genetically programmed placement of chemical gradients. These gradients guide the migration of specific cell types during neuroembryological development (Rakic, 2009). Cell types associated with dorsal and ventral streams – pyramidal and granular, respectively – also originate in different regions of the embryonic proto-brain (i.e., ganglionic eminence and the ventricular zone). This process reflects the evolutionary development of the mammalian neocortex from primordial pallial and subpallial architecture.

From these bases in neurotrophic and gliotrophic chemoaffinity gradients, change is activity dependent. Only synapses that are engaged by ongoing brain activity are retained. That is to say, the brain is learning at all times, and that learning is isomorphic to brain growth. Changes in neural architecture, even in the womb, reflect tension between the consolidated learning (stability) and the experience-dependent specification of synaptic connections (plasticity). Among many examples of environmentally sensitive neural plasticity in ontogeny, the formation of ocular dominance columns in the visual cortex requires some interface with the fetal environment (Markham & Greenough, 2004).

Even the initial design of neural connections is *self-organizing*. It is largely spontaneous behavior in the womb that induces sensory and motor activity and drives synaptic differentiation. In post-natal development, self-organizational processes expand beyond innate rhythms of arousal, sleep, feeding, and elimination. More and more, the brain must work to integrate complex states of attention, memory consolidation, and social interaction. Tracing the self-organizing brain function through developmental phenotypes, we see that neuroembryological change is isomorphic with cognitive processes in adulthood. It follows that evidence from neurodevelopment provides important insights into the psychology of intelligence, in general.

EMBODIED COGNITION: MOTIVATIONAL BIASES AND CONCEPTUAL STRUCTURE

In this section, we follow the functional trends identified in evolved neuroanatomy and neurodevelopment into an exploration of higher order psychological constructs, such as assimilation, accommodation, attachment, and autonomy. We reintroduce the concept of cybernetic self-regulation, thoroughly addressed in the structural work of Piaget, but also attempt identify its neural root. A cybernetic framework, localized in neuroanatomy, then provides clues to how action is motivated, guided, and constrained in a self-regulatory system. We then suggest that cognitive ability emerges from this neural self-regulation in a social context. As a result, Piaget's descriptions of learning behavior and of cognitive growth can be understood as reflecting the neurodevelopmental processes of brain behavior and growth.

Cybernetics of Action-Regulation

In the mid to late 20th century, learning research was dominated by the behaviorist perspective. Focus was placed on the formation of passive associations and the information processing capacity required to support these formations. Though largely absent in academic psychology, concepts of control theory were meanwhile taking root in more technical scientific fields such as robotic machine learning (Wiener, 1961). Perhaps by addressing problems in domains outside of psychology, theoreticians were better able to define the nature of a self-regulating systems.

Originating in the early days of ship navigation, the concept of *cybernetic* regulation provides a systematic model of internal control through opposing feed-back mechanisms. Piaget borrowed heavily from cybernetic theory in order to describe how self-regulating systems function to maintain equilibrium. He claimed that "cybernetic models are, so far, the only ones throwing any light on the nature of autoregulatory mechanisms" (Boden, 1994, p. 130). Piaget used a cybernetic model to account for evolutionary phenomena as well as psychological systems (including intelligent behavior), which also contain the structure of purposeful behavior and its adaptation. In both of these cases, however, his primary focus was on abstract logical structure. He largely avoided the physical substrate of these mechanisms, leaving that to the physiologists, and he did not focus heavily on the social and emotional contexts, leaving those to Freud. Similar to engineering cyberneticists such as Wiener, who attempt to define equilibria in algebraic equations, Piaget seems to have anticipated the computational approach to distributed connectionist representations in cognitive science (Boden, 1994). In neuroscience, the cybernetic approach helps to explain how visceral motives can regulate somatic adaptations, and how these visceral and somatic processes combine to create cognitive schema.

Cybernetic theory is perhaps most easily applied to behavioral mechanisms in the context of action regulation. Take, for example, the programmatic needs of a robot that is designed to self-regulate its exploration of an environment. Navigation might begin through *feed-forward* control: the robot executes action (e.g., speed and direction) according to an estimate of the environmental features. When an exception to this predictive model is detected (e.g., an obstacle), *feed-back* control has become necessary. These informative sensory data are then integrated with the initial behavioral plan. This tension and modification is continuous.

In mammals, the dual modes of feed-forward and feed-back control seem to have become elaborated within dorsal and ventral frontolimbic networks, respectively, and these modes appear be integral to human self-regulation of action (Table 13.1). For example: you reach to pick up a cup of coffee. You begin with an urge, and with a ballistic (feed-forward) motor trajectory that serves as a best estimate of the gross motor navigation required to target the goal. Both the urge and the initiation are motivated by positive affective bias, optimism, and anticipation of reward. As the hand nears the cup, the cybernetics change: The initial motor plan must be adapted to the visual constraints (feed-back). This adaptation requires vigilance and concern for environmental information that is incongruous with the assumptive plan. This negative emotion (e.g., anxiety) further motivates the refinement of the ballistic plan from its initial trajectory to fine adjustments near the goal.

We should recognize here that in conventional neuroscience the terms of feed-forward and feed-back are more typically used to describe neural projections that extend between cortical layers in the sensory (mostly visual), association, and limbic areas. A close inspection reveals that this conventional usage of the terms actually implies opposite directionality from what is intended by the terms in a cybernetic context.

What is particularly exciting about this very simple example is that control theory provides a stable theoretical frame for both the behavior and the underlying neurophysiology. This theoretical frame also includes the affective bias and constraint that is implied by the involvement of specific limbic-cortical regions and their cell-types. From this elemental basis, we propose that a neurocybernetic framework can help us understand how the brain self-regulates (Table 13.1)

We have identified two action control pathways: a mediodorsal path and a ventrolateral path, and each contains visceral and somatic aspects. The visceral momentum is derived from limbic cortices. Differing evolutionary origins of the limbic core of each system implies a great deal about how they function to motivate and constrain the somatic aspect. Many structures of the mediodorsal pathway evolved from the hippocampus

(Sanides, 1970). Dorsal premotor and motor areas receive input from the medial frontal and dorsolateral frontal cortices, which are regulated by the cingulate gyus. In this way, internally derived predictions appear to guide action in a feed-forward, projectional fashion. The projectional mode of the mediodorsal pathway requires a positive affective bias to motivate action according to a predicted outcome (Tucker & Luu, 2007). Indeed, symptoms of depression (loss of positive hedonic tone) are related to hypo-activity in these mediodorsal structures (Goldapple et al., 2004).

The ventrolateral pathway begins in the olfactory cortex which projects to the ventral motor areas via the orbital frontal lobe to the lateral frontal cortex. With phylogenetic origin in the olfactory cortex (Sanides, 1970) the ventrolateral pathway appears to constrain action progress by integrating external feed-back received by the senses. The pathology of the ventral-lateral limbic cortex (e.g., amygdala) is related to clinically significant anxiety and deficits in fear-based learning. Indeed, the primary affective force driving ventral functionally is anxiety. The influence of these structures provides a driving negative affect bias associated with the detection of threat or discrepancy (Tucker & Luu, 2007).

Cybernetics of Self-Regulation: Dorsal and Ventral Control of Assimilation and Accommodation

Having established the neurocybernetic framework in the context of basic action regulation, we can now begin to explore these concepts in psychological constructs. Each pathway is compelled by visceral functions (need states) at the limbic core, as it is simultaneously constrained by the environmental demands (reality testing) at the primary sensory and motor cortices. The visceral and somatic functions at the boundaries of each cortical pathway are not simply related unconscious activities of the brain. Cognition must emerge from the dynamic neurophysiology of these linked cortical regions (limbic, association, primary sensory, primary motor). Indeed, these processes describe the neural substrate of memory and cognitive representation, more generally.

Learning involves both discrepancy detection (fast learning) and the gradual development of new models (slow learning). Consistent with control theory, the organism develops an expectation and then checks incoming stimuli for discrepancy against this model. Ventral stream functioning seems more important for rapid learning and dorsal stream for slow learning (e.g., Gabriel, Burhans, Talk, & Scalf, 2002). Certainly, the limbic core of the dorsal trend (i.e., hippocampus) is essential for long-term memory, while the ventral limbic structures (i.e., amygdala) play an important role in the rapid consolidation of highly informative concepts. Complex learning is an emergent property of the whole cybernetic system, however, so it is productive to view these processes as complementary control systems, as opposed to separate memory streams. Very likely, the requisite stability and plasticity required to accomplish both fast and slow learning create an ongoing tension in the brain. From the perspective of the brain, memory (i.e., *schema*) is a dynamic process: memory *is* learning, and a schema is consistently being updated. This tension is radically apparent in the developing brain, but it may remain as a key principle of brain function throughout the life span.

As it turns out, there are particular aspects of this functional brain architecture that map easily to Piaget's observed assimilation and accommodation. The organization of the child's psychological representations through assimilation and accommodation can thus be understood to be achieved through specific learning mechanisms described earlier (Table 13.1). Although these mechanisms interact closely, they have different cybernetic bases. Here, we find it useful to reintroduce the terms "impetus" and "artus." These constructs represent the dual functional and motivational features associated with a neurocybernetic framework. They also represent a theoretical leap. Here we attempt to utilize an evolutionary developmental model of brain function to explore more conceptual structure in cognitive science.

The function of assimilation appears to be supported most closely by the dorsal cortico-limbic system that operates in a feed-forward fashion, elaborating internal urges from existing expectancies. The child's existing schema is a good fit to environmental events, and it shapes the expectancy for new information through feed-forward control. This cybernetic mode can be described as the *impetus*: an ongoing hedonic expectancy supports an agentic, even impulsive, form of behavioral control, motivated through the child's sense of agency and competence. The integral positive affect of the impetus mode supports exploration and flexibility, even as it rapidly habituates to unchanging input.

In contrast, the function of accommodation appears to be supported most closely by the ventral cortico-limbic system that operates under feed-back control through sensory guidance. This ventral cybernetic mode appears integral to changing internal representations when expectations are discrepant with actual environmental events. This mode can be described as the *artus*: the representations of external criteria provide active constraints on cognition and behavior. The artus engages inherent motivational controls, including anxiety and frustration, that are congruent with the focused, sustained attentional control necessary to change working memory when expectancies are incorrect.

In the organization of psychological development, both the impetus and the artus provide essential regulatory influences, shaping assimilation and accommodation, respectively. These influences operate within the domain of the child's own self-regulation (which may be isomorphic with the concept of a self), and they also integrate the social influences that shape the development of self-regulation skills, in the domain of the social context. It may be useful to consider the impetus and the artus as cybernetic vectors in each of these domains.

COGNITION AS ONTOGENETIC PROCESS: IMPLICATIONS FOR ATTACHMENT AND AUTONOMY

Activity-Dependent Specification

Changes in neural architecture reflect tension between consolidated learning (stability) and experience-dependent specification of synaptic connections (plasticity). Indeed, this is how the fetal brain develops, but also how the brain continues to change and elaborate with experience throughout the life span. Massive connections are formed according to the architectural structure outlined earlier, but only those strengthened by use are retained. The fetus generates its own activity, including spasmodic actions in the womb that help to shape activity-dependent specification before birth. Cognition appears to be a continuation of this process after birth, as each conceptual process exercises and shapes the neural architecture.

Cognition is not just the episodes that we discuss in psychological theory. It is continuous, including in sleep, and it exercises the visceral-somatic architecture through ventral limbic and dorsal limbic constraints. From the perspective of the brain, neural development and learning (and by extension cognition) are the same processes. Human functioning in its simplest form involves adaptation to the environment (largely social) and regulation of internal homeostasis. We are particularly good at these (especially the former) relative to our phylogenetic ancestors because we have evolved exquisite memory capacity. We can therefore learn from experience (i.e., develop predictive models) and inhibit immediate drives in the service of longer-term goals (i.e., self-regulation). In this way, cognitive talent associated with the human species is also tied to memory enhancement. This also implies that cognition is better understood as a functional component of learning, in general. Although the consequence of these processes is most apparent in childhood, a developmental model of brain function applies as well to the entire life span.

From a neural perspective, a single cognitive event is a developmental process. Making a simple decision, for example, may engage the same cybernetic, self-regulatory processes implicated in accommodation and assimilation. More generally, to quote Piaget, "An organism is a machine engaged in transformations" (as cited in Boden, 1994, p. 140). Evidence from neuroscience was indeed preceded by Piaget's suggestion that cognitive development is *mental embryology*, sharing attributes with the higher-order mental activities from which it derives (Flavell, 1963). Piaget also saw value in viewing all of human development in terms of ontogenetic processes, including cognitive functions. In some of his writing, he expressed concern that the study of ontogenetic processes and adult psychology were viewed as separate (reviewed in Flavell, 1963). In our formulation, we pick up on these sentiments to explore constructs in cognitive psychology from the perspective of functional neuroanatomy. It should be noted, however, that in his conceptualization, Piaget, differentiated between learning and development, and this was in keeping with his more narrow definition of learning behavior (Boden, 1994). We define learning more broadly, as the process by which experience alters an organism's expectations (i.e., predictive models, schemas) and responses to experienced stimuli. This cognitive functionality is achieved by the neural apparatus through ever-changing dynamics of self-regulation and is thus considered neurodevelopmental across the life span. When cognition is so "embodied" in neuroanatomy, we recognize that it is entirely activity dependent; ever changing within a tension of stability and plasticity.

Self-Regulation within the Attachment Relation

In addition to their self-regulatory functions, the motive-cybernetic systems provide unique modes of engaging in significant attachment relations (e.g., with parents and peers). These are complementary, in a somewhat paradoxical way, with the self-regulatory functions.

The motive and cognitive functions of the impetus are integral to social dependency. The child's love and sense of security and belonging are projected in feed-forward fashion in the schema of the other. Just as assimilation operates to integrate new events in line with the child's existing heodonic schema in many contexts, the impetus charges assimilation to integrate the self and other within a single hedonic representation. The schema fuses self and other in a hedonic package.

In dialectical contrast, in the context of the dependency relation, the artus provides differentiation of self from the social context. Just as accommodation is engaged generally when events are discrepant, the artus provides the child with the motivational control of cognition. In time, the model of self (fused with the attachment relation) fails to predict the behavior of others. The theory of neural self-regulation suggests that autonomy begins at this stage, when the social constraint of the parental figure becomes more aligned with artus. Though attachment is still a necessary component of the child's self-regulatory ability, her impetus now represents the visceral drives of an individual who is separate from the attachment relation. The theory further suggests that the motivational mechanisms of the impetus (anxiety, hostility, and negative affect) are integral to the negativism of autonomy strivings at key developmental stages, both for the 2-year-old and for the young adolescent.

The Self-Regulation of Autonomy

In the child's internal self-regulation, the impetus provides the essential motive engine of autonomy. Personal schemas for the nature of the world make successful predictions, and a strong sense of agency and forward momentum of behavior are supported by positive affect. This is the mode of assimilation, allowing interactions with the world to be organized within the child's existing schema.

An unbridled impetus, of course, leads to impulsivity and selfish action, the degraded behavioral effects of the child's sense of agency. The artus provides important constraint, internalizing the feed-back not only from objective, practical facts of the behavioral context, but the feed-back from the social context as well. Once the practical and social constraints are internalized, the child's self-regulation can be organized through a dialectical interchange of both impulse and constraint. The result is that autonomy becomes effectively organized within the social context. It is less a primitive struggle to actualize impulses in the face of social punishment, and more a patient exercise of individual self-direction within the context of others' perspectives.

Dialectics of Autonomy

There thus may be quite different implications of the fundamental self-regulatory modes, depending on whether the child's behavioral trajectory is congruent with the social context or not. In conditions of congruence, the impetus supports both the agentic impulse and the dependency of the attachment relation (whether with parents or peers). In conditions of incongruence, the artus supports self-constraint, as appropriate to the social conflict, but also negativism and its role as the engine of individuation from the attachment relation. This later mechanism is critical to enduring autonomy. It is perhaps paradoxical that the artus engages the same motive and cognitive mechanisms that are used to internalize the constraints of social influence to reject external social influences in the process of individuation.

CONCLUSION

In this brief review, we have attempted to apply now classic constructs from developmental psychology to the formulation of a general theory of brain function. Once this is established, we place more abstract psychological constructs within the neurophysiological frame. The work of Jean Piaget is particularly amenable to this treatment for several reasons. First, his logical observation of behavioral trends was intended to generalize across the human species. Thus, it is reasonable to think that the phenomena he characterized are also highly embodied. Second, we emphasize evidence from brain evolution and brain development in constructing a model of neural self-regulation that is continuous through all stages of development. This is very much in keeping with Piaget's concepts of learning and intelligence that were intended to apply across the human life span. Piaget may have anticipated fundamental features of human brain function that have been made known by more recent advances in neuroscience. Piaget provided an observed system (e.g., learning) from which we are able to investigate brain function. In the spirit of functionalism, we propose that a new synthesis is possible in which the discipline from an evolutionary developmental analysis can integrate the emerging information to cast new light on the process of psychological development.

REFERENCES

Barbas, H., & Pandya, D. N. (1986). Architecture and frontal cortical connections of the premotor cortex (area 6) in the rhesus monkey. *Journal of Comparative Neurology*, *256*, 211–228.

Barbas, H., & Pandya, D. N. (1989). Architecture and intrinsic connections of the prefrontal cortex in the rhesus monkey. *Journal of Comparative Neurology*, *286*, 353–375.

Boden, M. A. (1994). *Piaget* (2nd ed.). London, UK: Fontana Press.

Butler, A. B., & Hodos, W. (2005). *Comparative vertebrate neuroanatomy: Evolution and adaptation* (2nd ed.). New York, NY: Wiley-Interscience.

Flavell, J. H. (1963). *The developmental psychology of Jean Piaget*. New York, NY: Litton Educational Publishing.

Gabriel, M., Burhans, L., Talk, A., & Scalf, P. (2002). Cingulate cortex. In V. S. Ramachandran (Ed.), *Encyclopedia of the human brain* (pp. 775–791). Amsterdam, The Netherlands: Elsevier Science.

Goldapple, K., Segal, Z., Garson, C., Lau, M., Bieling, P., Kennedy, S., & Mayberg, H. (2004). Modulation of cortical-limbic pathways in major depression. *Archives of General Psychiatry, 61*, 34–41.

Herrick, C. J. (1948). *The brain of the tiger salamander.* Chicago, IL: University of Chicago Press.

Markham, J. A., & Greenough, W. T. (2004). Experience-driven brain plasticity: Beyond the synapse. *Neuron Glia Biology, 1*, 351–363.

Mayberg, H. S., Liotti, M., Brannan, S. K., McGinnis, S., Mahurin, R. K., Jerabek, P. A., Silva, A. S., Tekell, J. L., Martin, C. C., Lancaster, J. L., & Fox, P. T. (1999). Reciprocal limbic-cortical function and negative mood: Converging PET findings in depression and normal sadness. *American Journal of Psychiatry, 156*, 675–682.

Pandya, D. N., & Seltzer, B. (1982). Association areas of the cerebral cortex. *Trends in Neural Science, 5*, 386–390.

Pandya, D. N., & Barnes, C. L. (1987). Architecture and connections of the frontal lobe. In E. Perecman (Ed.), *The frontal lobes revisited* (41–72). New York, NY: IRBN .

Pandya, D. N., & Yeterian, E. H. (1984). Proposed neural circuitry for spatial memory in the primate brain. *Neuropsychologia, 22*, 109–122.

Piaget, J. (1971). *Biology and knowledge: An essay on the relations between organic regulations and cognitive processes.* Chicago, IL: University of Chicago Press.

Rakic, P. (2009). Evolution of the neocortex: A perspective from developmental biology. *Nature Reviews Neuroscience, 10*, 724–735.

Sanides, F. (1970). Functional architecture of motor and sensory cortices in primates in the light of a new concept of neocortex evolution. In C. R. Noback & W. Montagna (Eds.), *The primate brain: Advances in primatology* (Vol. 1, pp. 137–208). New York, NY: Appleton-Century-Crofts.

Steinberg, L. S., & Silverberge, S. B. (1986). The vicissitudes of autonomy in early adolescence. *Child Development, 57*, 841–851.

Tucker, D. M., Derryberry, D., & Luu, P. (2000). Anatomy and physiology of human emotion: Vertical integration of brainstem, limbic, and cortical systems. In J. Borod (Ed.), *Handbook of the neuropsychology of emotion* (pp. 56–79). New York, NY: Oxford University Press.

Tucker, D. M., & Luu, P. (2012). *Cognition and neural development.* New York, NY: Oxford University Press.

Tucker, D. M., & Luu, P. (2007). Neurophysiology of motivated learning: Adaptive mechanisms of cognitive bias in depression. *Cognitive Therapy and Research, 31*, 189–209.

Wiener, N. (1961). *Cybernetics, or control and communication in the animal and the machine.* Cambridge, MA: MIT Press.

Index

THE JEAN PIAGET SYMPOSIUM SERIES (*continued from page iii*)

Language, Literacy, and Cognitive Development, edited by Eric Amsel and James P. Byrnes, 2003.

Reductionism and the Development of Knowledge, edited by Terrance Brown and Leslie Smith, 2002.

Culture, Thought, and Development, edited by Larry Nucci, Geoffrey B. Saxe, and Elliot Turiel, 2000.

Conceptual Development: Piaget's Legacy, edited by Ellin Kofsky Scholnick, Katherine Nelson, Susan A. Gelman, and Patricia H. Miller, 1999.

Change and Development: Issues of Theory, Method, and Application, edited by Eric Amsel and K. Ann Renninger, 1997.

Piaget, Evolution, and Development, edited by Jonas Langer and Melanie Killen, 1998.

Values and Knowledge, edited by Edward S. Reed, Elliot Turiel, and Terrance Brown, 1996.

Development and Vulnerability in Close Relationships, edited by Gil G. Noam and Kurt W. Fischer, 1996.

The Nature and Ontogenesis of Meaning, edited by Willis F. Overton and David S. Palermo, 1994.

Development in Context: Acting and Thinking in Specific Environments, edited by Robert H. Wozniak and Kurt W. Fischer, 1993.

Piaget's Theory: Prospects and Possibilities, edited by Harry Beilin and Peter B. Pufall, 1992.

The Epigenesis of Mind: Essays on Biology and Cognition, edited by Susan Carey and Rochel Gelman, 1991.

Constructivist Perspectives on Developmental Psychopathology and Atypical Development, edited by Daniel P. Keating and Hugh Rosen, 1990.

Reasoning, Necessity, and Logic: Developmental Perspectives, edited by Willis F. Overton, 1990.

Constructivism in the Computer Age, edited by George Forman and Peter B. Pufall, 1988.

Development and Learning: Conflict or Congruence? edited by Lynn S. Liben, 1987.

Thought and Emotion: Developmental Perspectives, edited by D. J. Bearison and H. Zimiles, 1985.

Moderators of Competence, edited by Edith D. Neimark, R. De Lisi, and Judith L. Newman, 1985.

New Trends in Conceptual Representation: Challenges to Piaget's Theory? edited by Ellin Kofsky Scholnick, 1983.

Piaget and the Foundations of Knowledge, edited by Lynn S. Liben, 1983.

The Relationship Between Social and Cognitive Development, edited by Willis F. Overton, 1983.

New Directions in Piagetian Theory and Practice, edited by Irving E. Sigel, David M. Brodzinsky, and Roberta M. Golinkoff, 1981.